MISSION, CHURCH, AND SECT IN OCEANIA

MISSION, CHURCH, AND SECT IN OCEANIA

ASAO Monograph No. 6

Edited by

James A. Boutilier
Daniel T. Hughes
Sharon W. Tiffany

UNIVERSITY
PRESS OF
AMERICA

LANHAM • NEW YORK • LONDON

Copyright © 1978 by the
Association for Social Anthropology in Oceania

University Press of America,™ Inc.

4720 Boston Way
Lanham, MD 20706

3 Henrietta Street
London WC2E 8LU England

All rights reserved

Printed in the United States of America

Co-published by arrangement with the
Association for Social Anthropology in Oceania

ISBN (Perfect): 0-8191-3838-X
ISBN   (Cloth): 0-8191-3837-1

All University Press of America books are produced on acid-free
paper which exceeds the minimum standards set by the National
Historical Publications and Records Commission.

To Pacific Islanders

CONTENTS

Figures x

Tables x

Abbreviations xi

Editor's Preface................................. xiii

1. Introduction: Missionary Occasions 1
   Kenelm O. L. Burridge

   PART 1: MISSIONARIES AND ANTHROPOLOGISTS
   Introduction by Gottfried Oosterwal 31

2. Foreign Missionaries in the Pacific Islands during the Twentieth Century................................. 35
   Charles W. Forman

3. Mutual Biases of Anthropologists and Missionaries 65
   Daniel T. Hughes

   PART 2: MISSIONIZATION IN HISTORICAL PERSPECTIVE
   Introduction by James A. Boutilier.............. 83

4. The Impact of South Sea Islands Missionaries on Melanesia 91
   Sione Lātūkefu

5. Civilizing the Heathen: Missionaries and Social Change in the Mortlock Islands 109
   James D. Nason

6. Missions, Administration, and Education in the Solomon Islands, 1893-1942 139
   James A. Boutilier

7. Competition for Baegu Souls: Mission Rivalry on Malaita, Solomon Islands 163
   Harold M. Ross

   PART 3: LOCAL-LEVEL MISSIONARY ADAPTATION
   Introduction by Daniel T. Hughes 201

8. Mission, Church, and Sect: Three Types of Religious Commitment in the Torres Strait Islands 209
   Jeremy Beckett

9. Intercultural Communication in the Western Solomons: The Methodist Mission and the Emergence of the Christian Fellowship Church 231
   Frances Harwood

10. Indigenization as a Missionary Goal in the Caroline and Marshall Islands 251
    Francis X. Hezel

11. The Impact of Vatican II on the Marists in Oceania 275
    Gerald A. Arbuckle

    PART 4: INDIGENOUS RESPONSE
    Introduction by Sharon W. Tiffany 301

12. The Teachings of Father Marino: Christianity on Tobi Atoll 307
    Peter W. Black

13. Christianity in Kaliai: Response to Missionization in Northwest New Britain 355
    Dorothy Ayers Counts

14. After the Missionaries Came: Denominational Diversity in the Tonga Islands 395
    Shulamit R. Decktor Korn

15. The Politics of Denominational Organization in Samoa... 423
    Sharon W. Tiffany

16. Conclusion: Retrospect and Prospect 457
    Sione Lātūkefu

    References. 465

    Contributors 497

FIGURES

1. The Genealogy of the Story: Manu Pirao and Manu Vogi . 380
2. Denominational Differences among the Core Members of Two Stem Kindreds in Motulahi 412

TABLES

1. Survey of Schools (Population 130,000-140,000). 155
2. Baegu Population and Religious Affiliation as of 1967-1968 186
3. East Baegu Census Area Data 187
4. Baegu Hamlet Size and Composition. 188
5. Synthesis: Kaliai Tradition, the Story, and Genesis. 387
6. Adherents of the Major Denominations in Tonga, 1931-1966 398
7. Denominational Affiliation of Adults in Motulahi. 400
8. Adult Change in Denominational Affiliation, Classified by Sex, Motulahi 416
9. Denominational Affiliation, Western Samoa, 1921-1966. . 426

ABBREVIATIONS

The following standard abbreviations are used throughout the text.

ABCFM	American Board of Commissioners for Foreign Missions
ABM	Australian Board of Missions
ACC	Australian Council of Churches
ASAO	Association for Social Anthropology in Oceania
BSIP	British Solomon Islands Protectorate
CCCS	Congregational Christian Church in Samoa
CFC	Christian Fellowship Church
LMS	London Missionary Society
LMS, IC	London Missionary Society, Islands Committee
MC, CSID	Methodist Church, Correspondence Solomon Islands District
MCA, BM	Methodist Church of Australasia, Board of Missions
MCA, FDS	Methodist Church of Australasia, Fiji District Synod
MCA, MMSA	Methodist Church of Australasia, Methodist Missionary Society of Australasia
MCNZ	Methodist Church of New Zealand
MH	*Missionary Herald*
MM, FDCC	Methodist Mission, Fiji District Chairman's Correspondence

ABBREVIATIONS

MN	*Missionary Notices*
MR	*Missionary Reports*
MRMCA	*Missionary Review of the Methodist Church of Australasia*
NZMC	New Zealand Missionary Conference
NZMFMB	New Zealand Methodist Foreign Mission Board
PCNH, GA	Presbyterian Church of the New Hebrides, General Assembly
PIC	Papua Industries Company
PMSNH	Presbyterian Mission Synod of the New Hebrides
QKM	Queensland Kanaka Mission
SDA	Seventh-Day Adventist
SMSM	Sisters of the Missionary Society of Mary
SPMC	South Pacific Missionary Conference
SSEC	South Sea Evangelical Church
SSEM	South Sea Evangelical Mission
VPPC	Vicariate Pastoral Planning Council
WPHC, IC	Western Pacific High Commission, Inwards Correspondence

EDITOR'S PREFACE

The inhabitants of the Melanesian, Micronesian, and Polynesian islands have been subject to more intensive missionization, by Europeans and indigenous missionaries, during the nineteenth and twentieth centuries, than almost any other peoples in the world. The chapters in this volume highlight the enormous complexity and variability of this missionizing process in Oceania—examining how the missionaries acted as agents of European colonialism, how they sought to westernize as well as Christianize the islanders, how the missionary personnel and their message varied from time to time and from place to place, how they themselves were affected by the Pacific experience, how the islanders perceived the missionaries, pragmatically assessing and exploiting the material and cultural advantages inherent in the missionary presence, how Christian theology and traditional Oceanic cosmologies were blended syncretistically, and how indigenous churches and sects came into being.

This volume, the sixth in the Association for Social Anthropology in Oceania monograph series, is the result of an ASAO symposium on missionary activity in Oceania held at Stuart, on the Atlantic coast of Florida, in March 1975. Participants from the Pacific region, North America, and elsewhere assembled there to hold formal sessions, sit in the sun, and wander by the sea, debating the complex dynamics of missionization. On that occasion, I and my two coeditors, Daniel T. Hughes and Sharon W. Tiffany, selected fourteen of the papers available and commenced work on this volume.

I am particularly indebted to them for their editorial assistance. I have also been extremely fortunate to have had the steadfast and cheerful cooperation of all the contributors, whose support made my task infinitely easier and more rewarding. I would like to thank Kenelm Burridge and Sione Lātūkefu for their stimulating and finely honed contributions, as well as Alan Tippett, whose sage advice and vast knowledge of missionary activity in the Pacific were of great benefit to me. My thanks go to the United Church Board for World Ministries and to the U.S. State Department for underwriting the attendance of participants from the Western Pacific. Without the able and unstinting assistance of Eileen Taylor, Peggy MacDonald, Pat Steele, and Jean Merritt, who did so much to prepare the typescript, this volume would have been long delayed in its completion. And lastly, I would like to acknowledge the prompt and professional support which I, and the contributors to this volume, have received from Mac Marshall, the series editor, and from The University Press of Hawaii.

James A. Boutilier

Royal Roads Military College
Victoria, British Columbia
Canada
December 1976

INTRODUCTION: MISSIONARY OCCASIONS

Kenelm O. L. Burridge

Some years ago the *Journal de la Société des Océanistes* (December 1969) devoted a volume of nearly four hundred pages to the general topic of Christian missionary activity in Oceania. Containing a wealth of statistical data on mission organizations and their adherents, it also provided original archival material and ten essays on a variety of matters relating to missionary labors: histories of first contacts and later consolidation; educational questions; the translation of theological terms; economic development and welfare. Three of the contributors to the journal (Sione Lātūkefu, Charles W. Forman, and Gerald A. Arbuckle) have also written essays for the present work. And since that volume of the journal will long remain the authority for missionary studies in Oceania, it may well be asked why another book should be thought necessary or apposite now.

The answer is simple. There is a growing consciousness among students of society and culture—whether they call themselves historians, economists, anthropologists, sociologists, or missionaries, and whether they study their own or exotic peoples—that the missionary contribution both in action and in reflective scholarship should be reevaluated. The next decade, it is safe to say, will see a host of publications by missionaries and others about Christian missionary activities in Oceania and elsewhere. Within that future context this volume is a pioneering effort.

The contributors met for a symposium in the spring of 1975 and opened themselves and their prejudices to the kind of honest criticism and appreciation that is possible only when professional positions evaporate in the stinging surf of Atlantic rollers and the shared meals of a seaside hotel. Formal presentations and subsequent discussions finally resolved themselves into the themes addressed by this book. And since each set of contributions is separately introduced in the body of the work, my task and privilege is to provide a general perspective to some of the problems involved in assessing missionary activities.

Sociologically, as I perceive it, Christian missionaries form a class of persons whose moral stance and attitudes are significantly different from those among whom they work and to whom they address themselves. This is the central problem; and its details are richly adumbrated in the chapters that follow. In this introduction, however, the contingencies attending this or that kind of Christian missionary in a specific social milieu at a particular time must needs be dissolved into the more general constitutive relations generated by the presence of those with peculiar and special moral concerns. There seem to be four primary areas of interest: the general sociohistorical context in which missionaries and others have gone about their business in exotic cultures; the relations between missionaries and social scientists, particularly social and cultural anthropologists; what missionaries set out to do and what they actually achieve; and the nature of the missionary situation itself.

GENERAL PERSPECTIVE

Claude Levi-Strauss (1966:126) has remarked that ethnology or social or cultural anthropology—the sustained and systematic study of other cultures—is a European phenomenon. And I have suggested (Burridge 1973:1-42) that the enterprise is rooted in the Greco-Christian synthesis working in the Roman ambience of a hegemony of diverse interacting indigenous cultures. On the one hand there was an intellectual tradition: rationality, objectivity, the collection begun by Herodotus and Alexander of materials on other cultures, and that intellectualized model of an alternative and supposedly more perfect society provided by Plato's *Republic*. On the other side was the significance attached to the events and experiences of the New Testament: the participatory values grounded in love; the Resurrection which gave hope where there had been little or none; the Pentecostal experience which taught that, with love and the guidance of the Holy Spirit, a particular form of laws or social order could be transcended; the exhortation to "teach all nations"; and the basic tenet that God was for all humankind. The New Testament experience flourished in the soil of the Greek intellectual tradition. What could be imagined, intellectualized, and ordered might be realizable in fact. New earths might stretch out to meet the new heaven.

Yet if the impact of early Christian missionaries was a message of love, hope, fellowship, enlightenment, salvation, and the conquest of death, the follow-up required an intellectual effort of some magnitude. And the effort, a centripetal flow from differing cultural traditions into a more or less common mode of scholarship centering upon the sacred scriptures, was made. But the Bible, for so long the focus of all reading among European people, was not only a collection of sacred scriptures. It was also an anthropological monograph. To understand it required a knowledge of Hebrew, Greek, and Latin. With increasing emphasis, the neophyte was asked to learn other modes of articulate communication and to seek the will and face of God in the history, customs, images, and figures of an exotic people who, after the fall from grace, knew hunting, herding, slavery, nomadism, and cultivation and (becoming a warlike and conquering people) formed a kingdom that was eventually dominated and finally destroyed by the Roman imperium. God was for all, man was made in God's image, and Christ was in everyone. Before the question "Who or what am I?" could be answered the question "What is humankind?" had to be faced.

This is an enormous question. It contains the notions of universality, trans- or cross-cultural unities, and epistemological validities. The direct and simple message which can cut the Gordian knot when edged with love and spiritual presence becomes a scientific and intellectual question of almost impossible complexity when burred with the skepticisms of scientific method and formal logic. For over a thousand years Europeans addressed themselves to this conjunction of the humanly simple and the intellectually most complex. And it took a remarkably simple man of impressive intellect, Saint Thomas Aquinas, to formulate a synthesis on a higher plateau of understanding. Yet that synthesis could only be uneasy and temporary. No sooner had Aquinas completed his work than missionaries, merchants, and explorers were going out to the ends of the known world and encountering new faces, new customs, new histories, new images and figures: attempting to complete the synthesis necessitated a reach into the strange and unfamiliar. Biblical studies, which required the exploration of other languages, customs, and social situations, habituated scholars and other interested persons to these things and reinforced the attempt to achieve a synthesis in universal terms. That missionaries should seek the face of the universal God in other cultures was, in hindsight, to be expected. Nor was that reach into other social spaces confined to missionaries, seen as professional religious persons. It permeated as it still permeates the cultural tradition. Travelers, merchants, and explorers, in addition to seeking trade links and establishing the ties of empire, also wrote accounts of other cultures. Missionaries led the way in this respect and brought to their observations and accounts an intellectual quality unusual in laymen for some centuries. Las Casas, Ricci, De Nobili, Sagard, Lafitau, de la Créquinière, the Abbé Dubois, Junod, Codrington, Roscoe, Smith, and Fox are just a few names from among the many missionaries who, in their various times and places, have led the way in constructing the huge reservoir of knowledge that Europeans have of other cultures.

From the middle of the nineteenth century, when anthropology as such began to take form, anthropologists used missionary materials as a matter of course. By the early years of this century, particularly in Oceania, missionaries, administrators, and anthropologists, however else they may have differed, cooperated in the intellectual endeavor of finding out as much as they could about the peoples they encountered. But the break in the partnership was bound to come. Malinowski's letter to Rentoul in *Man* (1932:33-38), which was addressed to administrators and admonished the layman for attempting to interfere in professional scientific concerns of which he could know little, was an explicit signal to missionaries as well. European or Western society was going through another complex phase of further differentiating social roles and specializations. Moreover, as we can now appreciate, even if there was much common ground in the methods of anthropological study being used by both missionaries and anthropologists of the time, the deep opposition between those who grounded their work in the activities related in the New Testament and those who took their departure from science seemed impossible to reconcile. Yet in Malinowski's diaries (1967) it is clear that there was more in his dislike of missionaries than a recognition that professionalism and science must succeed amateurism; there was also an animus, the overtones of an unresolved oedipal problem. Missionaries had fathered the work to which he was dedicating himself with typical missionary zeal—on the other side of the fence. Moreover, missionaries were changing the cultures he and other anthropologists were investigating, and they were dedicated to particular kinds of change—something that could not but alarm the archpriest of functionalism and his followers. For though the practitioners of what might be taken to be the dynamic universalism of Christianity are often accused of being conservative and static, they are surely not more so than scientists who identify themselves with the dogmas of their methodologies.

Missionaries bring about many changes in an indigenous culture, but they do not necessarily bring about those that may seem, with hindsight, to have been inevitable. What informed and educated Roman of the day would have judged Saint Paul a successful missionary or a man who was pursuing a path that would lead to all that has happened since? Few missionaries are, or even can be, thought "successful" by their contemporaries. They can only suffer, as their chief exemplar did, and do what they feel and think they have to do: teach, learn, aid, reorganize. The critique of their activities always has been far weightier than a dubious appreciation can ever be. And yet all missionaries did what a whole army of functionaries are now doing in most places. Besides preaching the gospel, learning languages, and recording customs and traditions, they introduced literacy and learning, were physicians and surgeons, taught new skills and crafts, brought new goods—combined in themselves, in short, all those roles and activities which, organized into a variety of aid and development agencies, are now to be found cluttering the capitals of the lesser-developed countries. It is a facile rejection of history to assert that the vast and complex apparatus of developmental agencies would have come about anyway. Christian missionaries were in the forefront, providing the exemplar. To use an evolutionary idiom, the missionary has been differentiated into a variety of specializations which now require complex bureaucracies to organize and maintain.

Saint Paul worked among communities that, in an urbanized and civilized ambience, were as technologically and intellectually competent as he himself. They knew all about money and so he was able to confine himself to moral and spiritual matters. The earlier Christian missionaries in North and Central Europe no doubt had more book learning than the peoples to whom they addressed themselves. And in attending to moral and spiritual concerns they could allow time to deal with technological and cultural innovations. But for Las Casas, settler turned priest and missionary in a colonial situation, time was no ally. He had to make it clear, there and then, that the simpler peoples of the world were not as animals to be exploited and used: they were, like their conquerors, children of God, fellow mortals with immortal souls who should be loved, treated morally and mercifully, and given the opportunity to enter fruitfully into the new ambience of culture and learning. He was not the first nor was he the last missionary to earn the enmity of his fellow countrymen on the spot—settlers, merchants, political administrators—as well as the antagonism of professional scientists and the developmental experts of the day for saying such things. And in the great debate at Valladolid in 1550-1551 we see Las Casas championing the simplicities of the Christian message against the vast intellectual apparatus that seemed necessary to understand it. Indeed, this opposition is one which no Christian can or has escaped. Its imprint still infuses the work of social scientists within the Western heritage. As Tylor pointed out more than a century ago, anthropology—or "ethnology" as he called it—is a "reformer's science" (1958:539).

As scientists, anthropologists find objectivity by relating their observations to a variety of intellectual constructs. But involved as they are in the assumptions and consequences of that traditional reach into otherness, their paradigms are morally loaded.

And they themselves, implicitly or explicitly through their paradigms, assume a moral stance indicative of moral reform. In this respect anthropologists become like their prototypes: missionaries. And reformers with different ends in view are likely to be at odds with one another.

MISSIONARIES AND ANTHROPOLOGISTS

Although they may branch out in different directions, missionaries and social scientists share the same heritage in their moral address and exploration of other social spaces. Certain general features, moreover, characterize the relations between anthropologist and missionary: the opposition between an empirical outlook and a transcendent one; professionalism versus amateurism; and the pace, direction, and substance of sociocultural change. The first point requires little adumbration. While most agnostics and non-Christians regard the opposition as decisive, anthropologists and social scientists who are Christians find little difficulty in overcoming it. As to the second, the opposition is similar to that in any other walk of life. The amateur may have flair and penetrating insights but usually lacks the training, technical vocabulary, control of comparative materials, and systematic apparatus of the professional.

On the last point, anthropologists are caught in two dilemmas: while wishing to preserve other cultures in their variety, they have to acknowledge the fact of change. In acknowledging change, what kinds of change is it their duty as professionals to encourage or oppose? These dilemmas, which echo those of Las Casas and de Sepulveda in the great debate at Valladolid, and which anthropologists share in their way with missionaries, add to the difficulties inherent in the former being fathered by the latter. For on this point let there be no mistake. In the suggestion that there were oedipal overtones to Malinowski's attitudes toward missionaries is the implication that the relations between missionaries and anthropologists have in them something profound and elusive.

During 1972 I had the good fortune to visit a variety of missions in Oceania. My intent was to investigate the situations and problems of missionaries just as one might investigate the situations and problems of any class or tribe of people. Doing so, of course, involved talking to all sorts, including anthropologists, about missionaries and their work. A stereotype quickly emerged.

First and foremost was the general assertion that missionaries changed the culture undesirably. Discussion yielded the popular view that although governments, development, and United Nations agencies might make silly mistakes and were, like missionaries, changing the culture, they were on the whole making beneficial changes whereas missionaries were not. Even those who called themselves practicing Christians subscribed to this view. On the other hand, almost everyone interviewed admitted to knowing one or two missionaries who were "doing a good job well." Somehow, whether a person was a physician, an agricultural expert, a technician, a schoolteacher—whatever—the fact that he or she was also a missionary seemed to neutralize the expertise being proffered. One was left with the impression that it was the rarely articulated "Christian" in the general label "missionary" that was the prime target of objection. Nevertheless, it has to be admitted that when this point was put more respondents countered with a demurrer.

The general condemnation of all missionary activity followed by the exception of particular individuals or a particular mission body known to the respondent is, of course, a well-known syndrome: "Some of my best friends are Jews/Catholics/Negroes/missionaries." It goes along with that other popular image: the comic figure blundering about in a situation he or she completely misunderstands. But again, frequently though this image was evoked and articulated, almost as often was it followed by excepting one or two well-known missionaries who appeared to understand the situation extremely well.

The fact that missionaries are also people who preach was much resented. But a general indication in the direction of two of the universities in the Pacific and the speeches of development officers was usually sufficient to force at least a partial withdrawal of the charge. Only partial because there appeared to be an unarticulated but nonetheless perceived difference between "preach" and "speech": a distinction which seemed to refer to moral exhortation on the one hand and technological advice on the other. After all, anyone may confess wryly or even proudly that he or she is not quite moral, but nobody likes to be told that an apparently satisfying and materially profitable set of activities is wrong, morally wrong.

Implicit in the foregoing is "Heads I win, tails you lose." A missionary confining himself to spiritual matters was frequently castigated for filling the heads of ignorant natives with ideas on equality and universal brotherhood when he could be doing something positive like starting a hospital. Yet mission hospitals or schools were regarded as "lures to religion" and should, more properly, be run by secular professionals, not missionaries. Or again, if a missionary happened to be a hardheaded businessman this was grounds for reproof: as a man of God he should be doing other things; he should not be outdoing or undercutting proper merchants who had their living and profit to make. On the other hand, a missionary with a woolly head for business should not be allowed to make such a mess. Finally, there were assertions that missionaries taught a pristine and honest people how to lie and thieve, that missionaries were parasites, social climbers who had become missionaries to gain a status they could not otherwise have obtained, that they were imperialists and—particularly of single female missionaries—sexual perverts.

I do not suppose that any one person to whom I spoke would subscribe to all the particulars of the composite image so produced. Certainly the anthropologists and other academics, who bore their part in building the stereotype, would never dream of committing to paper as a considered opinion the things they actually said. Yet there is nothing strange in the stereotype. Malinowski's diaries reproduce it; it can be picked up in sojourners' works over the past century dealing with places where missionaries have been active; and Robert Louis Stevenson (1900, 1973), who started his adventures in the South Seas prepared to be critical of missionaries but ended their champion, paints much the same picture. Studies of race and ethnic or religious minorities over the world have yielded similar attitudes held by politically dominant majorities. Christian missionaries, in short, are seen as some kind of threat, though the precise nature of that threat differs with particular respondents. For some it will be their Christianity, for others their denominational affiliation, nationality, transcultural characteristics, intellectual qualities, economic activities, personalities, or political views.

The objections can be legion. Let us say for the moment, however, that the threat itself arises from the variously defined opposition: in relation to others in the situation, missionaries are seen as ambiguous, variable, and different. While the roles, material interests, and personalities of others can yield reasonably sure predictions of their behavior, the same cannot be said of missionaries. Expectations of them remain essentially ambiguous and ambivalent.

The relationship which may be derived from the stereotype—itself a classical mode of attempting to resolve an unresolvable ambiguity—is a dangerous one which needs to be aired if it is to be neutralized. At one level we may deplore the things that are said. At a deeper level we ought to find out which relations can result in what are, for the most part, unreasoning untruths. First, however, it may be instructive to see what acceptance of the stereotype can lead to. It happened that one mission station I visited was associated with people being investigated by an anthropologist. Like flocks with like: hospitable and generous entertainment went along with gossip, academic talk, and information about the mission. Most of the stereotype appeared. Later, visiting the mission, which happened to be one that was strict about no smoking and no alcohol within its compound, it emerged in conversation that the anthropologist concerned had been in the habit of smoking on the premises and, adding insult to injury, had urged some of those who lived there to accept free gifts of cigarettes.

Why? What anthropologist would offer pork chops to the caretaker of a mosque or eat hot dogs in a Hindu temple? Perhaps it is the confrontation between a missionary's ambiguity and the ambiguous position of an anthropologist in relation to the people being investigated (see Burridge 1973:229-232) that makes it difficult to draw the line between blissful ignorance and culpable blindness. Yet, and this must be said, there is something about the moral stance of many missionaries, of whatever denomination, which is totally exasperating. And confronted by it normal courtesies and a sense of fair play simply evaporate.

It is thus all the more ignominious to discover that if the coin is turned certain common criticisms emerge but no stereotype. Anthropologists and other social scientists constitute a class in the eyes of missionaries only insofar as they are social scientists who carry out an investigation using funds which often might be better used in some other enterprise, who write a thesis or publish articles or a book mainly for their own professional advancement, who repay material help and hospitality with unhelpful criticisms of missionary work, and who, if they become involved in an imbroglio, may at once retire to the security of their universities.

Wryly put, such views can come too near the bone. Material interests, making a name, and gaining status and security are pitted against their negation. Missionaries remain missionaries, and although few can allow themselves to speak as freely and recklessly as laymen, they have ordinary human feelings and failings. And beneath their charitable remarks, so often edged with sarcasm, it is still possible to detect a certain bitterness. For the most part they have been forced to abandon their traditional scholarly pursuits. The adventurous pioneer in every missionary, the continuing challenge to ingenuity and personal resourcefulness materially as well as morally, has had to give way to secular expertise and bureaucratic organization. Further, if a missionary usually knows more about the personal circumstances of most people in his area, in a few months the well-trained professional will have pieced together an overall picture of the social structure which, for all its naivete, has the look of a reality which years of patient ministry without that specialized training simply cannot yield. Moreover, in those few months the professional usually establishes a rapport and intimacy with the people which a missionary might envy if only because his own role, as we shall see more clearly, demands just that kind of opposition to traditional ways which an anthropologist, in his role, must initially at least sympathize with and find admirable.

Complex because it is derivative and competitive, the relationship between missionaries and anthropologists is crucially affected by the general relations between missionaries and others as well as by the ultimate achievement each has in view. Anthropologists seek a "sociological language," a vocabulary and grammar for describing a culture which, transcending partisan moralities, will have transcultural ontological validity. Missionaries seek the same kind of universal on an action projection, and they prescribe the general terms of a common epistemology which would make that universal possible. If missionaries were entirely successful, the anthropological problem (well-nigh insoluble while cultures have differing epistemologies) would be solved. Moreover, if at one time all or most Christian missionaries were Europeans, today they form one of the largest classes of interethnic and transcultural people. Missionaries, unlike anthropologists whose field experiences yield a series of unique and schizoidal epistemologies, reveal and are themselves exemplars of the diversity of cultural forms which a common epistemology can yield.

ACHIEVEMENTS

What a missionary says he or she wants to do, does, and ought to be doing in the circumstances often coincide but usually extend in different directions. Moreover, each missionary has a large range of alternative "ministries" or "apostolates": scholarship or teaching in an elementary school, scientific research or the teaching of varied skills and crafts, agricultural advisor, printer, carpenter, newspaper editor—the vocations are many. Even the cultivation of what are taken to be the Christian virtues is liable to vary with denomination, place, and time. Still, every missionary has a deep commitment to Christianity and being a Christian. The entailments of this commitment projected onto the sociological plane form a structure on which a variety of contingencies and particulars may be hung and more deeply understood.

Whether they settle in an area by invitation or at their own behest, Christian missionaries have usually commenced operations by preaching, establishing a school for teaching elementary doctrine and Bible stories, and setting up a trade store or plantation to help pay for their own upkeep and that of the mission itself. Learning the local vernacular and translating parts of the scriptures into that vernacular have traditionally gone along with recording local customs and usages and teaching European languages. Once adequate communications are established, promising young pupils at the bush school are passed on to central establishments where there are usually more sophisticated, comprehensive, and better-equipped institutions.

Through the years these institutions become larger and more diversified, instructing in a variety of trades, crafts, and rural skills as well as the more formal scholarly curriculum. Young men go to work in plantations or centers becoming urbanized and, in return, if the mission is well funded from the home population in Europe or America, more sophisticated equipment requiring more personnel to use and maintain finds its way to the bush station. Administrations become involved, the area is more or less policed, and the peace is more or less maintained. Traders and merchants also become involved. The general process, differing in its particulars from place to place, is familiar. These matters can no doubt be measured: so many students trained to such and such a standard in this or that subject at a cost of such and such per capita over so many years; all funding being subscribed by the faithful at home, helped in some instances in later years by government and developmental grants.

Such educational, developmental, and social works may be measurable and even, in a particular context, rated as successful or otherwise. But it should not be forgotten that these endeavors are secondary to the ultimate aim: the creation of a viable indigenous clergy and support personnel capable of maintaining an authentic Christian identity. Yet this is not so simple a matter as armchair critics often seem to think. Holiness, piety, and devotion to God and community do not in any way depend upon literacy and a formal education. On the other hand, continuities of doctrine and the apparatus for a sustained critique of charlatans and pretenders, who can often appear holy, inspired, and charismatic, require more than an ordinary education. Some denominations are satisfied with casual standards; others insist on five or six years of postgraduate work. Achieving such levels has never been easy, and the difficulties of avoiding a third-class clergy are exacerbated by the fact that so many of the best-educated Christians coming out of the mission schools and seminaries have in the end opted for a secular career with its wider opportunities for material benefit, status, prestige, and secular achievement in a developing social and political process.

Although a missionary has to ask himself how many pseudoconverts are worth one true Christian, looking at the missionary strictly as a communicator of Christianity, the significant proportion of what is being done is either scarcely visible or too pervasive to be measurable. At least part of what is actually being communicated, for example, often only emerges in a disturbance, a cargo cult, or similar activity. On the other hand, a smart young postal clerk, carpenter, or mechanic may admit that he learned his three Rs and trade at a mission school. The local jail probably houses more of the baptized than pagans, not only because there happen to be more baptized than pagans in the local population.

One retired catechist or church elder impresses the visitor as an undoubted scoundrel. But another, though not formally schooled to any high degree, has a manner that evokes the idea of holiness in its more admirable facets. He, we may learn, was at first a "rice Christian," one who became a Christian only for the material benefit that it seemed could obviously be derived from being baptized. But during the course of his life something happened: nothing necessarily dramatic or mysterious perhaps, and yet, infinitely slowly, he became more and more truly a Christian. Or an ex-sorcerer, eyes brimming with mischief, admits that in the past he fought against the mission and manipulated people's fears, envies, hates, and ambitions for his own ends. Then, he says, manipulating such manifestations began to lose its savor, so he became a Christian and turned his attention to the manifestations of love. Or one is introduced to a priest with degrees in philosophy and theology whose knowledge of European languages is surer than most European professors but whose father and mother were what we carelessly call "savages."

The results of missionary endeavors are scarcely measurable. Judging whether a particular missionary or mission body had succeeded or failed would require some sort of equivalence rating between an ordained Christian minister and so many Christian jailbirds. Besides, few missionaries would claim that they were any more than instruments through which anyone might accept or reject the divine will and purpose. Missionaries do what they feel they have to do; and the results of that doing have a bewildering variety.

Is it possible to distinguish what a missionary is doing from what the general secular ambience of material goods, trade, money, administrators, and so on are doing? Certainly not within these few pages. The acceptance of monotheism in itself would seem to require a continuing expansion of the boundaries of thought and social action. But to demonstrate it would take more space than is available. Still it is possible, I think, to pick out some of the features which most directly express the Christian contribution to the European experience and achievement.

The sustained and systematic study of other cultures has been cited as a European phenomenon, and I have suggested that the impetus to this study arises from the Greco-Christian synthesis. It is precisely this attempt to understand other social orders that Christian missionaries have been communicating. It involves establishing the self as a discrete and responsible entity. And from this flow successive attempts to achieve an at-oneness with a wider and wider range of communities. Cargo cults and germinating political movements are surely evidences of one mode of attempting to realize wider comprehensions. One may go further. The initial Pentecostal experience, reexperienced in some small way in each true Christian life but also publicly and more dramatically reenacted with every Christian generation in countless millenarian, enthusiastic, and similar activities in the European experience, is clearly related in some way, again, to such things as cargo cults, and the establishment of indigenous churches. That is, much that may be understood by just those events in the New Testament from which missionaries take departure tends to be reenacted on the missionary scene. Moreover, the sociological dimension of the Pentecostal experience represents the (attempted) transcending of one social order so as to realize a new one: to put on the new man. And again we are back to Plato, the events of the New Testament, and Biblical studies.

Nor is this all. In the "new man," directly related on the sociological level to the Resurrection, we find the result of the interplay of the features mentioned. With the establishment of the self as a distinct entity, the person—a parcel of prescribed customary rights and obligations—is capable of becoming an individual. In time, individuality may become institutionalized and generalized: within the grasp of each single person who, from cultural instruction, is invited to make the effort to become an individual. Now by individuality I do not mean entrepreneurial activity, egotism, selfishness, or anti-social behavior, though these are often some of the consequential aspects. I mean the capacity to deliberately step outside custom, tradition, and given social roles, rights, and obligations, scrutinize them, formulate a moral critique, and, without relinquishing participatory values, envisage a new social order governed by new moralities.

In the European tradition this moral innovation is institutionalized and enjoined on all. Indeed, it is a process which all within the European tradition have experienced if only in momentary flashes. The movement from person to individual and back again, to accept given traditions as a temporary accommodation and also to subject them to moral criticism without foregoing participation in community values, is the basis, I suggest, of that ongoing developmental process characteristic of European history. New social orders are always in the offing, even when economic and political conditions seem to preclude the realization of the conceptions themselves. The conceiving of an alternative social order, a new morality, is what is important. And doing so entails concomitant alienations from what is given and traditional. Whether attempts to realize what has been conceived are judged to be failures or successes must depend upon viewpoint and a perception of the deeper issues involved. At any rate, they are contingencies, variables dependent on what may be seen either as the cultural capacity to enter a moral critique or the ingrained cultural instruction that such a critique should be entered.

The consequences are various: holiness, spirituality, entrepreneurial activity, criminality, social reform, terrorism, rebelliousness. The positive moral critique may easily turn sour and negative; the instruction to make a positive moral critique may be read or received in a variety of ways. When institutionalized and generalized, when it is habitual and incumbent on each member of society to move from person to individual and back again—as it is in the European tradition—social change becomes endemic and a succession of different forms of social organization becomes part of general expectations. History—as distinct from myth—becomes possible.

While there may be many Christian missionaries who are exemplars of spirituality, we do not often hear of them. What we do hear about, encounter, and observe on many occasions is missionaries urging new discriminations between what is right and what is wrong. And because these moralities are related to a movement between the positive and transcendent corresponding to the movement between person and individual, they are distinctively not necessarily attached in their entirety to an extant form of social organization. I suggest that because missionaries are themselves exemplars *par excellence* of individuality (the capacity to move from the position of conformist to that of critic), it is this individuality together with its discrepant moralities that they actually communicate. The recipients may make of it what they will in the circumstances. A farmer or fisherman may become an entrepreneur, a trader, or a jailbird; a sorcerer may become a pastor; catechists and seminarians may become rogues, priests, trade union leaders, or cargo cult activators. And it follows, too, that when institutionalized and generalized individuality is adopted, various forms of alienation also become institutionalized in the sense that they are implied or inevitable.

All cultures would seem to have forms of individuality, institutionalized means of mediating, renewing, or changing traditional moralities. It is more easily observed and achieved in organizational configurations determined by kindreds or, as in Melanesia, where the basic pattern is determined by brother-sister relations and affinal exchanges. Lineal descent groups, the Hindu caste system, and the Australian section system exemplify conditions in which achieving individuality is difficult. For the most part, however, outside the European or Christian tradition the kind of individuality spoken of here is not generalized, incumbent on each, but prescribed to particular positions: shaman, pawang, manager or bigman, sorcerer, sanyasi, leopard-skin chief, mullah. The ethnographic record is replete with such figures. Belonging to the same family of sociological niches as the Old Testament prophets, they are the alienated or different ones whose dress, speech, and behavior are singular and who provide the moralities of their generally conformist communities with their necessary dialectical edge of moral critique. Only within the European heritage, however, do we find the roles of these figures distributed into each member of the community so that generalized individuality becomes a continuing part of social life. Indeed, the Christian tradition, particularly the lesson of Pentecost which teaches the transcendence of a given set of laws of moralities, insists upon it. Yet no amount of insistence could have brought about this individuality without one enabling condition: money. This medium of exchange, which becomes a measure of differentiated statuses and roles, missionaries bring on the scene whether or not there are traders, merchants, or administrators about. Christianity was founded in a monied environment. And Christianity's internal problems are intimately related to the tensions inherent in the coexistence of the moral implications of a subsistence economy (which demands participatory values) on the one hand and a cash economy (which differentiates them) on the other (see Burridge 1969:41-46, 143-149).

It might be argued at this point that individuality and its concomitants, the whole apparatus of differentiated and competing economic and political interests, would have come into being whether Christians or missionaries were a part of the scene or not. This is much the same as saying that the course of European history would have been much the same since that time had there been no French Revolution. The historical fact is that Christianity and Christian missionaries were significant parts of the situation and remain so. And the purpose of this volume is to assess in some measure just what this significance has been. As an individual, a missionary is an exemplar and communicator of the basic dimensions of institutionalized individuality: the built-in instruction to each to enter a critique of present moral being. And since money appears as the enabling condition, and missionaries bring money with them into the situation, they also communicate the fact that money can be put to a variety of uses. Moreover, it is precisely the varieties of moral alertness inherent in individuality which, emphasized and frequently expressed by missionaries, account in great part for the ambiguity in missionary behavior in relation to others. This, the situational predicament of the missionary, we may now examine in more detail.

MISSIONARY SITUATIONS

The Christian missionary's qualities of ambiguity and ambivalence in the eyes of others are certainly not unique to European cultures. But the reasons probably are. At bottom the Christian denies the validity, reality, or rightness of an existing social order; it is but a temporary, if necessary, corruption which must give way to a more perfect order in correspondence with the 'body of Christ." Grounding themselves in love and mercy, which any social order apart from the most perfect must corrupt, Christians reach a compromise by transforming love and mercy into a notion of justice which is secreted in and administered by those joined together in an organized community. The original Pentecostal experience negated an existing social order, transcended it, and posited a new one. Similarly, each simulacrum of that experience negates the existing social order and manifestation of justice; and then, because human beings must live in some kind of social order, attempts to present a more perfect realization of mercy and love through a more satisfactory and more perfect notion of justice. Things often go awry, of course. That is to be expected. There have been many abominations in the course of European history, all in the name of justice.

Still, there has also been much to honor and admire. And whether seen subjectively as a force for good or a force for evil, at the sociological level the negation of a present social order, which is contained in the notion of individuality, coupled to the necessity for creating a viable social organization, remains the central paradox and dynamic of Christianity. Correspondingly, or as consequence, communities which have called themselves Christian reveal a bewildering variety of forms of social organization. Or, to put the same point more forcibly, there is no social order that could be described as specifically Christian. Further, denominational differences and local custom show almost as great a variety of rituals and forms of service. What is common are the Bible and a few major tenets centered on the Christ figure, Pentecost, the Resurrection, and other significant events in the New Testament. Nor is this inconsistent in a faith which, in asserting universality, seeks the image of God in the faces of all humankind and affirms the world as the necessary raw material for a new earth.

Not bound to a particular social order, but formally set the task of negating all extant forms of organization in order to realize a better one, the missionary has to face a series of dilemmas. His first task is to communicate a negation of the existing social order through a series of metanoias and then negate each successive ordering through further metanoias. And a metanoia, essentially and for our purposes in secular idiom, entails the negation of the past and present, a "no" to the sinful ways of the past and present, a change of heart and mind, and, thus transformed, an entry into new ways and new moral discriminations with a positive affirmation. But if a missionary is not to be disappointed the metanoia must be mutual. The missionary should participate in the metanoia and be transformed as the other is transformed. Yet missionaries, not so ordinarily human, but with human faults and virtues, tend to take as a model of at least the first stage of creating the perfect social order the kind of organization in which they themselves have been reared. They fail to realize a *mutual* metanoia. And when a missionary fails to transform himself in relation to the transformation of the other, communication evaporates and there is merely an exchange of words. The others' moral, economic, and political initiatives and developments continue to surprise and scandalize. With the realization of a mutual metanoia, on the other hand, a missionary begins to appreciate that the steps toward the perfect social order do not necessarily include a replication of his or her own native environment. On the contrary, their variety is such that only those who have experienced a mutual metanoia are not wholly bewildered.

In the past some missionaries in a hurry have sought to wrench a community out of its traditional ways and create a Christian community overnight as it were. Mostly, however, they have had to content themselves with the slow grind in a mixture of the apparently haphazard together with the more systematic. If some parts of the culture must go, some continuities with the past must be retained. Yet what should be retained, what abandoned? A clean sweep has often seemed, and often been, the best answer. For in this way a Christian identity is achieved with prospects of retention. The alternative seems fraught with pitfalls leading eventually to the loss of such identity. The experiences of Ricci and De Nobili, the first in China and the second in India, have repeated themselves over and over again. Ricci found himself mired on two main grounds: whether the indigenous Confucian ancestor rites were more properly social and political than religious; and whether the ideogram and term for God which he had chosen indicated agnosticism (Rowbotham 1966:133). De Nobili, basing himself on the ways in which the early Christian missionaries in Europe had operated, tried to maintain that so long as Hindu Brahmins accepted Christian doctrine, made the confession of faith, and received the sacraments in good faith, they should continue to wear the sacred thread, tuft of hair, sandal paste, and so on (1971). For these usages were social not religious; they were matters of status in the secular community and did not refer to the condition of the immortal soul.

Neither case, well argued though it was, was acceptable in Rome. Overtly, this outcome might seem to be merely the result of political infighting between rival missionary bodies: Jesuits against Franciscans and Dominicans. But the issue was as deep and divisive as that which separates the Soviet Union and China today: the extent to which particular cultural forms were the necessary vehicles of a defined process of social and moral renewal. Dominated by their experience of nonliterate peoples in the Americas, Franciscans and Dominicans tended to prefer the clean sweep and so transform their converts into one or other kind of European. More impressed with their experience of literate peoples with centuries of civilized traditions behind them, Jesuits such as Ricci and De Nobili chose to graft Christianity onto what was already there, thus taking a cultural approach which is now most favored. Further, of course, while the operations of Dominicans and Franciscans could not but be affected by their being a part of an overwhelming material, political, and intellectual power in a colonial situation, missionaries such as Ricci and De Nobili were at the opposite pole. They had only themselves and were at the mercy of their hosts.

A mutual metanoia involving both missionary and those addressed certainly helps a missionary avoid the pitfall of attempting to transform the other into his own image and likeness. But the almost insuperable conceptual and symbolic difficulties inherent in different rituals and the translation of key terms would seem to demand a unilateral decision of some sort of clean sweep in the total process. Such a solution is all the more tempting when there is the power to enforce it. Still, if putting on a Mother Hubbard or a pair of khaki shorts will not make a Christian, it is a matter of experience that a rice Christian can become a real Christian. So it is with the adoption of a whole range of European artifacts and usages. In a notable if obscure essay Max Muller (1875: 251-280) warned missionaries of the danger of trying to create Europeans instead of Christians; yet neither he nor anybody since has been fool enough to say that there is an ideal solution to the difficulty. For the believer with real faith the matter is best left to the Holy Spirit, which in practice usually means that events have to be followed and seized as they occur.

On one aspect of social organization, however, Christian missionaries have formally had to insist, though the practice has been more lenient: monogamy. And in this, as one might expect, a series of further paradoxes is involved. Despite and perhaps because of the weight of Old Testament usage, the commitment to monogamy is clear and direct even though it might seem to be based on what can only be indirectly inferred from passages in the New Testament. Indeed, many dissident Christian groups, basing themselves on the Old Testament, have opted for polygyny in the past (see Cairncross 1974). But this practice has never lasted very long. One might reasonably suppose that it has failed because of pressures exerted by orthodox Christian groups thoroughly scandalized by the usage. In addition, since secular law also has prohibited polygyny in states generally thought of as Christian, it has been difficult to persist in polygyny for more than two or three generations except in isolated conditions. The history of the Mormons of North America provides a good example.

A deeper and, in the orthodox Christian view, more important objection to polygyny and polyandry concerns the relation between the social and ontological statuses of men and women. In general, the evidence reveals that women in polygynous unions enjoy many social and economic advantages over their monogamous sisters: the burden of work is lighter, cooperation is assured, adversity is shared, the attentions of an obnoxious husband are usually more easily avoided, and the care and nurture of children are made lighter. Moreover, social status and economic prosperity are more secure: a husband could not have more than one wife if he was not successful, and his economic solidity and social status are themselves strengthened by having additional wives. On the other hand, in polygynous conditions the ontological status of women is defined as inferior to men. In Mormon doctrine, for example, a woman's final and eternal salvation depended on being a married wife, on the moral status and final salvation achieved by her husband, and on the number of wives the husband had (Cairncross 1974:180-200). A superior or more advantageous social status was validated and buttressed by an inferior ontological status. So far as I am aware, in no polygynous society do females have an ontological status equivalent or superior to males. And the same problem of reconciling social and ontological statuses occurs in relation to polyandrous societies.

The doubtful ontological status of women in polygynous or polyandrous conditions goes against the orthodox Christian grain, whatever social status may be predicated by a particular social organization and set of customary usages. A Christian marriage connotes ideally the union in love of initially equivalent souls each of which finds salvation in the love of God, each other, and others. Again the antithesis between Christianity and a form of social organization is demonstrated. Yet Christianity also affirms the world: "love each other," in any of a variety of modes but here and now and effectively and pragmatically and not in an abstract or theoretical way. A particular social organization is but a temporary expedient to be replaced by another and another until a perfect reconciliation is achieved between the world and the divine. Hence both the tolerance and intolerance of particular social organizations. And the missionary's dilemma, which cannot be escaped, focuses on the crucial institution of marriage. That equivalent ontological status, whatever the imperfections of the transient social order, is all-important. Yet the choice between a clean sweep or a gradual shift into monogamy over several generations is hardly a real one. Most missionaries have to content themselves with the long haul.

Sometimes, although missionaries have no more knowledge of God's purposes than anyone else, it may seem to an outsider that God is on their side. Most often, however, if the presumption and metaphor be permitted, He seems to put his servants through the hoop. Yet missionaries know that their lot is to suffer. Christ is their prime exemplar, Saint Paul another. They, like others in sacred or secular duty, do what they consider their commitment makes it necessary for them to do. If some rely upon themselves more than the Holy Spirit, they know they have only themselves to blame; and if others rely on the Holy Spirit more than they rely on themselves, they know they have been faulty instruments. Christian holiness is the human in tune with the godhead and other Christians and, similarly, a Christian society is a social order in tune with the godhead. Some individuals and missionaries have achieved the first of these syntheses. The second, so far as one knows, has yet to be realized. But desiring it, and even more so attempting to achieve it, entails that the Christian and more so the missionary not identify himself with a particular form of social organization in any permanent way. The goal is a different and better society with new moralities. And these new moralities, figured in a missionary's address but not necessarily linked to an extant visible social order, lie at the heart of a missionary's ambiguity. These features, not allying oneself in any permanent way with a particular social organization or faction within it, but intent upon another set of moralities, lie behind some further classic missionary situations.

Generally, the ritual expert, the explicitly professional religious person, the keeper and expounder of the eternal verities, stands aside from the political process in a sacrosanct position. He, or sometimes she, may legitimize the political process; may intervene to make peace or arbitrate an issue when otherwise mutual oppositions might destroy the society; usually stresses within prescribed formal contexts the common moral values which override partisan issues; may conduct communal ceremonies to emphasize the same; and attends on and advises those persons in the community who have psychological or moral problems. Sometimes but not often this ritual expert may, however, ally himself or herself with a certain faction. And when this happens great events, implying changes in the social order, are set in train. But the Christian, and more particularly the explicitly religious person—the priest, cleric, missionary, or minister—is in duty and vocation bound to do precisely the opposite of what most social organizations demand. His life becomes a series of continuing sorties from his protected position in order to steer events and relationships into that manifestation of justice which appears as a satisfactory expression of love and mercy.

Sometimes these interventions have been in the interests of what some might call the left of the political spectrum while at other times they have been in the interests of the right. But only the most jejune could think that left was always morally right. And if doubts may be raised about what may have been implicit in such interventions, the explicit motive has always been that more perfect expression of justice. Indeed, the most comprehensive terms in which to discuss the history of the European heritage must be those contained in the relations between the state and the church as moral guardian and innovator.

The colonial missionary's compulsion to steer the political process has been described many times. It is unavoidable. Every missionary has experienced it, yet it has no name. Briefly, the missionary sees himself as, and to a certain extent becomes, the protector of his charges against all others. But while the missionary identifies himself with his charges, the latter do not always identify themselves with him. They may play him off against administrative officials who compete with him for the role of protector. Yet, interstitial between people in the colonial or developmental apparatus, the missionary's concern on behalf of "his" people and his beliefs can never be permanently allied to any of the other interests present. They are transient and tangential to the great process in which the missionary sees himself involved. No sooner does an administrative official, for example, feel that he has secured the alliance of a missionary in some projected program than he begins to run into trouble. And other secular interests in the situation have much the same tale to tell (see Burridge 1960:140-146). The missionary has his own furrow to plow and welcomes temporary alliances, but he must always discard them when they affect his own independence. No wonder that in the eyes of others missionaries exasperate and are ambiguous. Clichés are readily voiced; it is a cliché situation. It irritates and always appears as obtuse and unnecessary. A missionary creates a situation in which he, with his peculiar moral address, is an actively ambiguous element in a structure of relations otherwise well defined and unambiguous to competitive economic, status, and political interests. On the other hand, place a missionary in a context where no interests conflict, or where such conflicts are temporarily suspended, or where local courtesies prohibit the barbed moral critique, and that missionary quite likely becomes "one of my best friends."

Another classic situation, which is a development and partial resolution of the one just described, is the missionary who becomes a quasi-king or tyrant in the local community. Faced with the task of building a more perfect society, the missionary with a forceful and energetic nature assumes the reins of power in a community and enters forthwith on his task. A missionary in such a situation who could not develop the necessary character and energy would be compelled to give way to a successor more fitted to the work. The missionary who attempts to become a "king" against the wishes of the people usually asks for home leave in fairly short order. The situation not only invites a "king" but eventually manipulates a missionary into becoming one. And few such "kings" have not been "successful" in their time. Kwato mission in Southeastern Papua is an example. Yet as Lord Acton reminded us: "Power tends to corrupt and absolute power corrupts absolutely." Something of a scandal to metropolitan missionary headquarters, it has to be admitted more often than not that the "king" is doing a fine job. The bane of adminstrations which are successfully defied in a multitude of small matters, the "king" invites admiration. The rival of the merchant whom he undercuts, his custom and patronage are still required. Visitors to the mission are invariably complimentary, though they may have second thoughts when they return home. Yet if they want to visit the mission again they had better keep those second thoughts to themselves. When the "king" retires the edifice he has built does not necessarily crumble. For even though it seems to have rested not on a principle but on the presence of the missionary himself, the memory lives on. The metanoia communicated seems to be genuine and the seeds of yet another kind of social organization seem to be immanent. In short, a missionary who becomes a "king" becomes, on a minor scale perhaps, much like any other successful reformist charismatic figure in history.

Though the personal qualities of a missionary can color the situation, the situations themselves are easily identifiable and repetitive and arise out of the nature of Christianity and its zealots. Involvement in the world and the political process goes along with the sentiment that each political or social organization is a temporary affair which, through successive metanoias, must give way to another. At the same time, however, the situations described seem to be buttressed contingently by some further sets of conditions. Not every missionary can be a Saint Francis or a Mother Teresa, two Christian missionaries who have possessed that kind of spirituality which has preserved them from the corruption of politics while they have immersed themselves in the political process. No doubt when every missionary sets forth he or she has an image in mind which corresponds to the achievements of Saint Francis or Mother Teresa. But almost at once, and certainly as the weeks and months roll by, the frustrations of the spiritual task—occasioned by attempting to teach spirituality instead of being spiritual—transform the task into an explicitly moral one. In turn, the frustrations of the moral task begin to force a missionary to spend more and more time in very ordinary worldly pursuits. The motorboat or truck must be overhauled; radio schedules must be maintained; there is paperwork to be done; an extension to the schoolhouse must be built; accounts have to be balanced.

Such tasks have to be done. And as missionaries point out, the people participate and learn in each case. Yet an outside observer cannot but note that each of the varying tasks seems addictive, the address obsessive, and the teaching role minimal. Most missionaries will readily admit that apart from the general routine of pastoral work and teaching in school, the frustrations of time spent in positive evangelism are such that they could not survive without the aid of positive technological tasks. Inevitably, more and more time is given over to these more immediately rewarding and satisfying areas. Traditionally, evangelical frustrations were overcome by attacking them in intellectual pursuits: recording and learning the languages and customs and reflecting on what was being discovered, thereby giving that mutual metanoia a chance. Today, however, most of the creative fire in that intellectual, spiritual, and moral effort is absorbed into the impersonal routines of bureaucracies and channeled into a variety of practical skills which, even in innocence, place a missionary in a position of power over his charges. They come to rely on his knowledge of bureaucracies and on his skills as a social worker and technical expert. They begin to enjoy advantages quite disproportional to the contribution they have made themselves. Quite simply, the missionary ceases to be the determined Christian he or she should be. By discounting the communication of explicit new moralities the Christianity in him or her becomes irrelevant. What becomes valued are the variety of technological skills and the market and status they can command. And most of those who are not missionaries, who are almost totally engaged in forwarding their own status and economic and political interests, would prefer to have things that way. It removes the sting from moral reminder.

Aiding and abetting this power and status through mastery of technical skills is the fact that financial support for the mission comes from overseas. Particular missionaries and missionary bodies may not be overly endowed. But, whether poor or rich, money and goods not produced by, worked for, or earned by the local community keep coming. In some ways it may seem an enviable situation. Mostly it corrupts. The missionary is maintained in power or allowed, so long as the money and goods keep flowing in, to retain the forms if not the substance of power. Moreover, local political processes become adapted to the presence of the expatriate, and despite or because of his ambiguities the missionary becomes an integral part of the local scene (see Burridge 1960:140-149). Caught thus, no time seems appropriate for cutting the umbilical cord. Creating a wholly indigenous clergy becomes progressively more difficult; the aptest recruits prefer the glittering prizes evident in a secular career. For the expatriate the end comes when subscriptions from the faithful at home dwindle and die or when a newly independent government flexes its muscles on easy prey.

That expatriate missionaries have succeeded in creating viable indigenous clergy and churches in many areas is beyond dispute. Elsewhere, however, such achievement is either negative or at least doubtful. Still, even in circumstances where indigenization is at its weakest, a missionary must see in indigenous diplomats, civil servants, merchants, trade union leaders, and professors the fruits of much of his labor. That these same persons might seek to eject him from his country of adoption is an irony the expatriate missionary should have come to expect. For, as educators and social works, expatriate missionaries are already an anachronism—a fact which suggests that missionaries should do to themselves what they have advised others: renew themselves and find a new space. They have their exemplars.

CONCLUSION

It has often been asserted by churchmen and others that the missionary situation differs from the established Christian community and that missionary and pastor have quite different tasks and roles. Indeed, many Christian clerics and ministers object to being called missionaries. Yet it is doubtful whether any churchman would deny that a Christian could ever cease being a missionary of a sort. Certainly, explicit missionaries are usually more adventurous and determined than their brothers and sisters in established Christian communities. The explorer, intellectual and otherwise, is built into them. Composed as they are of dogged individuals, missionary bodies tend to squabble among themselves with a frequency and in a way which their confreres thoroughly deplore. But then they live where issues have not become blunted by time and the desire for a quiet and settled life. Many missionaries seem more bigoted, more authoritarian, less understanding, and less flexible than others. Their motives for becoming missionaries are often thought to be less than godly or honest. Still, for a churchman to object to being called a missionary seems but a superficial if understandable reaction to the reputation missionaries have acquired. Missionaries, morally intent as they are, are troublesome people.

Christianity is a missionary and troublesome faith. Because it seeks new and more universal moralities it cannot rest on a single achievement. It has an innate capacity, which is also instructional, to transform itself. And the means of its self-transformation is largely through generalized individuality. As soon as one denomination attains local stability, new movements develop from within. This capacity for renewal is, indeed, the prime challenge in a sociology of religion. The experience of a Christian missionary, and the situations he finds himself involved in, derive directly from the fact that he is a peculiarly determined Christian. Buddhist and Muslim missionaries have had quite different experiences, and they generate quite different situations. There is no doubt that where Christianity is well established the professional religious person is inclined to relax. And in that moment he begins to be corrupted. Decay sets in. But let political authorities and economic interests take certain steps, and the sleeping dogs wake and bark. The energetic and determined Christian, whose target is not so much particular persons but the moral renewal of whole social environments, begins to create missionary situations.

If only because missionaries are individuals, exemplars of institutionalized individuality, it would be a truism to assert that every missionary is different and every missionary situation unique. As members of a class of transcultural and transethnic persons they span the spectrum of human diversity. Nevertheless, they are a class. And it is because missionaries do constitute a class that I have attempted to outline some of its major formal properties. If the differences of character, ability, proclivities, and aptitudes between Mother Teresa, Bishop Codrington, Gabriel Sagard, Daisy Bates, Saint Paul, and a former U-boat captain seem greater and more important than their family resemblances, each in their own time and place took the same departure with the same landfall in mind. Their courses were different and each had different tools to work very diverse soils. Still, down the ages in Europe, Asia, Africa, Oceania, Australasia, and the Americas the same sorts of missionary occasions have repeated themselves. It is these situations which, sociologically, define the Christian missionary through time. Christian missionaries are not simply morally strenuous, though that might be sufficient. They are so in a specific socioreligious context whose long history and development have been characterized by transcendent moral values. An achieved set of moralities rarely contents them. They pursue perfection with renewed vigor. They offend, disturb, and perturb all those who would prefer to rest in, or who can take advantage from, the status quo. Which makes them subjectively objectionable. Transcending such circumstances is most of what is entailed in sociological analysis and at least a part of what is entailed in Christianity.

NOTES

I acknowledge with thanks the support of the John Simon Guggenheim Memorial Foundation for this project.

PART 1: MISSIONARIES AND ANTHROPOLOGISTS

INTRODUCTION
Gottfried Oosterwal

Though the Christianization of Oceania began long before the end of the eighteenth century, it was Captain James Cook's voyages between 1768 and 1780 that really challenged European Christians to send out missionaries to "the islands of the South Seas" (Jaspers 1972). In order to disprove Cook's prophecy that the island of Tahiti would never become the scene of a Christian mission, the London Missionary Society purchased and equipped a ship, the *Duff*, which sailed for Tahiti in August 1796. On board were thirty missionaries (only four of whom were clergymen), six wives, and three children. The little mission vessel sailed via the Cape of Good Hope, New South Wales, and New Zealand before arriving in Tahiti in March 1797.

The original plan was for the group to stay in Tahiti and establish a model Christian community there. But the heated theological discussions which had taken place during the ten-month voyage seemed to render that scheme impossible. So the group split, the missionaries Crook and Harris journeying to Tahuata Island in the Marquesas, ten others moving to Tongatabu, the main island of the Tonga group, and the rest settling in Tahiti. The story of these men and women contains all the elements that characterize the spread of Christianity in Oceania. Harris stayed only one day and one night on Tahuata. Crook remained there for a year, all by himself. Then he moved to Nukuhiva, where he lived and worked for seven months. English whalers brought him back to England in 1799. The missionaries on Tongatabu took up residence with Chief Tukuaho. This arrangement aroused the jealousy of the other chiefs, who resented the immense prestige which the missionaries' presence gave their rival. To dispel that jealousy, and to spread the prestige their presence created more evenly, the ten mission workers went to live with different chiefs. That decision proved fatal, for the missionaries soon became involved in a civil war in Tonga. Three of them were killed; others were tortured and threatened with death. Shortly thereafter, an escaped "criminal" from the penal colony of New South Wales set foot on Tonga and accused the remaining missionaries of being agents of the British crown and of bringing evil to the people of Tonga. Those allegations destroyed the first Protestant mission there. Weak, exhausted, and disheartened, all the missionaries left the island for Australia, except one, who "went native."

Of the eighteen missionaries in Tahiti, eleven took the opportunity afforded by a passing ship to go to New South Wales. Two of those who remained married non-Christian Tahitian wives and were cut off by the mission. The rest became the nucleus of a Christian community, from whence missionaries, Western and indigenous, spread the Christian religion throughout much of the Pacific.

In various forms and at different times and places, the story of the men and women of the *Duff* has been repeated all over Oceania. In chapter 2 Charles Forman speaks of these different missionaries, English and French, Australian and American, Protestant and Roman Catholic, and of the effect of their work on the island communities of Oceania: the spectacular spread of Christianity throughout the whole Pacific world, largely by mass conversions; the construction of new societies; the impact of the Christian religion on the life of the people, from what they eat and wear to the way they build their houses and organize their society; the protection these missionaries offered against fellow Europeans, such as traders and whalers, hunters and sealers, adventurers and beachcombers, who invaded the island world of Oceania for wholly different reasons; and the fact that the missionaries often formed a buffer between the settlers and the government officials on the one hand and the indigenous populations on the other. Forman speaks of these missionaries therefore as "helpers of joy."

But this is a missionary's view. In anthropological literature these same men and women, who spread the Christian religion, established schools and clinics, introduced new agricultural methods and reduced languages to writing, are described at best as "agents of change" but more often as "destroyers of culture." As a result of this difference in outlook, in role perception, and in the evaluation of change, anthropologists and missionaries have tended to view each other's work—and persons as well—with suspicion and hostility. Daniel Hughes, in chapter 3, takes a critical look at these mutual biases and offers a basis for greater understanding, if not respect and admiration, for each other's activities and goals.

On the whole it is true to say that missionaries have had little appreciation for indigenous cultures. Thus where a majority—or even a powerful minority—of the people accepted the Christian faith the indigenous ways of life largely disappeared. This can be an extremely frustrating development for the anthropologist who attempts to conduct fieldwork after a Christian mission has been established, a fact illustrated by the work of Elbert and Monberg on the islands of Rennell and Bellona (1965). "I was especially interested," Monberg wrote, "in religious concepts and rituals, and in this respect my stay on Rennell was a disappointment. The Rennellese readily admitted that almost all the ritual formula had been forgotten. . . . Thus we decided to leave for Bellona, although I had originally planned to work only on Rennell" (ibid.:3). But on Bellona the anthropologists ran into difficulties with the leaders of the two missions operating on the island, who did not want their people to remember "the old ways" and fall back into the old sins of dancing, singing, and other heathen practices.

It is not merely personal interest or the anthropologist's academic work as such which is at the core of the antagonism between missionaries and anthropologists. Hughes points out that it is the anthropologist's concepts of cultural relativism and functionalism that are at the heart of the controversy. Functionalism is based on the premise that societies and cultures are integrated wholes, all elements serving to maintain the equilibrium of that society and its preservation. As long as this view persists, anthropologists cannot but speak in degrading terms about the missionary as an agent of change.

In recent years, however, anthropologists have become aware of the limitations of functionalism. Whereas a few decades ago acculturation was not considered a respectable topic in anthropology, today it is a focus of research and study. Some anthropologists have even done away with the concept of cultural relativism and insist that anthropologists should themselves become involved in changing "traditional" society according to certain ideological viewpoints. These changes in orientation may also help the anthropologist to look differently at Christian missionaries and evaluate their work more as successful acculturation, a process whereby "alternative systems," "meaningful substitutes," and "functional equivalents" have inevitably replaced the old cultures and societies.

For their part, as both Forman and Hughes have pointed out, missionaries are also changing their attitudes toward anthropologists, their discipline, and their work. Forman attributes this change to a shift in theological orientation—from a conservative to a more liberal view—and also to the missionary's greater awareness of the significance of anthropology to the work of the mission. Another reason is the cultural nationalism which characterizes the new nations of Oceania. As a result of these changes in outlook and understanding, missionaries may become principals in the process of indigenizing churches in Oceania, even over and against the older indigenous leaders. And the anthropologist may recognize in missionary labors not only a cause of the collapse of traditional societies but above all a work of successful acculturation—and thereby evaluate the missionary as indeed a "helper of joy."

FOREIGN MISSIONARIES IN THE PACIFIC ISLANDS DURING THE TWENTIETH CENTURY

Charles W. Forman

The first Christian foreign missionary was in all likelihood Saint Paul. He was the first, as far as our records show, who moved beyond his own people and inaugurated a mission to the wider world. His description of his relationship to the churches where he served as a missionary may therefore be taken as something of a standard for foreign missionaries of succeeding generations. To one of these churches, the Corinthian, he wrote: "Not . . . that we have dominion over your faith, but are helpers of your joy" (2 Cor. 1:24). The foreign missionary and the mission organization are seen in this perspective not as rulers to dominate but as helpers of the indigenous people, providing a kind of scaffolding to aid in the construction of an indigenous church. In the South Pacific, however, there is no doubt that the scaffold has often appeared more important than the structure. Most people speak of the "mission" rather than the "church." In this chapter we are to examine the mission, but it is well to remember that what we are looking at is only the scaffolding and that beyond our immediate consideration lies the more important question of the indigenous church. We shall consider the numbers and origins of the missionaries, their religious and social outlook, their life-style and work, and their relation to other foreigners and to the indigenous people. But they are, though we may often forget it, only the "helpers." Whether *they* also have tended to forget it will be one of our concerns.

The great age of Christian missions in the South Pacific is usually considered to be the nineteenth century. It was then that missionaries converted whole archipelagoes at one time and proceeded to play a major role in the conduct of public affairs. The twentieth century has seemed less spectacular, with fewer stories of mass conversions and less room for missionary influence on public affairs because colonial regimes have spread over the islands. Nevertheless, the twentieth century has actually seen a larger number of missionaries and a larger number of conversions to Christianity than did the nineteenth, and through much of this century missionaries have continued to play an important role in society.

MISSIONARY NUMBERS

At the beginning of the twentieth century there were some 1,277 foreign missionaries at work in Polynesia, Micronesia, and Melanesia (excluding Hawaii, New Zealand, and Dutch New Guinea). By 1930 the number had gone upt to 1,702, and in the 1960s it had swollen to 4,503.[1] Since the number of persons outside the Christian faith was steadily shrinking during these years, it may seem anomalous that the number of missionaries, sent presumably to bring their religion to those who were outside it, was steadily growing. By the 1960s, when the missionary force was at its largest, there remained only small pockets of people who were not at least nominally Christian. (The Indian immigrants to Fiji provide an exception to this statement, which applies only to the indigenous island inhabitants.)

This anomaly is partly explained when we realize that the growth in the number of missionaries took place largely in New Guinea, and this was indeed an area where new groups of non-Christians were being discovered. The total number of missionaries in New Guinea grew from 319 to 3,010 during this century, and this growth accounted for seven-eighths of the overall missionary increase in the Pacific.[2] The small increase in missionary numbers on the other islands came mostly among the Roman Catholics and, to a lesser extent, among the Mormons and Seventh-Day Adventists. Except for these three groups the number of missionaries on the islands other than New Guinea has remained quite stable throughout this century.³

New Guinea attracted not only new missionaries but also new mission organizations. Previously unknown bodies such as the Church of the Nazarene, the Assemblies of God, and the Four Square Gospel International Church appeared on the scene in the years following World War II. Altogether thirty-three new missions started work, and New Guinea gained something of an international reputation as the "happy hunting ground" for missionary endeavor. These groups should not be given undue importance, however. They were all small missions. The great bulk of the enlarged missionary staff in New Guinea (five-sixths of the increase) came from the established missions—Catholic, Lutheran, Methodist, Anglican, and Congregationalist—which had been there since the beginning of the twentieth century.

The Roman Catholics took the lead in missionary numbers everywhere. They far surpassed any Protestant body and even all the Protestant bodies put together in the islands as a whole in every period of the century. In New Guinea they had an enormous lead at first, but by the 1960s the Protestants had almost caught up with them. In this respect the newly introduced missions did play a significant role, for though they accounted for only one-sixth of the total New Guinea increase, they accounted for over one-third of the Protestant increase.

DENOMINATIONAL AFFILIATIONS

Lest the large number of groups working in New Guinea in recent times give the impression of a confused and highly variegated operation, it should be said that in the islands as a whole during most of this century there were only a very limited number of missions at work and these conformed closely to two or three types. There were only two Protestant missions and two Catholic missions which spread throughout a large part of Oceania. For the Protestants it was the London Missionary Society and the Methodist Missionary Society of Australasia which were widespread. Between them they worked in all the territories except Micronesia, the New Hebrides, and the French possessions. For the Catholics, the Marist and the Sacred Heart missions were the main ones. They covered all the areas except Tahiti and the

Marquesas, where the Picpus Fathers worked, the north coast of New Guinea, where the Divine Word mission operated, and Micronesia, where the Capuchins were followed by the Jesuits. But these other orders were not greatly different from the Marist and Sacred Heart Fathers. Most of the other Protestant groups, each of which worked in a limited area—the Paris Evangelical Mission in the French territories, the Presbyterians in the New Hebrides, the American Board Congregationalists in Micronesia, and the Lutherans in New Guinea Territory—were quite similar to the two more widespread Protestant groups. This meant that over most of Oceania the missions were very much of two types: Roman Catholic missionary orders of nineteenth-century origin and standard Protestant denominations.

The only deviations of major significance during most of this century were those provided by Anglicans in the Solomons and Papua and the South Sea Evangelical Mission in the Solomons. The former represented a High Church style of non-Catholic mission quite different from the Low Church evangelicalism that characterized the usual Protestant groups, and the latter was the only representative prior to World War II of the nondenominational, conservative evangelical type of mission which was spreading widely elsewhere in the world. The Seventh-Day Adventists and Mormons (scattered widely but nowhere of much size until the recent Mormon growth) also represented very distinctive kinds of missions. Except for these latter two groups, Protestants normally recognized and made no efforts to infringe on each other's areas of work. Among Catholics, too, each group had its own area (assigned by the Propaganda) so that there was no overlapping among them. But between Protestants and Catholics there was, until recently, no mutual recognition of territories and much competition.

The threat involved in competition and overlapping was more serious in these islands than almost anywhere else in the world because, for their population, the Pacific islands have had a higher number of foreign missionaries than any other part of the world. Only the North American Indians have had a higher concentration of missionaries, and in their case the missionaries were not strictly foreign since they were working within their own country. There was one missionary for every 1,018 people in the

Pacific at the start of this century. This ratio increased to one for every 768 in 1930 and in recent years it has been one for every 608.[4] By contrast, during the early part of this century Africa had one missionary for every 50,000 people and China had one for every 132,000 (Beach 1906:19). The reasons for this heavy concentration in the Pacific must be seen as both historical and geographic. Historically, it was here that the nineteenth-century missionary movement saw its earliest and most publicized successes and therefore the churchgoing population of Europe took a disproportionate interest in the area. Geographically, the area was of special interest to the people of Australasia because of its propinquity and they concentrated their missionary efforts on the islands.

MISSIONARY NATIONALITIES

If we examine the national origins of the missionaries it is evident that as the twentieth century advanced, geographic interests loomed much larger than historical ones. European involvement gave way increasingly, though not totally, before Australasian. In the beginnings of mission work in the South Pacific all the Protestants were from England and all the Catholics from France. The Americans came in only north of the equator in Hawaii and Micronesia. The Australasian Methodists were the first of the southern churches to take wide missionary responsibilities when, in the mid-nineteenth century, they took over all the English Methodist areas of work in the Pacific and then added considerable ones of their own. Presbyterians and Anglicans of Australasia likewise developed work of their own, the former in the New Hebrides and the latter in Papua before the end of the century. In the twentieth century even the London Missionary Society agreed to an arrangement whereby half its missionary force in Papua would be recruited from Australia (see chapter 8). The Australian Protestant churches in recent years have concentrated nearly two-thirds of their 2,300 foreign missionaries in the Pacific islands (ACC 1966:25). New Zealand has had no such concentration, primarily because it does not share Australia's huge involvement in New Guinea, but it has still done much work in the islands (NZMC 1926:51-55).[5]

Australasian Catholics were much slower than Protestants in coming into foreign missions, but they advanced rapidly after World War II. Even before that time the old French monopoly of Catholic work had been broken by other European groups. Germans developed the strong missions in the Rabaul area and on the north coast of New Guinea around the turn of the century. Dutch, English, Irish, American, and Italian workers also came in, as well as the Australasians, so that during the twentieth century all the Catholic missions outside the French colonial territories became truly international ventures. The French dropped out of these areas for the most part. No French missionaries came to Fiji after 1935 and only two came to the Solomons after 1937, though both these missions had been entirely French in earlier days. No longer was it possible to have the kind of concentration from one French locality whereby, during the first two decades of this century, one-half of the missionary sisters in the New Hebrides and three-fourths of the priests and sisters in the Solomons came from the single French diocese of Nantes (Douceré 1934:390; De Bigault 1947:30). Australasian Catholics, who formerly had been absorbed in establishing themselves in their own land, turned their attention outward and more than offset the losses from France. In 1948 the Australian Catholics had 278 foreign missionaries; a decade later they had 609; and by 1966 they had 1,044, nearly three-fourths of whom were serving in Oceania.[6] Similarly, New Zealand priests and nuns spread out into the islands, particularly workers from the Marist order, which was exceptionally strong in New Zealand and was able to fill many posts in Tonga, Samoa, Fiji, and the Solomons. During recent years the American presence has also become more and more pronounced in Catholic work.

The increasingly international mixture in these Catholic missions suggests the possibility of a decline in national feeling among the missionaries. This has in fact been a characteristic of the twentieth century. Those who were serving at the beginning of the century still gave expression occasionally to nationalist sentiments. Arthur Hopkins of the Melanesian Mission wrote of the "possibilities of serving God, church and country" (n.d.:1), while Bishop Darnand in Samoa quoted with evident approval the dictum that the happiest days for French missionaries are those when "in serving religion and humanity they can serve and honor the name of France" (1920-1943:28 February 1920).[7] But such statements were not heard from later generations. What nationalism there was among the missionaries was usually tacit and assumed rather than vocal. They could anticipate that their contacts with the indigenous people would contribute to a favorable impression of their home country; and when their country was at war, most of them expected to be of service to it. But there was no longer the close association of national power with missionary expansion which had characterized at least the French Catholic missions in the nineteenth century. The strong anticlerical direction of the French government at the beginning of the twentieth century made that impossible in any case. In the New Hebrides the Presbyterians did seek to advance the cause of British or Australian annexation and the Catholics did the same for the French, but in all of this, as in much of what went on in the nineteenth century, it seemed to be more a case of the missionaries trying to use national interests to serve their ecclesiastical purposes than of themselves trying to serve various national interests.[8]

RELIGIOUS OUTLOOK

The missionaries' major concerns were, not surprisingly, religious. Though investigators have often been prone to emphasize the political or economic factors which were, without doubt, operative in their work, such an emphasis usually reflects the interests of the investigator more than the interests of the missionary. The key concepts in the missionaries' work, as they saw it, were providence and vocation. They felt themselves to have been called into their work by God rather than to have acted on their own initiative. In the circumstances that confronted them they saw not process or coincidence but the hand of God and the leading of God. The letters and addresses of the Anglican bishop of New Guinea through the 1940s and 1950s, for example, referred constantly to the protection God had provided in specific dangers and interpreted the protection received not as good fortune but as a call from God for further service.

It may be possible to detect some lessening of the intensity of religious conviction during the course of the century, though this is hard to prove. The mid-nineteenth-century Marists when undertaking a new mission seemed to think that careful preparation or investigation of the area to which they were going was inappropriate for those who trusted in God. Their twentieth-century successors had no qualms about such precaution (Laracy 1969:23-24, 145-147). In the 1890s, an enthusiasm for martyrdom was often still reflected in the writings of the Catholic missionaries, but it seems largely to disappear in the twentieth century.[9] The great decrease in strictly religious interests among Catholics came after the Second Vatican Council, as is shown in the survey reported by Arbuckle in this volume (see chapter 11).

Certainly among Protestant missionaries there were significant developments of liberal theology, going back to the late Victorian era, which reduced the importance of strictly religious concerns. Henry Adams noted the beginnings of this trend in 1890 and foretold trouble on that score between the missionaries and the conservative, religious, Samoan pastors (Adams 1930: 445). The Australian Methodists became particularly sympathetic to a liberal emphasis on the fatherhood of God and the brotherhood of man as a sufficient religious message and an end to the "hellfire theology" which older missionaries had represented.[10] The leader of their mission in the Solomons, Reverend John Goldie, declared that Christ's gospel "is a gospel of health and happiness—at least that is the Methodist interpretation of it" (quoted in Brash 1948:30). The most brilliant thinker and strategist of the Lutherans in New Guinea, Christian Keysser, discounted the teaching of religion in favor of what he called a style of life and took on other liberal ideas to such an extent that, when he started to instruct the new missionary recruits in Germany, the old head of the New Guinea mission refused to accept any of the men he trained (Keysser 1921:10; Pilhofer 1963 II: 102).

The clearest examples of decreased religious interest come from two Congregational missionaries in Papua (Butcher 1963:6, 287):

> I wonder [wrote one] what would have happened if instead of formulating the unprovable creeds and doctrines about Jesus... the priests and clergy had sought to know and practice the religion of Jesus which is summed up in one great sentence, "Thou shalt love."

> It is too early to make any true converts [said the other], but if the example of our way of life among these peoples improves their own way of life at all . . . if we can heal some of the sick, reduce the appalling infant mortality . . . and generally make them happier and healthier natives, our work will not be in vain.

These statements are extreme, but even the major Conference of South Pacific Protestant Missions in 1948 quoted favorably a British opinion that "the missionary's aim is not to gain the nominal acceptance of Christianity by pagan peoples, but to try to safeguard, enrich and ennoble their whole way of life in a rapidly changing environment" (SPMC 1948 II:15).[11]

At the same time there continued to be many missionaries who maintained a greater importance for religion. The conservative evangelical types represented by the South Sea Evangelical Mission were still prepared to risk the introduction of epidemic diseases in order to bring "the blessings of the gospel and the Bible" (Hilliard 1966:393), and the Presbyterian, Anglican, and most Lutheran and Catholic missionaries represented a greater emphasis on religion than can be found in these last statements.

CULTURAL ATTITUDES

The gradual changes in religious outlook ran parallel to changes in attitude toward indigenous cultures. A more liberal religion and a greater appreciation of the island cultures seemed to go hand in hand. Earlier missionaries were quite consistently antagonistic to the traditional cultures. Their writings monotonously employed the words "cannibals" and "child races" when referring to the island peoples, and many of them believed that they should treat the people as children. Some would not let "natives" into their homes or deal with them socially as equals (Hames 1972:9).[12] Few of them made any effort to understand the cultures in which they worked. Restrictions on the people were many, exemplified most strongly by the Presbyterians in the New Hebrides, where the famous Peter Milne, who worked there from 1870 to 1924, said:

> I forbade the betrothing of children when young; the selling of their girls to husbands; the making of feasts at funerals; the putting of superfluous

calico and other things into the grave along with the body of the deceased; also the making of a feast at the birth of a child (Don 1927: 279).

Plentiful examples of such attitudes could be found in the twentieth century and from most of the major churches.[13] Government officers and anthropologists who questioned the ethical right of the missionaries to destroy a people's way of living and tried to defend the much harassed traditionalists were giving in some respects a very Christian challenge to the representatives of Christianity.[14]

As the twentieth century has progressed it is noticeable that these negative expressions have decreased. After the 1930s they were seldom heard. Positive appreciation for the traditional cultures became the usual, perhaps the invariable, attitude among the missionaries of the major churches. Men like Reverend George Brown and Reverend John Burton of the Methodists, Reverend Christian Keysser of the Lutherans, and Reverend Ben Butcher of the London Mission, all exponents of a more liberal theology, were among the early leaders of a more appreciative ethnology.[15] The Anglican mission in Papua was infected from an early date with a romantic idealization of Papuan culture (Wetherell 1974: 405-406, 413). The 1948 conference on Pacific missions expressed the view that missionaries should not tell the people what to do about their culture but should try to build their own contribution into the old cultural life.[16] In Catholic circles spokesmen for the Vatican stressed the importance of "bringing out all that is beautiful and healthfully good in the different human races," and missionaries began to pay more attention to the values of native culture and to wonder "why has it taken so long to realize that the so-called savage is not as primitive as once assumed" (Costantini 1949:411).[17]

A strange situation sometimes developed: the foreign missionary trying to restore indigenous traditions which his predecessors had eliminated would meet resistance from the Christianized islanders, who felt that this was a return to heathenism. One missionary on the south coast of Papua tried to make a fresh study of old customs for possible inclusion in Christian life but found that the Christians thought of all the old customs as bad (Hurst 1937:28; cf. Wetherell 1974:403-405). In Tonga during the 1930s, there was much missionary pressure involved in the Free Wesleyan Church's decision to adopt traditional Tongan dress for its ministers. Since then it is only the churches which have broken away from missionary leadership, the Free Church of Tonga and the Church of Tonga, which continue to dress their ministers in the black frock coats of nineteenth century missionaries. Such situations are thoroughly anomalous. True indigenization can only mean adherence to the will of the indigenous people; any indigenization brought about by foreigners must be spurious.

The change in missionary outlook, while related to the general liberalization of Christian thought, was also a result of the increasing study of anthropology. It is hardly surprising that the missionaries had little appreciation for island cultures at the beginning of the century: the science of anthropology was still not widely recognized and they had had little opportunity to be introduced to it. The first professorship in anthropology in Australia was not established until the late 1920s. By the end of the 1930s, A.P. Elkin, an Anglican priest who succeeded to that professorship, had trained over seventy missionaries in anthropology and the effects were beginning to be felt in the islands (Hogbin 1939: 249; Keesing 1945:240-241). Both Catholic and Protestant mission leaders began to stress the importance of anthropological training for all missionaries (Winthuis 1929:34ff; Burton 1949: 209-210).

A number of missionaries undertook anthropological investigations of the people among whom they worked. Early missionaries often had the greatest amount of firsthand contact with traditional culture and wrote important descriptions of specific cultural traits, particularly recording languages, but they did not examine the culture as a whole or try to see how it functioned (Elkin 1953:6-7). Reverend R. H. Codrington's book on the Melanesians (1891) came the closest to being a full study. In the twentieth century, however, a good number of extensive studies were produced by missionaries. Among the best known of these were the writings of W.G. Ivens and Charles E. Fox, members like Codrington of the Melanesian Mission; George Brown, Lorimer Fison, and E. Colocott, all of the Methodist mission; Maurice Leenhardt of the Paris Evangelical Mission; Georg Vicedom and Christian Keysser of the Lutheran mission; Alfons Schafer and

Louis Luzbetak, of the Divine Word mission; and J. Winthuis, Carl Laufer, Gerhard Peekel, and Karl Neuhaus of the Sacred Heart mission. The Divine Word mission began early in the century from its center in Austria to issue the journal *Anthropos* for the publication of anthropological studies by its missionaries and others.

While many different nationalities and churches were represented among the anthropological writers, it is evident in considering all who were active in this field that the German missionaries made the greatest contribution. When one remembers that the Germans were largely limited to one area of the Pacific, the original German New Guinea, while other nationalities were spread widely, the quantity of their work becomes even more impressive. The difference between the two missions of the Sacred Heart order—the one, German, in New Britain and the other, French, in Papua—shows the German lead very clearly, though the French mission was certainly not devoid of some anthropological interests.[18]

PROTECTION OF THE LOCAL PEOPLE

It must be realized that the missionaries saw themselves more as the protectors than the investigators of the indigenous people. Whatever negative views they may have had about the indigenous culture and however much they may once have opposed and oppressed it, when it came to the land rights of the people or the exploitation of native labor, they often found themselves involved as protectors of the islanders against the power and rapacity of the Europeans (Morrell 1960:438; Grattan 1963; 338-342). The missionaries were closer than the government officials or most other Europeans to the daily life of the people and hence could learn of hardships more quickly (see chapter 13). It was the French Protestant missionaries from Tahiti, for example, who discovered about 1925 that an English adventurer had, through trickery, taken possession of the small island of Mai'ao, west of Tahiti, and was forcing the people to work for him. When the government, on the mission's complaint, sent an investigator to the scene, he was misled by his interpreter (who was in the Englishman's pay) and nothing wrong was discovered.

Not until 1935, through the continuing demands of the mission, was the adventurer expelled (Finney 1968:73; Vernier 1964:1-3).

In the Mai'ao case both of the two common issues, land and labor, were involved. At other times the two issues arose separately. Protection of native lands was itself a major interest of the missionaries. In Papua the leaders of the Protestant missions united early in the century to oppose compulsory purchase of lands by the government, which they claimed was contrary to the promise of free and undisturbed possession of land made by Britain at the time of annexation (*Sydney Morning Herald* 1907; Morrell 1960:405). The Presbyterian mission tried many strategies in the New Hebrides to block the acquisition of land by the big French commercial interests; the mission itself even bought tracts to hold as reserves for the people (Forman 1972:79-83; cf. Burton 1949:51-52; Laracy 1969:332-333).

Indentured labor as it existed on islands of the Western Pacific and the harmful effects it had on family life when the men went off to live on distant plantations were also a constant concern of the missions.[19] In general the Presbyterians, Methodists, and Congregationalists were more active in protecting laborers than were the Catholic, Anglican, and Lutheran missions. When the Australian government moved toward the abolition of flogging indentured laborers in New Guinea, the chief of the Lutheran mission objected (Rowley 1966:136); when in 1944 it considered ending the indenture system, the Anglican mission opposed the change. But the National Missionary Council of Australia, with Low Church groups in the majority, was vigorously against indenture and made proposals for abolishing it which were eventually adopted by the government in 1950 (Stanner 1953:45-47, 132). In the Solomons at this same time, the Anglicans of the Melanesian Mission were still supporting indenture within the area, although they had long opposed recruitment for foreign indenture (Fullerton 1969:224). In New Caledonia, earlier in the century, the Protestant missionary Maurice Leenhardt was notable for championing the cause of the indigenes and accused the Catholics of laxity in this regard (Leenhardt 1922:18). The Catholics were not as indifferent about such matters as he claimed, but they did try to defend themselves from any charges of stirring up trouble among the native population (Laurent 1900).[20]

RELATION TO OTHER EUROPEANS

It was the defense of the islanders which became the main cause of tension between the missionaries and the other Europeans, to whom they would normally have felt a considerable affinity (see chapter 6).[21] Not just defense against exploitation was involved here but also defense against what was seen as the moral laxity and religious skepticism of the other Europeans. One leader of Methodist missions declared that "the missionary's greatest problem is . . . the immoral lives, the evil influences and the greedy exploitation of his European brethren" (Burton 1949: 20). Understandably, the Europeans who left their homes and came to the islands were not usually those who were attracted to a strict morality or a traditional theology, and this often meant that the suspicions of the missionaries were both thoroughly justified and heartily reciprocated.

Other sources of tension arose in the missionaries' operation of small stores and in their great influence in society. The stores competed with white traders and so "brought odium on the mission" in commercial circles(see chapter 13). Stores had been started by the missions when other sources of supply were not available and were a way of getting supplies to the local employees of the missions. They were found in all kinds of missions in the western part of the Pacific where commerce was late in developing—where, as one missionary in Papua said, "you would have to go 50 miles to find a place where you could spend money and even there there would be very little to spend it on." The mission stores were not expected to make much profit and they usually lived up to this expectation. But this, of course, made them even more objectionable competition for the traders who were struggling to make profits. There were a number of attacks on mission stores in the public press in the early 1930s. But most mission stations closed their stores as the ordinary commercial channels for supply developed, and thus this source of tension gradually disappeared.[22]

The extensive influence of the missionaries in society led to tensions with another class of Europeans, the government agents. Prior to the coming of European rule the missions, as has been noted, played an important role in the public affairs of several island kingdoms, though certainly their influence was not as dominant as has sometimes been pictured (Gunson 1969:263-264). After European rule was established, missionary influence was still powerful, especially in the outlying areas where government control was less developed. Outstanding examples of this were to be found among the LMS missionaries in the Cooks, Niue, and the Southern Gilberts, the Presbyterians in the Southern New Hebrides, and the Catholic missionaries in Wallis and Futuna and also on part of the Papuan coast. Catholic missionaries were not excluded from the government in Wallis until 1910, and in Futuna the missionary continued to exercise the power of government under French suzerainty until 1957.[23] Even in central areas like German Samoa and parts of Fiji the government found mission power to be a problem. In Fiji, through the first half of this century the president of the Methodist mission could never enter a government office without all the clerks rising in his honor.[24]

This power declined gradually, but as long as it continued it resulted inevitably in strained relations with government officials. A British representative in the New Hebrides spoke resentfully of the "autocratic power" and "old oppression" exercised by the missionaries and added that though their power was declining the missionaries seemed "unable to accept the change with good grace" (WPHC, IC 1907). In the Territory of New Guinea there was still evidence of rivalry between missionaries and government officers well past the middle of this century. This was not always because the missionary was dominating the people. Sometimes he was too dependent on the people and so involved with his community that he was expected to help them against the administration (Burridge 1960:142-146).

The existence of so many tensions should not hide the fact, however, that missionaries had a good relationship with their fellow Europeans in many instances. After all, the missionaries often depended on government for protection and on traders for their supplies while on the other hand traders and governors found that the missionaries introduced a degree of welcome stability into their environment. Also, despite the frequent differences over morality and religion, there were many shared cultural traits that smoothed the relationship and many common problems and circumstances of life which drew them together.

MISSIONARY LIFE-STYLES

Missionary life in the islands, while released from most of the serious hardships and dangers which had once made it seem so adventurous, was still attached by plentiful problems in the twentieth century. Some reporters have spoken of it as a life of ease, but this hardly fits the average case (Davis 1935:218; Burnett 1910:162-165). It is true that in the older missions the missionaries had well-built homes set in attractive gardens; but even in the oldest of the missions, Tahiti, missionary life required such constant work that one observer complained that the missionaries were too busy to think about what they were doing (Schloesing 1952:24-25). And in the newer missions accommodations were not so comfortable. The traditional grass and thatch dwelling of the islanders was the common residence for Lutheran missionaries in New Guinea and American missionaries in Micronesia until after World War I and among the Catholic missionaries in the Solomons until after World War II. The Anglican bishop of New Guinea maintained in 1917 that "on no account would he live in a European house" (Sharp 1917:29).[25] Since the beginning of the century, however, most missions began to provide frame houses, often prefabricated in Australia. Some of them were huge residences like those of some LMS stations on the Papuan coast.

Even where living conditions became easier, however, traveling conditions for the missionary remained difficult. The commonest way of traveling around the smaller islands was by sailing canoe or, later, by motor launch. This often required long, strenuous effort, especially in the case of sailing craft. Writing in the Marshalls in 1913, C.R. Heine gave as a routine report the story of being caught in a heavy storm, losing part of the rigging, and fighting for two days and nights to keep the ship from swamping. Finally, on the third day, he got a faint view of the sun which made it possible to discover his location and reach his destination that night, only to have to wait until morning to find the passage through the reef. On the larger islands travel was usually on foot. An Anglican nurse in New Guinea in the 1950s told of one trip to a village where she had to cross eighteen rivers: "Thigh deep mud and waist high water was often too deep for me to stagger through" (Clarke:n.d.). Probably the most intrepid walker was A.H. Voyce of Bougainville, a Methodist, who retired in 1958. He regularly tramped 50 to 60 kilometers in a day over rough hills and covered as much as 1,200 kilometers in a single walking tour (NZMFMB 1958). Even where the conditions of travel were apparently more congenial, as in the larger oceangoing ships which three of the missions owned—the *John Williams* of the London Missionary Society, the *Morning Star* of the American Board, and the *Southern Cross* of the Melanesian Mission—the work connected with the travel could be grueling. Missionaries in the Gilbert Islands tell of traveling on the *John Williams* from island to island working often twenty and sometimes up to thirty-six hours continuously while the ship was at an island, getting only one hour of sleep, and then being up for a three-hour boat trip down the lagoon to the ship for breakfast. "This kind of thing week in and week out," they said, "is very wearing" (LMS 1920:25).

The difficulties of travel affected a smaller proportion of the missionaries as the years passed because more schools, training centers, and other institutions were being established and consequently more missionaries were involved in work which kept them in one location. As the number of islanders who were trained for the work of the churches increased, there was less call on the missionaries to visit every village, a fact which further reduced their travel. These developments not only affected travel, however. They also meant that the missionaries were not so closely in touch with the life of the people in the villages. They knew better the institutional life of the mission centers, which could be small towns in themselves—places like Vunapope ('Village of the Pope') near Rabaul or Kokeqolo in the Western Solomons, which included various schools and industrial and commercial enterprises as well as residences and mission headquarters, led a style of existence that was far removed from village life.

Despite these institutional developments, mission life in the islands tended to be a very isolated existence, especially during the first half of the century. Each island was a world unto itself, and even though it might have some institution of importance in the mission, it had little contact with the outside world. An

American in charge of a mission school was, in February 1913, still waiting to hear the results of the presidential election held in the United States in November 1912 (Baldwin 1913). Isolation bred conservatism; without new contacts there was no reason to think new thoughts.

Gradually some change occurred. When steamship lines began to move through all the main island groups early in this century, it meant that once a month there might be regular contact with the outside world. The 1930s witnessed the widespread use of radios on mission stations so that they could learn the world's news in an instant rather than in months. Later still came two-way radios on which they could hold conversations with their headquarters at a specified hour each day, and it was not unusual for the missionary family's routine to be built around that hour. Missionaries' children could even go to school daily via the radio. Fully as revolutionary for missionary life was the introduction of air travel. Both the Lutherans and the Divine Word mission bought planes in 1935 in order to reach the newly "discovered" peoples in the New Guinea Highlands. Journeys to their up-country stations were reduced from two weeks of strenuous effort on foot to three hours of relative comfort in the air. As one Divine Word missionary observed, only someone who had made the trip on foot would know "how rightly to value this new treasure" (Sterr 1950:121-123; Frerichs 1957:190-193). After mid-century, air travel brought the whole world to the major centers of the Pacific and isolation was largely broken down except in the outlying islands. In New Guinea a new organization, the Missionary Aviation Fellowship, created to serve all the missions, tried to establish regular air links with even the most isolated posts.

The increasing use of furloughs for missionaries also brought them back into touch with the wider world and allowed them to keep better health. In the beginning of mission work, the missionaries had come to the islands for life. In some places it might better be said that they came for death. Of the first thirty-three missionaries who came to work in the Lutheran mission around Madang, New Guinea, one-third died within a short time and another one-third had to be invalided home. When, in 1914, the French missionaries of military age in Papua had to present themselves for possible mobilization, they were found to be so badly affected by fever and overwork that they were rejected to a man (Dupeyrat 1935:392). Because of such experiences, regular furloughs began to be adopted, especially in malarial areas like New Guinea and the Solomons. The Protestant missions were the first to move in this direction. By 1916, the London Missionary Society had regular furloughs after every three years of service in Papua (Viner et al. 1916:251). In the more salubrious areas further east, regular furloughs came later. A visitor to a Protestant school in Tahiti in 1930 reported that the headmaster had had two furloughs in thirty-five years and another missionary had worked forty years without a furlough (Allan 1968:3).[26] Catholics were generally slower than Protestants in this respect. Marists were not granted furloughs even in the most unhealthy areas until after 1925, and even then they worked for fifteen years between these breaks (Laracy 1969:149). Catholics in the Gilberts still knew nothing of furloughs in 1939 (Sabatier 1939: 267). But in more recent years regular furloughs for Catholics after six or seven years and for Protestants after four or five years have become the norm even in the better climates. Clearly, missionary life was becoming much less isolated and more comfortable.

FINANCIAL SUPPORT

The financial situation also improved. In the first half of the century, missionaries were generally forced to live very frugally. The famous doctor Sylvester Lambert, who did so much under the Rockefeller Foundation for the improvement of health in the islands, often stayed in missionary homes as he traveled about, and though he found a few which he regarded as luxurious, his general comments were that life was "so bitterly hard and so meagerly paid" and they were "poorly fed" (Lambert 1941: 68-69, 328). This poverty was on the whole more marked among the Catholics than among the other missions. Protestant missionary agencies took full responsibility for the support of their missionaries and sent regular, though modest, remittances to them. Catholics, on the other hand, sent out their missionaries expecting them more or less to make their own way and find their own support. Rome dispatched small supplemental payments, but local resources or personal contacts had to be used for the major funds. This is why so many Catholic missions developed plantations and timber mills and other businesses while the Protestants did so only in the case of the Methodists in New Britain and the Solomons and the Lutherans in New Guinea. The Lutherans in fact were the one Protestant group which at the beginning of the century maintained the Catholic policy of self-support for the mission; missionaries vied with each other consequently to hold down their costs of living, the prize going to one family who lived on fifty pfennigs (12 cents) per person per day. But later the Lutherans sent out to New Guinea practically all the funds needed for missionary support. In this way they acceded to the usual Protestant pattern, though they maintained a communal system of provisioning, each missionary being allowed to order certain supplies from the common stock, which was not the usual Protestant pattern (Pilhofer 1963 II: 98-99; Schiotz 1950: 1).[27] The Catholic missionaries were very conscious of their financial limitations vis-à-vis the Protestants and felt that in consequence their work was seriously handicapped in any competition.[28]

For a time during the world economic depression of the 1930s, the financial situation worsened and in some missions the workers were proposing salary cuts for themselves in order to keep the work going.[29] But after the mid-century the general rise in affluence began to affect the missions noticeably. The income of the mission-sending agencies increased. The Australian Board of Missions (Anglican) was able to maintain annual budgets of Ł50,000 to Ł80,000 as compared with Ł3,000 to Ł10,000 before World War II (ABM 1964:12-13). The Paris Evangelical Mission, which maintained 68 missionaries at the beginning of the century, was maintaining 359 by 1967 (Spindler 1967:9). Catholics reached a new level of comfort and efficiency with more adequate tools for work. The most marked change came in Micronesia, where the poverty-stricken, undernourished, slow-moving Spanish missionaries of prewar days were replaced by the magnificently equipped, well-fed, and vigorous American Jesuits (Hernandez 1955:2).[30]

TYPES OF MISSIONARY WORK

After looking at the missionaries' standard of living, their style of life, religious and cultural outlook, and relationship to other groups, we must consider, finally, their work: the whole raison d'etre of their presence in Oceania. Here a distinction needs to be made between the work of initial presentation of the Christian faith to non-Christians (the work which originally brought missions to the islands) and the many other kinds of work which went alongside this and continued long after it, when conversion to Christianity was completed. The first work was confined to an ever smaller area of the Western Pacific during the course of this century (see chapter 7). The other kinds continued, spread, and grew through the years.

The Christian message was presented in many ways. Most common was for the missionary, in the course of a visit to a village, to speak about his religion and to pray with the people. This was often accompanied by the giving of presents, the giving of medicines, or, with some Catholics, the distributing of religious medals. The presentation of gifts was a standard way of approaching new people in the cultures of the islands; to be parsimonious in this regard was taken as a sign of indifference or pettiness, so gifts were presented. But often the missions learned to regret this approach since it led people to think of the mission primarily as a source of goods. Much depended on the size of the gifts. Where they were large and repeated, much damage was done to later work. Where they were only enough to satisfy formalities, the response was less eager but the relationship was on a firmer footing. The commonest gift was stick tobacco (a black and sticky mixture widely used as currency in the Western Pacific), and some missions saw their path through the villages as one paved with tobacco.

After the presentation of gifts and some talk about religion, the most common thing was to ask whether the village would accept a teacher—an islander trained by the mission to provide the rudiments of education in "the three Rs" plus a fourth, religion, in the form of daily Christian worship for the village. Often villages sent to the mission asking for teachers since they had heard of the work they would do. These teachers and their wives provided the real spearhead of the mission's approach to new areas and were just as truly missionaries as their European leaders (for an analysis of their work see Forman 1970).

If the village was not prepared to take a teacher or the mission could not provide one, the offer might be made to take some youths of the village for education in a central mission school. An alternative followed by some of the Catholic missions which operated plantations was to recruit young men of the village for plantation work rather than for school. In such cases the presentation of religious beliefs or of gifts might be omitted and the mission's approach would be simply that of a labor recruiter. Occasionally, especially when youths were taken for schooling, a payment was made to the families. Sometimes a higher level of payment was made for girls since their labor was more valuable to their parents. But this system of buying recruits was not the most common one. Normally the transaction was made in terms of the interest of the village or of the youths themselves in going with the missionary. Young people brought to the mission in this way often proved to be the initial group of Christian converts who spread new ideas when they returned to their villages. The Lutherans in New Guinea, under the influence of the missionary Christian Keysser, modified this approach by refusing to baptize any such youths until their home villages indicated their approval and willingness to move toward the new religion. This policy caused, as can be imagined, great heart-searching among the missionaries since they had scruples about refusing baptism to those who asked for it, but it was intended to maintain the unity of village communities and in the long run it doubtless made for a more effective spread of the faith. In these ways the missionaries made contact with new groups of people who gradually came into the church and by their entry brought this kind of work to an end.

Other types of work then came to the fore: the administration of the new church, the training of pastors, the education of members. In addition, efforts were made through educational and medical services and projects for industrial and agricultural development and training. Missionaries were no longer reaching new groups with their religious message (except in the furthest parts of New Guinea, the Solomon Islands, and among the Indians of Fiji) but were moving into a wide variety of tasks related to the advancement of church and community. Their greatest field was education (see chapter 6). Native teachers handled the elementary village schools, but missionaries operated the central boarding schools and during the latter half of the century built some of them up to full secondary level. As the level advanced, more foreign workers were needed and this explained some of the increase in missionary personnel. Medical, industrial, and agricultural services were fewer and smaller, but they too called for foreign staff.

ADMINISTRATION OF THE CHURCH

Within the life of the new church the missionary usually became a supervisor or trainer of pastors rather than himself serving as pastor for a congregation. This was not precisely true in the churches which still lacked an ordained native ministry of any size; in them, the foreigner had to provide the sacraments for the individual congregations. But even in these cases the missionary served really as a traveling supervisor who celebrated the sacrament when he was visiting but otherwise left the care of the congregation to an indigenous teacher or catechist. Missionaries served almost universally as bishops or heads of churches until late in the 1960s, and many continued after that time. They felt that the administrative operation of the church was beyond the capacity of the local people. In most cases they also held onto the financial operations of the church (Burton 1930:20). They feared that islanders might be careless in handling the funds or succumb to pressure from relatives and let the money be used for family purposes. Island customs of generosity would make it very difficult to turn down a relative in need. Beginnings were made in a few churches with the use of local people as treasurers, but in general financial operations remained with the missionaries.[31]

All the mission agencies that sent missionaries to the islands were committed to the establishment of an indigenous, locally self-governing church, so these tasks which the missionaries performed were seen as only temporary (Burton 1949:105-112).[32] But it is clear that the missionaries were not moving rapidly and vigorously toward turning over their responsibilities to the indigenous leaders. Until very recently progress in this direction was slow (see chapter 10).

There are at least three basic reasons for this slowness. One is rooted in the colonial mentality which prevailed wherever foreign powers were in control. In this atmosphere there was little sense among missionaries of the need to advance local people in responsibility. The islanders themselves wanted to keep missionaries in charge as long as the church had to deal with European governments. The missionaries would know better how government officials might think and would be able to handle them more as equals. In a similar vein, as long as there were other churches in the vicinity which were staffed with Europeans, islanders thought it would be good to have some Europeans in their own church who could compete more effectively. In the colonial atmosphere missionaries also provided a certain prestige for the church (Forman 1969a).

Another reason is that the whole structure of the church was a very Western creation and therefore seemed to require Westerners to handle it. The islanders could certainly have handled the administration of a church run on indigenous patterns, and in fact the local congregations, which they did handle, were operated in very indigenous ways. But the larger church organization built up by the missionaries was a complex operation looking after many different programs and services. Perhaps the increasing westernization or "modernization" of the islands and the presence of European commerce and European government made this alien type of church structure necessary. In any event the missionaries, though they talked about indigenizing the church, certainly assumed that the Western structures would have to be maintained by and large and that the islanders would have to learn to operate them.[33]

But the education which the missionaries provided during most of the century did not equip islanders to handle so complex an operation. Mission schools in the villages were at a very elementary level. The central institutions that trained pastors likewise provided a fairly simple education, students spending half of each day in gardening, fishing, and building. This was an education designed to make good and faithful pastors or catechists but not to produce national church leaders. There were serious reasons for these limitations. This simple education could be provided without large injections of outside funds. It also kept students in close touch with the people and obliged them to make their living as village people did, rather than raising up a privileged elite trained to spend all their time in study and self-advancement. But such education did not prepare men for complicated church operations, and those consequently had to be staffed by foreigners. In the second half of the century, island governments, with not a little injection of outside capital, started building up education in a more elitist style and the missionaries then moved in the same direction in order to keep up. A whole new level of education for church leaders, with much higher academic requirements, was established throughout the Pacific (Forman 1969b: 156-166). Then, at last, top-level local leadership began to emerge. It must be said that the churches for the most part moved faster than the governments in turning over the highest responsibilities to these new leaders.

There is no doubt that the missionaries had been caught in a difficult situation. They wanted an indigenous church, but one that could deal with the modern world, and they wanted an indigenously based education, but one that could produce major leaders for the churches. These things could not go together. An indigenous church in the traditional isolated island scene was not one that could deal with the large-scale, bureaucratic complexities of modern organizational life. An indigenously based education in which students spent half their time producing their own food, boats, and houses could not produce leaders intellectually alert and resourceful, equipped for the modern world. The problem the missionaries faced was very much like the problem faced more recently by Maoists in their debates over making people "Red" or "expert." A choice had to be made. And the result of the missionaries' choice was that the operation of the church at its top levels continued, until very recently, completely in the hands of foreigners.

The situation is changing rapidly today. Thanks to the introduction of an elitist type of education, most churches now have indigenous leaders in their top offices or have local men almost ready to take up those appointments. We may expect to see in a few years a Pacific church life which is entirely in the hands of the islanders. This development will constitute the most important change that has occurred yet in the place and work of the missionaries.

CONCLUSION

When the island scene is viewed over the past three-quarters of a century, it is impressive how great the change in the missionary picture has been, even in so stable a part of the world as the South Pacific. The religious outlook has been transformed from one that was very dogmatic and traditional to one that is increasingly liberal and open. This has carried with it a new ecumenical spirit in relationships, especially between Catholic and Protestant missionaries. The Second Vatican Council marked a sharp turning point in these relations. Where there was once bitter rivalry, there is now cooperation.

In the same way there has been a great change in the missionary approach to local cultures. The old opposition and repression have been replaced by an increasing interest in these cultures and a desire to preserve and develop them. Of course this change came only after the cultural traits to which the missionaries most strongly objected, such as polygamy, infanticide, cannibalism, and intertribal warfare, had been eliminated. Missionaries had absolutely no interest in reviving those traits.

The changes in standards of living and ease of communication have revolutionized missionary living. In the most obvious respects these changes have made life more comfortable. At the same time, all the problems and challenges of the wider world have been rapidly communicated to the islands, thereby rendering the missionaries' work enormously more complicated and difficult.

But the greatest change has been in the structure of the missionary task. The first stage, as we have seen, was the presentation of the Christian faith to the islanders, though in the twentieth century this stage was still to be found only in New Guinea and Melanesia. The next stage was that of building up the local church and preparing it for self-government and self-support. This was the stage, long overextended, which covered most of the islands at the beginning of this century and all of them in more recent years. The stage of turning over responsibility for church life to the local leaders has arrived and will soon be completed.

MISSIONARIES IN THE TWENTIETH CENTURY 61

The church is now replacing the mission as the center of importance and decision making. This transition was symbolized by the formation of the Pacific Conference of Churches in 1966 where there had only been conferences of missions previously. As this stage comes to an end, the missionaries who remain in the islands will be there as assistants in the work of the indigenous churches. They will finally be playing a role which corresponds to Saint Paul's original prescription: "Not . . . that we have dominion over your faith, but are helpers of your joy."

NOTES

1. These figures include the wives of missionaries since they were often as active as their husbands. The Protestant numbers for the beginning of the century are taken from Beach (1906 II:21-22), the Catholics from *Missiones Catholicae* (1907:713-739). The 1930 figures are from Burton (1930:88-90). Burton's figures for the Catholics seem somewhat more reliable than the lower ones given in *Missiones Catholicae* (1927:344-345) since, in the case of certain territories, they correspond more closely to the locally reported figures available from other sources. The figures given for the 1960s are taken from *Journal de la Société des Océanistes* (1969b:1-41), supplemented by reports from certain churches whose foreign personnel are not included there. The number of Mormon missionaries has been added into the totals for each of the years on the basis of information from the Historical Department of the Mormon church (S. G. Ellsworth 1974, personal communication). It should be noted that the figures given in the *World Christian Handbook* (1962) are not entirely reliable. The number of Protestant missionaries in New Guinea, for example, was, according to the *Handbook*, 548, while official government figures for the same period cited 1,422. The *Handbook's* figures may not include missionary wives, but it is inconceivable that addition of these persons would increase the total to anything near the government figure.
2. The 1930 figure was 663. These figures are taken from the source listed in note 1.
3. There were 315 missionaries from Protestant missions in 1900, 349 in 1930, and 499 in 1965.
4. These proportions are based on population figures for the area, taken from the *World Almanac* (1900:367, 375), of 1,300,000 at the beginning of the century and also in 1930 (1930:589-593) and 2,740,000 in 1960 (1960:333-335, 354). Beach (1906:19) and Burton (1930:86) calculate a proportion of one missionary for 2,500 people, but this does not accord with the absolute numbers they give when set against these population figures.
5. In 1926, 80 of New Zealand's 388 Protestant missionaries were in the Pacific. One further, minor case of geographically related missions was that of the small Japanese Protestant mission with four or five missionaries in Micronesia in the 1920s and 1930s (Japan 1925:95; 1933:57; 1937:54).
6. Figures provided in January 1967 by Brian Cosgrove, editor of *Catholic Missions*.
7. See also Gunson (1964) on the generally unenthusiastic stance of British missionaries toward the expansion of British rule. A well-known exception was the

Reverend George Brown, the most famous Australian Methodist missionary leader at the beginning of this century (see chapters 4 and 9).
8. On the case of the New Hebrides, see Forman (1972). It was remarked that German influence continued in New Guinea Territory after German rule had ended, thanks to the fact that 391 of the 658 missionaries in the area about 1940 were German (Reed 1943:235-236). Although some of these Germans were Nazis, an anthropologist working in their area found no trace of anti-British propaganda from them (Hogbin 1947:3).
9. However, the famous war aviator, Leon Bourjade, who came to Papua in 1921, was one who wrote of the "ardent desire at the bottom of my heart" to be designated for martyrdom (Goyau 1938:113). For earlier examples, see Douceré (1934:203) and Goyau (1938:89).
10. For example, the liberal emphasis was evidenced by the Reverend George Brown, the leader of Australian Methodist missions, in his address to the Methodist General Conference in Brisbane (1913) and by his foremost successor, John Burton (1949:11-12).
11. For similar views see Hilliard (1966:206-209, 248).
12. Wetherell (1973:35) and Parratt (1975:185) give examples of fraternization which were remarkable because of their unusualness. Laracy (1969:248-250) tells of harsh treatment of the people by one missionary.
13. See also Valentine (1958:320-324) on the early views of Bishop Leo Scharmach; Scarr (1967:235-237) on the proportion of "narrow-minded bigots" among the Presbyterian missionaries as late as 1912; Cadoux (1953:263); Wilson (1935); Lebeau (1911:255); Luxton (1955:50-51); Nottage (1940:25); Nicholson (1925: chaps. 1-3); Brendt in Lawrence and Meggitt (1965:104); and MRMCA (1910). Somewhat more balanced are Lehner (1922:374) and Dupeyrat (1935:390, 427, 434-435). Although Winthuis (1929:152-155) attacks almost everything indigenous as evil, in other parts of the same work (1929:18, 63) he speaks of the need to accept the people as they are and to live in real fellowship with them.
14. See, for example, F.E. Williams (1944-1945:141) for a critique of the Kwato mission. For a report on the breaking of taboos by missionaries, see WPHC, IC (1913a, 1913b).
15. See Brown (1910:199), Burton (1949:12-13), Keysser (1921:21), and Butcher (1937).
16. SPMC (1948 II:7-8, 17).
17. See also Laufer (1959:51-59). Similar views are expressed by Laufer (1961: 324-325), Cato (1947:147), Wench (1961), and Lehner (1922:363-373).
18. For more extensive lists of missionary contributions to Pacific anthropology, see Eilers (1967:18-19), Pilhofer (1963 II:310-312), and Elkin (1953:46-140).
19. See Danks (1912:1-3), Flierl and Hopkins (1928:538-549), Wylie (1955: 128-129), Freytag (1940:32-35), and Wetherell (1974:272).
20. For examples of free-church Protestant views in support of native rights see MCNZ (1920:12-13); PMSNH (1907); PCNH, GA (1958); Forman (1972:79-81); Goward (1902:9-10); LMS, IC (1943:163-164); Lenwood (1925:11) and MM, FDCC. (1907). An example of the Lutheran defense of native rights is reported in Wagner (1964:97-101), but the context suggests that the missionary may have been opposing the head tax chiefly because it interfered with church collections.
21. See also Williams (1935:32), Reed (1943:243), and Leenhardt (1922:134-135).
22. See Jacomb (1914:185-188); Burnett (1911:100); ABM (1966:25-27); MCA, BM (1933:5-9); Viner et al. (1916:244-245); Wetherell (1974:279); and *Pacific Islands Monthly* (1932:14).

23. See Fullerton (1969:83); Burnett (1911:60, 169-173); WPHC, IC (1907); O'Reilly (1963:26, 30-34, 43); and *Annales de Notre Dame du Sacré Coeur* (1963:138).
24. See Keesing (1934:94) and Grattan (1948:138). A former president of the Methodist mission, the Reverend S. Cowled, has spoken of the public recognition associated with that office and has also noted that during the 1930s the Methodist missionary, the Reverend A. D. Lelean, so dominated the area around Ba in Fiji that even people who were offered positions in business would secure his approval before accepting.
25. See also Pilhofer (1963 II:86-88) and De Bigault (1947:84).
26. In 1909, when the Reverend A. J. Small was chairman of the Fiji Methodist Mission, he had to make a special request for his third furlough in thirty years (McHugh 1965:55).
27. For a full account of the development of plantations as a source of support in one Catholic mission, see Wiltgen (1968).
28. See also Dubois (1928:404-405) and Darnand (1920-1943:26 January 1923).
29. See also Lewis (1935:27) and MCA, FDS (1930).
30. As another example the Australian Methodist missions showed an increase in annual budgets from a usual Ł50,000 to Ł75,000 in the 1920s and 1930s to budgets of over Ł250,000 in the 1960s.
31. Samoans associated with the London Mission asked for a Samoan treasurer for their church in 1923 but were refused by the missionaries (LMS, SDC, 1923:275-276). The South Pacific Missionary Conference of 1948, however, reported a successful experiment with Samoan treasurers in this church, starting in 1930 (SPMC 1948 III:27). The Methodists in Fiji also started associated Fijians with a missionary in handling the funds of the circuits (the major divisions of the Fijian church) in 1930 (MCA, BM 1932). The New Britain Methodists introduced this policy about 1959, according to an oral report from their district chairman in 1967, but instead of associating a local man with a missionary they associated two local men together in the task. The Protestant churches in Samoa, Fiji, and Tonga were the earliest to move toward the appointment of islanders to their higher administrative offices.
32. See also Paton (1913:138); Lenwood (1925:30); Ahnne (1931:56); Viner et al. (1916:82); Wheen (1923:2-3); MCA, BM (1931); and Oliver (1961:176).
33. The South Pacific Missionary Conference held in Australia in 1948, representing all the major Protestant missions, expressed dissatisfaction with the way Pacific churches, with the exception of the Samoan Congregationalists, uniformly followed the organizational pattern imported by the missionaries, and the "Commission re: the Native Church," appointed by the Australasian Methodists in 1923, expressed a desire for the creation of island churches which would not be a reflection of the mission-sending churches. However, no great change came as a result of these statements (SPMC 1948 III:7-8; MCA, MMSA 1923:11).

MUTUAL BIASES OF ANTHROPOLOGISTS AND MISSIONARIES

Daniel T. Hughes

Having worked both in Micronesia and in the Philippines as a professional missionary, as a professional anthropologist while still a missionary, and as an anthropologist after leaving the priesthood, I have been asked to discuss the mission process from the points of view of the missionary and the anthropologist. Reflecting on the many anthropologists and missionaries I have seen become close and lasting friends, I find that one party often refers to the other somewhat as an American middle-class white boasts that "some of my best friends are black."

This chapter examines some of the basic differences between the missionary and the anthropologist that might bias their views of one another. At the risk of oversimplifying a very complex relationship, I shall divide the discussion into a consideration of differences in world view and differences in role. At the most basic level the missionary and the anthropologist differ in their attitude toward the sacred and the profane. From this distinction there follow significant differences in role. The missionary is essentially a teacher and, to some extent at least, an agent of culture change. The anthropologist is an observer and a preserver of culture.

DIFFERING VIEWS OF SACRED AND PROFANE

Perhaps the most fundamental difference between the missionary and the anthropologist (and the foundation of many other differences) is the way that each views the nature and the relationship of the sacred and the profane. For the anthropologist, the supernatural is a phenomenon to be observed and analyzed like any other. He can observe and describe a religious ritual in terms of the ideology of the participants. But there he stops. He cannot view the ritual in terms of a supernatural reality which has any substance beyond the behavior of the people he observes.

For the missionary (and for any individual of faith), the supernatural is not primarily an object of analysis but an object of faith. It may or may not be an object of analysis, but it must be an object of faith. For the missionary, the most significant fact about a Christian ritual is not the exact manner in which it is performed or even the way it relates to the ideology of the participants. For him the most significant fact about a Christian ritual is its ability to link the participants with the realm of the supernatural.

Although it is true that all Christian missionaries are men of faith who accept the supernatural as an object of faith, not all of them regard the supernatural and the profane in the same light. There has been a wide variety of thought on this issue, ranging from puritanical and Jansenistic views of the profane that are hostile to the sacred to the more humanistic stand expressed in the Teilhardian dictum that "nothing here below is profane for those who know how to see" (Teilhard de Chardin 1965:66). This latter view, increasingly prevalent among Christian missionaries, enables them to relate to anthropologists more easily than did earlier less humanistic theological views.

MISSIONARY AS TEACHER

A Christian priest or minister is ordained to teach or to preach Christian doctrine. If anything, the missionary apostolate assumes a stronger teaching role than a home apostolate. A minister dealing with people of a European culture, a Judaic-Christian tradition, and a thorough grounding in church teachings could well expect to learn something about Christianity from the members of his congregation. Not so the missionary. The task that his church has commissioned him to perform is to spread divine truth to people who do not yet have it.

The missionary is cast in the role of teacher and dispenser of truth not only by his church but also by the people themselves. Even in a nonmission area a priest or minister is called on constantly to tell the parishioner what should be done about a wide variety of problems, many of which are not questions of faith or morality at all. In a mission area there is often an even stronger tendency for people to look to the priest or minister for direction. Even if he wants to do so, the missionary cannot ignore the expectations of the people that he will be their teacher and their leader. These expectations, as well as the mandate from his church, generally cast the missionary in a role of teaching rather than learning, giving rather than receiving.

In fairness, I must hasten to add that there are, and have always been, individual missionaries and even missionary movements that have seen the task of the missionary as one of learning as well as of teaching. The most outstanding to my mind was that begun by Matteo Ricci in 1583. Ricci, an Italian Jesuit, was the first Christian missionary allowed into China and he followed a policy of adaptation which was remarkable. One of Professor Ralph Linton's students said that Linton used to refer to Ricci as the first cultural anthropologist. Ricci was convinced that Christianity could be properly presented to the Chinese only by missionaries who understood and appreciated Chinese language, literature, art, and philosophy: in short, the total culture. He set out to master the fundamentals of Chinese culture and did so with astonishing success. He became a Chinese mandarin, one of the most renowned of his time, and his writings were soon considered Chinese classics.

There are two significant facts about Ricci's approach: first, it was a group effort within the Catholic church and not just the work of a single individual; and second, it was officially condemned by Rome later. When Ricci first entered China, his Jesuit superior, Valignano, gave Ricci and his companion explicit orders to adapt themselves as far as possible to the Chinese way of life. With Valignano's approval Ricci lived first in the style of a bonze and later became a mandarin. When Ricci died, he was replaced by other priests who shared his respect for Chinese culture. This approach was not, of course, adopted by all missionaries who entered China after Ricci. Some of them followed more direct methods of preaching Christianity. They went through the cities holding their crucifixes aloft to attract a crowd. When one gathered, they would tell the people (usually through interpreters) that all the Chinese emperors were burning in hell and a similar fate awaited everyone who followed the teachings of Confucius instead of the words of Christ. These missionaries were scandalized that Ricci and his followers allowed converts to continue to honor Confucius and the tablets of their dead ancestors. Thus began a controversy of utmost importance to Christianity. This Chinese Rites Controversy, as it became known, was not settled until 1704, after a trial by a commission of nine Italian cardinals held in Rome where all documents were in Latin and all arguments in Aristotelian categories. The cardinals decreed that Christianity must be free of superstition and even from the suspicion of superstition. They forbade the continuation of the practices Ricci and his followers had allowed.

The significance of the Chinese Rites Controversy was that a prolonged, successful, and viable effort to expand Christianity beyond the limits of Roman or European culture and Aristotelian philosophy was condemned officially. The world is poorer for the destruction of this bridge between two great cultural and philosophical traditions. Other bridges were built by other missionaries, but not until much later. It is only in this century that papal pronouncements have exhorted missionaries to understand the indigenous culture and adapt Christianity to it. But hundreds of years of rigidity were not so easily put aside. It has only been since World War II, and particularly since Vatican II, that we have seen any large-scale attempts at adaptation. Also, it is important to keep in mind that even with policies that are most open to learning local cultures and adapting Christianity to them, both the mandate of his church and the expectations of the people keep the missionary in his role as teacher.

The missionary as a teacher of divine truth can be offended by the indifference of the anthropologist toward religion. Although it was never an issue in my group of seminarians, I am sure that the question of evolution was a major concern to many Jesuit missionaries who had received their theological training at an earlier date. It was never an issue for my group or later groups of seminarians (at least not in the Jesuit seminaries), because our training in Sacred Scripture was more literary than literal and our rationalization of faith was based on the reasonableness of the act rather than on its logical demonstrability. Previous generations of seminarians had been taught that the act of faith followed closely knit arguments, some of which had rested on rigid interpretations that scholars of scripture could no longer uphold. When we visited parishes and talked to older priests (even Jesuit priests), they often denounced the new professors of theology who were rejecting arguments the older priests had once accepted. The whole notion of evolution, which of course contradicts any literal interpretation of Genesis, was just as abhorrent to such priests as the new approaches in scripture. And their fears were given a substantial amount of official encouragement. Remember that Teilhard de Chardin, the French Jesuit paleontologist, was prohibited by his religious superiors from teaching in France in 1926 because of his ideas on human evolution. He never succeeded in obtaining his superiors' permission to publish his major works. His most brilliant and controversial works came to light only after his death in 1955 when such permission was no longer required.

Whatever the source of their bias, I know that during my three years with the Catholic mission on Truk (1955-1958) a number of missionaries with whom I was associated assumed that anthropologists were hostile to religion. Everyone admired one anthropologist who had been converted to Catholicism while working on Truk some years before. But he was regarded as the exception that proved the rule. The most bizarre example of this bias that I experienced concerned the staff anthropologist for the district administration. I had visited him several times in his office and was very impressed by his knowledge of Trukese culture. We became friends and I had dinner one evening with his family in their home. A short time later I was on my way out of the mission school on a Sunday morning, intending to go to the base and play some tennis. The principal of the school, my religious superior, saw me leaving and asked if I would be playing with the anthropologist. When I replied that I would, if he showed up, my superior said that he did not want me to play tennis with the anthropologist. He said the man was a fallen away Catholic who had divorced and remarried. He claimed that to associate with such a person would scandalize the Trukese. I replied that it did not seem possible for me to walk onto the tennis court and then refuse to play with one person on the grounds that he was a divorced ex-Catholic. So I was allowed to play tennis, even with the ex-Catholic. But the prohibition against visiting the anthropologist's home or associating with him in any way remained. This prohibition was approved by the religious superior of the Truk district and, when I appealed to higher authority, by the superior of the whole missionary territory. I recount this incident with great reluctance because, as with all such anecdotes, it can leave a distorted picture of the people involved. The priest who laid down the prohibition is one of the kindest and most truly Christian men I have known. This prohibition not only contradicted his basic principles but also his ordinary way of dealing with people. He was acting out the very strong feeling of ill will against this man shared by a number of the priests on Truk. I am convinced that a major part of this ill will was directed against the image of the anthropologist as hostile to religion.

ANTHROPOLOGIST AS OBSERVER

If the primary role of the missionary is to teach, the primary role of the anthropologist is to observe. His task is to observe, record, and analyze the indigenous culture and to do so objectively. The goal of objectivity for the anthropologist derives from several sources. It derives in large measure from the doctrine of cultural relativism, which makes him wary of the kinds of value judgments he sees the missionary making.

Certainly anthropologists would agree that it is their job to try to understand the values of the people they study. Most would probably agree as well that it is their proper task to try to discover universal moral principles in the common conditions of human society. Beyond that, anthropologists would generally agree with Firth (1951:183-184):

> The anthropologist... is not concerned directly with questions of ethics—the abstract, philosophical examination of the bases of right and wrong in general, the assumptions on which such notions are founded, the problem of the existence of intrinsic good and evil, and their relation to human conduct and destiny.

If asked what type of value judgments are proper to an anthropologist and how he should reach them, most anthropologists would respond with the principle of cultural relativism. Cultural relativism holds that the values and cultural patterns of a society can be properly understood only within the total cultural context in which they occur. So far, so good. But many anthropologists would push the principle further and say that the anthropologist cannot value one culture pattern over another. They would agree with Herskovits (1948:63) that since everyone makes value judgments according to principles received by the process of enculturation, there can be no basis for the anthropologist's preferring one model of behavior over another. I agree with Redfield (1953:145) that this argument is a complete non sequitur. Because people by and large act according to principles they have been taught, it does not follow necessarily that the anthropologist cannot, upon reflection, prefer one set of values over another. Nor does it follow that ethnographers must be entirely neutral toward what they see in the field. It is obviously necessary for an ethnographer to maintain as much objectivity as possible. But surely Redfield is correct in suggesting that this objectivity must be balanced by an attempt to understand and appreciate the people and their values.

Anthropology is not the study of people by machines; it is the study of human society by human beings. A good ethnography must reveal something of the observer as well as the observed. Anthropologists cannot be bound to be totally neutral toward all cultural patterns or all sets of values. And they are no more required to see all of them as good than they are to see all of them as bad. Anthropologists are required to be open and explicit when they make their value judgments and to make as clear as possible the basis for their preference. Redfield (1953:154): has expressed this view aptly:

> Objectivity requires that I hold in suspense each formulation I make about the native life. It requires me to become aware of the values I have that may lead me in one direction rather than another. It demands that I subject my descriptions to the tests of documentation, internal consistency, and if possible the evidence and judgments of other observers. But I do not think that it asks of me that I divest myself of the human qualities, including valuing. I could not do my work without them.

The cultural relativism that many anthropologists espouse, but few if any practice, is in complete conflict with the missionary's professional dedication to a set of religious values and his expressed commitment to inculcating these among the people with whom he works. Thus professional stance and rhetoric can easily be a source of conflict between the missionary and anthropologist. It is unfortunate that this is so, because when one looks at what is done and forgets what is said, one not infrequently finds that the anthropologist is more condescending and shows less respect for the indigenous people than the missionary does.

The anthropologist's stress on objectivity comes not only from his doctrine of cultural relativism but also from the anxiety he often shares with other social scientists about proving that his discipline is truly a science. Many social scientists are extremely sensitive to the charge that their disciplines are entirely different from the "hard" sciences and are at best pseudosciences. Social scientists often are pitifully anxious to divorce themselves and their disciplines from anything that might compromise the objectivity they consider requisite for playing in the big league of true science. Their attitude toward religion and religious ministers (whether missionary or not) frequently is one nothing short of mere tolerance. One of the most blatant examples of this attitude that I have experienced occurred when I was being interviewed for a position at a major university. While I was in the office of the dean of social sciences for the university, the conversation turned to my being an ex-priest. The dean assured me that this would present no problem to my joining the faculty, and then he added that of course it would be different were I still a priest. I asked with rather open puzzlement what difference that would make. He said he would never appoint a priest to the faculty of the social science college: in some other areas, perhaps, but certainly not in social science. He explained that the religious training and commitment of a priest made him so dogmatic as to preclude the objectivity that is so necessary for a social scientist. I told him that I agreed with him completely; that the study of dogmatic theology frequently produced in priests a dogmatic attitude in areas other than theology. But I added that I had met many people who were not priests who were terribly dogmatic in outlook. I then said that I was surprised he could adopt such an absolute policy on a question like this. I suggested that if Teilhard de Chardin were still alive and applied for a position in this college, he would have to reject Teilhard de Chardin with obvious loss to the institution. If this example is extreme, it is extreme only in the bluntness with which the bias was expressed. The same bias, springing from an excessively defensive position about the objectivity of social science, is found in many social scientists and it obviously affects their relationships with religious ministers.

MISSIONARY AS AGENT OF CULTURE CHANGE

The missionary usually performs not only the role of teacher, but also that of agent of culture change or, more precisely, agent of westernization. Jeremy Beckett explains in chapter 8 that the very concept of mission, "a sending forth of spiritual agencies to spread divine truth," implies a discontinuity and inequality between the main body of believers and those to be missionized. This inequality is due not only to the latter's ignorance of Christianity. It is due also to their ignorance of so-called civilized living and the economic and technological means of attaining it. Thus missionaries have often been willing to enter almost any sphere of society and their influence has frequently been quite extensive.

In chapter 10 Francis Hezel makes basically the same point in describing the approach of both Catholic and Protestant missionaries throughout most of the mission period in Micronesia. In reviewing missionary correspondence he finds that the missionaries have from the beginning sought to convert the people not just to a religion but to a civilization as well. Until quite recently missionaries there have considered themselves as performing a civilizing task. Traditional island cultures were considered to be incapable of nurturing Christianity once it was established. So the missionaries tried to remake these island societies in the image of their own.

The missionary's role as agent of westernization can affect his relationships inside the mission group as well as outside it. During my year and a half (1968-1969) working with a Jesuit group in Manila, the spirit of nationalism was very much in the air. Within the Jesuit order itself there was a strong agitation by Filipino members toward a "Filipinization" of the order. The objectives of this movement were, first, to adapt the work of the Jesuits to coincide with the goals of national development and, second, to replace American Jesuit superiors and administrators with Filipino personnel.

The general reaction of the American Jesuits to this push by the Filipino Jesuits for Filipinization was simply to label it as "anti-Americanism." There were constant and sometimes bitter misunderstandings between the two factions because entirely different meanings were attributed to the same statements about "Filipinization." The Jesuit superior in the Philippines, a Filipino, called in an American anthropologist to study the problem, especially at the Ateneo de Manila, the largest Jesuit university in the Philippines. The anthropologist's approach to the study was from the beginning strongly pro-Filipino and was seen by the American Jesuits as being simply anti-American. The recommendations in his final report were never implemented, at least in part because so much ill will had been stirred up among the American Jesuits toward the study.

Anthropologists are fond of discussing the missionary's role in the process of westernization in the Pacific, and missionaries are often resentful and defensive on this topic. This is quite understandable, since such discussions rarely examine the anthropologist's role in the westernization process and usually ignore the historical context of the missionary's work and the positive fruits of his labor. From chapters 10 and 11 it is clear that some missionaries themselves are examining this aspect of their work and are modifying their approach to the mission apostolate.

Even though missionaries have been agents of westernization, they usually do not identify completely with other Westerners in their mission area. There is a strong group spirit among almost all the missionaries with whom I have been associated, even among the rugged individualists described by Gerald Arbuckle in chapter 11. Of course, some degree of group identity is found among the members of almost any group. Among missionaries the group identity is particularly strong, however, not only because they share the same beliefs and the same training, but because they are put in a unique category by the people they deal with. I have no knowledge of the training programs for Protestant missionaries, but beyond high school the training of Catholic missionary priests generally includes one or two years of spiritual training in a novitiate, two years of study in the humanities, two or three years in philosophy, and four years in theology. Some orders add other requirements such as the three years of teaching experience acquired by most Jesuit seminarians between their study of philosophy and theology. Indoctrination, concerning the goals of the order and the ideal of obedience, helps to develop a group loyalty but so also does the common experience of such prolonged training.

The sense of group identity is also fostered for members of a mission group by the fact that they are put in a special category by the people they deal with. The missionaries themselves and their projects are usually viewed, officially and unofficially, differently from other aliens and their projects.

It is not surprising that the missionary's view is affected by this treatment. On Truk between 1955 and 1958 and on Ponape in 1966, several Jesuit priests were stationed close to the headquarters of the district administration, where they had frequent contact with large numbers of American personnel. On Truk several Jesuit priests and four seminarians also staffed a high school about one hour's drive from the district headquarters. Other priests were stationed in more remote villages on Ponape and on other islands in the Truk lagoon. One priest was stationed on an atoll about 180 miles south and another on an atoll about 150 miles west of Truk. Both on Truk and on Ponape the conversations of many Jesuit missionaries were sprinkled with references to quite distinct groups: "the people" (meaning the Trukese or the Ponapeans), "the Americans" (meaning all Americans other than the mission group), and "the mission." The missionaries clearly looked upon themselves as being in a distinct category from the other Americans in the islands. This was just as true of those missionaries stationed on distant atolls.

ANTHROPOLOGIST AS PRESERVER OF CULTURE

I conducted a graduate seminar in 1974 with six or seven anthropology majors and three or four majors from other departments. In the first session we all introduced ourselves and said something about our background and interests. One of the non-anthropology majors introduced herself as a missionary who had worked for several years with a group learning the local language and translating the Bible in a remote village in New Guinea. She said that she was on leave in the United States for a short time and would be returning to her mission work. Later in the quarter this young woman gave a class report on role changes among the women of the village where she had worked. She had hardly begun her report when some of the anthropology majors began to ask her what right she had to impose her religion on these people and whether she realized that she was destroying the culture of the people she was working with. Unfortunately, the missionary was too gentle or too surprised to respond in kind and the discussion quickly degenerated into an inquisition. I finally intervened with an assurance to the graduate students that not all missionaries fitted their stereotype. These particular graduate students happen to be very bright, and I am convinced they will become competent anthropologists. In all probability their negative stereotype of missionaries will be favorably altered when they meet missionaries in the field and come to know something of their work. But I find this type of bias against missionaries to be quite common among graduate students.

One source of antimissionary bias among graduate students is the approach of functionalism that prevails in much of the literature to which they are exposed. As Merton has pointed out (1957:46-47), there is nothing new in interpreting data by analyzing their consequences for larger structures in which they are implicated. Such an approach is found in every human science. While this is true, the contribution of the early functionalists in anthropology in the 1920s and 1930s was that they established functional analysis as a practical approach to the study of cultures. Boas and the historical group had acknowledged the principle of functionalism in theory, but they had not put it into practice on any large scale. Thus the contribution of the early functionalists in anthropology was significant, but it was not without its limitations.

In his critique of functionalism, Merton lists three assumptions that were stated or implied in the works of such early functionalists as Malinowski and Radcliffe-Brown: the postulate of the functional unity of a society, the postulate of universal functionalism, and the postulate of indispensability. The postulate of functional unity of a society assumes that standardized social activities or cultural items are functional for the entire system. As Merton points out (1957:25-27), that all human societies must have some degree of integration is a matter of definition, but the degree of integration is an empirical variable changing for some societies from time to time and differing among various societies. Not all societies have that high degree of integration in which every culturally standardized activity or belief is functional for the society as a whole and uniformly functional for all the people living in that society. Social usage may be functional for some groups and at the same time dysfunctional for other groups in the same society.

The postulate of universal functionalism assumes that all social items fulfill social functions. Merton rejects this postulate and offers instead a provisional assumption that "persisting cultural forms have a net balance of functional consequences either for the society considered as a unit or for subgroups sufficiently powerful to retain their form intact, by means of direct coercion or indirect persuasion" (1957:32). Finally, the postulate of indispensability states that all standardized culture items are indispensable to the maintenance of the society. Merton criticizes this postulate because it ignores the fact that alternative social structures and alternative social forms can serve the functions necessary for the persistence of a society. He therefore proposes that greater attention be given to functional alternatives, equivalents, or substitutes.

I have dealt with Merton's critique of functionalism in some detail because it explains assumptions found in past anthropological literature. But there is an even more basic assumption involved in functionalism, one that Merton makes as well: the teleological assumption. Functionalism is teleological insofar as it assumes that the purpose of a society is to preserve itself in equilibrium and that the function of any part of that system is to maintain the system in relative equilibrium. In terms of Hagen's logical requirements for system analysis the functionalist approach assumes that a social system is closed and in a state of equilibrium. Although in reality social systems are neither closed nor in complete equilibrium, the assumption is a valid one and, as

Hagen points out (1962:507), it is often useful to construct an analytical model based on such an assumption. However, it may well be useful at times to make another assumption. Thus I could construct an analytical model based on the assumption that the society I am studying is an open, changing system. The model (and the analysis) would obviously be quite different from that based on the assumption that the society is a closed system in equilibrium, but it would be no less valid.

The teleological assumption of functionalism is apparent in much of our ethnographic literature, and it is often accepted as reality rather than as an analytical assumption. Thus a society in perfect equilibrium is considered the ideal, and change, particularly change induced by contact with some external agent, is harmful. Of course the anthropologist found no such societies because none has ever existed. He found only societies undergoing various degrees of change from many sources. So he postulated his perfectly balanced "Edens" (Oliver 1961:xxi) as the societies that had existed just before extensive contact with outsiders—Orientals and Europeans in the case of Pacific island societies. Destructive changes taking place within the society were attributed, often with great justification, to the foreign agents that have come into these societies: traders, planters, merchants, administrators, and, of course, missionaries.

Missionaries, along with other foreign agents of change, have been harshly judged by the anthropologist, and this harshness has certainly affected their mutual relationship. With such a low regard for agents of change, the anthropologist has been understandably slow to place himself in this category. Anthropologists have been much more comfortable with a "fly on the wall" image of themselves. Only recently have some come to examine critically their own role as external agents of change. This is a healthy development, because the anthropologist obviously affects his environment as does any other external agent. There are, moreover, more than a few anthropologists who piously denounce the evils of external agents changing a society and then do not hesitate to try their own hand at cultural tinkering while they are in the field.

MUTUAL FRUSTRATION, MUTUAL ADMIRATION

In the field, the individual missionary and the individual anthropologist interact directly and their mutual stereotypes often disappear or are at least considerably altered. Here, however, the relationship between them is frequently influenced by the fact that each finds the other engaged in work that he himself identifies with in some way. This overlapping of interests can cause a whole gamut of emotions, ranging from resentment to admiration, which may provide a basis for warm or for strained relations.

In recent years there has been an increasing stress in missionary training on the need for the missionary to adapt to the local culture. Courses on such subjects as cultural anthropology and linguistics have become common for seminarians preparing for mission work. Official documents have stressed the importance of missionaries taking and applying such courses. So today many missionaries go to the field with some knowledge of cultural anthropology and linguistics and a strong desire to apply it. But it is often difficult for them to study the culture and the language in any organized way, and it is particularly hard to do so quickly. First of all, the missionary rarely has a thorough training in these disciplines. Secondly, he is often assigned immediately to work that makes it impossible for him to devote much time to studying the language and the culture. Finally, even when he has the time, the missionary normally is limited in the extent of his contact with the people. The anthropologist, on the other hand, has much more thorough training in this regard. Moreover, he usually has almost unlimited time to devote to studying the language and the culture and can do so with fewer restrictions. So the missionary sees the anthropologist do in months what it takes him years to accomplish. It is perhaps not surprising that, under these circumstances, many missionaries have at least some feelings of resentment toward anthropologists. The anthropologist also finds the missionary engaged in work that the anthropologist considers of special concern to his research. Religion, after all, is an important segment of any culture. The contemporary anthropologist finds that in many societies throughout the Pacific the people are Christians. Of course, Christianity here (as elsewhere) contains elements of the traditional religious system. But that does not change the fact that in most Pacific societies the people are Christians and their world view is largely centered on their Christian faith. The missionary participates in this significant area of culture in a way that the anthropologist cannot. He remains much more of an outsider in this crucial area of culture than does the missionary.

The anthropologist, of course, finds the missionary actively engaged in working for the people in many areas other than religion, and in these areas too he may find himself as more of an outsider than he really cares to be. Most anthropologists have a benevolent and often paternal attitude toward "their people" or "their village." The anthropologist is not immune from the human desire to be liked and appreciated by people he cares about. Often the anthropologist is liked by the people he works with, but ordinarily he cannot develop the same relationships and evoke the same appreciation that an effective missionary can. The anthropologist usually goes to the field for one year. Sometimes he returns to the same place much later for another year or less. Although his practice often differs from his officially stated position, he is professedly interested only in studying the people, not in helping them.

Because of the length of a missionary's stay in an area and the nature of his relationship with the people, he is often highly respected and very popular. The missionary's popularity and the type of relationship that fosters such popularity is frequently envied by the anthropologist subconsciously. The anthropologist also wants to be popular, and more often than he would care to admit he shares the missionary's "do-good" instincts. Such instincts are obviously in conflict with his vaunted objectivity. But then why should the anthropologist alone be free of inner conflict?

Once again in this chapter I find myself dwelling on the negative aspects of the relationship between anthropologist and missionary. Of course their overlapping interests can lead to mutual frustration and misunderstanding. But they can lead to mutual admiration as well. I have certainly noticed a tendency among anthropologists who befriend missionaries to see and portray their missionary friends in larger-than-life terms. I once met an anthropologist who had some reputation as being strongly anti-missionary. He had just returned from fieldwork in Micronesia, where he and his wife had resided for several months with a missionary I knew. He asked me if I had heard anything from his friend, Father X. As we were talking, a third anthropologist joined us. The first anthropologist introduced me to him and said that I was a friend of Father X. He then proceeded to describe the priest and his work in a manner that portrayed him as a combination of Jesus Christ Superstar and Jack Armstrong, the all-American boy. I have observed among a number of anthropologists this same tendency to idealize their missionary friends. I think it is partially, at least, a result of an identification process that takes place when the anthropologist comes to know a missionary as an individual and not as a stereotype. He then sees the missionary as a person doing the sort of things for the people that he himself would like to do and he idealizes his missionary friend. Some missionaries lend themselves to this idealization more than others, of course.

CONCLUSION

If we, as anthropologists, wish to understand the missionary's role in the Pacific (or any other area), we ought to begin by examining some of the missionary's basic attitudes, particularly those that relate to his view of the anthropologist. These attitudes frequently influence the missionary's behavior toward the anthropologist and therefore, to some extent, will determine the anthropologist's data. But we should also go a step further and try to "anthropolize" ourselves as anthropologists. We must try to understand and explicate our own attitudes toward the missionary. The second task is much more difficult than the first but no less important, for these attitudes may strongly influence our interpretation of the data concerning the missionary's role.

In this chapter I have focused on differences in the world views and roles of the missionary and the anthropologist, differences which can lead to mutual bias. These views are based on two completely different conceptions of the sacred and the profane. These different world views can obviously occasion misunderstanding, as can the missionary's role as preacher and agent of culture change and the anthropologist's role as observer and preserver of culture. I am convinced that these differences between missionary and anthropologist, though perhaps oversimplified in this chapter, are real and significant. Still they portray only part of the relationship between them: the complete picture would involve a full discussion of the elements they both hold in common.

Over the past twenty years I have noticed an increasing tendency among anthropologists and missionaries to forget their stereotypes sufficiently to deal with each other as individuals rather than as members of a group. The more this has happened, the more they have found that they share a deep concern for the fate of the people with whom they work. Surely this mutual concern is a basis for the lasting friendship that often develops between them.

NOTES

I am very grateful for the encouragement and many useful comments I received from Karl Heider, Francis X. Hezel, Jay Dobbin, and James A. Boutilier when they reviewed the first draft of this chapter.

PART 2: MISSIONIZATION IN HISTORICAL PERSPECTIVE

INTRODUCTION

James A. Boutilier

The chapters in this part are essentially historical in character and address themselves to a number of fundamental issues which have been discussed or alluded to elsewhere in this volume: the impact of South Sea Islands missionaries on Melanesia, changes in individual/clan relationships among the Mortlockese of southern Micronesia as affected by the missions (as the principal agents of nontechnological, noneconomic change), the provision of "formal" education by various missions in the British Solomon Islands Protectorate, and denominational rivalry and the interplay between pagans and Christians on the island of Malaita.

Pacific islanders played an important part in terms of spreading the gospel in Oceania, as James Nason (chapter 5) and Sharon Tiffany (chapter 15) note with respect to Ponapean teachers in the Mortlocks as well as Tongan, Samoan, and other island converts and teachers in Samoa. In chapter 4, Sione Lātūkefu examines the practical and philosophical considerations which prompted the Methodist General Conference of Australasia to employ Fijian, Tongan, and Samoan missionaries in Papua New Guinea, and the Solomon Islands; the question of their fitness for the missionary undertaking; the problems they faced; and the remarkable impact they had on the peoples of Melanesia.

The Reverend George Brown, a veteran of Methodist mission labors in Samoa, advanced the idea of using island pastors in the

1870s. He argued that they would be able to speak sympathetically and effectively about their own conversion experiences, that they would be able to relate easily to Melanesian cultures, and that they would make few demands on the mission's meager resources because of their ability to live like their hosts.

Brown's experience in recruiting missionaries in Fiji, taken in conjunction with the continued willingness of Fijian missionaries to serve in Melanesia (despite disease, deprivation, and death), revealed, as Lātūkefu observes, that "most, if not all, of these men and women were not blindly following the wishes of their missionary teachers, but had taken up the challenge with a full understanding of the risks involved and the important task entrusted to them."

South Sea Islands missionaries had a profound impact on the cultures of Melanesia. By their patient, persistent, and stern (though sometimes arrogant) example they encouraged peaceful conditions, introduced new forms of feasting, promoted agriculture, altered architectural styles, and erected churches. They were successful in these endeavors (despite occasional conflicts with their European colleagues) because of their devotion to duty and because the changes they were advocating were, according to Lātūkefu, "easily comprehended, readily welcomed, and quickly adopted by the Melanesians."

Nason examines two related problems in chapter 5: the attitudes and methods employed by early Christian missionaries in converting the inhabitants of the Mortlock Islands and the degree to which these attitudes and methods had a bearing on the "emergence of native individualism vis-à-vis traditional kin group organization." The focus of his study is the microcosm of Etal Atoll, where roughly four hundred people live in a single compact village on an atoll 1.8 square kilometers in extent. Everyone on Etal was a member of one of the eleven matrilineal clans and was bound, in precontact times, by a set of behavioral values which reduced the potential for conflict, discouraged individual autonomy, and facilitated group task performance.

Nason describes five contact periods through which the Mortlockese have passed. During the first two (1795-1850 and 1850-1899) Etal was under Spanish jurisdiction, though the practical effects of that administration were "nonexistent" and what changes there were occurred as a result of the sporadic introduction of Western material culture and the activities of the missionaries, in this case representatives of the American Board of Commissioners for Foreign Missions (ABCFM).

From 1899 to 1914, Etal fell under the control of a German colonial administration, supported by the German Protestant Liebenzell mission, but it was not until the fourth (Japanese, 1914-1945) and fifth (American, 1945-present) periods that substantial changes took place. Massive off-island labor recruitment, new economic systems, missionary attacks on the belief in ancestral spirits, the decision by the clan chiefs to suspend corporate clan ownership of property in the 1930s—all altered Etal society significantly. The basic ideology of clanship was retained but in an "almost reminiscent and ineffectual way." It was not, Nason observes, simply that the clans per se were no longer effective social units but that "the basic notions of cooperation and sharing [were] no longer effectively in force."

What role, he asks, did missionary activity play in bringing about this "radical change?" The Protestant ABCFM sought not only to promulgate Christianity but also to civilize the Mortlockese, advancing, as Beidelman has noted with respect to missionary activity in Africa (1974:238), contemporary American concerns with temperance, cleanliness, godliness, and hard work. Spurred on in their evangelical endeavors by the imminence of the millennium, the missionaries attempted to promote the political and economic individualism to which they were accustomed at home, advancing the causes of Western education and individual ownership of property.

The biggest changes occurred during the 1920s and 1930s when Father Espinal labored on Etal as Father Marino was doing on Tobi (see chapter 12). Espinal attempted to stop many of the practices that were directly associated with clan chiefs, thereby promoting individualism in a different way. By reducing the role of the clan chief as an intermediary with the ancestral spirits, he fostered the Christian notion that individuals were inherently responsible for their own actions.

Despite these changes, Nason argues that governmental and commercial interventions played the central role in promoting the "basically anticlan individualistic orientation" within Mortlockese society. What the Christian message did do, however, was to provide "an ameliorative symbolic context within which such changes could be undertaken without massive interpersonal disruptions within the community." The adoption of Christianity would not have occurred, he concludes, had not conversion seemed advantageous to the islanders in their efforts to adjust to changing conditions.

This pragmatism (an aspect of the missionization process highlighted by a number of chapters in this volume) was also apparent in terms of the islanders' assessment of the value of mission education, a theme I deal with in chapter 6. Nason describes Mortlockese traveling to Ponape to learn reading and writing, while Harwood (chapter 9) refers to the inhabitants of New Georgia seeking to exploit the political, social, and economic advantages associated with mission schooling. Tiffany also notes (chapter 15) that the early establishment of the London Missionary Society seminary in Samoa fostered the rise of an educated indigenous elite.

In chapter 6 I examine the more formal aspects of education as provided by missionary bodies in the South and Central Solomons from 1893 to 1942. In addition, I explore the relationship between the missions and the British administration with respect to education.

Education was entirely in the hands of five missions during this period: the Melanesian Mission of the Church of England, the Marist mission of the Roman Catholic church, the Methodist mission, the South Sea Evangelical Mission (presently the South Sea Evangelical Church), and the Seventh-Day Adventist mission (SDA). They came to the islands at different times, worked in different places, were perceived by the islanders in different ways, had different objectives, were staffed by personnel from different social backgrounds, and advanced different Christian messages. Nevertheless, they did have common concerns. Each mission, in its own separate way, sought to convert and civilize the islanders, and education was seen as a part of these processes. Yet education in a formal sense was not an end in itself but a means to an end: the production of pious, upright Christians. The Methodists looked upon education as a way of encouraging industry and dispelling laziness; the South Sea Evangelical Mission regarded education as a way of rendering the islanders sufficiently literate to read the Bible and preach to the pagans.

The administration came to rely upon the missions to provide educational services because they had qualified personnel and organizational structures which reached to the smallest villages. Unfortunately, the government's reliance became an "institutionalized excuse for its unwillingness or inability to tackle educational problems more resolutely." In the final analysis, the fact that the missions provided an educational service which was not only timely but advantageous to the administration must be seen as "little more than a happy accident of history."

What education existed was of a lamentably low standard, and by the 1930s the British resident commissioner had come to realize that the future development of the protectorate depended largely on a government program of education. Only Ł54 was allocated each year (out of an annual budget of Ł60,000) toward education. It seemed—in the words of an educational survey—"inconceivable" that such a state of affairs should be allowed to continue. The protectorate was penniless, however, and attempts at greater cooperation with the missions were doomed to failure. The missions resisted strongly any government involvement in their activites, fearing dictation and "secularization." These problems, compounded by personal, organizational, and philosophical differences, were still unresolved when the Solomons were overwhelmed by war.

While chapter 6 examines one aspect of missionary activity throughout the protectorate, Harold Ross (chapter 7) deals with most aspects of missionary activity in one small area of the most populous and politically significant island in the protectorate, Malaita. Specifically, he studies the problems of mission rivalry among the Baegu people of Northern Malaita and the relationship between Baegu pagans and Christians. In terms of the first consideration, mission rivalry, his discussion warrants comparison with Tiffany (chapter 15) and Decktor Korn (chapter 14), who explore the issues of denominational multiplicity and affiliation.

A little more than half the 1,800 to 2,500 Baegu are Christians, and whereas Nason tends to minimize the significance of missionaries as agents of change, Ross maintains that they are the "chief agents of cultural change . . . and . . . provide the dominant role models for acculturation" among the Baegu. The missions enjoy a virtual monopoly on education; and the missionaries have, in many instances, come to play the part of the bigmen on whom the people traditionally depended for leadership and social order (see chapter 9).

Ross observes that each of the four missionary enterprises on Malaita (Melanesian Mission, Marist mission, SSEM, and SDA) brings with it "unique theologies, organizations, purposes, forms of worship, clergy/laity relations, and social policies." He provides an extremely valuable analysis of the theological, sociological, and administrative backgrounds of each of the missions, exploring their *modus operandi* and their strengths and weaknesses as perceived by the Baegu people. The universality of the Roman Catholic church, for example, is seen as a source of appeal to the Malaitans, who are philosophically disposed to concepts of brotherhood as exemplified by the post-World War II Marching Rule movement which united much of the island in opposition to the British administration. By the same token, however, the Roman Catholics have maintained high, and fairly inflexible, standards in terms of admission to the priesthood (a problem examined in the Micronesian context by Francis Hezel in chapter 10), and so the development of indigenous church leadership has been discouraged in Marist mission areas, while the reverse is true in SSEM areas where limited funds, a reliance on the authority of the Bible, and a class disposition to the devolution of power have promoted local leadership. Thus the interaction between the missions and the Baegu Christians is complex, syncretic, dynamic, pragmatic. Indeed, Ross goes so far as to advance (with proper caution) the hypothesis that there may be psychological factors underlying denominational affiliation, a view which contrasts interestingly with Decktor Korn's (chapter 14) and Tiffany's (chapter 15) discussions, which stress the economic and political strategies underlying denominational choices in Tonga and Samoa. Roman Catholics and Anglicans, for example, are seen as attracting "more conservative, tradition-oriented types, people who are comfortable in a client/patron relationship," while the SDA attracts the "most progressive and ambitious types, who are ready to give up the old without regret."

Paganism is still fairly strong among the Baegu but is, Ross maintains, slowly and inexorably on the wane. Both pagans and Christians are tolerant of one another's theologies, but each group believes in the superiority of its own deities or spirits. Pagans and Christians tend to live apart but not entirely so. Pagans fear the ritual contamination which association with Christians entails and are reluctant to face the expense involved in the pig sacrifices necessary to expiate the guilt resulting from such contamination. Nevertheless, kinship obligations and moral ties cut across this pagan/Christian cleavage and tend to bring the two groups together on ceremonial occasions.

Membership in a Christian faith, however, is seen to confer very real advantages. Christian ethics promote peace and discourage death feuds, free women from the worst sex-associated taboos, and liberate men and women from the fear of ghosts and sorcery. Moreover, Christianity implies access to the white man's power and education, while adherence to paganism is expensive in terms of being denied access to a wide range of European goods and services and in terms of regular pig sacrifice.

In chapter 6 I remark that in some ways denominational rivalry undermined mission endeavors in the field of education. To a degree this is true with respect to mission activities among the Baegu, but from the islanders' point of view sectarian rivalry maximizes the options available to them—a state of affairs the Baegu favor, since the crosscutting of kindred ties and sectarian loyalties maintains areal and social integration, multiplies the sources of power to which the lineages have access, and maximizes the likelihood of protection against misfortune.

THE IMPACT OF SOUTH SEA ISLANDS MISSIONARIES ON MELANESIA

Sione Lātūkefu

Christ's command, given to his disciples two thousand years ago, "Go ye therefore, and make disciples of all the nations, baptizing them into the name of the Father and of the Son and of the Holy Ghost: teaching them to observe whatsoever I commanded you," has fired the enthusiasm of outstanding missionaries such as Saint Paul, Saint Augustine, and thousands of others over the centuries. John Wesley, leader of the Methodist movement in England, which was responsible for the evangelical revival that gave rise to most of the Protestant missionary societies of England and America, declared that the whole world was his parish. Many other missionaries were prepared to give their lives for the cause of their Master. The South Sea Islands Christians had their share of this enthusiasm. Most of the missions operating in Oceania employed island converts as missionaries to other Pacific Islands. This chapter examines the impact of the islanders employed by the Methodist mission in Papua New Guinea and the Solomon Islands.

From the beginning, South Sea Islands missionaries played an extremely significant role in the work of the Methodist mission in these areas. They were with George Brown when he established the mission in the Duke of York Islands in New Britain and New Ireland in 1875 (Brown 1908:69-104), with W. E. Bromilow in Papua (then British New Guinea) in 1891 (Bromilow 1929:57-76), and with Rev. J. F. Goldie in the Solomon Islands in 1902

(Goldie 1914:559-586), but the story of their involvement has never been fully examined. This chapter considers their impact on the social, economic, political, and religious aspects of the societies in which they lived, worked, and in many cases died.

EXTENDING THE METHODIST MISSION

For forty years after the opening of the Methodist missions in Fiji and Samoa by missionaries from Tonga in 1835, there was no attempt to extend the work of the mission to any new fields in the South Pacific.[1] This was not consistent with the sentiments of the mission's founder, John Wesley, particularly since parts of the Pacific had not yet been missionized by any Protestant mission. Since 1855, however, responsibility for mission work in the Pacific area had been transferred from the British Methodist Conference to the newly independent Methodist General Conference of Australasia, and the meager resources of the latter in both money and men were barely sufficient to sustain the existing missions in Fiji (Fijian and Indian), Samoa, Tonga, and in New Zealand among the Maoris.

Dr. George Brown, a man of vision, resourcefulness, and drive, conceived the idea that the first of a new series of ventures, the New Britain mission, could be established and maintained inexpensively by employing missionaries from the South Sea Islands, with or without European supervisors on hand. These island missionaries were expected to build their own houses with the help of the local people and to make their own gardens for their keep, thereby reducing costs considerably. Brown, a missionary in Samoa at the time, had been urging the Board of Missions in Sydney for several years to extend the operation of the mission in the Pacific. He had also been in correspondence with his counterparts in Fiji on the subject. But nothing had eventuated by the time he left Samoa in 1874. On his arrival in Sydney, however, he began "to agitate the matter on every occasion" (Brown 1908:70). As a result, he was given an opportunity to address the Executive Committee of the mission at its September 1874 meeting on his plan for the establishment of a mission in New Britain. The members of the committee received his address enthusiastically and approved of the plan in principle, pending further investigation of the area. They also recommended that missionaries be recruited from Fiji, Tonga, and Samoa. Brown was requested by the committee to tour New Zealand and the colonies of Australia to raise funds for the new venture. In the colonies he was greeted with great enthusiasm. One man, Henry Reed of Launceston, Tasmania, even went so far as to donate a new steam launch for the use of the mission (Brown 1908:70).

MISSIONARY RECRUITING IN THE ISLANDS

In April 1875, Brown departed in the mission ship *John Wesley* for New Britain via Fiji, Samoa, and Rotuma to collect missionaries for the new field. Nine missionaries, six of them married, were selected in Fiji, and two married teachers were selected in Samoa. Two of Brown's former schoolboys went with them as well. Over the following decades, through the mid-twentieth century, many others, including Tongans, were sent not only to the New Guinea and Papuan Islands but also to the Solomon Islands and, from the early 1950s, to the New Guinea Highlands as well.

THE SUITABILITY OF MISSIONARY RECRUITS

Questions are often raised as to the fitness of these South Sea Islanders for the work they were assigned. Did they really understand the meaning of Christianity or were they only drawn to their vocation by the persuasive powers of the missionaries, by mass hysteria, or by the appeal of heroism?

With respect to general education and theological training, the Tongans, particularly those trained at Tupou College under Dr. J. E. Moulton, would have been much better qualified for the task than the Fijians or Samoans. In 1869, the members of a deputation from the Board of Missions in Sydney described Tupou College as "a positive wonder" and Moulton as "a cyclopedia of accomplishment" (MN 1869:48; MR 1870:22). It is interesting that no Tongans were included in the first missionary recruits to go to the New Guinea Islands. According to Threlfall (1975:27), the Tongan missionaries selected to join this first team were asked to go to Samoa and wait there for the *John Wesley,* but they were not there when the ship arrived. This seems strange, for Tonga at that time had no regular communication with Samoa and it would not have been difficult for the *John Wesley* to stop at Tonga on its way to Samoa. Furthermore, while Brown remarks in his autobiography that he had been in correspondence with the missionaries in Fiji on the subject of extending the work of the mission, there is no mention of such correspondence with the missionaries in Tonga (Brown 1908:89). Moreover, it would have been easier or more sensible to recruit missionaries from Tonga since almost one-third of the population of Fiji had been wiped out by influenza only a short while before Brown went to Fiji to collect his Fijian missionaries. It seems more likely that the Tongans were deliberately excluded because Tongans who had been sent as missionaries earlier in the century to Fiji and Samoa had been accused of meddling in political affairs there. In addition, Tongans had something of a reputation for "big-headedness." At the same time there were problems among the missionaries in Tonga, especially between Rev. Shirley W. Baker, chairman of the mission, and Dr. J. E. Moulton, principal of Tupou College, which could have made communication difficult (Lātūkefu 1974:195-203).

Although the standard of education of teachers and pastors in Fiji and Samoa was not very high, the men who were recruited there were trained teachers. Quite possibly some were former warriors, for there were still tribal wars in Fiji in the 1860s, and there was a very serious civil war in Samoa from 1869 to 1873. Perhaps Fijian and Samoan recruits were willing to volunteer for this perilous venture because they hoped to become heroes in the eyes of their people. The available evidence, however, indicates that these men fully understood what they were undertaking. Their complete dedication to their calling is beyond any shadow of doubt.

When Brown arrived in Fiji he found that the men who had been chosen to go with him to New Guinea had either died or been prevented from going by the influenza epidemic of 1875. New recruits had to be found. On 1 June, Brown met the students of the Fijian Navuloa Training Institution. He explained to all of them that he "knew of the place [New Guinea], and of the character of the people who lived there; of the ferocity of the natives; of the unhealthy character of the climate; that they would be exposed to dangers on every hand; that in all probability many of them would never see their own Fijian homes again." He warned them that "they might be left there alone without any white missionary to look after them." Then he urged them to consider their decision carefully and give him an answer the following day (Brown 1908:75). Next morning every one of the eighty-three students volunteered to go.

Nine students were chosen. After hearing of this, the new colonial government determined to make sure that the men really understood the situation before they left Fiji. The administrator lectured the recruits on the fact that they were now British subjects, that their welfare was of concern to the government, and that the people of New Guinea 'were great cannibals and very fierce; that the islands were very unhealthy, so that almost everyone that went there suffered much from fever and ague; . . . that they would be left alone without protection or support." Then they were asked to decide whether they were still willing to go. The recruits consulted together and their spokesman, Aminio Bale, after summarizing the administrator's address and thanking him for his interest and advice, said:

> We wish, however, to inform your Honour that this is no new thing to us. Mr. Brown told us all that you have told us about the character of the people, the unhealthiness of the climate and the dangers we will probably have to encounter. . . . We wish also to thank your Excellency for telling us that we are British subjects, and that you take such an interest in us, and that if we wish to remain you will take care that we are not taken from our homes in Fiji. But, sir, we have fully considered this matter in our hearts; no one has pressed us in any way; we have given ourselves up to do God's work, and our mind today, sir, is to go. . . . If we die, we die; if we live, we live (Brown 1908:79-80).

Another example of the understanding these men had of the nature of their calling may be seen in a sermon delivered by Elimotama, one of the Fijian members of the group, on 8 August 1875 aboard the *John Wesley* as it was passing the Solomon Islands. His text was from Rom. 15:20-21. His sermon made three points. Firstly, the path that Saint Paul had followed had been marked out for him by God and not by himself. Secondly, this path had been a new one—a missionary venture—for while others had remained at home to preach the gospel Paul had gone to foreign lands. Thirdly, Paul's path had been the path of the Book. God had promised through the Bible that the gentiles should share the blessings of the Lord and Paul had been called to fulfill that promise. Brown reports that Elimotama applied each point to the Fijian's own situation, drawing parallels between Saint Paul's endeavor and their own with tremendous force and effectiveness (Brown 1908:85-86).

Many of the warnings given this pioneering group proved only too correct. The ferocity and treachery of the people were soon demonstrated in the murder of four Fijian missionaries. Three years after the establishment of the mission on the Gazelle Peninsula of New Britain, these four Fijians were killed at the instigation of a headman, Talili. Talili pretended friendship toward the missionaries, but he is said to have personally severed the head of the last surviving teacher, Peni Luvu, as Peni unsuspectingly drank water from a coconut. The bodies of the four were cut up and eaten by the villagers. When the news of these murders reached Fiji, many more Fijians and their wives volunteered to go to New Guinea to continue the work left unfinished by their dead compatriots. One volunteer was a brother of one of the murdered teachers. When the wife of another volunteer was asked about the prospect of meeting the same fate, she replied quite simply, "I am the outrigger of the canoe; where the canoe goes I go" (Threlfall 1975:47).

Later, in 1891, Seluvaia, the wife of a Tongan missionary was murdered on the island of Panaeati in Papua by a man who had just learned that one of his wives had eloped with a policeman from a distant island. The aggrieved husband went berserk and vowed to attack the first foreigner he met. This was Seluvaia (Bromilow 1914:555). Before she died, Seluvaia urged the people around her to ask her husband, who was visiting another island at the time, to plead for her assassin's life on the grounds that he had not been in possession of his faculties.[2]

It seems clear from these examples that most, if not all, of these men and women were not blindly following the wishes of their missionary teachers, but had taken up the challenge with a full understanding of the risks involved and the important task entrusted to them.

PROBLEMS ENCOUNTERED

Perhaps the most serious problem the missionaries had to face concerned their health. Before World War II more than one hundred and fifty men, women, and children belonging to the mission died of disease in New Guinea alone. Malaria was the most common killer. Because all the missionaries came from a region free of malaria, none had any firsthand experience with the disease; nor, more importantly, did they have any immunity to it. The white organizers of the mission expected these missionaries to live like the local people in houses made of bush material, unprotected from mosquitoes. The Polynesian home islands of these missionaries were mosquito-ridden, and they were accustomed to being bitten by mosquitoes. This made them less appreciative of the fact that the bite of one particular variety of mosquito could be so deadly. Furthermore, the idea of preventive medicine was absolutely unknown to them. Sorcerers in Fiji or medicine men and women in Tonga and Samoa did apply magic or medicine (whatever the case may be) to cure sick parts of the body and prevent spirits from entering the body and aggravating the sickness; but the idea of taking medicine in advance of sickness was not known. For this reason many South Sea Islands missionaries ignored their supervisors' instructions to take a prophylactic dose of quinine regularly.[3] They usually waited until they fell ill; by then, however, they felt too sick to take their medicine and often succumbed.

Another factor was psychological. At home when a person became sick, many of his relatives would fuss over him and give him every attention. There were always "experts" in whom one could conveniently place one's confidence, and often this confidence brought positive results. In Melanesia, a missionary and his wife were frequently sent to remote areas, sometimes among hostile local people. Illness quickly brought homesickness and despair, particularly when the healthy spouse became despondent in the absence of moral support from relatives and loved ones. Strong faith in Jehovah often overcame fear and despair, but in many cases this faith was not sufficient.[4] One former European missionary has remarked that the South Sea Islands missionaries had "a fatalism which is characteristic of Pacific peoples . . . a tendency when they become ill . . . 'to throw in the sponge,' to give up, and in some cases this resulted in death."[5] Often, too, these people had absolute trust in the will of God. They believed that if it was the will of God for them to die, nothing and no one on earth could prevent it.

Although social relationships between the missionaries and the local people were, on the whole, very close and happy, there were minor sources of friction due partly to certain attitudes peculiar to the South Sea Islands missionaries as a group and partly to individual idiosyncrasies. The Tongans and Samoans had no doubt whatsoever of their physical, mental, and cultural superiority to the Melanesians, an attitude that was reinforced by their role of "bringing light to the darkness of Melanesia." The Fijians were closest to the local people. Since they were Melanesians themselves, there were few barriers between them and the people, either racially or culturally. Marriage between Fijian missionaries and local women was quite common, especially among missionaries who became widowers during their term of service, but marriage between Samoans or Tongans and local people was extremely rare. Where it occurred, it was usually with a person of mixed race. There were occasional affairs, but I have not come across any recorded marriage between a full-blooded Melanesian and a Polynesian missionary. Had such unions occurred they would have been severely censured at home.

Of the three groups of South Sea Islands missionaries, it appears that the Samoans experienced the most difficulty in adjusting to their situation. Perhaps the most plausible explanation for this was that the Samoans had (and still have) a tremendous pride in their culture, the *fa'a Samoa* 'Samoan tradition.' Believing themselves to be the cream of the Pacific, they tended to look down on others, particularly the Papua New Guineans and the Solomon Islanders. The special place of the Samoan pastor in Samoan communities was another contributing factor. Pastors in Samoa had their material needs completely taken care of by the villagers. A pastor's house was usually the best in the village, built for him by the villagers, and practically all food and other necessities were provided by the community. Frequently the Samoan missionaries expected the same treatment from the Papua New Guineans and Solomon Islanders, and they became infuriated when their demands were not met. In one place members of the local congregation were denounced from the pulpit on Sunday mornings for neglecting their duty to the mission and to God. The same Samoan pastor had the habit of visiting people's gardens and taking whatever he wanted without asking. Others refused to accept food unless it had been cooked by the local people in the Samoan manner, which normally meant preparing it with lavish amounts of coconut cream.[6]

According to my local informants the people found these demands irritating. Almost every informant said that the Samoans were hot-tempered and quick to resort to violence when the people failed to follow their instructions.[7] The only missionary in recent years to be seriously wounded by local people in the Papuan Islands was a Samoan stationed at Bwaruada on Normanby Island during World War II: a young man attacked the Samoan for having broken his older brother's arm with a spear during an argument.[8] The tendency to resort to such tactics was by no means peculiar to the Samoans. A story is also told of a rather large Tongan who used to shake the huts of those members of his congregation who failed to attend early morning church services.[9]

Another group peculiarity that caused minor irritation, more often among the European missionaries than the local people, was the Tongans' insistence on wearing black suits to preach on Sunday despite the intense heat.[10] This was a tradition of the Tongan church, where the same formal dress was maintained in an equally unsuitable climate despite efforts by such outstanding European missionaries as Dr. A. H. Wood to allow the preachers to dress more simply and comfortably. An old chief in Tonga told Dr. Wood that if he insisted on trying to change this custom, he should return to Australia. At least one church in my area of Tonga still does not permit anyone to preach from their pulpit unless he wears long trousers, a coat, and tie.[11]

One of the problems worrying island missionaries was the attitude of their European colleagues toward them, particularly when a mission had become firmly established. The Europeans condemned the superior attitudes of the South Sea Islanders toward the local people. They looked upon these missionaries and Melanesians alike as black and tended to regard both as "natives." A Maori missionary was rejected by the chairman of the Solomons District in 1935 because the latter would only accept him under the same conditions of employment as other Polynesians, even though the New Zealand church had stipulated that a Maori missionary should be treated no differently from a European.[12] The Fijians, Samoans, and Tongans were not called missionaries officially; they were known as "native teachers." Like local people they were excluded from meetings discussing mission finances. During the early 1950s a newly arrived Australian missionary invited a very senior South Sea Islands missionary (who had been in charge of a mission area during the war years when the Europeans had been evacuated) to such a meeting only to be reprimanded and told by the chairman that the islands missionary must leave the meeting, for he was not entitled to attend and knew it.[13] Even islanders who were ordained ministers were not permitted to perform certain ministerial functions. As late as 1952, the Solomon Islands District Synod was able to pass a resolution saying that Tongan and Fijian ministers, fully ordained, should not be allowed to administer the sacraments except on the instruction of, and under the guidance of, a European superintendent.[14]

Though it would be an exaggeration to maintain that racial discrimination was widely practiced by European missionaries toward South Sea Islanders, there were certainly racist overtones in their relationship. In extreme cases it was quite overt. One Tongan missionary, on the rare occasions when he and his wife were invited to the mission house for afternoon tea, was told to bring his own cups and saucers. In other instances it was a general attitude held by European missionaries who could not accept the fact that their South Sea Islands colleagues might be more expert in some respects than themselves. An Australian missionary visiting the gardens at a training institution instructed students, supervised by a South Sea Islander, to build their sweet potato mounds closer together so that they could plant more in the area cleared. The South Sea Islander informed him that if this were done, the plants would yield a great many leaves but only a few small sweet potatoes. The Australian kicked the mounds, leveling them with his shoes, and then ordered the men to do as they were told.[15] Apart from the humiliation of such a scene in front of his students, it must have been galling for a man who had been growing sweet potatoes most of his life to be contradicted by someone so inexperienced in tropical agriculture.

Fortunately, however, there were others who behaved quite differently. A couple from Tonga who had come to a mission field in the late 1930s could not get over the way they were treated by the district superintendent while waiting for a boat to take them to their post. There was only one mosquito net in the house: the wives and the European couple's young child shared it while the husbands braved the insects.[16]

THE IMPACT OF THE MISSIONARIES

In spite of these problems, the impact of these men and women has been significant. It is not very difficult to find reasons for their success. While the European missionaries generally settled in headquarters away from the local populations, the South Sea Islanders lived among the people. They were able to communicate almost on the same level, and indeed many became fluent in the vernacular. The gap between their own culture and that of the people was not nearly as great as the gap between Europeans and villagers, a fact which greatly facilitated mutual understanding.

When the four Fijians were murdered in East New Britain in 1878, the future of the mission was in serious jeopardy. One of the main reasons for Brown's decision to carry out a reprisal attack on the murderers was the determination of the Fijians and Samoans to march inland, punish those responsible, and demand compensation as an admission of guilt and a token of a genuine desire to effect reconciliation (Brown 1908:287). This determination arose from their understanding of the local people's sense of justice and deep respect for strong leadership. While the expedition was condemned from many quarters—there was even an official inquiry—it was accepted by those responsible for the murders as a just reprisal and resulted in a reconciliation between Brown and the chief, Talili (Brown 1908:286-287). This occasion marked the turning point in the success of the mission as the people developed a deep respect and even affection for the missionaries.

The Samoans and the Tongans tended to be impatient with the character, traditions, and customs of the local people. The Fijians showed more tolerance and understanding of them and their culture. In New Ireland, for example, a Fijian teacher named Ratu Emos Verabasaga, instead of forbidding the traditional *malanggan* 'ceremonial feast,' joined in it and gradually extended his influence through it. He was later invited to offer prayers as part of the ceremony.[17] The Reverend Benjamin Danks tells of another Fijian: "Migieli, a man of Christ-like patience, occupied Waira, a place of murderers, liars and thieves. He was despoiled of his goods, his plantation was robbed, and he was treated with derision. When [the Reverend Mr. Danks and his colleagues] sympathized with him he said: 'Wait awhile, sir, they will know better soon. At present they are ignorant, but light will come to them, and then it will be different' " (Danks 1914a:515).

Another technique profitably employed by the South Sea Islanders, particularly by the Samoans, was to have themselves adopted by one of the clans and become involved in its social activities, thereby gradually extending influence over the community. The people of Taibe'u village on Fergusson Island in the Milne Bay District still talk with tremendous feeling about the Samoan missionary, Joel, who belonged to their clan. Philmon Faiteli, another Samoan, was adopted too, in the village of Nemunemu on Dobu Island.[18]

Feasting was also used by the South Sea Islands missionaries to bring together people who had been hostile or traditional enemies. Informants said that while the European missionaries only visited the village occasionally and in a rather formal manner, the South Sea Islanders would sit down with them, share betel nuts, and discuss their problems. Local people who happened to be in a South Sea Islands missionary's house at mealtime were invited to share the meal with the family.[19] Gradually the South Sea Islands missionaries introduced the concept of feasts to mark important occasions and invited people to participate in them (Tinney 1892-1902:17). When I visited Munda in the Solomons in 1968, a feast was held, and during one of the speeches, the speaker pointed to me and said that it was the Tongans who had introduced this type of feasting. He imitated the traditional way of eating: people hiding themselves and eating furtively, looking around nervously to see whether anyone was watching them and waiting to attack or procure food remains to prepare sorcery against them. After the Tongans had introduced the new way of feasting, everyone sat together, even those who had been traditional enemies, and enjoyed a well-prepared meal without fear of attack.[20] At Tonu, in Southern Bougainville, the people told of Taani Pālavi, a Tongan missionary who had prepared a feast soon after his arrival and invited all the people to partake of it. According to their account, it was the first time in the history of Tonu that men and women had eaten a meal together in public. The following Christmas the people of Tonu prepared a big feast under Taani Pālavi's direction, and he invited the leaders of the Roman Catholic faction in the area, with whom the Methodists had not been on speaking terms, to participate.[21] Feasting Polynesian style has now become traditional throughout these areas of Melanesia.

In their attempts to convert the people to Christianity, the South Sea Islanders, often from recently converted societies themselves, could point to the dramatic effects that the acceptance of Christ had had on their own lives and their own societies, which were similar in some ways to the Melanesian societies among which the missionaries worked.

TECHNICAL, ECONOMIC, AND SOCIAL CHANGES

The South Sea Islands missionaries used materials familiar to local people, such as pandanus, coconut fiber, and timber, and thus more advanced island technologies were readily adopted and absorbed into local cultures. Throughout much of Melanesia the traditional dwellings were fairly crude. They were usually temporary structures, shelters that could be abandoned easily during times of war, head-hunting raids, or other trouble. They were usually without floors and were shared with pigs and other animals. In some areas, such as Misima, the Tongan style of housing was adopted, but more commonly it was the Fijian style. On Teop Island, Bougainville, my wife and I were shown a traditional house built in 1972 to celebrate fifty years of mission presence there. The contrast between that house and the Fijian-type house adopted by the people of the island is quite marked.

We were told that the first Fijian missionary, stationed there in 1922, had taught them how to build this variety of house. The wives of the missionaries had shown the village women how to weave mats for flooring and bedding, thereby improving the cleanliness and appearance of their houses. In many areas they are called "Samoan mats." The people proudly displayed them to me recently on a visit to the East Papuan Islands region.

Informants told me that although their people had gardened before the arrival of the South Sea Islands missionaries, they learned better methods of cultivation from these missionaries and began to plant a greater variety of crops, many of them introduced from Polynesia. In the Solomons the Tongans are regarded as particularly good gardeners. Informants told me that the Tongans had taught them to plant sweet potatoes and new varieties of yams and bananas—one large variety of yam was still called the "Tongan Yam." As a result of this education, more food was produced and crops were better than before. In his autobiography, Brown (1908:199-200) tells the story of Mijieli (Migieli), who was sent to Waira village, 6.5 kilometers from the local mission station. There the people had never cultivated their land, claiming it to be bad, and they lived mainly by thieving. After a while the people

> saw that Mijieli planted the kind of food, sweet potatoes, which would grow best and give the earliest returns; so they began to follow his example and to plant little patches of their own. But the climax came when he took one of their little yams and planted it in proper soil, and cared for it . . . then when he dug up in due season some yams of which they said "one man could not carry two of them," the fame thereof went far and wide, and the men of Waira began again to plant, and in a short time were able to sell large quantities of their surplus produce.

The local people were experienced fishermen, but they were able to learn new techniques of fishing that are still practiced in many places today. They also adopted the Polynesian-style outrigger canoes, which proved highly popular for fishing and traveling short distances.

Sports of various kinds were introduced as well—rugby and cricket were especially popular. Teams were not limited to regulation size, but took on as many players as wished to join the game. In a way these sports were peaceful substitutes for tribal conflicts. Games and Polynesian dancing (stripped of its old association with traditional religion and sexual license) were introduced and brought the people much enjoyment. Improved standards in gardening and fishing, together with more peaceful and entertaining village life, helped improve the health of the villagers.

By encouraging local people to contribute to the work of the mission as a sign of their acceptance of Christ and the responsibilities accompanying true conversion, the South Sea Islands missionaries helped indirectly to improve the material well-being of the people. Some, such as Sione Tāufa of Tonga, saw it as an integral part of their job to help the people improve their living standards. He encouraged the mountain people near Kieta, on Bougainville, to plant coffee; and during his pastoral rounds he visited their plantations, giving them advice and encouragement. After successfully breeding chickens from a pair given him by a planter friend, Sione gave a pair to each village church leader to breed. Later he helped promising young farmers, using loans from their own local mission fund, to purchase land and start farms. My family and I were entertained on one of these farms, and the people warmly praised Tāufa's work and his love for them.

Many of the South Sea Islands missionaries were able teachers. Having no other way of communicating with the people among whom they were stationed, they were forced to learn the local languages. As most of these languages were Austronesian, like the Polynesian languages, they mastered them quickly and were able to teach people literacy in them. They also taught arithmetic and music, including, in one case, the playing of band instruments. One gifted Fijian translated hymns and Bible stories into the language of the area in which he was working (Metcalfe n.d.:16). The Tongans were skillful in teaching music and taught *tu'ungafasi* 'their own system of notation.'[22] Some Tongans introduced choirs to well-known choruses from the *Messiah* and to other classical works; some are still sung today. One Tongan minister, Paula Havea, much respected and regarded with warm affection by the people, taught English, geography, arithmetic, scripture, and music at the main school in the head station of Kokeqolo in the Solomons. In the thirteen years prior to World War II, he was bandmaster at the school, and one of his pupils was Belshazzar Gina, the first Solomon Islander to become bandmaster of the Solomon Islands Police Band.

The island missionaries were strict disciplinarians. My informants, most of them former students of these men, claimed that neither they nor their parents minded the discipline since they were convinced that the punishment was administered for their own good. Of course, strong discipline, including corporal punishment, was an integral part of the indigenous cultures, hence its unquestioning acceptance. Some of Dr. Moulton's former students took with them their academic gowns, received after graduating from Tupou College, and wore them at local school functions and important occasions. European missionaries tended to frown upon this practice, but it was very much admired by the local people. My informants on Matupit Island near Rabaul lamented the mission's decision to discontinue appointing South Sea Islanders to their schools. They claimed, with strong feeling, that their school would never again attain the high standard reached during the time of the South Sea Islands teachers.

Everywhere they went the South Sea Islands missionaries encouraged the construction of sturdy permanent churches and organized fund raising to buy the European materials needed for them. The Samoans came from a land of huge and beautiful churches, and no doubt they were keen to build on the same scale in the new mission fields. The Matupit people told me how Taniela Finau, a Tongan minister, made them buy fishing nets from another part of the Gazelle Peninsula, where people specialized in making nets from strong local material. Under his direction they put the nets across a narrow passage of deep water running close to the village. They caught hundreds of fish and sold them for *tambu* 'shell money' which was stored up in a great pile in his house. Later, as others needed *tambu* for ceremonies, it was sold for cash at a good profit. With this money they bought building materials for the first permanent church on the island, and over the years such churches have become a focal point for the social and religious activities of various communities throughout Melanesia.[23]

CONCLUSION

It is clear from these examples that in spite of their failures and limitations, these men and women from Fiji, Tonga, and Samoa had a tremendous influence on the way of life of the various peoples among whom they worked. Almost every facet of traditional life was affected by their presence. Not only were they dedicated to their calling but the changes they advocated were easily comprehended, readily welcomed, and quickly adopted by the Melanesians.

NOTES

1. The Methodist mission, known in Samoa as Lotu Tonga, had its origin in Samoa when a Samoan named Saiva'aia, who was converted in Tonga, returned to establish the mission on his own island of Savai'i in 1828 (Danks 1914b:483).
2. Informant: the late Rev. David Mone.
3. Informant: 'Ana Finau, widow of a Tongan missionary to the Solomon Islands.
4. Bromilow (1929:158-159) tells of a Fijian missionary by the name of Mosese Nasalo who died from malaria in Papua: "As one Sunday morning dawned, he said to his friends around him, 'I shall die today. Dress me in my best preaching suit . . . oil my face and comb my hair, that I may be ready when the call comes.' . . . Toward evening he cried, 'Look!' 'What is it?' asked his friends. 'There is a beautiful white canoe coming from the skies . . . it gleams like pearl; and when it comes nearer I will step on board. Do not weep. All is clear.' So passed Mosese Nasalo, humble and 'called, faithful, and chosen.' "
5. Informant: Rev. G. Carter, former chairman of the Solomon Islands Mission District, now general secretary of the New Zealand Methodist Overseas Mission.
6. Informant: Rev. Robert Duigu, United Church, Salamo, Fergusson Island.
7. Informants: Rev. Wilson Yareki, United Church, Bunama, Normanby Island, and Rev. Robert Duigu.
8. Informant: Lebega Yarudile, Bwasitolobwa village, Normanby Island. As a young man he speared Noah, the Samoan.
9. Informant: Rev. G. Carter.
10. Informant: the late Rev. J. R. Metcalfe, former chairman, Solomon Islands Mission District.
11. In December 1970 the writer was present in this village church when an old local preacher from another village was barred by local church officials from preaching that evening on the ground that he was not properly attired: he wore no suit.
12. Informant: Rev. G. Carter.
13. Informant: Rev. 'Isikeli Hau'ofa, former missionary to the Eastern Papuan Islands.
14. Informant: Rev. G. Carter.
15. Informant: a retired Tolai pastor who was a student at the time at the training institution.
16. Informant: Rev. 'Isikeli Hau'ofa.

17. According to my informants, when the people brought pigs for the *malanggan*, the Fijian missionaries used to contribute shell money toward the cost of the pigs. They were then allowed into the enclosure where the ceremony was held. There they helped to distribute the pig meat among the participants. The people were thrilled about this, feeling that these missionaries identified themselves with the people. But when the Tolai missionaries took their place they denigrated these traditional ceremonies. (Informants: Timot Kaipeng and Mesulam Pasingus, Lauan village, New Ireland.)
18. Informant: Vabati Gariauna, Dobu Island.
19. It is unthinkable not to do so in Fiji, Samoa, and Tonga.
20. Author's field notes, 1968.
21. Informants: a group of elderly men at Tonu village, Bougainville.
22. See Lātūkefu (1974:79) for detailed information on the origin of the *tu'ungafasi*.
23. Informants: elders of Matupit Island.

5

CIVILIZING THE HEATHEN: MISSIONARIES AND SOCIAL CHANGE IN THE MORTLOCK ISLANDS

James D. Nason

Any consideration of modernization in Micronesia must inevitably focus on the rise of the individual as a social, political, and economic force standing apart from traditional kin groups.[1] This is a matter of some consequence. It is notable because contemporary modernization theory usually posits the development of individualism as an identity relation with the introduction of foreign technology, material culture, and economics, especially the foreign-derived market system and its associated liquid currency. Individualism is thus a matter of concern because of the results that may occur: first, the diminished influence of traditional kin groups, which in turn affects other aspects of the prechange society and culture; or second, the nonalteration of primary individual affiliations with, or operations of, traditional kin groups, which provides us with adaptive change of theoretical importance.

Of associated interest in the study of modernization, regardless of the outcome for traditional kin group organization, is the delineation of how individualism is fostered by foreign change agents, particularly those who are not immediately concerned with technological or economic change. In Micronesian history, this change agent is represented almost exclusively by the missionaries. Their primary objective can be clearly identified as the Christianization of the native Micronesian population. The aim of this chapter is to examine the attitudes and methods employed by early Christian missionaries in the Mortlock Islands to achieve their primary objective. Of special interest is the degree to which these attitudes and methods also had a direct or indirect bearing on the emergence of native individualism vis-à-vis traditional kin group organization.

ETAL ISLAND: CLANS AND CHIEFS

The geographical focus for this examination is Etal Atoll, the smallest and northernmost of the three coral atolls that are called the Mortlock or Nomoi Islands. Positioned at lat. 5 degrees 34 minutes N, long. 153 degrees 35 minutes E, Etal has a land area of only 1.8 square kilometers and an aboriginal population that was probably in excess of five hundred persons in the early 1800s and is now about four hundred (Nason 1975). The island community has always lived on one of Etal's fifteen islets in a single compact village.[2] Everyone on the island was a member of one of eleven matrilineal clans, which were ranked, totemic, named, exogamous, and corporate. Clan rank derived from the purported order in which clans arrived on the island. Each clan held a homestead plot of ground in the village (each of which was further divided into lineage plots) with additional holdings in coconut-breadfruit "bush" lands, taro garden plots, and sections of reef or lagoon. Each clan's land was marked by a large canoe house qua men's house where canoes owned by the clan and its members were maintained when not in use. These clan houses also served as meeting houses for the clan.

Every member of a clan was ideologically a sibling of every other member, a system which obligated clan members to a behavioral set of fundamental importance not only to each clan but to the island's society as a whole. This behavioral set included the following basic concepts: all individuals were basically equal as persons; every clansman must support and cooperate with every other clan member; no aggressive behavior, either verbal or physical, may be shown to any other clan member. While these behavioral principles of interpersonal relationship were generally diffused so as to be inclusive for everyone on the island, they were most importantly maintained by the members of each clan. These principles reduced the potential for conflict within this geographically constrained society and, in addition, served as a leveling mechanism to counteract expressions of individual autonomy and as a clustering device to facilitate group task performance.

The clan chief was always a male who succeeded to this role by virtue of genealogical position (as the senior male of the senior lineage of the clan) rather than by virtue of ability.[3] His duties were marked by the expectation that his conduct would exemplify the general behavioral ideals expected of everyone. Specifically, a clan chief had to show in his demeanor that he was humble, concerned for the welfare of the group, fair-minded, and solicitous of the favor of the clan ancestors. A clan chief who was argumentative, attempted to redefine his role or make decisions without clan consensus, was haughty or greedy, or who otherwise acted improperly would quickly lose the respect and obedience of his clan mates. It would also be anticipated that he would be punished by clan ancestors. Theoretically at least, no clan chief could be deposed except through death, whether natural or caused by spirits.

The proper duties of a good clan chief revolved primarily around the allocation and protection of clan rights. He held clan meetings of the adult members to discuss and approve continuations or allocations of land usufruct tenure titles or of potential land transfers outside the clan (in payment of clan debts, for instance). The clan chief had to organize and initiate group work tasks, including certain fishing endeavors, clearing clan lands, rebuilding clan structures. He approved any proposed marriage involving a member of the clan, ensured that clan rights to property were maintained by clan members, saw to it that restitution was made for injuries done a clansman or his personal property, and settled disputes involving clan members. He also organized clan contributions for the exchanges that marked the end of the mourning period and approved the acquisition or disposal of important properties, including land, items like canoes, and specialized knowledge either possessed by a clan member or sought by one. As the direct intermediary between the living and dead members of the clan, the clan chief transmitted the proper first fruits to the appropriate island leaders at the correct times (to validate clan title to lands originally received as "gifts" from the island's founding two clans); organized the proper burial and mourning for clan members; and ensured that clan members who were ill or in danger received whatever assistance the clan spirits and living clansmen could provide. And, finally, the clan chief had to see to it that the men of the clan were prepared both spiritually and materially for either offensive or defensive combat with other islands.

This account of the clan chief's responsibilities makes it clear that his position was quite different from that of the lineage head: the latter was concerned primarily with the ordinary trials and tribulations of lineage members, while the clan chief's obligations were more inclusive and decisive. This differentiation is especially marked in that it was the clan chief who was the religious head of the clan as a whole—the nexus point between living clansmen and their deceased ancestors, at least some of whom continued to play an important role in human affairs. The clan chief is also more generally differentiated from other men by virtue of his uncommon obligations to live up to the behavioral ideals held to be proper for any islander. For example, the egalitarian ethic was maintained in several ways: a clan chief had to seek consensus decisions, he must not act arbitrarily, and he must continue to work his own lands (unless prevented by age) thereby being no better nor worse in status than anyone else. As chief, however, he was due special respect that clearly separated him from other men and women. One had to speak respectfully when addressing him and pay attention to, if not always obey, his wishes. He was due any unusually large or good fish and a token amount of the first taro or breadfruit. A clan chief could also expect others to demonstrate respect by bowing when they passed his dwelling or his person. The intention of these respect behaviors was not so much to honor the man as an individual, as it was to honor the clan's living representative. Respect shown was symbolic of the obligations any individual had to the clan for lifelong sustenance, in both a physical and spiritual sense. Failure to observe any of these proprieties would not only merit the displeasure of the community at large but would also open up the possibility of an angry reprisal by clan ancestral spirits toward some member of the clan (not necessarily the offender) or the clan as a whole.

Two of the eleven clans on Etal also held chieftainship positions with powers and duties extending beyond and cutting across clan lines. These clans, ranked first and second in importance, controlled the two districts that divided both Etal village and Etal Atoll. The clan chief of the second-highest-ranking clan was thus not only chief of his own clan but also chief of one of these two districts, while the chief of the highest-ranking clan was also district chief of the other island district and paramount chief for the entire atoll. In their roles as district chiefs, these two men were responsible for the arbitration of intradistrict disputes, particularly those involving two or more clans settled in their district, and for organizing and implementing food gathering and other labors associated with district or island feasts.

The paramount chief's position was of much greater import. He held the final veto power over any action that might affect the island's food supply, whether the planning of a feast, the offer of assistance to a typhoon-damaged neighboring island, the levying of island-wide labor to recondition gardens damaged by storms, or any enlargement of taro gardens. His rights over food lands specifically included the right to taboo any island food resource for any period of time. The paramount chief's position also encompassed the right to settle any dispute which could not otherwise be resolved, to approve any marriage planned by any member of the island community, and to direct the external relationships of the island community to the outside world, whether in war, diplomacy, or trade. As head of the clan that first "owned" all of Etal by right of first occupation, the paramount chief received first fruit from each clan via the district organization, thereby symbolically validating the original ownership and "gift" transfer of land rights from his clan to others who came later. His due included respect gifts, particularly of fish and turtles; moreover, others had to be especially cautious in language and bearing in his presence. While any lapse in respect shown to a clan chief would anger the clan's ancestral spirits and bring illness, death, or some other calamity to the clan, any transgression with respect to the paramount chief would bring misfortune to the entire community.

Of particular note in both the district chief and paramount chief roles was the obligation both men had to maintain harmonious relations between island citizens, provide for the well-being of islanders, and ensure the proper maintenance of custom and tradition. Men occupying either role were expected to know island genealogical data well enough to render wise decisions in land conflicts and in approving marriages (avoiding, for instance, the possibility of "accidental" incest). The special prerogatives that adhered to their prestigious positions in the society were simply that: prerogatives due their positions. As individuals, they were not economically supported by their fellows nor were they excused from the ordinary labors of life (unless age so excused them). Were it otherwise they would be guilty not only of laziness, which is contumacious for a male, but also of being *lamelam tekia* 'haughty and overbearing,' an attitude that merits disdain.

INDIVIDUALISM IN THE TRADITIONAL SOCIETY

Individualism can mean several different things in an analysis of a society. In this chapter it refers to the freedom of persons to make decisions which reflect their own unique assessments of the situations they encounter. In other words, individualism is the degree to which a society allows its members to ignore the social implications of their decisions. Of particular interest here is the manner in which the society may socialize members with a set of obligations toward others, since such obligations directly affect the individual's ability to interact with others.

Any attempt to assess degrees of individualism in this society by using historical data and informants' memories alone has to be approached with caution. We have no "hard" observational data with which to check statements that could be categorized as either "normal" or "normative" evaluations. Nor, for that matter, can we always detect biases in historical commentaries by early foreign observers. Indeed, some historical statements can have several possible interpretations. For example:

> At Mortlock the power of the chiefs is very limited; public affairs are reasoned upon and discussed, and those who are the best reasoners and orators have exercised the greatest influence (Sturges 1881:19).

And:

The Mortlock native cringes to no man, seems to respect himself, and to expect others to respect him, yet is teachable and ready to be moved by reason. There is not so much in the life on these low islands to stimulate activity as on Ponape, yet I think these people will not be found lacking in energy and aggressiveness when opportunities are offered them (Sturges 1881:143).

As preceding data have shown, clan chiefs (including district and paramount chiefs) were quite different from other men by virtue of their positions and yet circumscribed, ideally, in the degree to which they could actually exercise authority over their fellow islanders. The reference in the quotation above to decisionmaking seems to confirm other data that point to consensus as the structural form for decisionmaking. Not cringing to any man, however, has to be weighed against the respect behavior due chiefs, behavior well supported by other available data. This reference might stem from this missionary observer's comparison of social equality in this society and in Hawaii (the scene of earlier work by the same missionary group), or it may simply be a faulty interpretation based on limited exposure to this society.

In considering the role of the individual in traditional Etal society, the available data from islanders themselves direct our attention to the ultimate importance of clan and lineage as opposed to any single person. This is analytically substantiated when we consider three different sorts of data already discussed: first, the functional effect of the basic behavioral principles requisite for all members of this society; second, the degree to which clan membership required the subordination of individual interests to group cooperation, sharing, and concern; and third, the *primus inter pares* social position of chiefs as leaders whose actions and powers were clearly circumscribed by custom. Further substantiation of the view that social groups rather than individual interests were primary in the society comes from an examination of various roles for specialists. There were a number of specialist roles based on the acquisition and utilization of esoteric knowledge in traditional Etal society. The individuals who occupied these roles of prominence were always men who had begun to obtain their knowledge at a mature and responsible age, normally thirty-five or older.

The *itang* was responsible for military strategy and training, a man knowledgeable in magic and oratory (with a special "language"), an agent of the island community in situations requiring foreign diplomacy, and a holder of the traditional history of the island. Contemporary informants stated that the man occupying this position was only slightly less important in the community than the paramount chief. This status appears to be a reflection of the *itang's* importance in military affairs and his knowledge of magic (particularly the ability to give magical protection for combat and to place a killing taboo on property).[4]

The position of the navigator was also prominent, probably due to the importance of interisland trading relationships maintained by the community both with nearby atoll villages and with high islands further away (such as Truk). Like the *itang*, the navigator required specialized training and the acquisition of esoteric knowledge, including the native system of celestial and noncelestial navigation, general and specific skills in seafaring, and magical knowledge relevant to seafaring and protection. Recent studies on Micronesian navigation have clarified our understanding of this role and its critical place in island affairs (see Lewis 1972; Gladwin 1970). We also have a traditional historical account from Etal of the accidental killing of the entire population of Namoluk Atoll (just to the north of Etal) caused by a navigator practicing his magic, as well as the islanders' general high regard for seafaring men (see Burrows 1963:91-149). Other roles that required the acquisition of specialized knowledge and training include the knot diviner, canoe builder, and healer, all of fundamental importance within the island community.[5]

Each of these roles required some knowledge of magic as well as special training. The individual filling each role merited esteem within the community, and the associated knowledge was important enough to be considered valuable owned property. Such individuals were therefore controlled somewhat in the use and disposition of their knowledge by the chief and other senior members of their respective clans. Thus a canoe builder would be under some obligation to pass along his knowledge to a member of his matrilineage or clan rather than sell it to someone outside the clan (although this was possible with the clan's approval). In other words, respected specialized skills, while held by an individual, were also considered to be of primary interest to the possessor's clan and lineage. This may also reflect a past practice (which we cannot now verify) of clan apportionment of payments received for services provided outside the clan by one of these individuals. This would be quite reasonable given the basic principle of sharing required between kinsmen (a principle stated time and again by the two oldest men on Etal, one the paramount chief, during my field research).

To what extent, then, can we gauge the range of personal autonomy in this society? Based on contemporary conditions and the statements of older informants, the following general picture emerges. Any man might well decide who he would like to marry, but the actual marriage would depend on the wishes of the couple's lineages and clans, particularly their clan chiefs. The paramount chief would also hold a final approval or veto power. The wishes of these individuals and groups, focusing on both a concern for a lasting relationship and an interest in potential land inheritances, could be completely ignored. But to do so would mean public disapprobation, alarm that anyone would so jeopardize the well-being of the community by courting the anger of the ancestors, and, in an extreme case, exile.

Any man could anticipate spending the bulk of his time engaged in tasks alone, with lineage mates, or with members of his extended family (including in-laws) that benefited both his own family and his lineage. One suspects that for most of the year a man would be engaged in routine tasks agreeable to him. The lineage head or clan chief might, in the casual early morning or evening meetings of men, suggest that fishing be done or that the materials be gathered for the repair of a house and so on, but these suggestions would hardly be orders for immediate execution. One is simply working with one's kinsmen for the benefit of each and all, as things ought to be. But it is equally true that each man is held accountable to his kinsmen and particularly to his clan chief (and therefore to the clan's interested ancestors) for his behavior. Anyone who is lazy, unwilling to cooperate, unwilling to share, or fails to attend regularly to the suggestions of a family head, lineage head, or clan chief would quickly face the censure of the group. By the same token, any man who was in need (legally, medically, or otherwise) could expect to receive support from his kinsmen. And this means, by extension, that any member of a clan would be liable for service when called upon to render assistance either to the members of his own lineage or clan or, as in times of war, to the island community itself. In short, I am suggesting that socialized behavioral principles of interpersonal obligations and structured kinship group expectations were such that individual autonomy in decisionmaking was sharply delimited and contingent upon, ultimately, group rather than personal wishes. And, further, this subordination of individual to group was based upon a belief system centered on clan ancestors with mediating human agents: clan chiefs.

WESTERN CONTACT AND CULTURE CHANGE

The traditional system described in the preceding section no longer exists intact on Etal Atoll. It was changed as a result of direct and indirect contacts the islanders had with members of Western societies from the early 1800s until the present time. These contacts and their effects on the island's culture can be analyzed by historical time period and by the type of change agent which operated in the island's sphere of concern. To evaluate the role that missionaries played in the history of contact and change for Etal, it is first necessary that we review, briefly, the full chronological sequence.

For the Mortlock Islands, the period from 1795 to approximately 1850 was one of initial "discovery" and first contact with Westerners. These contacts took place between the islanders and Western vessels on exploration voyages or those ships which made contact while on a trading or whaling enterprise. From the reports of the four actual landings of foreigners that took place in the Mortlocks, we can derive two important pieces of information. First, the islanders were already aware of some foreign materials, especially metal tools (probably via trade connections that ultimately stemmed from the Spanish settlement of the Mariana Islands). Second, aside from the sporadic introduction of Western material culture in limited amounts, these contacts had virtually no effect on island society and culture.

This state of affairs changed in the next period of contact, from 1850 to 1899, with the advent of more varied agents of change and more intensive interactions. First, there was a dramatic increase in the number of foreign vessels active in the Central and Eastern Carolines. These were initially whaling ships, primarily American, that began to stop at the major islands (particularly Ponape) for relaxation and replenishment. By the 1860s and 1870s, the area was also in frequent contact with trading ships. These contacts led mainly to changes in the material culture of the islands as quantities of foreign tools, cloth, and weapons were introduced.[6] Also introduced into the island scene were tobacco, alcohol, and, on the large islands, resident foreigners themselves. Because of Etal's position at the periphery of this activity, it seems reasonable to conclude that few basic alterations in native life occurred aside from the introduction of new materials (which apparently had no effect on social organization).

Technically, the whole of this area was under the formal jurisdiction of the Spanish government, but the practical effects of this administration in the Mortlocks were nonexistent. Indeed, the actions of foreign governments appear to have had no direct effect in the Mortlock area until World War I. The arrival of missionaries, however, did have an important impact between 1850 and 1899. Although a small group of American Protestant missionaries and their Hawaiian counterparts arrived on Ponape in 1852, it was not until twenty years later, in 1872, that they initiated their first contacts with the Mortlock Islands. These missionaries of the American Board of Commissioners for Foreign Missions (known colloquially as the "Boston" Mission) were active in the Mortlock Islands until 1908; the details of their influence on island life will be taken up later.

From 1899 until 1914 this region experienced for the first time the actions of a concerned and active colonial regime, the German administration. The Germans were represented by a relatively small number of personnel and were concerned primarily with the commercial possibilities of the islands. To regularize their administration of the native population and promote commerce, they introduced a system of "flag" chiefs, the Deutschmark as the official currency, better and more extensive land development for coconut trees, and measures designed to provide islands such as the Mortlocks with emergency relief during times of hardship (after typhoons, for example). They ended warfare, intensified trade, and recruited native labor from Truk District for work on

Nauru and elsewhere. Aside from these measures, the German administration had the American missionaries still in the area replaced by German Protestant Liebenzell missionaries (with the approval of the American Board of Commissioners for Foreign Missions). Most of these actions had only slight effects on the political and social autonomy of islands like Etal, which was maintained much as it had been prior to German intervention. This period is also notable in the Mortlocks for the establishment of Catholic missionary activities, which came about at Lukunor islet, Lukunor Atoll (one of Etal's neighbors in the Mortlocks) in 1916, following the first contacts in 1911.

The next historical period is that of the Japanese administration: from 1914 until 1945. Like their German predecessors, the Japanese concentrated on commercial development of the islands' resources. Wage labor jobs far from Etal became commonplace. A majority of island men spent time away as recruited labor throughout the 1930s and 1940s, and islands like Etal were required to expand and improve existing land resources (particularly taro gardens and coconut groves). The combination of wages, complete acceptance of foreign currency, and the presence of a Japanese trade store on Etal promoted the rapid emergence of a much wider variety of foreign products. Long-distance trading voyages (or voyages of any sort) were banned by the government and Japanese marine transport was instituted throughout the area. Japanese schools were established alongside foreign missions. A system similar to the German "flag" chiefs was developed along with the introduction of a variety of administrative edicts that sought to control land ownership, inheritance of property, and customary law and behavior. While the government was engaged in these actions, missionary work in the Mortlocks intensified with the advent of Spanish Jesuit missionary work in 1921 and, following a period of no contact, the reentry of the Liebenzell missionaries in 1927.

By the end of World War II, life on Etal had changed to a marked degree, a change resulting from administrative and missionary work. Of particular importance was the effect of changes on the native sociopolitical system that had been traditionally vested in clan organization. Government regulations regarding land ownership, massive off-island labor recruitment with subsequent changes in available island manpower, the new economic system, intensive missionary attacks on the belief in ancestral spirits and everything associated with that belief (first fruit presentations, mourning customs, tabooing of land, respect gifts to chiefs, native medicine, divining, native dancing)—all resulted in a significant erosion of clan organization. This disintegration was confirmed in the 1930s by the decision of clan chiefs on Etal to suspend corporate clan ownership of property. At this time, all such properties were transferred to individuals or groups of siblings. This transfer reflected a basic change in the regard for the clan and set the stage for the decline of clan chiefs as community leaders.

The last period of historical contact with foreigners is that of the American administration, which began in 1945 and continues up to the present day. The total effect of the changes either introduced or continued during this administration are too many to list, ranging as they do from basic alterations in the native economy, political system, and social organization to changes in education, transportation, communication, worldview, and religion. For our purposes, it is sufficient to note that present-day life on Etal bears only slight resemblance to that of the traditional period. Of particular interest are those changes that have affected the position of groups versus individuals in island life. Clans are now primarily of consequence in community affairs only insofar as membership in a named clan regulates who one may or may not marry. Clans own no property and in few other ways remain of interest to the population. This is emphasized by the almost nonexistent status of clan chiefs. Individuals who occupy these positions are still known as such, but their influence in the political, social, and economic life of the community is virtually ended. Clan chiefs are neither given respect gifts nor asked about marriages, as a rule, and so serve no organizational purpose. Clan canoe houses no longer exist; clan meetings are no longer held. The basic ideology of clanship—that everyone is a theoretical sibling—is still retained but in an almost reminiscent and ineffectual way. Instead, we find today that the primary unit for production and consumption is the family: either the small nuclear family or the attentuated extended family composed of siblings, their spouses, and children; young adults and parents; or some other combination of kinsmen drawn from one's immediate kindred. Services and resources are contracted and paid for on a primarily individualistic basis, whether we are talking about having a canoe built or obtaining part of a neighbor's catch of fish. In other words, it is not simply that clans per se are no longer effective social units, but that the basic notions of cooperation and sharing are no longer in force. This is true even though leaders at island meetings continue to exhort community members to cooperate with one another and most men will wistfully and readily inform the visitor of how sad it is that clans no longer govern personal relationships. This is well illustrated by the following statements of island men:

> Every clan should have a men's house and land. They should cooperate with each other. We [his clan] do not have a men's house. It was given away with the land [in the 1930s]. This shows we do not cooperate so it is not a clan.

> The desire for money is lessening cooperation since men with stores don't help their clansmen and men working their own lands or copra don't help each other. If this goes on then people won't care any more about clans.

> People don't care today about learning about the clans, where they came from and things. Before, whatever the older man [clan chief] says it is done. But no longer is this done since if a man wanted help he'd ask another man and get help but no one asks now. They have money now and just don't care about men—they just buy help and things.

> Cooperation is obeying what the clan chief says to people and working together on things. No one does this anymore. I do not see any cooperation any more in clans so everyone should just think about their own family.

It should be pointed out that these are only representative samples of statements made by virtually all the adult men on Etal and, as such, reflect a general opinion.

Associated data include, in this review of group versus individual, the absence of a number of traditional social roles and the presence of a number of new roles. Gone from the island scene are the *itang*, the knot diviner, the long-distance navigator, the magically oriented medical practitioner (but not other kinds), and, for all practical purposes, clan chiefs.[7] It is also relevant to note that the traditional respect for senior men has begun to give way in the face of new social roles that are filled by younger, Western-educated men. At present these roles are related to the new educational and political systems, but in coming years they will almost certainly include a variety of economic roles as entrepreneurs.

In other words, both the structure and ideology that traditionally made clans and lineages of more importance than individuals are now so effectively diminished that we find ourselves examining a society much like other Western societies in which individuals have a primary obligation to make decisions of limited sociological impact. Young men in the wage labor market system, for example, are essentially responsible only to their own families, not to their affinal kinsmen or to lineage or clan kinsmen. Of course the community as a whole still exerts pressure through gossip, scandal, and other general social control devices over individual behavior. But the traditional context for individual action has changed radically.

THE IMPACT OF MISSIONARY ACTIVITY: THE PROTESTANTS

We may now seek to determine the role that missionary activity played in bringing about this radical change in island life, examining both the actions of early Protestant and later Catholic missionaries and attempting to understand their rationales for such actions.

The first missionaries to arrive in the Eastern and Central Micronesian area were American Protestants with Hawaiian allies supported by the ABCFM. They established "home" mission stations at Ponape, Kusaie, and Ebon where, after years of difficulty, they were successful not only in converting numbers of these populations but also in establishing schools. During their seminary training, the Americans had been taught that their first task was to establish schools and train catechists, teachers, and ministers (Crawford and Crawford 1967:204-205). If an early history of the American Board and its missions is representative, the tasks these men and women faced were formidable, if for no other reason than their own attitudes:

> The Micronesians were all liars and thieves. They were in the main approachable and friendly; markedly kind to strangers; at the same time cruel and revengeful by nature and sly in their petty thefts.... To the missionaries, fresh from Christian America, the look of these raw heathen was appalling. "The people were nearly naked, sitting or lying around in their huts or in the sun, filthy as possible, appearing more like apes than human beings. I thought I was prepared for all the hardships I should meet, but the question came to me again and again, how can I endure life for months and years amid such surroundings as these?" (Strong 1910: 234).

Here is another, even earlier, view from the missionary side:

> These various groups differ in language and in the details of their customs and superstitions, but agree in the general characteristics of their native occupants. They are the natural homes of indolence and sensuality, of theft and violence. The warmth of the climate renders clothing a superfluity, and the houses needless except for shade; while the constant vegetation of the tropics dispenses with accumulated stores of food. A race of tawny savages stalk round almost or quite naked, swim like fish in the waters, or bask in the sunshine on shore. They prove as ready to catch, as vile sailors are to communicate, the vices of civilized lands. Intemperance is an easily besetting sin; and licentiousness is, with rare exceptions, the general and almost ineradicable pollution of the Pacific Islands (Bartlett 1869:23-24).

And, finally, from yet another early missionary observer:

> At first view so degraded a people as this would seem fit only for destruction, like reptiles or ravenous beasts, or like the Canaanites of old. But deep as is the ocean surrounding their reefs and high as the heavens above them, so deep and high, and more glorious, is the Divine Mercy that would save so wretched a race; and the hearts of Christian people were moved to seek to save and reform them (Alexander 1895:209-210).

These perspectives on the native Carolinians that were to be the converts of the first American Protestant missionaries, all written after successes were obtained, perhaps exaggerate the desperately pagan situation they encountered. But whether or not these are representative attitudes about the islanders, they do provide us with a valuable datum. All contain a basic litany of what was bad about the islanders and their lives. Specifically, they all cite the following points: indolence, nakedness, lack of respect for private property, intemperance, sinfulness. We can easily see that some of these evils were rather standard ones that might have occurred to any civilized Westerner of the time, but others are more a matter of degree. After all, one of the most perplexing problems early missionaries dealt with had to do with the whites who were already in the islands: the beachcombers, ship captains, traders, and others whom they saw as corrupting elements counterpoised to the Christian effort. In fact, what we can derive from all this is that the Protestants were equally interested in civilizing per se as in promulgating Christianity.

This equation of civilizing with Christianizing was not new in the American Board but stemmed from historically important theological events in early America. The development of foreign missions, in fact, began within the context of what has been called the Second Great Awakening in the United States, a revivalistic and evangelical ferment that occurred at the beginning of the nineteenth century. Influenced most strongly by the theology of Jonathan Edwards and Samuel Hopkins in what became known as "New England Theology," this movement focused on an evangelical religious philanthropy made urgent by the imminence of the millennium (Phillips 1969:2-5). Best expressed within the Congregational sect, the movement emphasized religious duty in combination with the evangelical doctrines of the Bible and a Calvinist approach of practical faith and morality. The millenarian influence, although short-lived, added urgency to the evangelical efforts. In speaking of 1999 as the awaited time, a minister in 1817 said: "Before the commencement of the Millennium the Gospel must be preached to every creature. . . . And should the whole Christian world immediately engage in this glorious work with all their might, one hundred and eighty-two years would be time short enough to accomplish it" (Whitman 1817:19). Added to this, by 1827, was the notion that social conditions as well were proper objectives, since foreign missions were to seek "no less than the moral renovation of world. Wars are to cease. All the domestic relations are to be sanctified. Every village is to have its school and its church; every family its Bible and the morning and evening prayer. The tabernacle of God is to be pitched among men" (ABCFM 1827:159). This, then, was the beginning of the civilizing goal as a fundamental part of Christian activity.

The instructions given the first American Protestant missionaries to Hawaii by Secretary Worcester of the American Board illustrate this goal:

> You are to aim at nothing short of covering those islands with fruitful fields and pleasant dwellings, and schools and churches; of raising up the whole people to an elevated state of Christian civilization; of bringing, or preparing the means of bringing, thousands and millions of the present and succeeding generations to the mansions of blessedness (Phillips 1969: 94).

While accepting and reinforcing the notion that Christianity and civilization go hand in hand, it was nonetheless true that the former had to take precedence over the latter. Thus the Christian message of the Hawaii mission was described in 1833 as preceding "civilization and . . . leading the way to it. Twelve years ago, the people were enveloped in thick pagan gloom; but the Sun of Righteousness has risen" (Phillips 1969:96). But, given the task, this was a bit over optimistic, as we can see in a letter from an early missionary to Hawaii written in 1838:

> This people have much idle time on their hands, which we feel anxious to have employed to some valuable end. It is a most difficult task to teach industry to an idle people. But it is necessary to the promotion of their Christian character. An idle, improvident Christian is a contradiction in terms. And such have ever been the lazy habits of this people that they cannot improve on themselves without the influence and example of those who are willing to persevere in teaching and encouraging them to work. A little labor will suffice to provide a supply of food for their own consumption and, besides this, the wants of nature's children are few. Our Hawaiian Christians find themselves in consequence in possession of much idle time, and their previous habits make it sit easily upon them. . . . Their time must therefore be spent in indolence or, what is worse, in exposure to corrupting influences to which their fondness for each other's society peculiarly leads them. To this influence our churches will continue to be exposed until some means of employment can be devised which shall tend to raise them from their poverty and degradation (Gulick and Hinckley 1918:161).

What civilization meant, aside from the specifics mentioned time and again in passages such as the one above, has been admirably summarized by Berkhofer (1965:6-7) in his study of

American Protestant missionization of the American Indians:

> Comprising civilization was a cluster of institutional arrangements that Americans sought to achieve between the Revolution and the Civil War. Economically, they moved toward allowing economic individualism free rein under the liberal state. Politically, they first realized republicanism, then democracy. Lastly, the liberty of the individual was foremost in their minds; hence all social institutions were assumed to exist solely for the benefit of the individual.

The conjoining of temperance ideals with evangelical Protestant missionization developed with the temperance movement in New England in the early 1830s and was again related specifically to concepts of Calvinist and evangelical Christian duty. The strict prohibitions against both drinking and smoking, and particularly drinking, were based not only on an expectation that drinking led to quarrels and homicides, but also because it wasted time and funds. "Idleness was condemned, as was gossip. Native dances ... and 'frolics' violated the dicta against intemperance and idleness. All church members had to pay their debts promptly or face expulsion" (Berkhofer 1965:61). Regretfully, the first American missionaries in Micronesia had a good deal to contend with when it came to temperance matters, since both whalers and traders commonly used tobacco and alcohol along with tools, weapons, and cloth as trade items (Marshall and Marshall 1976). As noted by Loomis in her history of the Micronesian mission (1970:71):

> Red flannel and fishhooks and hatchets had some slight value in the trade, but these items neither served the chiefs in their tribal fights, as did firearms, nor satisfied desperate appetites, as did liquor and tobacco. Smoking and chewing, indeed, seemed to the missionaries, as they observed the natives, fully as disastrous as drinking.

Seen from this perspective of missionary concerns, it was small wonder that early missionaries asked how life could be endured. They found a native population in the Mortlocks which, as on Ponape, was not only idolatrous but also indolent, intemperate, and in various other respects apparently unconcerned with success in life. It must have been hard for them to know where to begin. Confirmation of Christian attitudes about individualism in native society at this time comes from several sources. Frederick Moss, who visited the Mortlocks in 1886 and spoke with the American missionary there, said later: "They [the natives] need more useful occupation, more healthy pastime and recreation mental and physical, wider instruction, a healthier public opinion, and a steady but cautious attack on their deadly communism" (Moss 1889:175). On the same tack, yet another American Protestant missionary in the Mortlocks wrote about the situation on Ponape: "Humanity here is a slushy mass, melted down and run together. . . . We are obliged to work upon the whole, the *mass* as such, because we cannot find an *individual*. In fact there is no such thing here as individual action and individual responsibility" (Sturges 1854). In 1873, Sturges again observed in regard to Ponape that *"want* of *authority* and *ownership* greatly hinders our work in reconstruction here. Everybody *owns* and does everything in general but nothing in particular" (Sturges 1873). "This law," he noted later in reference to a homestead law, "is the most radical of any they need, as it strikes at the root of the great evil here—a kind of socialism, quite destroying all our efforts to *fix* them as to place or property" (Sturges 1873).

From yet another of the early American Protestant missionaries, we gain an idea of how the attack on individualism was to be conducted on Ponape. As reported by O'Brien (1971:61):

> At this time [1872] Doane wrote of "the great work of civilizing this debased people." This work included the reorganization of the traditional land ownership by the tribe, and a "democratic" form of trial and punishment which did not rely on custom or the will of the chiefs. It encouraged the housing and dressing of the natives in a way more acceptable to the missionaries, a way which made them more vulnerable to commercial exploitation than they would have been in their native way of life.

At this juncture it is worthwhile summarizing what had to be done from the point of view of the American Protestant mission. First, they viewed native life as inherently lazy, with too few tasks to occupy "idle hands." To remedy this required that natives be trained in a host of new tasks through the mission schools that were opened up on home mission islands like Ponape. Thus, in the 1870s, we find Mortlock Islanders going to Ponape to learn to read, write, do arithmetic, study the gospel, and also learn sewing, carpentry, how to build Western-style houses, and farming—in short, to learn a variety of new technological and social roles, particularly that of native catechist or deacon. The wearing of long hair by men and the use of turmeric as a body paint were stamped out because these practices were not hygienic, indicated a pagan life, and were related to a belief in spirits. The people had to stop believing in spirits and ghosts in order to receive the Christian message. Drinking, smoking, and native dancing had to be eradicated since these were not only intemperate and sensual pleasures of the body but also wasteful of a good Christian's time. Clothing had to be worn since nakedness led to sensuality and depravity and probably promoted adulterous relations. And, finally, the native communities had to be encouraged in the development of a love for, and respect of, privately owned property, with an emphasis on the accumulation of individual property rather than group property (that is, clan ownership of lands).

At the same time, it seems clear that none of these early missionaries attempted to destroy outright the native political system itself. Nor did they always seek the complete destruction of the traditional religious system. Their rationale is admirably explained by Albert Sturges, one of the first of these missionaries:

> It is to our great advantage that we recognize the religious faith of these people. Paganism is infinitely more cultivable than atheism. The heathen who sees God in everything is a much more hopeful subject for the missionary than one who sees no need of a God. We do well to study the religious thoughts and habits of these people. We ought never to attack their beliefs or worship. It will not compromise us nor our religion to recognize them as fellow religionists. It will pay to be on friendly terms with their priests (Crawford and Crawford 1967:74).

In another context:

> The Christian missionary's job is not to sweep away heathenism and build something entirely new in its place but to mend up the religion already there. Conserve the much good in it and build up on it as a foundation. They abhor murder, adultery, stealing and lying as we do, and they have something of an idea of deity. Do not try to break down and discredit their sense of religion, but show them the true God, as we see Him, where and how He may be found and how He may be worshipped and truly served (Crawford and Crawford 1967:220).

The successes of this approach were only partial. Men did not, in the Mortlock area, entirely give up the wearing of long hair, the use of turmeric, smoking, and the system of clan ownership of property at any time during the Protestant period (from 1872 until 1908). Nor did they adopt completely Western clothes and Western education. Belief in clan ancestors remained important in native life throughout the Japanese period, as did the prominence of clan chiefs and the traditional political system. What did happen was the development of actual churches with sizable congregations on each of the Mortlock Islands. The missions in these islands that were established in 1872 were staffed by Ponapean couples trained by the American Protestant missionaries, who also oversaw their activities in regular visits from Ponape. These churches in the Mortlocks, supported by the tithes of the faithful on Ponape, did remarkably well. Etal's church was built in 1875 and by 1877 Etal had a school, regular church services, and a permanent minister—all due to the efforts of the island paramount chief, who picked up a trained Ponapean for Etal and its fifty church members. By 1879 more Etal people were in the church and even the paramount chief's son had been to Ponape (the year before) where he acquired Western clothing.

But the genuineness of the Etal conversion came into question in 1882 when a visiting missionary reported that the islands were being continually "reinfected" in sinful ways by young men returning from work on foreign vessels (Sturges 1882:498). In fact, during the 1880s the mission's work in the Mortlocks seemed to collapse: one of the native ministers had been dismissed for becoming a trader and many people had fallen into sin. Perhaps this falling away had more to do with the interruption of mission ship visits and the subsequent lack of mission goods for distribution than with a change of religious heart on the part of the community. Certainly the missionaries encouraged the activities of traders and the hopeful benefits of trade as part of the civilizing process. In 1873, for example, one of the missionaries reported after contact with a German trading company: "A change is coming over the business world. Men are beginning to see that the missions are a blessing to people. This heavy firm is seeing that, in a commercial point of view, missions pay" (Doane 1873:229).

The disruption in missionary activity that came about in 1908 with the transition from the American Board to the German Liebenzell mission resulted in only modest advances in the missionary endeavor. The missionaries had indeed acted as change agents, but not entirely in the manner they had wished. Their promotion of Western goods as part of the civilizing process had its effect. Trade flourished and expanded, both within and without the framework of German and Japanese government, all during and after missionary presence. The Americans had found their targets and set their sights. But the actual extent to which they were able to change the basic social organization of the island community on Etal appears to have been slight.

THE EARLY CATHOLIC ENTERPRISE

Earlier in this chapter it was pointed out that the most striking changes that occurred on Etal were during the Japanese administration of the islands. In this same period the first Catholic missionary efforts in the Mortlocks also began, following after and building upon the earlier Protestant attempts to convert these populations. In 1907, a serious typhoon struck the Mortlock Islands and a portion of the population was subsequently moved to Ponape. Mortlock Islanders first became acquainted with the Catholic church while in Ponape, and when they were ready to be repatriated to their home islands they requested a priest for the Mortlocks. In response to this, Father Gebhard Rudell, a German Capuchin, came to Lukunor in 1911 to establish a church. His time in the Mortlocks was short-lived, however, since the Japanese government repatriated all German religious personnel when they assumed control of the territory in 1914. It was not until 1921 that the Japanese government agreed to the entry of Catholic priests of neutral nationality. The Vatican requested Spanish Jesuits for this work and in that same year, 1921, Father Martin Espinal arrived on Lukunor to begin work. (Apparently a brother had already built a small chapel on Lukunor.) At the time of Espinal's arrival there were almost four hundred Catholics on Lukunor, the result of Rudell's earlier efforts. Using Lukunor as his base of operations, Espinal visited each of the island communities in the Lower Mortlocks. By 1927, the year when the government agreed to the reentry of the German Liebenzell missionaries (on Oneop islet, Lukunor Atoll, in the Mortlocks), Espinal had completed a large basilica on Lukunor, acquired a motor launch to facilitate his work, and converted almost one-third of the entire Mortlock population to Catholicism.

When he arrived, Espinal found Etal to be all at least nominally Protestant, but by 1935 over one-half of the island was Catholic. The people of Etal stated during field research that the permissive attitude of the church toward drinking and smoking swayed some, but most were converted by Father Espinal's dynamic evangelization. During the more than twenty years that Espinal labored in the Mortlocks a great many native customs and traditional beliefs were affected. Like his Protestant predecessors, Espinal apparently had no desire to change the political structure of the islands but intended to work through the native chiefs. He was not, apparently, so concerned about "civilizing" as a basic evangelical goal to accompany Christianization as were his Protestant counterparts. Indeed, it seems that most of the islanders' best memories of his work have to do with prohibitions of native customs and beliefs involving ancestors and spirits.

Espinal's attempts to change native beliefs were impressive. He tried to stop the practice of regarding some foods, such as totemic clan animals, as prohibited. He attempted to stop many of the practices that were directly associated with the position of the clan chiefs—the right of a clan chief to taboo lands belonging to a deceased clansman as part of the traditional mourning ceremony (related to a belief in the power of that person's ghost); the right of a clan chief to receive respect gifts from clansmen (a practice aimed ultimately at showing respect for clan ancestors); and the right of a clan chief to receive first fruits (a custom validating land rights and intended to show respect for clan ancestors). Each of these rights, in other words, in some way involved the belief in ghosts as active and potentially harmful agents in the lives of the people. If first fruits or respect gifts were not given, for instance, then the ancestral ghosts that remained active in a clan would be offended and cause trouble. So too with the tabooing of land or the eating of the clan's totemic animal. All matters related to ghosts were anti-Christian and therefore fair game. They were anti-Christian beliefs, in the first instance, because the belief in ghosts is basically antithetical to Christian dogma. Of perhaps equal importance, however, is that they were anti-Christian because—from the missionary perspective—they were based on the fear of retribution instead of the Christian ideal of God's mercy and love.

The extent to which Espinal realized the fundamental importance of many of these native customs as public manifestations of the authority of the clan and clan chiefs is uncertain. Perhaps he believed that the reciprocal rights and obligations of individuals in clans, and particularly of clan chiefs and clan members, would be continued through the clans as social institutions without religious overtones. In any event, the punishment for continuation of these practices was excommunication. The senior members of the Etal community maintained that many men were so excommunicated in the 1930s. There appears, in fact, to have been a general desire to continue these practices in secret up through the 1950s. Many senior men on Etal stated that in the 1930s the island elders (clan chiefs?) realized that such practices were more important to the clans than their removal, because of belief in ghosts, justified. Rather, such practices were carried out to maintain the social position of the clan chiefs. In other words, there is evidence to suggest a community maintained these customs to reinforce their ideals of behavior, especially group cooperation, by showing respect for the clan chiefs and therefore the clans themselves. As stated by one elder man when talking about Father Espinal, the presentation of first fruits was to show respect for the clan chief and this was stopped by Father Espinal not because of religion but because people said that if they failed to give them to the chief they would become sick. (This paraphrased statement sounds contradictory and it is; but it clearly points out the native separation of religion per se from these customs.)

Of course, Father Espinal was not alone in attempting to put an end to these beliefs and customs. The German Liebenzell missionaries also worked toward the same ends. One common thread that unites these Japanese-period missionary efforts with the earlier Congregationalist work is that although the missionary efforts were oriented toward slightly different targets, it was the individual who remained an important objective. In these later missionary endeavors, it should be clear, the attempts to deny the validity of ghost-related beliefs were, among other things, also destined to foster the Christian notion that each individual is inherently responsible for his or her actions. At issue was not simply the matter of to whom one was responsible but the basic concept of individual rather than diffuse, group-oriented responsibility, the latter being an important adjunct to clan organization.

The final impact of these missionary endeavors and other foreign interventions has already been outlined, beginning with the mid-1930s decision on Etal to suspend clan ownership of property. The final question, the one with which this chapter began, was how we can assess missionary influences as an integral part of the overall cultural and social changes that took place on Etal. It is to this question that we now turn.

CONCLUSION

Available data clearly indicate that missionary activity in the Mortlock Islands resulted in significant changes in native life. The focus of early Protestant activity on civilizing as well as Christianizing, along with later Catholic and Protestant attacks on customs and beliefs associated with clan ancestors, had an important effect on the decline of the group as opposed to the individual. In the process of almost completely changing the religious attitudes and beliefs of the community, there was an accompanying decline in the viability of the clans and clan chiefs. There was also a redirection of economic interests associated with the introduction of new social roles, material culture, and technology that was fostered not only by the government and commercial agents but also, in rather important ways, by early missionaries themselves. It seems fair to say, then, that the missionary position in civilizing as well as Christianizing did not determine but only contributed to the cultural and social changes that took place.

Would the changes in clan organization have occurred had there been no missionary influence? Would the same result have been achieved solely through the introduction of a market economy with money and wage labor, the impact of government regulations on behavior, work patterns, and landholdings, and the establishment of new governmental, educational, and economic positions and institutional structures? There is no definitive answer to such speculative questions, but general modernization theory argues that such a sociological shift from group to individual would indeed result. Rather than engage in an "if . . . then" argument, it is more to the point to see the missionary position in terms of the end results—the complete or near-complete replacement of the traditional religious system by a quite different system. It has been maintained in this chapter that one central ingredient of the Christian faith as it was introduced in Micronesia is the notion of individual responsibility. In the earlier Congregationalist mode, this implied a concentration not only on religious responsibility but also on economic and social responsibility. During the later Catholic and Protestant mission activities the focus appears to have been directly upon the religious aspects of individualism. This focus should not result in anything other than a decline in clan organization insofar as clans are based on traditional religious beliefs. Why anticipate the decline of clans as socially important and viable groups when the clan-based concepts of sharing and cooperation would be reinforced by similar Christian doctrines of interpersonal harmony?

We are dealing here with the classic arguments that have surrounded Weber's hypothesis about the "Protestant Ethic." Is individualistically oriented capitalism the precursor for and promoter of Christian, especially Protestant (Calvinist), doctrines in the practical world? Or is just the reverse true? I would argue that in the Mortlock Islands governmental and commercial intervention has played and continues to play the central role in promoting a basically anticlan individualistic orientation. It seems unreasonable to credit missionary activities with clan decline on Etal: in the first place, the practices that were directly related to clan organization that Espinal and his Protestant contemporaries attempted to stop were not in fact halted until much later, well after the dissolution of clan landowning; moreover, the same bases for clan organization as those related to work productivity and internal societal harmony remained significant and functional throughout the period of missionary effort. Thus I am suggesting that the disruption of clan organization was the result of governmental and commercial activity rather than missionary activity, even though the latter was carried out in such a way that it contributed to the end result.

If this interpretation is accepted as the most reasonable assessment of missionary influence, we can ask whether or not the missionary impact was inherently dysfunctional, as has occasionally been suggested. I would suggest that the answer must be a negative one. Changes in material culture, technology, economics, and political structure would (and in some cases did) occur regardless of missionary presence. What in the final analysis was contributed by the missionization of these island communities was a new religious framework within which change led to redirection of individualistic goals. In other words, Christianity contributed a religious doctrine that did not inherently change social organization but instead provided an ameliorative symbolic context within which changes could be undertaken without massive interpersonal disruptions within the community.

This chapter has focused primarily on the attitudes and motivations of missionaries and on their work as it affected native life on Etal Atoll. It has been argued that Christianity provided the native community with an ideological framework that aided their adaptation to new social, political, and economic demands. Micronesian communities like Etal have always sought to retain their autonomy and identity in dealings with foreigners. As indicated by other data, Etal has endeavored to condition the demands of outsiders to their own island interests. This datum is one we should not neglect. It implies, as a matter of speculation, that the adoption of Christianity would not have occurred had not conversion seemed advantageous to the members of the community in their continuing effort to cope with a changing world.

NOTES

The research on which this chapter is based was conducted in 1968 and 1969 on both Truk (Moen Island) and on Etal Atoll. Research support was received from the National Institute of Mental Health and from the University of Washington, for which the author is grateful.

1. This is well demonstrated by the numerous studies done in recent years in the Pacific that are primarily concerned with "Port Town" development, political change, economic development, and the like.
2. Readers who wish to find a more complete and detailed description of traditional life on Etal should consult Nason (1970). A demographic history of this community may be found in Nason (1975).

3. This does not include those cases where physical or mental defects would automatically disqualify an individual. This may be seen as an idealistic rule notable for exceptions in practice, but it stands clearly apart from the "capability" factor apparently taken into account by Ulithi lineage members when selecting a new lineage head (Lessa 1966:27).
4. Although data are not available to confirm this, it is always possible that the *itang* was also given respect as a result of the danger associated with his magical powers and the possibility that he might use them for sorcery.
5. I have no information on the existence of weather magicians per se, a role noted for other communities in the Caroline Islands. The *weitaoa* 'spirit medium' might be added to the list, but this was clearly not a role so much sought after as bestowed by the spirits.
6. The impact of foreign weapons on native conflict presents us with some intriguing questions that cannot be taken up here. It is possible, however, that they did have an important influence on the conduct of not only interisland relationships but also interpersonal relationships within the island community.
7. The exception to this is the paramount chief, but this is due largely to his advanced age.

6

MISSIONS, ADMINISTRATION, AND EDUCATION IN THE SOLOMON ISLANDS, 1893—1942

James A. Boutilier

Education was a fundamental feature of the interaction between the missions and the peoples of Oceania. The educational process operated on both formal and informal levels. The missions, as agents of change, utilized education in the formal sense as a means of advancing metropolitan ideologies and religious beliefs. Their own activities and attitudes served to educate the islanders in an informal sense. The latter, seen by many as the passive recipients of imported cultures, were for the most part pragmatic assessors of the value of mission education and sought to exploit it for social and political advancement.

This chapter is devoted primarily to a descriptive, historical examination of the more formal aspects of education as provided by missionary bodies in the South and Central Solomon Islands from 1893 to 1942.[1] It does not explore the impact of South Sea Islands teachers, a subject dealt with ably elsewhere in this volume by Lātūkefu (chapter 4). These missionary bodies differed from one another in terms of time period, *modus operandi*, theology, character of personnel, and attitudes toward education.

This chapter also examines the relationship between the missions and the British administration of the archipelago with regard to education. The islanders frequently, and not surprisingly, perceived the missions as extensions of the residential government and almost as frequently the resident commissioners saw the religious organizations in the same light. But these organizations were not one and the same. The fact that the missions provided an educational service which was not only timely but advantageous to the administration must be seen as little more than a happy accident of history. The missions were primarily concerned with their own ends, converting and civilizing the islanders, and they were often bitterly opposed to the administration despite the existence of common experiential and cultural bonds.

DECLARATION OF THE PROTECTORATE

The British declared a protectorate over the South and Central Solomons in 1893, and three years later the first resident commissioner, Charles Morris Woodford, arrived in the group to establish his colonial headquarters on the island of Tulagi. The administrative tasks confronting him were formidable. With one assistant, a tiny police force, and a meager budget he was expected to govern a sprawling array of volcanic high islands clad in dense equatorial jungle and inhabited by a Melanesian farming and fishing folk. These folk, moreover, were divided culturally, geographically, and linguistically, as well as being given to head-hunting and warfare.

Woodford's principal concerns were pacification and the provision of an adequate revenue for the protectorate by way of land leases and trading licenses. The administration was penniless from the outset, and what little money there was was defrayed by transportation and administrative costs. Government welfare services were practically nonexistent: after half a century of British rule the only progress that had been made was in the form of a forlornly inadequate medical service.

MISSION EDUCATION: HISTORICAL BACKGROUND

Education was entirely in the hands of five missions: the Melanesian Mission of the Church of England, the Marist mission of the Roman Catholic church, the Methodist mission, the South Sea Evangelical Mission (presently the South Sea Evangelical Church), and the Seventh-Day Adventist mission. It is important to note that the term "education," while a convenient one, encompassed a wide range of variables within the island context. The very words "school" and "teacher" had different meanings in the Solomons, depending on the missions involved, and their overall value was normally at variance with that understood to prevail in such metropolitan settings as London or Sydney. Moreover, educational facilities in the protectorate were extremely diverse in character, though, generally speaking, they fell into three broad categories: village schools, district or station schools, and special upper-level schools (Tippett 1967:122).

THE MELANESIAN MISSION

The Melanesian Mission, the senior mission in the field of education, enjoyed a free hand in the Solomons during the last half of the nineteenth century after the Marist mission failed to establish itself on Santa Isabel and San Cristobal at mid-century. One of the forerunners of Melanesian Mission schools in the group was Saint Andrew's at Kohimarama, New Zealand, where Lonsdale Pritt was headmaster in the 1860s. Pritt was "no linguist . . . but a man of his hands, a great organizer and a great disciplinarian" (Fox 1958:217). Mota was the only island language he knew and so, willy-nilly, it became the official language of instruction and remained so for some sixty years. The whole object of Saint Andrew's School was to teach "industry, regularity and responsibility rather than learning" (Fox 1958:217). Thus after two and a half hours of schooling each morning the Melanesian students were sent to work in the fields, the produce being sold in Auckland to finance the institution. Pritt made industrial work "the recognized rule of the school," Bishop Patteson observed, and all later Melanesian Mission schools were patterned on the Kohimarama model (Fox 1958:217).[2]

In 1867 the school was moved to Norfolk Island and located on a "plateau above high cliffs, grass covered and dotted with trees" (Fox 1958:218). There were four boardinghouses, a dining hall, a chapel (with Burne-Jones Morris stained glass windows sent out from England), workshops, houses for married men, a European and Melanesian hospital, and playing fields laid out on a 405-hectare site. There were also pastures for sheep and cattle as well as food gardens for the two hundred pupils. The students were taught reading, writing, arithmetic, singing, farming, and carpentry during a course which normally lasted six years. Robert Codrington, the philologist and anthropologist, was the first headmaster, followed in 1895 by Palmer and in 1902 by Thomas Cullwick, known to the students as "Hurricane," or "Matches" because his temper flared up so quickly. Saint Barnabas College "never had a high standard of secular education," but it was a "marvelous center for the training of Christian character" (Fox 1958:218). From this school came the teachers, priests, and missionaries who took the Word to the islands.[3]

On Saint Luke's day, 1893, Richard Comins purchased a block of land at Siota in the Solomons for Ł10 on behalf of the Melanesian Mission. The Nggela people had cut down the sacred groves, which stood on the spot, when they became Christian in 1881. A school was erected there in 1896 and a bull and two cows were acquired. The islanders had never seen such large animals before and treated the beasts with appropriate deference. The following year a lad from a trading vessel visited Siota. He brought with him dysentery and eleven of the forty-seven pupils died. Despite efforts to improve conditions the site was deemed to be unhealthy and the school was closed down in 1900.

THE METHODIST MISSION

Two years later the Methodists arrived in the Western Solomons. They did so at a time when the concept of the industrial mission was in vogue. This concept called for the acquisition of tracts of land large enough for the establishment of plantations and technical and industrial institutions, which were supposed to demonstrate to the inhabitants the "importance of industry and the reward of honest labor" (Tippett 1967:66). Reverend John Goldie, chairman of the mission, wrote of its aim to develop the islanders physically, mentally, morally, and spiritually. "I am convinced," he observed,

> that mission work amongst savage people if it is to succeed must be on industrial lines. I hope that I shall not be misunderstood when I say that the most objectionable creature in the Pacific today, with the exception of the white beachcomber . . . is the religious loafer. The loafer is at all times objectionable, but the half-civilized native who loves to strut around quoting passages of the Bible, singing hymns, and shaking hands on the slightest provocation but who has learned nothing of industry, honesty or cleanliness, is the most objectionable of all. He is a by-product

of Christian missions. He has been taught a Christian creed divorced from Christian conduct. He is to be pitied more than blamed (Goldie 1914: 583).

In short, it was necessary to teach the islanders that there was no such thing (in the words of a remarkable propaganda film made by the mission in 1914) as a "lazy Christian."

The industrial idea focused mission activities on the station, a place where islanders could participate in boat-building, carpentry, saw milling, and plantation work or have access to medical services, education, recreation, and religion in a world divorced from the village. Thus, though there were 105 mission schools with an enrollment of 2,642 by 1930, the main centers of education were the mission stations at Bilua on Vella Lavella, Patutiva in the Marovo Lagoon near Seghe, and Kokeqolo in the Roviana Lagoon.

There was a day school and a college at Kokeqolo, the mission headquarters. Primary education was given at the day school and secondary education at the college. Two hundred and eleven students were enrolled in the former and thirty-three in the latter by 1930. The college provided technical training, prepared pastors, and trained island teachers, some of whom possessed a "very fair degree of education" (WPHC, IC 1930b). Generally speaking, however, the island teachers were men of limited formal education who seldom went beyond simple arithmetic and English in the village schools. The hours of instruction in these schools were not fixed but were regulated by village life and rarely exceeded two hours a day.

THE MARIST MISSION

The Marists established a mission in the Solomons in the late 1890s, following an abortive attempt on the island of Isabel half a century before. Their main preoccupation was evangelism, an "activity which achieved its purpose when the convert was baptized, safely ensconced in a Christian marriage, and beyond the reach of Protestantism" (Laracy 1969:195). For the most part they were convinced that the population of the islands was caught up in an irreversible decline, and they saw their main function as trying "to send to Heaven the relics of the race" (Laracy

1969:204). Thus the religious and social advancement of converts beyond the minimum level was of "little concern to them" (Laracy 1969:195). They were generally unperturbed by their failure to provide sophisticated medical services, and education was intended to impart "a modicum of religious instruction to as many pupils as possible and to produce catechists, low level auxiliaries for the missionaries" (Laracy 1969:198). When the Marists did establish educational or medical facilities, it was frequently because of fears that the Protestant missions might forestall them or that the administration might attempt to enforce certain standards on their work.

Thirty-five young islanders were being educated in 1899 at the mission station on Rua Sura islet, off the northeast coast of Guadalcanal, and in the same year another station was opened at Avu Avu on the "weather coast" of the same island (WPHC, IC 1899a).[4] By 1928 the Marists had established boarding schools for boys and girls at Wanoni Bay on San Cristobal, Buma on the Langa Langa Lagoon, Malaita, and Rohinari in the Are Are district of Malaita. The Wanoni school became a plantation "where the pretended scholars made copra and supplied cheap labor, while their overseer earned an unenviable reputation for irascibility" (Laracy 1969:248). Eight years later a senior training institute was established at Marau Sound at the southern end of Guadalcanal. The school aimed to produce "a higher-calibre native teacher and leader for village and station work by adapting its work to local conditions and relating its program to native life" (Kent 1973:171). It was largely successful in this goal, and an educationist who visited Marau in 1939 considered the school the "outstanding educational institution in the Protectorate" in terms of relevance to the island situation and in the "quality of the scholastic side of its teaching" (Groves 1940:sec. 3, p. 6).

Elsewhere, however, the level of Roman Catholic schooling was low. "I do not think this Mission makes any pretence that its certified teachers are expected to do more than hold daily services in their respective villages," the district officer for Malaita observed in 1930. "A few of the teachers may be able to read and write but they do not appear to attempt to teach reading and writing in the villages and most of the teachers would be quite unable to do so, if they tried" (WPHC, IC 1930b). It was much the same story on Guadalcanal, where a survey revealed that the educational impact of the Roman Catholic school at Ruavatu was "negligible" as a result of "native apathy, limited mission resources and trained personnel," and the lack of any definite syllabus (WPHC, IC 1939d).[5]

THE SOUTH SEA EVANGELICAL MISSION

The fourth of the five missions involved in education in the Solomons was the South Sea Evangelical Mission. The SSEM, as it was known, owed its beginnings to the Pacific labor trade. When the established churches in Australia proved unwilling or unable to bring the Christian gospel to Melanesians working in Queensland, Florence Young decided to establish an undenominational evangelical mission for that purpose. This was in 1886 and the mission, the forerunner of the SSEM, was called the Queensland Kanaka Mission.[6] The QKM expanded its operations over the years, conducting classes and holding Sunday services in an ever-increasing number of towns and plantations throughout the state. "Schools" for laborers were particularly popular, and the Kanakas, roughly half of whom were Solomon Islanders, showed a "keen desire to learn reading and writing" (Hilliard 1969:44).

The flow of Pacific island labor to Queensland was curtailed in 1901, and three years later the QKM decided, if reluctantly, to establish a missionary outpost in the protectorate. Their first attempt was ill-fated, but in 1905 Miss Young journeyed to the islands for a second time and selected sites for future mission stations on the island of Malaita. Onepusu, a small peninsula south of the Langa Langa Lagoon on the west coast, was chosen as headquarters and in 1906 a small boarding school was established there for boys and girls. With the repatriation of most of the indentured laborers from Australia in the same year, the QKM ceased operations and the Solomon Islands branch was renamed the South Sea Evangelical Mission in 1907.

From the start the SSEM was able to build on the foundations laid by QKM converts who had returned to the islands prior to 1905. As early as 1892, a former laborer, Samson Jacko, had established a "school" at Malageti on the south coast of Guadalcanal, and another was founded after the turn of the century by

David Sango at Talisi, 24 kilometers to the east. In 1911 the SSEM established a station at Talisi, and a year later a mission house was erected near the newly founded Roman Catholic mission at Wanoni Bay, San Cristobal, on the site of another returnee's "school."

Like the Methodists, the SSEM also embraced the idea of industrial training. To this end Miss Young convinced her two brothers, Ernest and Horace, who had already had wide experience in operating a plantation at Bundaberg in Queensland, to establish the Malayta Company in 1909. Woodford, the first resident commissioner, welcomed the prospect of commercial development on Malaita and granted the Youngs a strip of land 24 kilometers long and 4,047 hectares in extent, centered on Baunani, 32 kilometers north of Onepusu. The Malayta Company made "generous provision for evening classes on its plantations," and so the SSEM transferred its training school to Baunani in 1911, only to return it to Onepusu in 1918 when the company shifted its operation to the Russell Islands.

Onepusu was the site of the main mission school, and Dr. Northcote Deck was accustomed to sail round the coasts of Malaita on board the mission schooner *Evangel* recruiting students for training there. The school was divided into two departments, "senior" and "junior." This arrangement bore no relationship to the age of the scholars but referred rather to the length of schooling that it was anticipated each pupil would undergo, those in the senior department remaining for three or four years, those in the junior department, who constituted two-thirds of the enrollment, for one or two years (WPHC, IC 1930b). Students in the senior department were taught, apart from religious instruction, reading and writing in English and the vernacular, English dictation and composition, and choral singing. The standard of academic achievement was not high. When the district officer for Malaita visited Onepusu he found that only half a dozen senior scholars could do elementary sums in simple arithmetic (WPHC, IC 1930b).[7] In the junior department students were taught reading and writing in the vernacular, reading in English (by the "look and say" method), and singing. In addition, practical instruction was given to selected scholars in such trades as carpentry and plumbing.

The primary object of this and other schools was not academic but religious. Northcote Deck's brother, Norman, described the philosophy underlying the SSEM most forcibly in a letter to Resident Commissioner Ashley in 1931. "Is it reasonable," he wrote,

> to expect missionaries to come to a tropical climate with its many disabilities, live here on an allowance of say Ł24 per annum plus keep (for that is what our missionaries agree to) and out of this Ł24 they pay duty on everything they get, to this add gun licence and on top of this the men folk have to pay a tax of Ł1 for the privilage [sic] of living here, all this to merely do *educational work?* There is one incentive and only one which will lead men and women to so sacrifice (in the world's estimate) their lives, namely—the Gospel. We missionaries do give education, but such education is secondary and incidental to our main objective, which is to preach the Gospel and establish an indigenous church on a knowledge of the word of God, and we are not ashamed of this objective. We believe that the *righteous character* which results from the acceptance of the Gospel together with a knowledge of God's word is the finest education in the highest sense of the term that is possible to man. It is the lack of such education that is at the root of so much lawlessness in the homelands of the present day (WPHC, IC 1931c).

The primary function of the SSEM "schools" was to train boys, and more often men "of proven character," in scriptures and to send them forth to propagate the faith. It is not surprising, therefore, that the purely secular education provided was "extremely rudimentary in quality and limited in quantity" (WPHC, IC 1930b). Indeed, as Norman Deck observed in a patronizing but prescient minute, the SSEM was "afraid . . . of a secular education which lifts a considerable proportion of natives out of their natural environment unless such natives can be usefully absorbed, lest such natives may form a disloyal and dissatisfied class" (WPHC, IC 1931c).[8]

An education survey in 1939 revealed that the SSEM had "innumerable small native-settlement schools" on Malaita, providing religious instruction "on the basis of rudimentary vernacular literacy"; regional schools, mainly for children; and two centers of higher training, Onepusu for men and Afio for women (WPHC, IC 1939c). Teaching methods were normally "universal and rigid": a system which, while leaving little room for individual initiative, had the virtue of simplicity. Textbooks and procedures were all standardized, thereby simplifying the problem of teacher training. The village teacher's responsibility was to promote godliness, cleanliness, and industry. Schools were for Bible study. As one observer noted, "all the teaching, except arithmetic, [was] directly related to religion" (WPHC, IC 1939c)—a state of affairs entirely in keeping with the old dictum "salvation before education or civilization" (Young n.d.:39).

THE SEVENTH-DAY ADVENTISTS

The Seventh-Day Adventists (SDA) did not arrive in the Solomon Islands until 1914, when they established a station at Gizo. They were even more fundamentalist than the SSEM, and, convinced of the imminence of the Second Coming of Christ, they were quite willing to entrust religious authority to the islanders. Medical work was a special interest of the SDA, but, as Laracy has observed, it was seen as "a proselytising device rather than a humanitarian activity." Soon after their arrival the SDA set up district boarding schools from which islanders were dispatched to spread the Word in neighboring villages. By 1930 the mission had seven village schools in the Marovo Lagoon area and a headquarters school at Batuna, Vangunu Island. There was also a "regional" or boarding school for boys at Nafinua. Kwai region, on the east coast of Malaita; a station school and medical center at Kwailabesi on the northwest coast of the same island; and a district headquarters school at Kopiu, near Marau Sound, Guadalcanal. The Seventh-Day Adventists, perhaps more than any other mission, enjoyed a reputation for devoting "much care to the education of the natives" (WPHC, IC 1926). The SDA was the "most active" mission educationally on the south coast of Guadalcanal, and the Kopiu school was a "well established and progressive" one which provided "an inspiring example to the natives of what may be attained by organized effort with its variety of gardening activity . . . and its improved methods of cultivation" (WPHC, IC 1939d).

THE MELANESIAN MISSION: LATER WORK

The Melanesian Mission continued its educational work after the failure of the Siota school. A boys boarding school was established in 1910 on the island of Bungana near Nggela with an enrollment of eighteen students from San Cristobal, Guadalcanal, and Santa Isabel (Fox 1958:229). The following year another boys boarding school was created on a 65-hectare site at Pamua, San Cristobal. "It was a difficult school to establish," the first headmaster recalled, "because of constant alarms from the hill men, still cannibals, and from marauding parties in canoes. The boys were uneasy and we had to watch over them through the night with a loaded shotgun, which did not leave one fresh for school next day. On one occasion going down to the shore in the morning I found a headless corpse" (Fox 1958:231).[9]

In 1916 Bishop Wood established a theological college at Marovovo at the northwestern end of Guadalcanal. Saint Mary's, as it was called, became the junior school for the Melanesian Mission in the Solomons in 1922. It was the largest and "in some ways the greatest" of the boys boarding schools established by the mission (Fox 1958:232).[10]

Six years after Saint Mary's was opened a senior school was established at Pawa on the island of Ugi. All Hallows School was designed to fill the gap created by the closure of Saint Barnabas College on Norfolk Island in 1919. The school language remained Mota; the customs and rules were those of its predecessor. Boys' houses were erected, gardens dug, fields fenced off for cattle, football and cricket pitches laid out, and a "small but beautiful" chapel built on the hill. The number of students rose to 110 and the school was considered by the administration to be the "finest in the Protectorate" (Fox 1958:238).[11]

In addition to these major junior and senior schools, the mission operated a considerable network of village schools. The district officer on Savo made a tour of island schools in 1930 and submitted this description of a Melanesian Mission school: "The school building is about twelve feet square. School daily from 7 to 8 a.m." At a neighboring village he found "a small school house which appeared to have been little used. [He] was shown a broken alphabet table, a few slates covered with cobwebs and a

Bible written Mota [sic] language. Four young men, fifteen girls and thirteen boys attend this school where there are two preacher-teachers" (WPHC, IC 1930b).

The teachers posted to the various Melanesian Mission village schools were all supposed to have qualified in reading and writing, chiefly in Mota, the lingua franca of the mission. But, as Fox points out, the word "teacher" was rather misleading—the name "catechist" would have been more precise, for their main function was to teach the Christian faith (Fox 1958:224). Most of them held daily classes in their villages during which they propagated the virtues of cleanliness and hard work, but in many cases the teachers gave the impression of being "dull and apathetic in manner and slovenly in appearance" (WPHC, IC 1930b). A survey of Melanesian Mission village schools on Guadalcanal and Malaita in the late 1930s tended to confirm this impression—the educational worth of the Marasa school on Guadalcanal being deemed "negligible," the mission village of Tasimboko being full of children without a school, and the A'ama and Gwounatolo district schools on Malaita being labeled failures (WPHC, IC 1939c).

ADMINISTRATION ATTITUDES TO EDUCATION

The resident commissioner reported in 1930 that there was "very little education of any kind in the Protectorate" (WPHC, IC 1930b). Village schools were attended by a few young men, mostly children, for an average of one hour each morning. Education was entirely in the hands of the missions, and Ashley was convinced that none of their village schools was worthy of the name (Solomon Islands 1934). The Moorhouse Report, which was occasioned by the murder of District Officer Bell in 1927, had concluded that the demand for trained islanders outside the mission field was not sufficiently pressing to necessitate the establishment of government schools. But after studying the quality of education provided by the missions, Ashley decided that the administration could expect no progress in the protectorate until it undertook to educate the islanders. There were very real practical reasons for doing so, quite apart from broader considerations. In a tropical and malarial possession, where it was necessary to incur the expense and inconvenience of offering leave, it was imperative to have "natives . . . to fill all the second class appointments in the Service" (WPHC, IC 1932a). "All our work in the Protectorate," the resident commissioner reported, "is seriously cramped by the fact that there has been no education such as would enable natives to hold any position in the lower branches of the Administration, or among the trading firms, with the result that in this native Protectorate . . . the outlook to the ambitious native is hopeless" (WPHC, IC 1930a).

The answer to the problem appeared to lie in the establishment of a central government school, an institution which would provide the protectorate with a "steady and regular supply of young native men who could be employed as sanitary officers, dispensers, nurses, vaccinators, etcetera" (WPHC, IC 1930a). The high commissioner concurred. "The whole question of [the protectorate's] progress and future prosperity [is] bound up in this matter," he informed the secretary of state for the colonies (WPHC, IC 1931d). The need for such a school was further reinforced when the high commissioner received requests for schooling from the people of Isabel and Nggela during a tour of the protectorate in 1931 (WPHC, IC 1932c).[12] By that time, however, the protectorate's financial problems had become acute and Ashley was forced to concede that there were "no funds to allow us even to contemplate embarking on a scheme of Government education" (WPHC, IC 1931c).

ADMINISTRATION ASSISTANCE TO THE MISSIONS

Once again the administration fell back upon its second line of defense, the missions. Resident Commissioner Kane had exempted eight categories of islanders from taxation in the early 1920s, among them "scholars attending schools presided over by European teachers," "native preachers," and "native preachers who conduct daily schools." Ashley felt that there was little justification for exempting these groups when there was hardly any evidence that exemption encouraged attendance at school and a great deal of evidence to suggest that the level of mission education was abysmally low. Instead the resident commissioner proposed that taxes be collected from the three groups involved in education and that grants-in-aid be made to missions which showed a genuine desire to promote secular education.

The high commissioner's secretary was critical of the plan. While conceding that the threat of taxation might be one way of bringing the missions' "present lackadaisical methods of education" to an end (WPHC, IC 1931b), he felt that it was extremely important for the government to avoid placing "any further burden or disability" on mission efforts at education (WPHC, IC 1930b). The mission methods might be "crude" but their schools were "the only means available to the natives of learning to read and write" (WPHC, IC 1930b).

Moreover, the missions were almost unanimous in opposing the scheme. "Is it likely," the bishop of Melanesia wondered, "that for the paltry grant proposed our mission will agree to these proposals or to seek for a Government grant at the expense of having its organization and teaching more or less controlled by the Government?" (Solomon Islands 1934).[13] For the Roman Catholics, government intervention in education was a "dire secularist threat" (Laracy 1969:209) to be resisted at all points. The right to educate without restriction was based on Pope Pius XI's encyclical *On the Christian Education of Youth* (*Divini Illius Magistri, 1929*):

> The Church has inherent in herself an inviolable right to freedom in teaching. She is independent of any sort of earthly power both in the origin and exercise of her mission as educator.

There were also grave objections to the size of the grants, and Bishop Wade of the Northern Solomons opposed the plan on the grounds that each grant represented only one-tenth the cost of supporting a pupil in a mission boarding school.

The SSEM refused to support the scheme on different grounds. "I remember Mr. Ashley," Norman Deck (1970) was to recall many years later.

> He had a long syllabus. He wanted us to adopt that syllabus. He said you can give the religious instruction as well. I said, "Mr. Ashley, you'll drive us into a corner. God has sent us here primarily with a gospel to win these people to the Christian faith. We give them education because they don't know how to read until we teach them to read. And central was the Scriptures. Our whole work is built upon the knowledge of the Scriptures. And they pay dividends. If we were to do as you said . . . our source of

income would dry up. You don't realize that this is a faith mission. We never ask for money. We never take up collections and we never make known the financial needs. But the money comes in answer to prayer. Now if we were to change the center of gravity to the secular, we couldn't get the money." There was no answer to that.

The plan was dropped.[14]

The administration did, however, decide to make grants of Ł100 each to the SDA training school at Batuna, Marovo Lagoon, and to the SSEM training school at Onepusu "with the specific object of encouraging the missions to impart technical education to their students." But when it was discovered that probably less than 10 percent of the pupils involved received any form of technical instruction and that those who did were almost all absorbed into the ranks of the missions, the grants were cut to Ł25 each (WPHC, IC 1932b).

A meeting was held in Tulagi in February 1934 at which the resident commissioner and representatives of the various missions discussed the problem of education at length. Eventually it was decided to refer the matter to the Advisory Committee on Education at the Colonial Office for advice. Two years later the secretary of state for the colonies was asked to consider whether funds might be made available from the Colonial Development Fund to assist in the establishment of a central government school along the lines of the King George V School at Tarawa in the Gilbert and Ellice Islands Colony. The application was received too late for consideration that year and the administration was instructed to renew its request when submitting estimates for 1936-1937.

EDUCATION SURVEY

In the meantime it was decided to mount a full-scale survey of education in the protectorate (see table 1). The secretary of state for the colonies, W. Ormsby-Gore, was entirely in support of the plan. "I am much impressed," he wrote,

> by the need for the adoption of a definite progressive policy in regard to education in the Protectorate. The need is urgent and the Government cannot escape criticism if active steps are not taken to meet it. . . . Means must be found for enabling the Government to take a more active share in

> both practical educational work and in organizing, assisting and directing the work which is at present being carried on by the missions. A situation in which, out of a total annual expenditure of over Ł60,000, the amount provided for education only amounts to Ł54 a year cannot be allowed to continue (WPHC, IC 1938).

"In all circumstances," he concluded, "I would suggest that as a first step arrangements should be made without delay for an expert to visit the Protectorate with a view to advising the Government on the whole question of future [educational] policy" (WPHC, IC 1938).

By February 1939 the administration had succeeded in arranging for the secondment of William C. Groves from the Victorian Government Service in Australia to carry out the survey.[15] The high commissioner's secretary outlined the nature of the problem for Groves. "Secular education as such is of little interest to the missions," Vaskess observed (WPHC, IC 1939a):

> except in so far as it is necessary as the foundation for religious instruction. Hitherto the Protectorate Government has done nothing towards the . . . provision of educational facilities, but it is becoming increasingly apparent that action cannot be further deferred. The general standard of education amongst the native teachers is extremely low and the teaching generally is haphazard, disconnected, and unsystematized.

Groves took up his appointment on 1 April 1939, charged with the responsibility of investigating and reporting upon the question of native education, formulating a scheme of government cooperation with the missions, and advising the government generally as to educational policy and effort, including the proposed establishment of a central government school. Groves toured extensively, investigated schools of every kind, wrote interim reports, and made his final submission in 1940. He found the educational prospects far from inspiring. In the circumstances, he opined, "the future provision of any useful and suitably adapted education for Guadalcanal as a whole will be a most difficult and thankless task even with the whole-hearted and understanding co-operation between Government and missions and amongst the different missions themselves" (WPHC, IC 1939d). "The only enduringly successful educational line . . . will be one of slow, carefully planned non-disruptive infiltration as far as influ-

TABLE 1 Survey of Schools (Population 130,000-140,000)[a]

1922	Boys	Girls	Total
Seventh Day Adventists	———353———		353
Catholic Mission			
North Solomons[b]	120	90	210
South Solomons	377	253	630
SSEM Boarding	90	30	120
Melanesian Mission	1,360	818	2,178
Methodist Mission[c]			
Total			3,491

1930-1931			
Seventh-Day Adventists	612	408	1,020
Catholic Mission			
North Solomons	100	88	188
South Solomons	447	345	792
SSEM Boarding	90	26	116
Melanesian Mission	———3,904———		3,904
Methodist Mission	———2,723———		2,723
Total			8,743

1938-1939			
Seventh-Day Adventists	548	362	910
Catholic Mission			
North Solomons	94	56	150
South Solomons	471	306	777
SSEM Boarding	116	164	280
Melansian Mission	462	77	539
Methodist Mission	———2,238———		2,238
Total			4,894

[a]The figures were drawn from the *BSIP Blue Books* (Solomon Islands 1922, 1931, 1939). Adequate statistics are not available for 1920. The figures listed for 1940 are as for 1938-1939.
[b]The "North Solomons" Roman Catholic diocese included Bougainville and Buka, islands outside the British protectorate, so the figures provided are slightly larger than for the protectorate proper.
[c]No return.

encing the mass of the people is concerned" (WPHC, IC 1939c).

"Education," Groves noted,

> must be organized to contribute, through the appropriate institutional programme towards the general development of the people as a whole, in health, in spiritual and mental outlook and in material life, away from their primitive ideas and standards.
>
> For to allow them to remain as they are at present is inconceivable; their development on sound lines presents a challenge to all civilizing agencies of which the Government and the missions (especially in their educational work) are the chief (WPHC, IC 1939c).

There was no question of implementing Groves' recommendations. The protectorate was in a parlous state financially and the copra situation was "calamitous" (Marchant 1940). The report was forwarded to London: there to be read, filed, and swallowed up in the confusion of war. Thus, as the result of parsimony, the pressure of priorities, the vagaries of world trade, the low regard for the islanders' ability, and the weight of official indifference, education throughout the protectorate was still elementary in character and limited in geographical scope after almost half a century of British rule.

MISSION-ADMINISTRATION RELATIONS

The failure of the administration and the missions to provide adequate educational services was in many ways a tragedy. Indeed, a perusal of the voluminous correspondence relating to education filled one high commissioner with despair (WPHC, IC 1937b). Yet the situation was understandable. In the early years the administration came to rely upon the missions because money was scarce, distances were great, and staff was limited. The missions had qualified personnel and organizational structures which reached down to the level of the smallest villages. But there were fatal flaws in this relationship. Increasingly, the government's reliance upon the missions became an institutionalized excuse for its unwillingness or inability to tackle educational problems more resolutely. For their part, the missions saw their mandate to civilize in terms of salvation. Education was given scant regard and in some cases was viewed as a veritable obstacle to the main task at hand.

Moreover, there was frequently tension between the missions and the government and between the various mission bodies themselves. "Wherever I went and whenever I tried to establish contact with the local natives," one district officer recalled,

> I encountered an invisible wall of silent suspicion and distrust. . . . In the end I was forced to the conclusion that it was the direct result of the deliberate policy of the European missionaries who were intensely jealous of the exercise of any influence or authority over the natives other than their own and who aimed at maintaining and fortifying their power by posing as heaven sent intermediaries between the ruthless oppression of an ignorant and hard-hearted Government and the rights of the oppressed (WPHC, IC 1933d).

It seemed, he concluded, as if the government officers were engaged in a "sort of perpetual trial of strength" with the ecclesiastical authorities in the conduct of island affairs (WPHC, IC 1931b).

Missionaries and government officers were often openly contemptuous of one another. The bishop of Melanesia in the 1930s considered most of the district officers quite unfit to be the resident commissioner's deputes or to inspect schools. Reverend John Goldie, one of the more outspoken critics of the administration, accused Resident Commissioner Kane of living in debauchery and one of the district officers of running a brothel.[16] The latter countered by drawing attention to the fact that he had known missionaries who had once been blacksmiths, tramway conductors, and attendants at "professional cyclist competitions in Melbourne" (WPHC, IC 1933d).

There were fierce antagonisms between the missions as well. Goldie appears to have consistently urged his followers to obstruct the activities of other missions, and there were such bitter exchanges between Norman Deck of the SSEM and Father Babonneau of the Marist mission that the resident commissioner was forced to order the former to desist.[17] On other occasions the administration appears to have actually fomented rivalries between the missions, as was the case when Woodford encouraged the Seventh-Day Adventists to establish a foothold in the Western

Solomons in order to spike "Mr. Goldie's guns" (WPHC, IC 1933d). Of course these rivalries and tensions did little to encourage cooperation between the administration and the missions with regard to education.

The missions were generally as hard pressed as the administration to find enough money to finance welfare services. The Marists spent Ł13,400 educating 4,178 children at station schools during the period 1929-1938, and when the price of rice trebled in the 1920s they were forced to close down their school at Rua Sura, Guadalcanal (Laracy 1969:220). The mission's inability to pay their catechists, as promised, led to a revolt among the students and widespread disenchantment at the way in which the Marists had "cheated" them. The provision of food for young students was a constant problem, and the mission's finances were so strained in the early 1930s that an approach had to be made to Ashley for a token ex gratia payment of Ł250 to keep the school at Marau open (WPHC, IC 1939b).

THE ISLANDERS' VIEW

Although they were frequently critical of the quality and character of European education, the islanders were often eager to be educated by the missions.[18] Their enthusiasm was based on a pragmatic assessment of the situation. For many of them the white man's god existed side by side with their own ghosts and spirits, and to embrace Christianity was to add to one's reservoir of *mana* "spiritual power." Moreover, the white man's education was seen as a passport to the European world and, more important, to European goods (Hogbin 1965:91). Yet there were aspects of Solomon Islands societies which hindered the educational work of the missions. Traditional religious beliefs were rigid, the islanders were at different stages of social development, and the various social organizations were sufficiently conservative that it was difficult for the islanders to accept change or adjust to the dislocations which resulted when change occurred.

The missions simultaneously promoted and prevented educational development. They confronted the islanders with a bewildering variety of attitudes to religion, an overweening intolerance to rival faiths, and a confusion of languages. The Melanesian Mission, for example, alternated between Mota and English as the language of instruction. The SSEM, Marists, and Melanesian Mission employed a host of Malaitan vernaculars while the Seventh-Day Adventists resorted to Marovo and the Marists to Tangarare on Guadalcanal (WPHC, IC 1939c). In addition, the missions often operated side by side, thereby compounding the confusion. Thus there were five missions located adjacent to the government station at Aola, on the eastern coast of Guadalcanal, where the population was about three hundred. Similarly, in the Makwano district of Malaita, the Roman Catholics, Seventh-Day Adventists, and SSEM operated in close proximity. The effect of such a situation upon the corporate life of the islanders, Groves observed, "must surely be disastrous" (WPHC, IC 1939d).[19]

CONCLUSION

The administration and the missions were frequently at loggerheads over the question of educational instruction. The former had an understandably low regard for the academic training the islanders received in the mission "schools," but the latter considered academic work only incidental to the propagation of Christianity and the virtues of cleanliness and industry. When the government tried to exert control over the school syllabi and schooling in general, the missions reacted strongly, complaining that there was no reason why they should be the subjects of such control when they provided all the money and all the staff. To have done so was to invite the seculaization of their activities and the denial of their primary task.

The government considered that the missions for "all their enterprise and enthusiasm [had] been largely wasting their time in misguided effort" (WPHC, IC 1931d). Yet for all its criticism of the mission bodies the administration had little of its own to offer. It did encourage peaceful conditions which enabled the missions to carry on their work but contributed almost nothing to educational welfare. "It is pitiful to observe how much in the Solomons has been left undone by the Government," the high commissioner, Sir Harry Luke, wrote in 1941 (Marchant 1941):

> How many of our obligations have been tacitly abandoned to the missions to fulfill. . . . How appropriate to the Solomons is the adage—Penny Wise, Pound Foolish.

NOTES

This chapter is a revised and abbreviated version of a paper read at the annual meeting of the Association for Social Anthropology in Oceania held at Asilomar, Pacific Grove, California, in March 1974.

1. By the Anglo-German Convention of 6 April 1886 the islands of Buka, Bougainville, Choiseul, Isabel, and the Bougainville strait fell within the German sphere of influence. The remaining islands in the archipelago were annexed by Britain in 1893. Rennell, Bellona, and Sikaiana were added to the protectorate in 1897 and the Eastern Outer Islands were added in 1898. By the Samoan Tripartite Convention of 1899 Santa Isabel, Choiseul, Shortlands, and Ontong Java were transferred by Germany to the British Solomon Islands Protectorate.
2. "At St. Andrew's," Patteson wrote, "all can acquire habits of obedience, industry and faithfulness in fulfilling responsibility; we are in school about three hours only a day, yet all are responsible for the employment of their time" (Fox 1958: 217).
3. At one time there were seven hundred graduates from the school at work in Melanesia. The first schools established by old boys were on San Cristobal, Ulawa, South Malaita, and Nggela in 1865.
4. See also WPHC, IC (1899a) and a WPHC minute on the establishment of the mission: "Having due regard to the proceedings of this sect in other parts of the Western Pacific, I cannot but view this proposed new step with anxiety."
5. A Dutchman, Father Engberink, was in charge at the time, assisted by two religious sisters. There were fourteen local boys and eight girls undergoing training. Schooling for the boys consisted of a 1½-hour session in the morning and a 1¼-hour session in the afternoon. Father Engberink was killed by the Japanese when they overran the school in 1942 (Horton 1970:98-99).
6. "Florence Young was a wealthy spinster and a member of a prominent Plymouth Brethren family . . . a woman of determination and drive. Stout and bespectacled, with a buoyant Evangelical faith and overwhelming assurance of the will of God, she was a striking example of that army of emancipated Victorian women who found an outlet for their crusading instincts in religious causes, preferably those in which they themselves could occupy a commanding position" (Hilliard 1969:42).
7. See also WPHC, IC (1939c). In 1939 there were 136 male students at Onepusu and 36 women (mostly the wives of male students and their families). All the students were adults between fifteen and fifty years of age.
8. It is interesting to note in this regard that a significant number of SSEM converts were among the leaders of the Marching Rule movement, a resistance movement on the part of some Solomon Islanders against the British administration following World War II. This matter is dealt with by Harold Ross in his study of the Baegu people (chapter 7).
9. Fox was the first headmaster. The school closed down in 1932.
10. A sixth junior school was established on the island of Ugi in 1936.
11. The mission established its first boarding school for girls in 1917 at Boromole on Nggela and moved it to Siota in 1918. Saint Hilda's was moved to Bungana in 1920, when the boys school closed down, and has remained there ever since, the oldest girls school in the mission. There were thirty-three pupils in 1922.

 A college for training Melanesians for the deaconate was started at Maka on Malaita in 1933 and was moved to Taroaniara on Nggela in 1939.

MISSION EDUCATION IN THE SOLOMON ISLANDS 161

12. The Isabel people wished English to be taught and technical instruction to be given in carpentry, boat-building, blacksmith work, and elementary engineering, (such as the running of engines both shore and marine).
13. The Methodist mission was the exception to this rule.
14. The "failure to get anything done," H. H. Vaskess, secretary to the high commissioner, observed in a characteristic minute, "is due mainly to lack of funds during the depression years and partly to Mr. Ashley's own inaction and failure to produce a scheme acceptable to the missions" (WPHC, IC 1937a). Elsewhere Vaskess criticized Ashley for lacking even a "modicum of vision" in the matter of educational grants (WPHC, IC 1931a).
15. Groves had just completed (as of 23 December 1938) a two-year appointment as director of education on the island of Nauru.
16. Richard Routledge Kane, an Irishman, was frequently accused of being a drunkard. He was once involved in a case of assault in Tulagi, and ran off with the wife of one of his district officers.

    "J. C. B. [Jack Charles Barley]," Sandars relates, "through his love of the local maidens waged constant war with the head of the Mission." Sandars tells the story of how Barley used to have assignations with island girls while his "cookie boy," nicknamed "Pig Face," stood guard at a distance with an old saucepan he would bang in the event of danger (Sandars n.d.).
17. A French priest described the SSEM as a "strange sect, with hardly any religious principles, [and] without a definite name" (Raucaz 1928:196).
18. But compare Groves' observation in his educational survey: "One fact is certain, the mass of the people have no faith in the existing mission village 'schools' as factors in their educational development" (WPHC, IC 1939d). See also Hilliard (1966:468).
19. See also WPHC, IC (1933b).

7

COMPETITION FOR BAEGU SOULS: MISSION RIVALRY ON MALAITA, SOLOMON ISLANDS

Harold M. Ross

The alert visitor to Malaita in the Southeastern Solomon Islands soon notices the plethora of Christian denominations there and the competition among them that can rival their joint antagonism to the island's pagan population. Without anthropological sophistication or intuitive brilliance, and even without leaving the conventional white man's circuit of Fassy's Auki Lodge hotel, the district commissioner's office, and the congenial Auki Club bar, one perceives that the ecumenical spirit has not prevailed here. There are no protocols delineating spheres of influence for the toilers in Malaita's missionary vineyards like those that reduced intermission competition in Southeast Asia and on other Pacific islands. Instead, the missions of several Christian sects compete with one another for the souls and loyalties of Malaitan pagans, and now and then even do a little poaching in one another's congregations.

MALAITA ISLAND AND MALAITANS

Malaita is the most populous district in the Solomon Islands. In the Southwest Pacific at 9 degrees south latitude and 161 degrees east longitude, it has a humid tropical maritime climate with seasons of prevailing southeasterly trade winds and a northwest monsoon. Malaita is a continental island 180 kilometers long and 20 to 40 kilometers wide, rising to 1,450 meters above sea level with rugged terrain and steep drainage gradients. Natural vegetation is an Indo-Malayan tropical rain forest, but most of the island is now covered with secondary bush forest fallowing between cultivation periods.

The almost 51,000 Malaitans are of Papuan-Melanesian race, darker than Polynesians but lighter than the people of Bougainville and New Georgia, with highly variable phenotypes. They speak Austronesian languages of the Eastern Oceanic branch. Inhabitants of the interior specialize in swidden horticulture (taro, sweet potatoes, bananas) and casual pig husbandry, while the coastal folk are fishermen who grow a few yams and other vegetables. A barter market system links the two economic interests, called in Solomon Islands pidgin *Bus Man* 'bush man' and *Sawara Man* 'saltwater man.'

Malaitans identify themselves by native languages or dialects. From northwest to southeast these are an unnamed language (that includes the dialects Lau, Toabaita, Baelelea, Baegu, and perhaps Fataleka), Kwara'ae, Langalanga, Kwaio, 'Are'are, and Sa'a. Baegu and Lau words are rendered by a phonetic orthography modified for standard typewriter keyboards (Ross 1973: 51, 293).

As of 1972, there were 1,800 to 2,500 Baegu, depending on where census boundaries were drawn and how the ethnic/linguistic category Baegu was defined. Baegu land extends across the island, bounded on the north by the Kwainafala and Takwea rivers and on the south by the Taeloa and Ata'a rivers.

All but a few Baegu are horticulturalists, living in hamlets of eight to sixteen persons or in slightly larger mission villages. Traditional social organization featured agnatic clans that held collective title to land, cognatic definition of social obligations and usufruct provisions, and leadership by *wane baita* 'big men': hereditary titular lineage heads, pagan priests, war leaders, or neighborhood organizers (Ross 1973). Baegu men have been going away to work on white-owned plantations since the nineteenth century, and steel tools came into their possession during that era. Today most of them are well acculturated and own a piece or two of clothing, a bush knife (machete), a few pots and pans, a pipe, and a few other Western items. Many are partially literate in the vernacular. A little more than half the Baegu are Christians, with the remainder a still vigorous and proud pagan population.

Malaita is a unique place. Generalizations about interaction between missions and traditional societies there may or may not apply elsewhere.

THE MISSIONS AND MISSIONARIES

Missionary activity among the Baegu is limited to four denominations: Roman Catholic (Marist), Anglican (Diocese of Melanesia), South Sea Evangelical Church, and Seventh-Day Adventist. The London Missionary Society, the Lutherans, and the Presbyterian mission bypassed Malaita altogether. The Methodists, who are strong in the Western Solomons because of Reverend John F. Goldie's work since 1902, never really got started there; nor did the Latter-Day Saints (Mormons), who have been so successful elsewhere in Oceania. Since World War II there has been some proselytizing by Jehovah's Witnesses. In 1967 a Baha'i businessman opened a store in Auki, the Malaita District administrative center, as the nucleus of a development that has expanded to include a cinema and small hotel.

Missionaries are the chief agents of cultural change on Malaita, and they provide the dominant role models for acculturation. Other agents of change are minimal or indirect. There is only one commercial plantation on Malaita (at Baunani in West Kwaio), and Baegu workers are not welcome there. Baegu who want wage labor must go to Guadalcanal or the Western Solomons. Nor are there any trade stores in Baegu territory. The Chinese, who dominate retail trade in the rural Solomons, have stores in Auki and Malu'u, from which they dispatch boats carrying trade goods to service consumers along the rest of the Malaitan coast. Government influence, too, is peripheral, while most Baegu live inland. The administration provides a small police force and magistrate's court system, and staff departments (agriculture, education, geology, land survey, medical, and so forth) send personnel on tours of coastal regions. The elected Malaita Council provides rural health clinics (at Fouia) and elementary schools (at Ata'a) on the coast, and in 1971 they built a coastal road that improved access from Auki to Baegu country.

There are two major reasons for missionary influence in acculturation and cultural change: missions have a virtual monopoly on education, which people value for its mobility potential; and missionaries have to some degree assumed the roles of big men, on whom people have traditionally depended for leadership and social order.

Roman Catholics were the first missionaries. In 1844, Pope Gregory XVI gave the Society of Mary (Marists) responsibility for propagating the faith in the Western Pacific; and in 1845, Bishop Épalle, first vicar apostolic of Micronesia and Melanesia, was martyred on Santa Isabel Island.[1] His staff, led by Pro-Vicar Père Frémont, moved to San Cristobal, where more Marist fathers and lay brothers succumbed to malaria or cannibals before Bishop Colomb ordered a retreat to less hostile New Guinea in 1847. The Marists returned in 1898, when, led by Bishop Vidal, they built a mission station on Rua Sura islet and began ministering to the people of Guadalcanal. In 1908 Father Bertreux did a reconnaissance of Malaita. At the invitation of dissident Anglicans in 1910, the Marists founded a mission at Tarapaina among the 'Are'are of Maramasike Island, where they were protected by Araiasi, the local big man. In 1912, they began work at Rohinari among the 'Are'are, under the tutelage of the war leader Arisimae; and in 1913 they settled in the Langalanga Lagoon at Buma, which grew into a school, timber mill, and port. Histories never identify these mission pioneers, referring only to *"le père"* or *"le missionaire."* Dutch and American Marists ultimately replaced the earlier French priests. In 1966, the Diocese of Honiara (which includes Malaita) lost mission status, becoming a diocese of the church province of Rabaul. That year the first Solomon Islander, Father Michael Aike, was ordained a priest.

Anglicans through their Melanesian Mission were the first Protestants in the area.[2] Bishop George Selwyn of New Zealand acquired responsibility for Melanesians through a typographical error—his episcopal charge from the archbishop of Canterbury read 34 degrees N. rather than 34 degrees S. Bishop Selwyn visited the Solomons in 1847, and in 1848 he began training boys from the islands at Saint John's College in Auckland. The first Anglican convert, Didi of San Cristobal, was baptized there in 1851. Overseas training shifted to Saint Barnabas College on Norfolk Island in 1867. Bishop Patteson, the first missionary bishop of Melanesia, became the first Protestant martyr of the Solomons when he and two assistants were killed in 1871 on Nukapu in the Reef Group; his memorial cross there reads: "His life was taken by those for whom he would gladly have given it." In 1876, John Still and Joseph Waté began mission work at Port Adam among the Sa'a and Lau people of Maramasike; and in 1901 (Wilson 1932:199-201) or 1902 (Fox 1962:116) Arthur Hopkins, under the protection of Kwaisulia of Adagege and with the help of Fijian assistants, began ministering to the Lau, Baegu, and Fataleka around Ata'a and Ngorefou. Led by such priests as Alfred Penny in the Florida Group, Dr. Henry Welchman on Santa Isabel and Guadalcanal, Walter Ivens in Malaita and Ulawa, Clement Marau in Ulawa and Ugi, and C. E. Fox on San Cristobal, the Anglicans became dominant in the Southeastern Solomons. They elected quite early to create an integrated expatriate and native clergy. George Sarawia was ordained a priest in 1873; Ini Kopuria and Bishop Steward created the Melanesian Brotherhood, a lay service order, in 1924; and in 1963, Leonard Alufurai of Malaita and Dudley Tuti of Santa Isabel were consecrated as bishops. What began as the Melanesian Mission of the Church of England in New Zealand, and became the Diocese of Melanesia of the Anglican church, is today becoming an independent church of the Anglican communion.

The South Sea Evangelical Mission (SSEM), now the South Sea Evangelical Church (SSEC), began among indentured Melanesian laborers in 1882 when Florence Young started a baptismal class for workers at the Fairymead Plantation in Queensland.[3] This mission was nondenominational but definitely fundamentalist. The Young family were dissenters of the Plymouth Brethren, Florence Young served with the fundamentalist China Inland Mission, and various Baptist groups were influential throughout. Her effort grew into the Queensland Kanaka Mission, which sought to convert Melanesian plantation workers who would in turn carry the Christian message back home to the Solomons. In 1892, Peter Ambuofa, a returning To'abaita man, established a Christian village among his relatives and neighbors at Malu'u on Malaita. Several amateur efforts to reinforce this native evangelism failed disastrously, with Charles Pillans in 1900 and Frank Schweiger and Joseph Watkinson in 1902 meeting defeat or death. But in 1904, Florence Young herself, A. Kelley Abbott, James Caulfield, and O. C. Thomas settled in Malu'u to oversee Malaita operations of the Solomon Islands branch of the Queensland Kanaka Mission. They founded Malaita mission headquarters the following year and a school at Onepusu in 1906. In 1907 the South Sea Evangelical Mission became independent. The SSEM was supposed to be self-supporting; and in 1909 the Young brothers, Ernest and Horace, incorporated the Malayta Company to manage plantations for the mission at Baunani and elsewhere in the Solomons. John Maedola started a boarding school to train Melanesian preachers in 1930, and under the leadership of such expatriates as the Baptist pastor William Mallis and the evangelist Northcote Deck, the SSEM developed into a thriving Solomon Islands church.

The Seventh-Day Adventists (SDA) were the last effective missionaries. In 1914, the SDA Union Conference Council of Australia voted to establish a Solomon Islands mission, and later that year Pastor and Mrs. G. F. Jones arrived to start a mission in New Georgia, where they were aided by the trader Norman Wheatley.[4] In 1924, Pastor and Mrs. J. D. Anderson began the first SDA mission on Malaita at Uru among the Kwaio. After a brief withdrawal during World War II, Adventists began a vigorous new spiritual campaign.

TRADITIONAL BAEGU RELIGION

Baegu paganism was animistic and emphasized filial piety or ancestor worship (Ross 1973:232-242). Everyone had a soul with one or more aspects. The ghosts of the dead were feared. There were *kwasi* 'wild ghosts' in the forest and sea. Most important were the *akalo* 'powerful ghosts of famous men,' who were dangerous to mankind and had to be worshipped and propitiated. Theology was perhaps cautiously optimistic, inasmuch as the gods intervened in human affairs largely in negative ways. Deities caused failure and catastrophe, so people had to placate them to ensure success.

An *aabu* 'taboo system' was in effect to prevent angering the gods. This system included avoidance of the names of important ancestral ghosts, a rich domain of curses, some protection for totemic animals (usually birds or snakes with the sea eagle being a pan-Malaitan totem) associated with patrilineal clans, and stringent regulations governing sexual contact and excretion.

The all-important ritual was the *maoma* 'mortuary ceremony' at *beu aabu* 'sacred groves' whereby people sought protection from the deities by sacrificing pigs and performing dances in their honor. This would transform the gods, over the long run, into otiose spirits no longer interested in mundane affairs. Lesser ceremonies included first fruit offerings from new gardens, funerals of commoners, and divination and curing rituals. People could also atone for their sins by offering sacrifices through the priests.

Magic, of both positive and negative valence, was widespread. There were magical techniques and prayers to assure success in gardening, pig husbandry, fishing, trading, and war. People could protect gardens, trees, or fishing holes by a taboo sign. Herbal remedies, divination, and prayers helped to cure the sick. Sorcerers who used *arua* 'contagious magic' and witches were threats to the public. Divination could diagnose unnatural deaths and facilitate vengeance by means of revenge killings. The concept of *mamanaa* 'truth or power' covered an array of supernatural and real-world efficacy, success, and potency.

True priests, ordained by popular approval and confirmed by their knowledge of sacred lore and ritual, were the leading religious practitioners and were classified as big men. Diviners, curers, genealogists, and sacrificial food allocators were quasi-religious functionaries. This was the traditional pagan background into which missionary Christianity intruded.

MISSIONARY SECTARIANISM

Missionaries and the messages they present are by no means a homogeneous lot. The net results of these very real differences are that, first, missions do different things; second, local people perceive them differently, and third, acculturation takes different paths depending upon the sect involved. To appreciate their colonial impact, we must understand these differences (Birnbaum 1969:23-25).

Each of the four missionary enterprises in Malaita brings with it unique theologies, organizations, purposes, forms of worship, clergy-laity relations, and social policies. These, of course, depend upon the nature of the churches themselves and are the result of nineteen centuries of church history. The various theologies are independent of the Malaitan situation.

Roman Catholic doctrine stems from the Bible, council-approved doctrines such as the Nicene Creed, writings of early church fathers, and the lives of the saints, as well as nearly two millennia of scholarship, compromises, and dogmas emanating from the apostolic succession from Saint Peter through the papacy, which claims infallibility when speaking *ex cathedra*. Inherent in it are even older traditions of Judaic and classical Greco-Roman thought. Periodic reevaluation and resynthesis by such scholars as Saint Augustine and Saint Thomas Aquinas have made it the most complex of all Christian thought; and it contains baffling Christian paradoxes such as the Trinity, sin and salvation, free will and determinism, and faith versus works.

The Anglican church has both Catholic and Protestant characteristics. It, too, claims to be a catholic (meaning universal and unitary) and apostolic church, building upon the wisdom of past and ongoing scholarship as well as the biblical foundation. Historically, Anglicans at their origin rejected the primacy of the Roman papacy in favor of national or local control while retaining a hierarchical or episcopal form of government, canon law, and the convention form of resolving disputes and making decisions. Recurrent reform movements, a natural character of Protestantism, keep alive a certain evangelical spirit and tend more in the direction of national, local, and individual responsibility than the Roman Catholic church is willing to accept.

The South Sea Evangelical Church is unashamedly fundamentalist and Protestant. The Bible, especially the New Testament, is its sole and complete authority. The Bible as the word of God is to be accepted absolutely in its entirety; subsequent interpretations are the fallible works of man. Roman Catholics and Anglicans are somewhat tolerant in their attitude toward human affairs and frailties, but the SSEC, in keeping with its Baptist and dissenter origins, is strongly puritanical. Although not strictly Calvinistic, there is an emphasis upon salvation and the state of grace. Evangelical zeal for spreading the Christian message is coupled with Pentecostal emphasis upon emotional worship and divine revelation.

The Seventh-Day Adventists are a reform messianic movement within the Protestant fundamentalist tradition. The Bible is the authoritarian foundation of faith, there is renewed interest in the Old Testament, and particular importance attaches to the Book of Revelation. Adventists see the history of Christianity as a series of steps from darkness into light, with later revelations approaching more nearly the full truth. Protestant leaders such as Luther, Calvin, Knox, and the Wesleys approached the truth ever more closely, but full knowledge awaited the revelations of the Third Angel and the establishment of the Seventh-Day Adventist faith, which awaits the imminent Second Coming. Adventists, too, practice a puritanical way of life, renouncing alcohol, tobacco, and the traditional Melanesian chewing quid of areca palm nut, betel pepper, and lime.

Mission organization also comes to the islands with the missionaries. Roman Catholic authority devolves, as it does everywhere, from the Roman papacy, through the cardinal princes of the church and archiepiscopal provinces, through the bishops of dioceses, to appointed parish priests. It is truly international, recognizing national sovereignties only through informal national hierarchies of bishops, and its unity is marred only slightly by the various clerical orders, themselves of international nature. Like a parish anywhere at any time, a Malaitan parish is tied through its priest, bishop, and archbishop to Rome; and through the apostolic succession back through time it is tied to Saint Peter and Jesus himself. Seen from the parishioner's level, the church is authoritarian where faith, morals, and doctrine are concerned.

The Anglican church, while rejecting the Roman pope as head of the church and successor to Saint Peter, retains its hierarchical organization of bishops and archbishops and its three degrees of clergy: deacons, priests, and bishops. National churches, with distinct national ecclesiastical hierarchies headed by a governing board, presiding bishop, or primate of the church, are its ideal form of governance. Separatism, linked to national independence movements (like the American Revolution and the dominions and successor states growing out of the British Empire's dissolution), prevents international union beyond the vague sense of an Anglican communion. The autonomy of local parishes vis-à-vis the episcopal hierarchy, the role of the individual parishioner, and laity-clergy relationships seem purposely vague as befits the Protestant tradition, although local parish affairs are run by lay leaders under the parish priest's direction. Most Anglican villages on Malaita lack a resident priest and have to rely upon these laymen to keep church affairs going.

The South Sea Evangelical Church has no hierarchy. Each local congregation forms its own church, is led by elected elders, and is autonomous. Clergymen are selected from educated members. They are called by the congregation they will serve, and they are "ordained" by their own congregations. Most congregations on Malaita do not in fact have a clergyman but rely upon their elders and their own devices. In this sort of organization, there is no higher temporal authority than the local congregation itself. The Bible is the ultimate authority. Each individual is expected to resolve moral and doctrinal questions for himself by reference to the Bible, but it is assumed that reasonable minds will agree upon its interpretation. Hence there is an emphasis upon vernacular translations of the Bible in the Protestant tradition of Zwingli, Huss, and Wycliffe.

Seventh-Day Adventists likewise rely upon local congregations linked by agreement in their interpretation of the Bible and latter-day divine revelation. Again each individual is expected to consult the Bible to resolve doubts, confusions, and controversies. Officials and teachers at major mission stations may correct erring congregations. They dominate but do not lead them as an ecclesiastical hierarchy.

By "purpose" of the missions, I mean their goals, their reasons justifying their activities. Both Roman Catholics and Anglicans feel their main purpose is to bring Malaitans into the church and, secondarily, to improve their way of life, both spiritually and materially. The SSEC seeks to save souls, although instruction as to a proper way of life and material welfare are not forgotten. Seventh-Day Adventists want to save souls, prepare for the Second Coming of Christ, and help the people lead a proper life. The millenarian aspect of Adventism distinguishes it from other missions.

Naturally, the typical ceremonies and rituals of the missions are somewhat different on Malaita, just as they are elsewhere. For Roman Catholics, the Mass, confession, and the usual duties are paramount. A priest says mass daily, and attendance at the Sunday mass is mandatory. The sacraments receive their international attention. Feast and fast days mark the calendar, sacred holidays are recognized, and people observe the usual Catholic rites of passage (christening, first communion, marriage, extreme unction, funerals).

Anglicans pay heed to fewer events, recognizing only the major church holy days plus national and local holidays. A typical Anglican village on Malaita, for example, might schedule communal feasts for Christmas, Easter, the queen's birthday, and the saint's day for whom their church is named. Church services would also mark lesser church holy days and seasons such as Advent, Epiphany, Lent, Palm Sunday, Good Friday, and Whitsuntide, as well as note in passing minor secular holidays. Morning and evening prayers in the Anglican tradition are daily events conducted by laymen. Holy Communion is offered only when a priest visits a local church. Anglican rites of passage include baptism and christening of infants, confirmation, marriage, and funerals.

SSEC congregations hold lengthy daily prayer meetings. Sunday services are interminable. Village elders lead these services, since there are so few clergy. Revival meetings take place when there is a visiting preacher available or at times just to renew and intensify faith. Services feature prayers, Bible study, hymns, frequent public confessions or witnesses of faith, and, occasionally, charismatic trances, Pentecostal talking in tongues, and faith healing. Baptism is given only to rational adults. Weddings and funerals occur within the church context according to Protestant formats.

Seventh-Day Adventists also hold daily prayer, Bible and hymn sessions. They recognize the Jewish Sabbath, doing no work from sundown on Friday until sundown on Saturday, and celebrate an extra service on the Sabbath Day. In addition, they observe Levitical food taboos against pork, shellfish, and certain other foods defined as wild and unfit for human consumption. Weddings and funerals follow Protestant customs.

The nature of the clergy and laity-clergy relationships also vary with sectarian practice. The Roman Catholic clergy consists of highly educated and formally ordained priests who are assisted by missionary nuns, lay brothers who teach or work on church projects, and teaching or nursing sisters. Catholic villages nearly always have a priest in residence and the village itself focuses on the church. The priest is, in fact, the head of the community while the laymen have little responsibility in church affairs. Dutch and American Marists have predominated the past several decades. Only since 1966 have Melanesians begun moving into clerical positions.

The Anglican clergy, also educated and formally ordained, includes parish priests and archdeacons (rural deans) who serve several Anglican villages in a general area. Clergymen use a circuit riding technique, periodically visting villages in their areas to offer Holy Communion, baptize and christen infants, confirm new communicants, solemnize weddings that have happened since their last visit, and conduct memorial services for the recently buried. Unlike the Roman Catholics, most of the Anglican clergy are Melanesians, who have been gradually taking over from British and New Zealand expatriates almost from the beginning of the Melanesian Mission. Anglicans use fewer lay missionaries, but members of the Melanesian Brotherhood are available, and there are a few expatriate teachers, nurses, and physicians. Lay leadership is important in both secular and church affairs, with Anglican lay leaders assisting local big men and conducting worship in the absence of a priest.

In the SSEC, Melanesian leadership is paramount, with expatriates serving not as clerics or mission officials but as teachers or technicians when qualified Melanesians are not available. The white missionaries who created the SSEM were notable more for their fervor than their erudition. They tended to come from working class and agrarian backgrounds in Australia and New Zealand, unlike Catholic and Anglican missionaries, who were often drawn from the gentry and intelligentsia of their home countries. Their Baptist and Pentecostal preferences predisposed them to democratic forms of congregational organization. Many early evangelists were Malaita men themselves, converted in Queensland and knowing scarcely any more Christian theology than those they hoped to convert. SSEC congregations have always been autonomous and self-supporting, managing their own affairs through indigenous elders who served as village headmen in secular matters and as lay leaders of the church. The few visiting clergy have acted as advisors and teachers, upgrading the quality of faith but leaving local congregations on their own. A handful of expatriate lay missionaries serve finite terms as teachers or technicians in major population centers. Expatriates working with the SSEC have tended toward moral paternalism and absolutism, perceiving their duty as leading the heathen out of darkness into a better life.

Seventh-Day Adventist missionary pastors are mostly Australians or Americans from working- or lower-middle-class origins. The numerous SDA lay missionaries include teachers, medical workers, and craftsmen. They work almost invariably in major stations that include a school, hospital, farms, and craft shops. They train Melanesian teachers for small SDA village schools that are satellites of the mission station itself. The SDA pastor or teacher is very much the leader of the local SDA community. These communities are independent but look to the mission stations for guidance in faith, religious matters, and general policy.

Given these varied characteristics of organization, doctrine, and personnel, one has to expect that the social policies and goals of the several missions will differ. Roman Catholics and Anglicans have adopted a policy of leaving the native cultures intact with minimal disturbance of traditional ways. They have sought to bring Malaitans into the church, teach them Christian ideals and doctrine, and let the people work out their own lives as a synthesis of Malaitan culture and Christian beliefs. Bishop Patteson, for example, said: "When the people become Christians they will decide for themselves which customs are evil and must be given up" (Fox 1967:31). Both sects use traditional Malaitan art motifs, take a flexible attitude on incorporation of Malaitan elements into Christian iconography and symbolism, and tolerate or even support Malaitan customs and aesthetics. In Catholic and Anglican church architecture and decorative art one finds the stylized frigate birds, porpoises, sharks, and eagles common to Malaitan art in general. Catholics and Anglicans continue to use shell bead strings of money for ceremonial exchanges, and they pay with clerical approval the traditional shell money and porpoise teeth brideprices. Some parishes use taro and coconut water in place of the symbolic bread and wine in Christian communion. Polygynously married men have not been forced to renounce and abandon their wives, although future polygyny is proscribed. Traditional songs and dances are performed for Christian festivals, and traditional craftsmen work for their churches.

On the other hand, Roman Catholics and Anglicans differ in rates of localization of their ecclesiastical hierarchies. The ultimate Roman Catholic goal is a truly catholic church with a Melanesian national and local hierarchy. There is no compromise in quality, however. A parish priest in Melanesia is as qualified and educated as a priest in Europe or America. Hence the rate of localization has been slow and there are few Melanesian priests. But Melanesians are now being ordained, and they will move up in the hierarchy as they acquire knowledge and experience.

The Anglican goal is an independent national church with a native hierarchy. They have been ordaining deacons and priests for a century now, and two Melanesians were consecrated as Anglican bishops in 1963. Today most of the Diocese of Melanesia clergy are Melanesians.

Catholics and Anglicans did not neglect the material side of life, although their main emphasis has been upon the spiritual. Anglican Bishop Walter Baddeley asked rhetorically: "It was right to build a fine house for God, but is it right for the sons of God to live in hovels?" (Fox 1967:33). Catholic missions usually are a busy complex of farms and workshops directed by the parish priest, who also runs a school and hospital. Anglican missions rely more upon parish congregations to run their own schools and economic projects through cooperative efforts on their own. The Diocese of Melanesia supports some larger schools and hospitals directly.

The South Sea Evangelical Church is almost wholly localized. Its goals—a native church with independent congregations—have been realized. Local congregations are autonomous and democratic. With the exception of a few expatriate teachers and technicians, leadership is Melanesian and local. On the other hand, the SSEC expects its adherents to give up native ways and live a Christian (westernized) life. Theirs is a functionalist assumption; the Christian religion must be accompanied by Christian (hence Western) politics, economics, and social policies. Education and material well-being have always been secondary to spiritual conversion. Early SSEM leaders followed a conscious policy of salvation before education and civilization; dogmatic purity based upon biblical sources was required, and the thrust of their educational efforts was toward qualifying candidates for baptism (Hilliard 1969:43-45). SSEM leaders insisted that baptized converts live in ways appropriate to Christians, as defined by scripture and white missionaries. SSEC members do not pay brideprices, and they must forgo native singing, dancing, and art. But by and large the tasks of education, material welfare, and social transformation to Western ways have been left to congregations to accomplish on their own.

Seventh-Day Adventists have been the most insistent of all upon giving up Malaitan customs and transforming society along the lines of a Western Christian model. But this model is a somewhat aberrant one, according to their scriptural reading and prophetic revelation. Converts must give up traditional customs, including art, literature, music, and dance, which are seen as unalloyed sinfulness. They forbid the payment of bridewealth, which they wrongly interpret as chattel purchase, even though this is in Malaitan terms simply a necessary solemnization of marriage. Symbolism, iconography, daily life-style, and morality are to be strictly Christian and Western; but unfamiliar elements are their imposition of Old Testament food taboos and the Saturday Sabbath. On the other hand, Seventh-Day Adventist missionaries do more than anyone else for material welfare. Their missions include schools, hospitals, workshops, and commercial enterprises that are exemplars of progress. Their white missionaries exert more direct influence on converts than others do, but they train Melanesian teachers who serve in satellite mission schools and who will take over mission activities when they are technically, doctrinally, and spiritually qualified to do so. The Adventist goal is the complete transformation of society in preparation for the Second Coming; theirs is a messianic and revolutionary movement.

BAEGU PERCEPTIONS OF CHRISTIANITY

Some aspects are common to all forms of Malaitan Christianity, regardless of sect. Malaitan Christianity is syncretic, a peculiar amalgam of Western and Malaitan beliefs. This is, of course, characteristic of the rank and file of the populace, not of Malaitan clergymen and well-educated products of mission schools.

Both pagans and Christians are tolerant of one another's theologies. Christians still believe in the ancestral spirits, calling them devils, but they argue that the Christian God and his Word make it no longer necessary to observe pagan taboos or sacrifice pigs to the pagan gods. Jehovah, God the Father, Jesus, the Holy Ghost, the Virgin Mary, or the saints can protect Christians from the anger and vagaries of pagan spirits. Likewise, pagans are willing to grant the divinity of Jesus, Jehovah, the Holy Ghost, or the Trinity and accept the holiness of as many saints as you care to name. But pagans argue that the Malaitan spirits are too powerful for Christian ones to overcome. One old man told me he had been a Christian when he worked on plantations overseas but reverted to paganism when he returned to Malaita. As he observed, white men's gods were best in the white men's country; but Malaitan gods were best in Malaita, and it would not be wise or safe to ignore them. There is also some syncretism of mythology. Noah and the Flood, Abraham and Isaac, the Garden of Eden—all have acquired Malaitan characteristics and are associated with traditional Malaitan figures in some oral traditions. Because of the differences described above, however, Malaitans perceive each Christian sect somewhat differently.

Their level of education and organization earn status for the Roman Catholic priesthood in Malaitan eyes. Malaitans know the Catholic missions are not part of the protectorate government; they are aware of the international associations of the church outside the British Commonwealth and of the ultimate supremacy of the pope in Rome. Most priests and nuns have been non-British (French, Dutch, or American), and Catholic missions have won local sympathy by being consistently for the common people of Malaita and occasionally against the government. Malaitans often turn to the Catholic missions as buffers against state power, and they admire the Roman Catholic claim to universality, which has analogs in Malaitan ideals of brotherhood and union similar to those that motivated the Marching Rule movement after World War II.

There is some confusion between church and state involving the Anglicans. Although there never was an established church in the British Solomon Islands, most early Anglican missionaries were influential Britons, most British officers have been members of the Church of England, and the Diocese of Melanesia has usually taken progovernment positions. Hence many Baegu think that the Anglican church is a state agency. People were puzzled, for example, in 1966 when some Anglicans destroyed an old pagan shrine in the Lau Lagoon and were subsequently convicted and fined by the magistrate's court for desecrating a religious site. At any rate, they admire the Anglican church for its aura of power and its effective organization. Even if not officially established, it is nonetheless an establishment church. On the other hand, there is local pride in the fact that the Anglican clergy are mostly Melanesians and the Diocese of Melanesia is a truly national church belonging to the people of the Solomon Islands rather than to foreigners.

The South Sea Evangelical Church occupies a more ambiguous position. Some Baegu may envy the sureness of their sense of salvation and their confident assertions of divine guidance through the Bible; but others resent what they perceive as sanctimonious smugness, and Catholics and Anglicans may hold SSEC fundamentalism and simplicity in contempt. Other Malaitans envy SSEC independence, but at the same time their lack of support leaves the SSEC lagging in education, health care, and economic development. That is not envied. SSEC evangelical zeal for converts sometimes antagonizes their pagan and other Christian neighbors. On the whole, they are a truly Malaitan religious body who enjoy the blessings and endure the hardships that come with self-determination, which is at once their strength and weakness.

Malaitans are also ambivalent toward the Seventh-Day Adventists. Adventist groups win admiration for their devotion, energy, and self-confidence. They get bad marks for being sanctimonious and pushy. Some respect their puritanism; others do not. Their stringent taboos make sense to Malaitans, who are used to living with a taboo system—once, that is, one accepts the validity of their particular revelation. The material prosperity of the Seventh-Day Adventists, based upon mission public health works and commercial enterprises, is envied by many. Yet, like the SSEC, their strident evangelism tends to annoy their neighbors. In balance, the Adventists form a strong and successful community. If one accepts their beliefs and their goal of a radical transformation of society along Western lines (which not all Baegu do), one admires them.

PATHS OF CHANGE

Conversion to Christianity brings with it some changes in life-style. Missionaries urge relocation to new villages on the coast or at lower altitudes because it makes people easier to organize and control. New villages permit Christian converts to focus their communities upon a church, and a concentrated population means mutual support for their new beliefs. Church officials find them easier to reach to reinforce conviction and root out heresy. Coastal residence offers better access to material welfare. Ships call at coastal ports, and government roads, dispensaries, and schools are all on the coast. Relocation also protects converts from bad (that is, pagan) temptations of singing, dancing, and pig feasts. Yet traditional forces and the tendency for new lowland villages to fission into smaller hamlets approximating traditional size and placement remain strong (Ross 1973:250).

Pagans and Christians tend to live as separate communities, as Keesing (1967) found among the Kwaio. Pagan and Christian Baegu rarely intermarry, a situation similar to Tikopia where conversion has also been a gradual process (Firth 1975:77). Christians form their own villages at the urging of missionaries, who hope to isolate them from temptations to apostasy and sinfulness. Pagans withdraw for their own reasons. First, they fear ritual contamination from Christians who no longer observe the taboo system; second, they could not afford the pig sacrifices entailed in expiating guilt stemming from constant exposure to ritually unclean persons.

Yet the two communities continue to interact to some degree. Kinship obligations and moral ties cut across the pagan-Christian separation. Both unite to make common cause for their lineages in the interminable Malaitan land title litigation. Men continue to contribute bridewealth to their younger male relatives, whether pagan or Christian. Although they do not generally take an active part, Christian Baegu will visit kin to watch the dancing and singing at a pagan mortuary festival and pagan Baegu will visit Christian kin at church feasts. Both go to the same markets along the coast, and pagan Baegu from the interior frequently spent the night with

Christian relatives near where I lived on their way to or from markets. Both pagan and Christian leaders held office in the old Marching Rule and continue to do so in the Custom movement that succeeded it.

For obvious reasons each mission experienced slightly different patterns of success and failure, and the effect of each on the Baegu has been unique. Roman Catholics moved northward around the Malaitan coast. In 1915, shortly after the British government came to Auki to bring law and order to Malaita, a Catholic mission was established at Auki Harbor (Langalanga and Kwara'ae). By World War II, missionary priests were working at Dala on the northwest coast (Kwara'ae and Fataleka), Takwa at the northern end of the Lau Lagoon (Lau, Baelelea, and Baegu), and Usu'usue near Ata'a (Lau, Baegu, and Fataleka). The church and school at Dala were under a Dutch Marist priest. At Takwa, two Marist priests (one American and one Dutch in 1966; but one Dutch and a Malaitan 'Are'are by 1968) and three nuns (one New Zealander and two American sisters) ran a church, school, hospital, dairy and swine farm, and workshops for making lumber and concrete blocks. A Dutch Marist priest at Usu'usue supervised a church, school, and medical dressing station and at one time the Ata'a mission ran a thriving business selling seashells to collectors around the world. Each mission station had its own motor launch. Converts formed clusters of villages, subdivided along dialect and clan lines, around each mission. These clusters were large by Baegu standards. In 1967, 335 Baegu lived in four villages near the Ata'a mission.

Beginning in 1901-1902 at Ngorefou, near Ata'a, the Anglican Melanesian Mission had success in the Lau Lagoon among the Lau and Baegu. Most of the Kwarande group at the south end of the lagoon became Anglicans, and by 1915 the entire island of Sulufou (around five hundred people) in the Tae Lagoon section had joined the Melanesian Mission, with other Lau Christians at Adagege (Tae Passage) and Foubebi in the Makwanu portion of the lagoon. On the west coast, Anglicans began working at Fiu in 1901 and at Auki in 1909; they established a hospital and leprosarium at Fau'abu (Kwara'ae, Fataleka, and Baegu) in 1929 (Fox 1962:249). From the Lau Lagoon, missionaries worked among bush peoples like the Baegu. Fouia, opposite Sulufou

Island, and Manule, on Urasi Cove, are mixed Lau and Baegu villages. Baegu Melanesian Mission converts formed churches in the west at Ferafalu near Fau'abu, in the southeast at Ata'a, and in the east at Ailali and Anoketo along the Sasafa River. In 1966, an English nursing sister was in charge of the leprosarium at Fau'abu, a retired Lau priest lived at Manule, and a Lau priest at Fouia had responsibility for parish churches throughout the Lau Lagoon and East Baegu area. There were Anglican schools with Lau teachers at Lilifia and Gwaunatolo (near Fouia) on the lagoon, schools with Baegu teachers at Ailali and Manule, and a school with a Baegu teacher at Rame'ai in Baelelea. Baegu Anglican converts did not congregate around mission stations; they created new villages. Some were considerably larger (Ferafalu 78, Ata'a 39, Ailali 93, Anoketo 49), but others approximated traditional hamlet size. In 1968, 151 Anglicans lived in my East Baegu census area, which included Ailali and Anoketo but not the other Anglican places named above. Anglican villages tend to be dialectically homogeneous and to segment along clan or lineage lines.

Spread by Malaitan converts themselves, South Sea Evangelical Church villages are scattered throughout Malaita. SSEC converts live in all ecological zones and dialect groups. Kofiloko, on Urasi Cove, is a mixed Lau and Baegu hamlet; Abuisaia (near Ailali) on the Sasafa River is a lowland Baegu village; and Faadile, up in cloud country on the central mountain ridge at 950 meters, is Baelelea and Baegu. There are SSEC schools at Unu'u at the mouth of the Takwea River and at Araki near Ata'a; in 1968 these had volunteer teachers from New Zealand, but Melanesian teachers had taken over by 1972. These schools were for children, and no major settlements have grown around them. Lacking the drawing power of major mission stations and being wholly under local leadership, Baegu SSEC communities stayed closer to the old small size and have shown the most marked tendency to fission along dialect and kinship lines. In 1968 there were seventy-five SSEC converts living in my East Baegu census area: at Abuisaia (twenty-six), at Kafo'ote'ote (seven) and Ngalianarufo (thirty-two) near Ailali, and at Adomose (ten) near Anoketo.

Seventh-Day Adventists built their first mission station in northern Malaita at Kwailabesi (Lau and Baelelea) at the northern end of the Lau Lagoon about 1948. In 1966 they opened a large, well-equipped new hospital at Uru (Kwaio) that serves all northeastern Malaita. At Kwailabesi, an Australian pastor, assisted by a staff of Australian volunteers and Solomon Islanders, runs a school, a medical dressing station, a model farm, several motor launches, and machine and other workshops. They sometimes collect Malaitan handicrafts to sell through the SDA College at Betikama on Guadalcanal. Melanesian SDA teachers, under the supervision of the pastor at Kwailabesi, run schools for converts at Newland in the Makwanu passage of the Lau Lagoon (where they have numerous recent converts) and in the bush at Whitestone (Baegu) and Ata'a (Baegu and Fataleka). SDA converts may translate local place-names into English; thus Ferafalu becomes Newland and the Baegu Faukwakwaoa becomes Whitestone. SDA hamlets are heterogeneous: they include residents from several clans, including converts from other missions as well as from paganism. In 1968, thirteen Baegu Adventists lived at Ata'a and thirty at Whitestone; by 1972 their numbers had grown to twenty-seven and forty-seven respectively.

The most spectacular happening in postmissionary Malaitan history was the Marching Rule movement of 1944-1954, and this bore directly upon the missions in several ways. Marching Rule was a nationalistic political-economic movement, not a naive cargo cult, although it did degenerate into cargoism among the less sophisticated at its fringes. It began on Guadalcanal in 1944 among Malaitans working for American military forces but reached its apogee on Malaita under the leadership of southern leaders such as the highly educated Timothy George of Walande and Hoasihau, Aliki Nonohimae, and Nori of 'Are'are (Laracy 1971:97-103). Their long-range goal was the revitalization of Solomon Islands society through increased brotherhood, social solidarity, and productivity. More immediate goals included a fairer deal for Melanesians, a higher standard of living, and some degree of national self-determination. The facts of life in the protectorate and the events of World War II in the Pacific made Marching Rule implicitly anti-British and pro-American. Typical activities (which continue today) included compiling genealogies called generations, preparing land title claims, and recording custom in order to conserve traditional ways. Marching Rule was well organized with an elaborate hierarchy of head chiefs (who formed an All-Malaita Council), chiefs, clerks (who recorded deliberations), custom chiefs (who debated and interpreted custom), and duties (who served as orderlies). In 1947 they called a general strike; and in 1949 they began a civil disobedience campaign in Malaita that involved nonpayment of the annual rate (a poll tax), resettlement in large native towns, and building fortifications with palisades, watchtowers, and sentries. Police raids, jail sentences for the leaders, and the creation of a British-approved Malaita Council (local self-government) suppressed Marching Rule in its active phases by 1953 or 1954.

Marching Rule ideology and underground activity continue in the Custom movement that still preoccupies many Malaitans. The Custom men inherited the Marching Rule hierarchical structure and interests in recording genealogies, land claims, and custom, which turns out to be a sort of ethnoethnology (Keesing 1968; Cochrane 1970:97-118). They are, however, less unified and rather more addicted to cargoism. Nevertheless, I erred in my Baegu ethnography (Ross 1973) in stressing the cargo cult aspects of the Custom movement. The cargo cult beliefs of unsophisticated adherents are not in fact held by the leaders. Blame my mistakes, if you will, on the fieldworker's pique at the thousandth time a delegation came to ask him when the cargo was going to arrive from America!

Marching Rule showed, among other things, the Trojan horse in the South Sea Evangelical Mission. Being used to running their own affairs through elected village elders and to making their own decisions after studying the Bible, SSEM Christians came to believe themselves capable of self-government. In the 1930s they expelled their white clergy, and during Marching Rule eight of the nine head chiefs of Malaita were SSEM members, the ninth being a pagan (Laracy 1971:104).

Anglicans and Roman Catholics, with their more dependency-oriented communities, had different Marching Rule experiences. The Melanesian Mission officially opposed Marching Rule, a lukewarm progovernment stand that cost them local support. Dutch Marist priests were more sympathetic toward the movement, and the Catholic church in Malaita grew from 5,410 members in 1946 to 7,694 in 1950 by attracting dissident Anglican Marching

Rule sympathizers (Laracy 1971:108). This new Catholic strength proved to be soft, however. In 1950, Father Van de Walle formed a Catholic Welfare Society as an alternative to Marching Rule for Catholics; this the British government later ordered disbanded (Laracy 1971:111). After 1954, Catholic missions quarreled repeatedly with Malaitan leaders over Custom claims to church-owned mission lands (Laracy 1971:113).

All told the missions have succeeded in converting 87 percent of the Malaitan population. According to Laracy (1971:103), of an estimated 1942 population of 40,000, there were approximately 9,000 SSEM fundamentalists, 5,000 Melanesian Mission Anglicans, 4,000 Roman Catholics, and maybe 1,000 Seventh-Day Adventists. The 1970-1971 Solomon Islands census reveals a Malaitan population of 50,659 with 15,655 SSEC, 12,464 Melanesian Mission, 10,110 Catholic, 2,563 Jehovah's Witness, 2,478 Seventh-Day Adventist, 325 Baha'i, and 75 United Church (Wesleyan) affiliates. Pagans then numbered 6,665; there were 123 others, and 194 did not specify a religious preference, leaving a discrepancy of 7 persons (Groenewegen 1972:331).

For the Baegu proper, official census data are useless, because census districts (like electoral wards) cross dialect boundaries and include both bush and saltwater people. My 1966-1968 ethnographic fieldwork yielded an estimate of 1,880 Baegu still in the hills with another 500 now on the coast (Ross 1973:94-99). All the coastal and part of the hill Baegu are Christians. Table 2 presents population and religious affiliation data from a 1968 census sample area in the Sasafa River valley and surrounding ridges, the southeastern area around Ata'a where Baegu assistants collected census information, and estimates for the interior hills and west coast lowlands.

Three ethnographic trends appear in my 1966-1968 data and in the changes that had taken place by my 1972 visit. First, there is a slow but steady drift toward Christianity. For 1966-1968, I counted nine conversions from paganism to Christianity and seven apostates who went back to paganism (Ross 1973:63). By 1972, nine pagans had converted to Anglicanism, there were three apostates, and ten pagans had become Adventists. This yields a net gain of eighteen converts for the period 1966-1972, not counting natural changes due to births and deaths. A severe

TABLE 2 Baegu Population and Religious Affiliation as of 1967-1968

Religion	Census Sample Area	Ata'a Area Census	Central Hills Census Estimate	West Coast Census Estimate	Estimated Totals
Pagan	267	178	400	0	845
Roman Catholic	0	335	0	0	335
Melanesian Mission (Anglican)	151	39	70	300	560
South Sea Evangelical Church	75	272	50	200	597
Seventh-Day Adventist	30	13	0	0	43
Christian subtotals	256	659	120	500	1,535
Totals	523	837	520	500	2,380

influenza-pneumonia epidemic in 1970 produced most of the converts, who turned to the missions seeking supernatural protection from the wrath of ancestral ghosts. Second, the Adventists are growing at the expense of other Christian denominations. From 1968 to 1972, ten pagans became Adventists at Whitestone, but seven new Adventists were former Anglicans. All fourteen new Adventists at Ata'a were already Christians. Third, there are opposing tendencies among the Baegu for both fusion and fission of settlements, as tables 3 and 4 show.

Christian sects want their converts in large, church-oriented communities, and Marching Rule ideology (carried on in the Custom movement) urges settlement in big new towns. Nevertheless, internal strains break larger villages into traditionally sized hamlets. The Neo-Marching Rule town of Fatakalie has fissioned into several hamlets. Since 1955, the Anglican village of Anoketo has sent out two nearby offshoot hamlets, Liufania and Matakwadolo. During my stay, four Ailali families left to form their own Anglican hamlet; this happened twice more by 1972. The SSEC village of Abuisaia segmented to form nearly adjacent Ngalianarufo. An older SSEC village on the Sasafa right bank fissioned into Adomose, Kafo'ote'ote, and a now defunct third hamlet near Anglican Anoketo.

TABLE 3 East Baegu Census Area Data[a]

Village	Altitude (meters)	Distance from sea (kilometers)	Religion	No. of Households	Total Population
Abuisaia	300	3	SSEC	5	26
Adomose	150	1	SSEC	3	10
Ai'aofia	300	5	Pagan	6	21
Ailali	150	3	MM	21	93
Anoketo	300	3	MM	12	49
Ao'ana	900	10	Pagan	4	13
Borumalakwa	750	8	Pagan	7	22
Faakwao'abu	600	5	Pagan	6	20
Fatakalie	600	5	Pagan	10	28
Fauboso	450	5	Pagan	3	17
Faukwakwaoa	300	3	SDA	9	30
Fera'inomae	300	5	Pagan	2	10
Gwaikabarai	600	6	Pagan	8	28
Gwasumoko	900	10	Pagan	2	6
Kafo'ote'ote	150	3	SSEC	3	7
Kilie	900	10	Pagan	1	8
Liufania	150	5	MM	1	3
Maelanafe	750	8	Pagan	3	12
Matakwadolo	150	5	MM	2	6
Ngali'abu	900	10	Pagan	2	9
Ngaliana'ago	600	3	Pagan	2	9
Ngalianarufo	300	3	SSEC	7	32
Ngalifulibeu	750	8	Pagan	5	22
Ngalikwao	450	5	Pagan	5	20
Rue	750	3	Pagan	3	9
Total				136	523

[a] Figures are as of June 1968; this table is adapted from Ross (1973:294-295), which also provides a Baegu hamlet map and gazetteer.

TABLE 4 Baegu Hamlet Size and Composition[a]

Area	No. of Hamlets	No. of People	Average Hamlet Size	No. of Households	No. of Households per Hamlet	Average Household Size
East Baegu						
Pagan (traditional)	14	189	13.5	48	3.4	3.9
Pagan (Neo-Marching Rule)	3	78	26.0	25	8.3	3.1
Anglican	4	151	37.8	36	9.0	4.2
Roman Catholic	——	——	——	——	——	——
SSEC	4	75	18.8	18	4.5	4.2
Seventh-Day Adventist	1	30	30.0	9	9.0	3.3
Totals and gross averages	26	523	20.1	136	5.2	3.8
Ata'a						
Pagan (traditional)	3	42	14.0	7	2.3	6.0
Pagan (Neo-Marching Rule)	5	136	27.2	31	6.2	4.4
Anglican	1	39	39.0	9	9.0	4.3
Roman Catholic	4	335	83.8	87	21.8	3.9
SSEC	4	272	68.0	61	15.3	4.5
Seventh-Day Adventist	1	13	13.0	3	3.0	4.3
Totals and gross averages	18	837	46.5	198	11.0	4.2

[a] Data from 1967-1968; adapted from Ross (1973:99).

Finally, despite sentiment for Christian cooperation, rivalry among sects is real. Everyone in the Solomons always felt that Christians ought to work together. The division between the Methodist west where Goldie worked and the Melanesian Mission in the Southeastern Solomons was a negotiated effort to prevent mission rivalry. As early as 1913, Resident Commissioner Woodford deplored the arrival of the SSEM missionaries and their consequent rivalry with the missions already there (Hilliard 1969: 49). Subsequent British officials continued to criticize mission proliferation as wasteful of effort and resources and confusing to the people, who were confused enough by white interference without being drawn into interdenominational squabbling. Today, educated Solomon Islanders believe they can demonstrate moral superiority to Europeans if they can overcome the sectarian differences they have inherited and create a unified church in the spirit of the worldwide ecumenical movement. The Solomon Islands Christian Association is a vital part of their modern life (Kent 1973:48).

This proves, though, to be a hard task, for sectarian jealousies and prejudices are deep-rooted and persistent. Back in 1907, an Anglican missionary contemptuously described SSEM efforts as "dissent in its barest and crudest form" (Hilliard 1969:49). Roman Catholic separatism in Malaita partakes of worldwide Catholic-Protestant misunderstanding. Catholic opportunism during Marching Rule left bad feelings. SSEC insistence upon "plenary and literal interpretation of scripture" (Hilliard 1969: 43) makes it hard for more tolerant Anglicans and Catholics to work with them. Pagans and Christians resent not only the Adventists' sense of moral superiority, which they derive from their more advanced revelations, but also their aggressive evangelism. A religious revival swept Malaita in 1970-1971 when SSEC congregations began having Pentecostal experiences, talking in tongues, and entering trances. Motivated by the Holy Ghost, SSEC evangelists harangued pagan gatherings with jeremiads against ancestral spirit "devils," disrupted markets, and invaded other Christian churches to preach their revival. This enthusiasm produced some SSEC converts, but it also created resentment against them.

ANALYSIS OF CHRISTIAN SUCCESSES

To some extent, all Christian-pagan relationships partake of the same character. Pagan communities are motivated by loyalty to Malaitan customs and deities, who are of course their own lineage ancestors. One pagan priest, whose congregation had dwindled to eight, told me he might become an Anglican when he grew old in order to get food and medicine; but, he insisted, he had a duty to care for the ancestors (spirits) while he was young and strong. All Baegu revere their forefathers and fear the 'powerful ghosts of famous men.' Marching Rule and the Custom movement offer renewed pride in Malaitan traditions. Baegu traditionalism and geographic isolation tend to inhibit change. Some older Baegu feel that Christianity brings a devolution of values, since capital punishment of adulterers and deviants is no longer possible and abolition of the brideprice undermines social exchange and solidarity. Pagans believe they have made the right ethical decisions; in fact, they feel a sense of moral superiority to the Christians.

Converted Christian communities, regardless of sect, have a common feeling of superiority over the pagans, whom they refer to as heathen or wicked people because of their ignorance or rejection of the Christian faith. Christianity has, after all, always been an exclusivist religion.

There is some momentum toward conversion. Reasons of faith are paramount. Jehovah and Jesus claim to be powerful divinities. Evangelists and the Bible offer protection from the 'powerful ghosts of famous men.' Despite historical exceptions, Christian ethics are essentially good and their God benevolent; as they say, God is Love. Christian ethics can stop death feuds with their unending rounds of compensation and revenge killings, women are freed from the worst sex-associated taboos (isolation at childbirth and total exclusion from some activities), and fears deriving from the taboos system, 'wild ghosts' and sorcery are ameliorated. Missionaries are of course salesmen—they sell by example as well as by exhortation—and most of them live exemplary lives that give the best possible impression.

Christianity shares the power and prestige of its white carriers. As the religion of the conquerors, it offers Malaitans a chance to identify with white power: government, commerce, and the missions. There is also a magical hope that practicing Christianity will enable Malaitans to get the material goods that whites have in such quantity. With some exceptions, white officials and businessmen do not like to work with pagans, whom they consider naive and unreliable; they prefer to deal with native Christians. Hence ambitious Malaitans may find paganism a handicap to success in white-dominated affairs. Melanesian converts tend to be more zealous than white Christians, and as national independence approaches, with mission-educated Solomon Islanders taking over the reins of power, there may be even more prejudice against pagans.

There are also compelling economic issues. Paganism is expensive. Christians need no longer sacrifice valuable pigs to placate the ancestors or atone for sins. Missions stabilize and lower brideprice payments (or eliminate them altogether); compensation payments for taboo violations and traditional curses are reduced. Pagan concepts of ritual purity require costly fines by apostates to counteract the ritual pollution encountered among Christians, and this restricts ease of movement from Christianity back to paganism. Thus the barrier between Christianity and paganism is differentially permeable. Missions provide medicines, food during emergencies, boat transport, and access to commercial outlets for produce. Finally, missions have a virtual monopoly on education in Malaita, and education is the obvious key to the high-paying government clerkships and commercial jobs that young Malaitans want. In Baegu usage the loanword *sukulu* glosses as both school and church. As France's Henri IV is reputed to have said, "Paris is well worth a Mass"; and Baegu pagans send their children to mission schools, even at the risk of having them baptized.

ANALYSIS OF SECTARIAN COMPETITION

The success of each mission depends upon its intrinsic characteristics, its relationship with the Baegu, and its history in Malaita. Anglican success stems from an early head start, an image as an establishment (albeit not established) church, and a productive attitude toward Melanesian participation. Melanesian Mission work in the Solomons from 1847 gave the Anglicans a half-century without competition from other Christian sects. As a white church led by a white missionary clergy, it attracted converts from a Melanesian culture suffering from introduced diseases, labor recruiting excesses, warfare stimulated by white weapons, traditional disorganization, and perhaps a loss of confidence in themselves. British power and wealth seemed to prove the validity of British religion; association with success is not a handicap in Malaita. Anglican Christianity offered hope for reform and revitalization without total loss of old traditions. Anglican doctrine, ritual, and church art were acceptable alternatives to traditional ones. Their permissiveness and understanding left Malaitan societies intact, and their tolerance of Malaitan customs facilitated conversion. Anglican missionaries had considerable anthropological sophistication: they wrote important ethnological surveys of Melanesia (Codrington 1885, 1891) and respectable ethnographies of San Cristobal (Fox 1925), Ulawa and Sa'a (Ivens 1927), and the Lau Lagoon (Ivens 1930). Early in the twentieth century, Fox, Ivens, and others translated parts of the New Testament and the Book of Common Prayer into Lau (a dialect mutually comprehensible with Baegu) as well as other Southeastern Solomons languages. Church services and schooling were in vernaculars; English was offered as students advanced.

Anglicans used the local system. Big men became leaders of Anglican communities, the clergy working through them. Most Anglican settlements do not have resident priests, and traditional-type leaders manage hamlet affairs under the spiritual guidance of priests or archdeacons responsible for neighborhoods or districts. Missionaries transferred to themselves traditional feelings of dependence upon pagan priests and other big men, whose roles always called for them to care for their followers (Hogbin 1939:73-74; Ogan 1975, personal communication; Ross 1973:55, 188-193). Anglican communities respect Baegu community values by forming church unions for cooperative labor and public welfare projects.

Finally, Anglicans stimulated new local and national pride and traditions. Melanesian Mission martyrs and saints for whom local churches are named are officially honored. The Melanesian Brotherhood and church unions give common people a sense of involvement with the Anglican church, and they feel pride in their Melanesian priests and bishops and in the growing independence of the Diocese of Melanesia from white control. An unusually large proportion of the emerging generation of Solomon Islands leaders comes from a Melanesian Mission background.

The Anglican Melanesian Mission has been an effective combination of white leadership and native Malaitan participation. While protecting traditional social organization, customs, and communities, the Anglicans have realized latent Malaitan ideals for effective leadership and social cooperation on a large scale.

Roman Catholics have been almost as successful in Malaita (although they have fewer Baegu converts) for reasons much the same as the Anglicans, with some pertinent exceptions. Catholic missions are less identified with the colonial establishment. Thus Catholics have less immediate access to secular power, but their independence from the administration lets them play an antigovernment role. Catholicism's international connections, particularly through Dutch and American Marists, give them alternatives to British models and permit them to appeal to anti-British sentiment, which is strong in rural Malaita. Judicious application of Saint Augustine's concepts about the City of God and City of Man and the biblical precept of rendering unto Caesar the things that are Caesar's have enabled Catholic missions to enjoy government tolerance (or even support) while tapping the resources of Malaitan tradition, Malaitan antigovernment feeling, and international Catholicism.

Catholic tolerance and understanding are at least as great as the Anglican's, and they have made effective use of traditional customs and symbolism. The Catholic Welfare Society of the 1950s was a manifestation of Malaitan ideals of cooperation and brotherhood, which the priests harnessed in the church's name and cause. Priests preach and hear confession in the vernacular, but until recently the Mass was perforce in Latin. Mission schools teach vernacular literacy and offer English for advanced pupils. Protestant zeal for translating scripture into local languages is missing.

Catholic missionaries are more authoritarian than the Anglicans, and Catholics are more sure (thanks to constant pastoral reassurance) of the rightness of their faith. Catholic missionaries are also more paternalistic, and the church is more involved with the material well-being of its parishioners. Large villages form around the church, school, medical aid center, farms, and workshops that comprise Catholic mission stations. More so than the Anglicans, Catholic priests directly replaced traditional leaders upon whom the people depend (Ogan 1975, personal communication). The resident priest is the community leader and its big man. Like the Anglicans, they represent an effective blend of continuity and change, but the two denominations base their appeals on different strengths.

The success of the South Sea Evangelical Church lies in an implicit appeal to nativism that has the potential for nationalism. Church services and such education as there is are in the vernacular. Its propagation by Malaitan missionaries, its organization into autonomous congregations, and its reliance upon biblical authority as interpreted by Malaitan elders have created from the old SSEM a Malaitan church run by Malaitans for Malaitans.

The preponderance of SSEC elders among Marching Rule leadership shows how easily nationalism grows out of traditions of community self-determination.

Conversion to SSEM Christianity involved little disruption in the general form of social organization. Small autonomous SSEC Baegu congregations led by local elders without superordinate political authority differ little in size and form from pagan hamlets or neighborhoods led by big men.

Someone who, like Ruth Benedict (1934), was interested in subjectively describing the quality of culture could describe the Baegu as simple and austere. With its fundamentalist purity, SSEC Christianity is, in a functional sense, appropriate: a simple and austere faith for a simple and austere people. Absolute biblical authority and evangelists' promises guarantee them a place among the elect in a state of grace. SSEC emphases upon being saved and Pentecostal enthusiasm give them faith and, therefore, communal strength.

Evangelical missionaries expected converts to lead a good Christian (that is, Western-style) life based on the Bible, but there were no programs or on-the-scene leaders to direct such a cultural transformation. Autonomous congregations led by elected Malaitan elders develop pride and, of necessity, self-reliance. Converts were supposed to find guidance for themselves by consulting the Bible. This meant no direct pressure from white leaders for change—but there was no help either. SSEC hospitals, schools, and economic development projects are few and far between.

SSEC weaknesses come from the other side of the coin of independence. Their relative weakness in education, health, and economics leaves them behind other Malaitan Christians in a materialistic sense. Their lack of a clergy and a wider-than-local leadership put them at a disadvantage in comparison with other, more organized Christian groups. The evangelical mandate to become Christian (westernized) workers and farmers forces people to assume roles they do not really understand and for which they do not have adequate models.

SSEC Baegu have lost their old leadership and culture without proper replacements. They are obliged to compete in a new world bearing some severe handicaps. They are more individualistic than traditional Baegu or Christian Baegu of other denominations, but they also seem less sure of themselves. Disorganization, lack of education, and absence of capital facilities prevent real progress in economic development, although they are willing (nay, eager) to prosper. Their tendency toward the simple life and independence (without power) make them easy prey for government, commerce, and more competitive neighbors. In essence, SSEC congregations are left on their own to evolve. Both their strengths and their vulnerabilities come from their independence and self-reliance.

Seventh-Day Adventists have been the most successful missionaries since World War II. They continue to proselytize effectively among the pagans, and, despite some bad feelings, to attract other Malaitan Christians to their sect. Their success comes from the obvious fact that they have been most attentive to the material needs of the people. Their mission stations are dynamic centers with hospitals, schools, workshops, and commercial activities that are widely admired examples of cleanliness, industry, and business acumen. Among the Baegu, the Adventists provide more medical care, better schools, and better business advice than any other Christian denomination.

Seventh-Day Adventists gain confidence from fundamentalist and unquestionable biblical authority, prophetic revelation, and effective leadership under Malaitan teachers and white missionaries on the scene. They are convinced that theirs is the only true faith, and their faith is strengthened by their messianic expectations. This gives them motivation and courage to spread the gospel as they understand it.

Adventist practices may enhance prospects for economic development. The pork taboo means no more pig feasts and thus no more incentives to divert resources to raising swine for sacrifice to the ancestors. Religious tithing stimulates cash cropping and wage labor, since missionaries generally do not relish offerings in kind (Ogan 1975, personal communication). The messianic puritanism of Adventist doctrine favors deferred gratification and entrepreneurial investment rather than consumption (Weber 1930; Ogan 1972). Finally, the general tenor of Adventist faith is an optimistic note that gives believers confidence in the future.

Adventist converts were always talking about new ways to

earn money, strategies to get or protect land, investment schemes, cooperative projects, and so forth. Most of these plans were as sophisticated as similar daydreams one might overhear in Europe or America, but some do grade into mystical cargoism. Indeed, I suspect that the millenarian and messianic aspect of the Seventh-Day Adventist faith, its expectation of the Second Coming and Last Judgment, is one of its virtues for Malaitan missionary work. It is in effect a European-sponsored cargo cult.

But the material progress comes at a cost. Adventist missionaries insist that the old ways must go, and conversion to Adventism entails extreme disruption in cultural practices. Traditional customs and leaders lose their power, the Bible becomes law, and white missionaries are absolute authorities on its interpretation. Adventist missionaries forbid brideprice payments, thereby undermining the legitimacy of Baegu marriage and the entire concept of social exchange and obligations. They forbid traditional singing and dancing, and Adventist converts lose pride in Malaitan art and knowledge. Observance of the Saturday Sabbath and tithing become obligatory. Tobacco, alcohol (which is not available anyway), and the ubiquitous betel quid are forbidden. (Anyone who knows the Malaitan craving for tobacco and betel will appreciate how this taboo is a test of faith for the Adventist convert!) Food taboos against pork, shellfish, and wild foods (such as grubs and spiders) aggravate an already marginal nutritional regimen. These prohibited foods are the only protein sources routinely available to the Baegu (Ross 1976). Other Christian Baegu continue to live in kinship-based patterns, either in detached hamlets of kinsmen or as kin-wards in larger mission centers. Adventists give up traditional kinship obligations and settle in heterogeneous villages with their loyalties going to other Adventists. Adventist schools stress English (although they may teach initial literacy in the vernacular). The converts use Christian names (as other Christians do, albeit with less consistency), but go even further and give English names to their villages (which other Christians do not). In a way, even this disruption of life is an Adventist asset. As Mead (1956:445-449) pointed out for Manus, sudden conversion and revolutionary change may be easier in the long run than piecemeal gradualism.

Is there any rational pattern to the results of mission competition for Baegu souls? Probably the critical factor has been the fortuitous circumstance of who worked where and when. One finds converts in the vicinity of mission stations; and the longer the mission has been there, the more converts there will be. People are converted by contact with a missionary. They join the sect of the person who converts them. How could it be otherwise?

Other random events—missionary character, local leaders, natural phenomena, social happenings, local history—affect mission success also. An energetic, intelligent, and tactful missionary will gain more converts than a lazy, stupid and insensitive one. No sect enjoys a monopoly on talent. Local leaders can bring people to a mission or keep them away. Hurricanes, crop failures, plagues, wars, local power struggles, unapproved marriages—all send people to missions for help or refuge.

Although I cannot prove it, I feel that the several mission sects appeal to different types of persons. That is, given exposure to different denominations, a person will be more apt to join one than another, depending upon character, values, and personality traits. Catholics and Anglicans attract conservative, tradition-oriented types, those who are ready to try the new but are unwilling to abandon their old ways altogether. They relish dependency, being comfortable in a client-patron relationship with their priests as they were with earlier big men (Ogan 1975, personal communication). They want leaders they can respect and depend on. If pro-British, they like the Melanesian Mission; if anti-British, they become Catholics. The SSEC appeals to those who are more comfortable with independence, who are self-reliant, and who can cope with being left alone to direct their own affairs without much help. Conservative in the sense that they are nativistic (they reject foreign leadership) and not progressive in a material sense (no one gives them aid and they lack all but the traditional economic and technical skills), they nevertheless are willing to cast off the old Baegu life, accepting the Bible as sole authority and making their way bootstrap fashion in a changing world. Seventh-Day Adventists attract the most progressive and ambitious types, those who are ready to give up the old without regret. Adventist converts have contempt for Malaitan tradition and revolutionary zeal for the new life they have chosen. They are enthusiastic about progress, eager to get rich, and confident that they will. If I were foolhardy enough to predict the results of psychological testing, I would guess that Baegu Catholics and Anglicans would score high on a dependency scale, moderate on willingness to accept authoritarianism, low on desire for innovation, and moderate on self-confidence; that Evangelicals would score rather lower on dependency, high on authoritarianism, moderate on innovation, and low on self-confidence; and that Adventists would score low on dependency, high on authoritarianism, and highest of all on innovation and self-confidence. (Pagan Baegu would probably score moderately on dependence, low on authoritarianism, low on innovation, and high on self-confidence.) Pagans who match one of the sectarian personality profiles would be more likely to convert to that sect and converts likely to switch to a more compatible one. This is of course more a problem for psychology than for anthropology. It could be verified by psychological testing, but given the moribund state of culture and personality studies, such testing is not likely.

CONCLUSION

Perhaps a forecast is the best way to sum up and evaluate the missionary position among the Baegu. Paganism will eventually disappear, but not soon. Baegu pagans are content, proud of their traditions, and respectful of ancestral ghosts. Lack of contact with the outside world, traditionalism, and inertia keep the conversion rate slow, and apostasy of Christian converts does occur. The presumed ethical value of Christianity, however, the association of the Christian religion with governmental and commercial power, economic factors (including the material advantages of mission life and the cost of paganism), and the urge for education as a pathway to success create a slow net drift toward conversion. On the other hand, political independence may generate more secular opportunities and weaken the present association of mission affiliation with social mobility (Ogan 1975, personal communication). The balance between Baegu paganism and Christianity is almost in equilibrium, but not quite. The tendency in favor of the missions will ultimately win out, no doubt, but not without difficulties and setbacks.

The several mission denominations will, despite ecumenical feelings, remain. And to put things in proper perspective, there is more Christian feeling and unity in the Solomons than in Europe or America. Most Baegu Christians feel that sectarian competition is unchristian, and this sentiment may prevail. Yet almost irreconcilable sectarian differences persist, and, furthermore, ecumenical decisions involve contexts far beyond the Baegu scale. Anglican association with the establishment is too strong to ignore; Roman Catholic internationalism and unity of viewpoint make church union impossible at present under any but Catholic terms. (As Pope Paul VI said at the 1974 synod of bishops, "Either the church is Catholic, or it is not.") SSEC fundamentalism and independence preclude union with liberal sects or ones with foreign hierarchies, and their rigorous evangelism breeds resentment. Adventist puritanism, theological extremism, and universal evangelism make it hard for them to work harmoniously with others. Christendom and the Western world themselves are not, after all, united. Finally, the Baegu find a degree of sectarian competition useful. A group of siblings or cousins, for example, may split up with one joining each sect and perhaps one remaining pagan. Kindred ties and sectarian loyalties thus crosscut. This strategy maintains areal and social integration, gives the lineage access to multiple sources of power or support, keeps individual options open, spreads the risk as a form of insurance, and hedges the supernatural bets. If one group of divinities does not help, maybe another will!

In sum, barring an unanticipated pagan revival or Armageddon itself, one can expect gradual conversion to continue until Baegu paganism is gone. Yet Christian sectarian differences will persist, as they have in the West, indefinitely.

NOTES

This chapter is based upon research sponsored and financed by the University of Illinois at Urbana-Champaign through its Center for International Comparative Studies (Professor Joseph B. Casagrande, director) in 1972 and by U.S. Public Health Services research fellowship MH-30017 and National Institute of Mental Health research grant MH-12647 during 1966-1968. Secretarial services were provided by the Department of Anthropology, University of Illinois (Urbana-Champaign), and the Population Institute of the East-West Center, Honolulu.

1. This account of the Marists' activity is based largely on the work of Verguet (1854) and Raucaz (1925).
2. This account of the Anglicans in the area is based largely on the work of Armstrong (1900) and Fox (1967).
3. This account of the SSEM is based largely on Hilliard (1969).
4. This account of the Seventh-Day Adventists in the area is based largely on Cormack (1944) and Kent (1973).

PART 3: LOCAL-LEVEL MISSIONARY ADAPTATION

INTRODUCTION
Daniel T. Hughes

From the following chapters certain generalizations can be made concerning Christian missionary activity in the Pacific. First, mission activity has been part of the expansion of Western culture and Western colonial power throughout the Pacific. Second, this activity has been a dialectical process between widely divergent cultural groups in which continuing interaction has been facilitated by "partial equivalence structures." Third, mission activity is a dynamic process that changes dramatically in response to the goals of the islanders and those of the missionaries.

The Christian missionaries who first went to the various Pacific islands were part of a wave of Western culture that was sweeping across these islands at an ever-increasing tempo. Western ships were more impressive, Western tools more durable, and Western arms more destructive than those of the islanders. There was no way that the people of these islands could hold back the tide of Western influence in their lands. The missionaries themselves saw the westernization of the island societies not only as inevitable but also as a necessary step toward the Christianization of the people. Traditional island cultures were considered poor soil in which to nurture the seed of Christian faith they were planting. The growth of such a delicate plant required an environment as close as possible to that of their own societies. Thus the missionaries not only attacked what they considered to be pagan practices and beliefs but also opposed many neutral elements in the traditional cultures. The industrial mission program described by Frances Harwood in chapter 9 was a typical attempt by missionaries to remake a native culture in the image of their own. The missionaries did not think it was possible to add Christianity to the traditional cultures. Rather they felt that it was necessary to replace them with Christianity and a Christian environment.

The very concept of mission, as Jeremy Beckett explains in chapter 8, assumes a discontinuity between the main body of believers and those to be missionized. This discontinuity was a consequence of a perceived inequality between the two groups. In the Pacific, the islanders were considered unequal or inferior not only because of their ignorance of Christianity but also because of their ignorance of Western civilization and their lack of the economic and technological means of sustaining it. Since the missionaries felt that the whole society had to be remade to form a solid foundation for Christianity, they were often involved in all aspects of the society. Their interests and their influence were all-pervasive. Especially in the earlier years, it was not uncommon for missionaries to establish petty theocracies with totalitarian tendencies.

Throughout the Pacific, missionaries have been agents of Western colonialism as well as agents of Western civilization. To be sure, they often opposed the government and the trader, but they rarely opposed the establishment of the Western market system or Western political control. Rather, the missionaries helped to legitimize these colonial institutions in the islands.

In portraying missionaries as agents of Western civilization and colonialism, both Beckett in chapter 8 and Hezel in chapter 10 caution against unfair generalizations. Beckett notes that missionary totalitarianism, even when it did exist, was often preferable to the social and physical breakdown that threatened some of these societies as a result of their rapid exposure to foreign elements. Hezel comments that one finds a wide range of attitudes reflected in the correspondence of individual missionaries and that some came to know and respect the traditional cultures. Also, cultural ethnocentrism and paternalism did not necessarily render a missionary ineffective with the islanders. Goldie's work in the Solomons, described by Harwood in chapter 9, is a good example of a successful missionary. Finally, the islanders themselves were awed by the power of the Westerners and often cast the missionary in the role of a paternalistic leader or substitute chief or big man figure.

The missionary process in the Pacific has been a dialectical process of interaction between cultural groups with widely divergent goals and with frequently differing interpretations of their interaction. For both Protestant and Catholic missionaries the major goal of the mission process has generally been to save souls from paganism and from each other. From the beginning, Protestant missionaries attempted to do this by establishing native churches which would be "self-financing, self-governing, and self-propagating." Initially, Catholic missionaries aimed only at the salvation of souls through the work of individual missionaries and mission groups. With various theological advances in the 1900s, the establishment of the church became an accepted goal of the Catholic missionaries too. However, for both Protestant and Catholic missionaries, the establishing of a native church did not mean that the church would in any way be an outgrowth of native culture and traditions. Their aim was to establish a church that, although staffed and financed by islanders, would in all essentials be a replica of the metropolitan church in their home country. As De la Costa has noted, this was "not a native church, but a church staffed by natives" (1972:119).

One of the primary goals of the islanders in their dealings with the missionaries, as in their dealings with other Westerners, was to achieve equality. From the beginning it was obvious to the islanders that the foreigners possessed a greater technology and more powerful arms. They wanted to acquire this new technology from the foreigners. However, the more contact they had with foreigners, the more they seemed to become second-class citizens. Thus the islanders found themselves striving for a social and personal equality as well.

To the islanders, knowledge and power were intimately linked. Thus they sought equality in power and technology and in personal identity by striving to acquire the foreigners' knowledge. They felt that a major part of that knowledge must be incorporated into the religion of the foreigners just as it was into their own. The conversion of the islanders to Christianity was certainly influenced by their desire to gain foreign power by sharing in foreign knowledge. In adopting a foreign religion the islanders were not necessarily rejecting their traditional system, as the missionaries thought they were or at least should be doing. They were simply acknowledging that their traditional systems alone could no longer cope with the reality of their expanded experience.

In view of the diverse goals and the differing interpretations of the meaning of their interactions, how was an accommodation reached between the missionaries and the islanders? Are not shared cognitions and goals a prerequisite for continued interaction? Harwood points out, in chapter 9, that shared cultural understanding can actually inhibit accommodation if the motives and goals of groups are widely divergent. The prerequisite for accommodation between interacting groups is predictability, and this can be achieved by what Wallace has termed "partial equivalence structures" (1970:36).

During the initial period of contact between two different cultural groups each group is constantly improvising its responses to the actions of the other. Improvisation, however, is highly unpredictable and therefore most unsatisfactory to both sides. If the interaction is to continue in the absence of shared motives and goals, mutual misconceptions and unpredictable responses must be minimized by limiting interaction. A set of partial equivalence structures evolves which allows both sides to share a minimum interpretation of events while adding their own interpretation to the shared meaning.

Harwood shows how Goldie and his fellow missionaries interpreted their interactions with the Solomon Islanders as the successful conversion of the people to a religion or church. The people themselves interpreted the same events to mean that they were actively selecting and elevating Goldie to the position of their leader and protector. Despite these differences in interpretation, a set of partial equivalence structures was developed that satisfied both groups. It was only the massive exposure to other Western contacts during World War II and the subsequent retirement of Goldie himself that finally shattered the established set of partial equivalences. Harwood suggests that the later rise of the Pentecostal Christian Fellowship church is best understood not as a rejection of Western presence but as the latest in a series of accommodations of partial equivalences, the main goal of which is still to achieve equality of power and of identity.

The missionary movement in the Pacific has been a dynamic process. In chapter 8 Beckett shows how the transition of the Torres Strait Islanders from mission to church to sect is best understood in terms of changing conditions and changing goals. Beckett's distinction of mission, church, and sect is essential to his analysis. For Beckett a church is a religious institution that reflects and transmits the values current in its own society. A sect, on the other hand, is a religious institution that stands apart from its own society and either rejects or attempts to change the current values of that society. Finally, a mission is the sending forth of spiritual agencies from a church or a sect to spread the divine truth. It assumes a discontinuity and an inequality between the main body of believers and those to be missionized.

In tracing the history of Christianity in the Torres Strait Islands, Beckett sees the islanders' acceptance, in turn, of the London Missionary Society, the Church of England, and the Assemblies of God sect as strongly influenced by concomitant socioeconomic changes in the islands. The mission approach of the London Missionary Society fitted the colonial situation of the islands in the 1870s when the islanders wanted protection against foreign boat crews and foreign diseases and when no formal colonial administration had yet been established. The Church of England fitted the later situation after 1900 when the colonial government became firmly established and the people were trying to integrate with the foreign system. Finally, a Pentecostalist sect, the Assemblies of God, suited the condition of the islanders on the mainland, where there proved to be no possibility of integrating into the larger society.

The mission process in the Pacific has responded to changing conditions and goals among the missionaries as well. In chapter 10 Francis Hezel traces the effects of the rise of nationalism and of independence movements in many colonial areas on theological thought and the codification of these theological developments in the pronouncements of the Second Vatican Council. He then describes the influence of Vatican II theology on the goals and policies of the Catholic missionaries in the Carolines and the

Marshall Islands. In chapter 11, Gerald Arbuckle examines the impact of these changes on the Marist missionaries in Polynesia and Melanesia.

A tide of nationalism swept across the colonial world and brought independence to many nations in the period after World War II. In the wake of these nationalistic and independence movements there followed an intense search for national and ethnic identity. Christian theologians were strongly influenced by such concerns and began to reflect on the importance of respect for people's cultural identity in the mission process. In the Catholic church these new theological trends were legitimized and sanctioned by the pronouncements of the Second Vatican Council between 1962 and 1965. Vatican II saw the church as being in dialogue with the local cultures. Missionaries were instructed to consider themselves as collaborators in the establishment of indigenous churches and not as their sole architects. Vatican II stressed the objective in the mission process of having ritual, worship, and theology grow out of the living culture of the people. Vatican II also placed increasing emphasis on the relative autonomy of local churches in contrast to the previous emphasis given to the unity and universality of the Catholic church. Post-Vatican II theology has gone beyond the notion of dialogue and has stressed the interrelation of the church and the world, developing further the humanistic trend set by Vatican II.

In chapter 11, Arbuckle reports the findings from his survey of Marist missionaries stationed in various islands of Polynesia and Melanesia. The survey reveals that the majority of these missionaries reflect strong Vatican II or post-Vatican II attitudes regarding the church and the goal of missionary activity. Their practice, however, lags behind their ideal in following such Vatican II directives as the adaptation of Christianity to local cultures and the participation of the laity in the administration of the churches. One reason for this gap appears to be the lack of effective leadership from bishops and regional religious supervisors, who have had no models for the dynamic leadership called for by Vatican II. Moreover, the rugged individualism of the missionaries themselves makes them reluctant to consult among themselves and with their bishops and religious supervisors. Nevertheless, Arbuckle sees signs in some regions of new structures that are fostering greater collaboration and planning among the missionaries and their leaders.

Vatican II directives have significantly altered the goals and approaches of Jesuit missionaries in Micronesia. Hezel describes the changes that have occurred in this order between 1970 and 1975. The Jesuits have come increasingly to see their goal as the establishment of a church that is not only staffed by Micronesians but is also an outgrowth of Micronesian culture. They are attempting to commit the church to the service of Micronesian society as a whole. Because they consider a sense of powerlessness and a loss of identity, resulting from rapid social change, as the most serious problems facing Micronesians today, they are shifting their focus from material works such as schools and housing programs to more social-psychological interests. They see their major task now as one of helping the Micronesian people to achieve a sense of self-confidence and mastery over their own destiny.

Missionaries are often stereotyped as being quite inflexible. The validity of this stereotype obviously varies from one missionary to another. The chapters in this part show clearly, however, that the missionary movement as a whole cannot accurately be described as inflexible. It has altered, and continues to change, in response to changes in the islanders' needs and the missionaries' goals.

8

MISSION, CHURCH, AND SECT: THREE TYPES OF RELIGIOUS COMMITMENT IN THE TORRES STRAIT ISLANDS

Jeremy Beckett

Christianity in the South Seas must, in the final analysis, be understood in terms of colonization. Its fortunes have been inextricably bound up with those of the market and the metropolitan power, and it has been important in the structuring of the people's relations with these institutions. Dependence on the introduced religion has complemented dependence in the economic and political sectors. But Christianity must also be seen as mediatory, though in ways that change as relations between people and colonialism change, standing with white civilization against heathen savagery, but with Christian natives against godless traders and government men. If it has been part of the colonial order, its representatives have always tried to determine what that part should be. For the people, then, conversion has always entailed a particular kind of commitment to the new order.

Christianity came to the South Seas in the form of a mission—that is, an agency of a church or sect. Church and sect, as I shall define them, occupy quite different places in the metropolitan society, and the strategy of their missions will vary accordingly. The mission, however, operating outside the metropolitan society, must be seen as distinct from either. In this chapter I shall analyze Torres Strait religion in terms of these three kinds of religious organization.

In its most general sense, mission means a sending forth of

spiritual agencies to spread divine truth. In common parlance it is the heathen who are to be the recipients of this message, but in ecclesiastical usage it may be Christians who have become separated from the main body—for example, the urban poor. The essential point is that there is a discontinuity between that main body of believers and those who are to be missionized. Here I define mission as a specialized agency of church or sect having the task of attracting, instructing, and directing people who are ineligible for immediate membership of the parent body. In most cases membership is at least the long-term objective. But in the meantime the people, however equal within the love of God, are deemed not equal within the *sight* of God.[1] This kind of charter allows the mission to organize itself along lines quite different from those of the parent body, creating roles and offices that have no currency in the outside world.

The inequality is due not simply to the people's ignorance of Christianity but also to their ignorance of civilized living and their lack of the economic and technical means for sustaining it. In the frontier conditions which are their typical milieu, missionaries find themselves undertaking uplift as well as religious work. They may themselves distinguish sacred from secular duties, but the people are not likely to do so. Thus the mission's influence becomes all-pervasive and, in the power vacuum which develops at the village level as a result of pacification, considerable. Petty theocracies are frequent in the history of the South Seas, and one may argue a tendency toward "totalitarianism" in missions which is lacking or much less pronounced in the parent bodies. (I shall suggest in a moment that they share this tendency with sects.) Having used the emotive term "totalitarian," let me add that mission regimes may be a welcome alternative to social and physical breakdown.

Much of the writing on sects is concerned with their internal structure and dynamics (as in Wilson 1967). Here I am concerned with the way in which they structure their members' relations with the wider society. On this point there is general agreement that a sect in some sense stands apart from the society which it either rejects or wishes to change. By contrast, a church or denomination "accepts the standards and values of the prevailing culture and conventional morality" (Wilson 1967:25). Viewed from the outside, a sect is deviant if not downright eccentric, whereas a church—even if it is not one's own—is normal and mainstream. As such, the sect is most likely to appeal to those who are deviant in terms of personality or social placement, since it explains and validates their alienation from the society in which they live. Thus, sects tend to recruit their members from one social stratum, ethnic minority, or subculture (see chapter 7).

Although missionaries are often narrower in outlook than the clergy at home, a church mission transmits at least some of the values current in the society it represents. A sect mission stresses those which mark it off from the majority. A church mission might be considered a better preparation for entry into the wider society, but a thorough grounding in religion alone is not sufficient to secure acceptance. This is because churches have only an incomplete hold over their followers: in other words, religion is not everything. Sects, by contrast, have a totalitarian hold over their followers: religion *is* everything—or almost. Thus, while a sectarian mission will not prepare its members for entry into the wider society it will prepare them for entry into the parent sect, where, whatever their other inadequacies, their religious accomplishments have overriding importance. For this reason the gulf between a sect and its mission is relatively small.

The Torres Strait Islands, the focus of this chapter, were evangelized by the interdenominational Protestant London Missionary Society (LMS) beginning in 1871. Having worked in the Pacific since the beginning of the century, the LMS was, by this time, a thoroughgoing mission. Its members were all products of British nonconformity, but coming from the Congregational and cognate churches they fell short of sectarianism.

The LMS withdrew in 1914, giving its flocks into the keeping of the Anglican Diocese of Carpentaria. The diocese was not organized for mission work and, unlike its predecessor, limited its activities to the religious sphere. In organization and policy it was a church. But because of the physical and cultural isolation, Torres Strait Anglicanism perpetuated certain elements of the mission at the community level. When, after World War II in the Pacific, islanders moved into white communities, they found standard Anglicanism unfamiliar and also unrelated to the problems of adaptation then troubling them. Instead they turned to a Pentecostalist sect, the Assemblies of God. Like a mission, the assembly sought them out and provided practical help in coping with their new surroundings. Difficulty arose when converts carried the new religion back to their home communities. Here the sect came into conflict with the missionlike features of Torres Strait Anglicanism. It also became the religion of political dissent, whereas Anglicanism remained politically neutral.

THE REGION AND ITS INHABITANTS

Torres Strait separates northern Queensland from the Trans-Fly district of Papua. In its waters are many islands, small and not so small, some twenty of which were inhabited when Europeans made their first surveys in the 1840s. The islanders were Melanesian in appearance and culture, though with a variable admixture of Australian traits. At the beginning of intensive contact, around 1860, they numbered some four thousand, falling to about half that figure by the turn of the century but thereafter increasing to a present figure in excess of eight thousand.

European vessels strayed through the strait from early in the seventeenth century, but the traffic did not become regular until the foundation of the Australian colony and remained transient until the middle of the nineteenth century. By the 1840s, Europeans had begun to exploit the rich sources of trepang and pearl shell, and within twenty years there was a thriving industry with fleets of schooners and luggers, shore stations, and a labor force of around a thousand. Most of this labor came from the Pacific islands, but islanders and aborigines soon played a part.[2] Thursday Island, which lies just off the tip of Cape York, became the center of operations and, presently, of government. The state of Queensland quickly established its jurisdiction over the offshore islands, but it did not annex the more distant ones until 1879 and had only nominal control until about 1885. Meanwhile the islands were dominated by the pearlers and trepangers and, after 1871, by the representatives of the London Missionary Society.

THE COMING OF THE LIGHT

In 1871, the Reverend Samuel McFarlane and the Reverend A. W. Murray arrived with eight Loyalty Island teachers. The teachers were to do the pioneering work of evangelization in the islands and along the Papuan coast, while their white directors set up the headquarters, which were to be the springboard for the Papuan campaign.

The teachers were themselves recent converts, but McFarlane argued that on this account they were better able to "get at the heathen of their class" (McFarlane 1888:138). Certainly there was a ready response. Just one year later, Murray declared that the Murray Islanders must be a people "prepared of the Lord" (LMS Reports 1872:33):

> The entire population . . . have attached themselves to the teacher. They treat himself and his family with great kindness, supplying their wants without charge so far as they are able and seeming ready to yield themselves implicitly to his guidance. No work is done on the Sabbath and the people come together from the three islands to attend the services, which except for the hymns and reading of the scriptures are conducted in the native tongue.

The work of the teachers was not everywhere so easy, and even the Murray Islanders had their moments of backsliding; but, seen in the long view, evangelization progressed steadily.

Present-day islanders describe the "coming of the Light" as though "heathen darkness" was dispelled in an instant. Closer enquiry indicates that, although the missionaries claimed a religious monopoly, Christianity long coexisted with indigenous beliefs. But the teachers destroyed the old shrines, took away the sacred paraphernalia, and put an end to the cults. By 1898, Haddon found difficulty in eliciting this kind of information and concluded that much had already been lost.

McFarlane believed that the islanders initially welcomed the missionaries as a protection against the foreign boat crews who were plundering their gardens and abducting their women. Attempts at resistance had brought sharp reprisals. An observer reported that "the once confident and fearless" people at Mabuiag had become "cowed and sullen," taking flight as soon as a sail was sighted (Somerset Magistrates Book 1872). Even when their intentions were peaceable, the foreigners disrupted the tiny communities, luring away the young people with the promise of cloth, metal tools, flour, and rice. Meanwhile epidemics were decimating the population. As so often happened in the Pacific, the missionaries won their converts in the midst of catastrophe, bringing into spiritual dependence people who no longer had the means of independent existence.

Whatever the reasons for their conversion, there can be no doubt of the islanders' commitment to the new religion. Not only did they come forward for baptism, but they went on to endure the rigors and abstinences required for church membership. Some even aspired to become deacons and teachers. Those who worked competed with one another over how much of their meager earnings should go to the mission, and by the end of the century each community had built for itself a substantial church.

The significance of this commitment emerges when we look at the social context in which it was taking place. Like most Melanesians, the Torres Strait Islanders had no ranking system. Moreover, ceremonial exchange was not highly developed among them. Traditionally, men acquired prestige through success in headhunting, and gained respect through the control of physical and supernatural powers. The arrival of whites put an end to headhunting and degraded other traditional skills. In the new order, islanders were always at the bottom of the scale, and there were few ways in which they could differentiate themselves from one another. The wages in the marine industry were small and went, at least initially, to the young men rather than to their elders. The mission opened up a hierarchy of religious worth and attainment, one which went some way toward redressing this economic imbalance, although it had no currency in the wider society.

THE MISSION REGIME

The Queensland government exerted little control over the islands until around 1890. Up to that time it did no more than back up the mission, which effectively ran the islands. Reverend Samuel McFarlane described the situation as follows:

> About 1878 Mr. Chester [the government resident] advised the chiefs to appoint magistrates and police. In the presence of the Rev. Mr. Chalmers and myself the laws were formally inaugurated and the officers appointed by Mr. Chester who publically *[sic]* requested Josiah [the pastor] to guide them in their administration (he being accustomed to a similar state of things in his own country) until they themselves were capable.

These laws were, on the whole, equitably administered, Josiah being occasionally required to interfere in the interests of mercy, the native judges being inclined to severity (LMS Correspondence: 17 July 1882).

In the same letter, McFarlane goes on to insist that it was the native judges and not the pastor that had had a colored seaman and an island woman flogged for adultery. But whatever the facts of this case, it is certain that such severities were inflicted—particularly for sexual offences—into the present century and that the pastors were closely involved. They may not have been formally responsible, but the authority of the "native judges" was not in practice distinguishable from that of the pastors. It is significant that when a government resident took over the running of one island, the pastor set up a rival court (Haddon 1908:179). The white missionaries may not have approved these developments, but several served as justices of the peace. One such was said to have shown marked partiality toward his church members (LMS Correspondence: 4 March 1889). It is worth remembering that the LMS had maintained some thirty years of stern theocracy in Rarotonga earlier in the century (Beaglehole 1957:62).

Between them, the white missionaries, the colored teachers, and the native judges assumed wide-ranging control over people's behavior. The bylaws which came into force during those years were by no means limited to the protection of person and property. Very early the mission set about stopping infanticide and the "revolting" mortuary practices; soon it was stamping out the old religion and whatever other traditional practices seemed offensive. The target was not simply paganism but anything, such as dancing, that seemed licentious or immoral. As I have already noted, the traditional sexual freedom was countered by severe sanctions. These, together with a number of religious observances, such as the Sabbath, were enforced by the island courts. But beyond the limits of the law, the pastors denounced sinners by name from the pulpit, threatening divine punishment. The white missionaries themselves believed that God vented his wrath upon the living; the Pacific islands pastors were forever predicting it (see Haddon 1901:78-80).[3] On one occasion the government resident on Thursday Island requested of the society that "threats of excommunication involving damnatory consequences should be sparingly applied" (LMS Reports 1897).

DECLINE AND FALL OF THE MISSION

The Reverend Samuel McFarlane, who directed the mission for its first fifteen years, had hopes that Torres Strait would become the springboard for the evangelization of Papua. Convinced that recent converts were "well adapted to fill the gap between the debased savage and the European missionary," he set about training teachers at a Papuan institute located on Murray Island (McFarlane 1888:138). His plans came to nothing. Of the 100 students who enrolled in 1878, few were still in mission work a decade later and McFarlane's colleagues thought little of them. More to the point, however, was the emergence of Port Moresby as an alternative springboard, and of the Reverend Mr. Lawes as an alternative director. McFarlane withdrew in 1885 and those who followed him spent much of their time wrangling, so that Torres Strait became a backwater. From 1890 until his death in 1900, the Reverend James Chalmers (the famous "Tamate") directed the mission from his headquarters on the Fly River. The pastors who were in effective control of the island congregation came mostly from Samoa and Niue, though a few islanders also served (see chapter 4).

By the time the Queensland government was in a position to assert its authority it had only Pacific islands pastors to contend with. By 1890, it had installed a senior official—in fact a onetime premier—on Thursday Island, providing him with the means of making regular tours. He, in turn, appointed white residents who would serve both as local magistrates and as teachers. The pastors held on tenaciously, but their superiors could not support them and alone they were no match for white officials (LMS Correspondence: 8 April 1914). In 1905, the society again installed a superintendent in Torres Strait, but by this time it was too late. Queensland had brought in legislation giving it extensive control over the local government, property, and movement of islanders, and it bluntly refused the mission's request to take over education (LMS Correspondence: 8 October 1908). As if this were not enough, it went on to curb excessively generous donations to the mission and extravagant displays of hospitality at the annual LMS meetings, which languished thereafter (Bleakley 1961:265-267). Prevented by its rules from starting economic enterprises, the society found little to absorb its energies.[4] Finally, in 1913, a government proposal to tax islanders' earnings brought the LMS superintendent into open opposition (LMS Correspondence: 18 August 1913). He secured a reversal, but also the enduring enmity of government officials. Further cooperation was impossible. The prospect of giving way to the Anglicans had been considered as early as 1907 (LMS Correspondence: 6 December 1907). The Papuan Committee of the LMS recommended it early in 1914 and the transaction had been concluded before the end of the year (Goodall 1954:420).

THE CHURCH AND THE GOVERNMENT

The Torres Strait Islands now came within the jurisdiction of the Anglican Diocese of Carpentaria, which had its headquarters on Thursday Island. The diocese was scarcely organized for mission work. In fact, it would probably not have taken responsibility for the islands had not the LMS completed the basic task of conversion and the Queensland government taken responsibility for all secular affairs. In the event, its resources were strained to provide for the people's spiritual needs.

The church, then, offered no challenge to the government's tightening control over the islanders' lives. By 1920, Queensland had effectively confined the people to their island reserves, taken charge of their pearling enterprises, and assumed control over any money they earned. They were allowed to elect local government councillors, but these were overshadowed by the white resident teachers.

The islanders did not welcome these restrictions on their freedom, and in the wake of the 1929-1933 depression they refused to work on the boats the government managed on their behalf. In 1937, a strike leader approached the bishop with the proposal that he take over the running of the islands. The bishop gently declined, and in the years that followed the church continued to stay out of political affairs. If there were differences they were settled in private. Publicly church and government appeared to be in harmony.[5]

The parishes were the islanders' one haven of autonomy between the wars. Government officials did not encroach for fear of offending the church, but the diocese could not maintain the control to which it was entitled. Anglican organization is not congregational like that of the LMS, but circumstances made it so in this case. The diocese could afford only two white priests to oversee thirteen island parishes, so that it had to rely on the native churchwardens to hold the ordinary services, preach, collect dues, and generally keep things going. This probably eased the transition from LMS to Church of England. By 1940, the bishop had ordained six island priests and a deacon, but these had been trained in a local seminary and were still imbued with the principles of congregationalism.

After 1936, the islanders restored another feature of the LMS regime. As a result of the strike, the government gave the island councils extensive autonomy. This they used to support the church and implement the old bylaws. Uniformed constables patrolled the village by night, armed with long flashlights for spotting courting couples or clandestine drinkers in the bushes. Those they apprehended came before the island court, though now the worst they could suffer would be fining or imprisonment. Once again religion had its secular arm.

TORRES STRAIT CHRISTIANITY

When Bishop White made his first tour of the islands, he concluded that under the LMS "the great mass of the people became not only Christians in name, but also to a large extent in practice" (White 1917:23). The conversion may not have been quite so thoroughgoing as the bishop supposed. In 1913, a cargo cult had flared up briefly on the islands off Papua, though without creating any long-term disaffection from the church. People still believed in sorcery and magic—as many do today. But the public religion was Christianity in a relatively orthodox form. The old teachers had begun working in the vernacular very early, and the gospels were in translation before the century had ended. A number of islanders had undergone religious training in preparation for mission work. Consequently, the people had a vast repertoire of Bible stories and some grounding in doctrine, even though the more exotic or complex ideas would not have passed through the linguistic filter.

Nevertheless, the island parishes were still a far cry from those of white Anglicans on the mainland. The LMS had destroyed a great deal of the traditional culture, but there were too few whites to fill the gap with the culture of Victorian England. Instead, the vacuum had been filled by the Pacific islands pastors and seamen who had lived alongside the people over many years. Thus Polynesian styles prevailed in music, dancing, cuisine, house building, and recreation. The hymns sung in church did not come from England but were Samoan polyphony, introduced by some pastor in LMS times and continued. Under the less puritanical Anglicans, religious holidays were celebrated by Polynesian-style feasts and dancing on the church grounds.

The island parishes probably surpassed those on the mainland for the frequency, regularity, and generality of religious observances. They probably also gave the church a larger proportion of their earnings. Finally, there was a far closer integration of church and local government.

MISSION AND CHURCH

The London Missionary Society in the Torres Strait was a mission not only in name but in the sense that I outlined earlier. Its congregations were not continuous with those in the wider society. It claimed to be nondenominational, though in fact it received most of its support from British Congregationalists, a group scarcely represented in Australia and not at all on Thursday Island. The government officials and master pearlers usually belonged to the Anglican or Roman churches, a fact that McFarlane and his successors felt told against the society. The pastors commanded small respect among the whites and were in no sense deemed the equals of white ministers. McFarlane himself thought of them "bridging the gap between the debased savage and the white missionary."

The society was also a mission in the sense of its totalitarian tendencies. It was ready to take on secular administration, education, and whatever else was needed. When the government pushed it out of these fields it withdrew. As we have seen, the Church of England had no such pretensions and carefully avoided political involvement.

Anglicanism was also a church in the sense of being equally for white and black. There were Anglicans not only on the mainland but among the officials and master pearlers of Thursday Island. It clearly had social importance, and it may have been for this reason that islanders regarded the change as an advance (Done 1960, personal communication).

In formal terms, black Anglicans were the equivalents of white Anglicans. The bishop had ordained the priests, appointed the churchwardens and Sunday school teachers, and confirmed the communicants in the normal manner. The forms of worship did not differ in essentials. Nevertheless, the church was part of a colonial order in which white dominated black. The priests were barely educated and had been trained at a local seminary: one white clergyman described them to me as "good chantry priests." They would not have been accepted in a white parish, still less their laity. They were inescapably placed on the wrong side of the color line. The full force of this segregation was cushioned, however, by the isolation in which the islanders lived.

THE END OF ISOLATION

World War II in the Pacific released the islanders from their isolation and overturned the established order. Although there was no actual fighting in the strait, it came under military administration and almost every able-bodied islander was drawn into a local defense force, which was based on or around Thursday Island. Here they came into contact with white Australian troops who were less imbued with prejudice than the local whites and who, in many cases, were ready to meet islanders on a footing of equality. They also heard talk of a "better deal" that would be due them when the war ended.

This experience had a profoundly disturbing effect on the islanders who went through it. Fifteen years later, they looked back on those days with nostalgia, and their view of their rights in society was markedly different from that of other islanders. With the war at an end, returning government officials discovered that the old order could not be restored in its entirety. There was a clamor for "citizen rights," access to alcohol, control of earnings. The government was slow to grant these rights, and long before it did so the ex-servicemen had come to regard it as their enemy. But, perhaps to provide a safety valve, the government did allow islanders to move onto Thursday Island and to settle on the mainland. For the first time islanders came to live alongside whites and to experience life in towns. Even those who remained on the reserves made frequent visits to Thursday Island for shopping and medical attention.

The situation on Thursday Island was unlike that on the mainland. The community was small, numbering about 2,500, and almost all employed in the marine industry or government service. Moreover, Thursday Island had a strongly hierarchical character. The small, all-white elite consisted of master pearlers, officials in charge of islanders' affairs, clergy, and medical personnel. Ordinary workers and small businessmen were predominantly colored, descendants of Pacific islanders, Malays, Filipinos, and Chinese who had worked in the pearling industry in bygone years. The islanders moved onto the bottom rung of the ladder and into the poorest paid jobs. Formally and informally, the groups stayed separate. Cultural differences were clearly recognized.

The Church of England went to considerable lengths to accommodate the islanders in its services and organization, catering for their distinctive likes and needs rather than expecting them to conform to those of whites. Senior clergy remained white, but island priests took their turn in celebrating communion and island lay readers alternated with whites. Island hymns alternated with English ones, and the organ was presently replaced with a drum accompaniment for both kinds. The church ground was opened for feasting and dancing on religious holidays. Some white Anglicans disliked these developments and withdrew. By 1958, islanders were in the majority at church services.

On the mainland, islanders were a small, little-known minority sometimes confused with the despised aborigines. Widely dispersed, often working in remote places, and coming to town only on weekends, there was no possibility of the church accommodating them as Thursday Island had done. If they attended a service they found the atmosphere alien and the congregations unwelcoming. Feeling out of place they did not come back.

Despite the rebuff, it was unlikely that the islanders could have stayed content with a purely secular existence. Uprooted from familiar surroundings and a highly organized way of life, they found themselves members of a migratory labor force that did not belong anywhere. A bewildering array of new opportunities and experiences surrounded them; they had more money than ever before. But there were no guidelines. With the government out of sight and the church ignoring them, life offered only the grossest kinds of restraints such as might come from the police. Religion, which had structured their world, legitimated their values, and engaged their emotions, was absent.

It is uncertain whether, in the long run, the islanders would themselves have organized to answer this lack. In the event, they were rescued by a Pentecostalist sect, the Assemblies of God, which had first emerged among uprooted and displaced rural folk in North America. Established in 1914 (Clark 1949:106), the sect reached Queensland in 1929, where it became the largest Pentecostalist group, though still numbering only 6,000 (Sommers 1966:167-169). In terms of Wilson's typology (1967: 27) it is a conversionist sect, putting a strong emphasis on the conversion experience and the acceptance of Jesus as a personal savior. It is fundamentalist, but not adventist, and while condemning worldly pleasures it is by no means opposed to the accumulation of property and material comforts. Meetings are enthusiastic and emotional, very much in the revival tradition. There is an absence of ritual and only the simplest of forms. Though a pastor conducts the meeting, he leaves ample room for the assembly to offer spontaneous testimonies, confessions, prayers, and occasional outbursts of glossolalia (speaking in tongues). There is much singing of revival choruses and time out for any sick to come forward for healing.

The assembly made warm approaches to islanders on the mainland and found a widespread response. Converts evidently enjoyed the exuberant services, so different from Anglican decorum. They welcomed, moreover, the prohibitions on drinking, smoking, and dancing and responded eagerly to the offers of healing. They claimed for their newfound religion more "power," greater "holiness," and, through the prohibitions, a sure way to save one's money. They also appreciated the friendliness of the white "brothers and sisters" who welcomed them into their halls and even their homes. This was "proper love."

The rally to Pentecostalism can be understood as a reaction to

Anglican coolness, but also as a compensation for low status in white society.[6] Islanders might be earning more than they did at home, but they were for the most part filling jobs that others did not want, and the world about them was impersonal and unfriendly. Yet, the whites who looked down upon them did not themselves live a Christian life—they broke the Sabbath, forgot their religious observances, and practiced adultery and fornication without check. The islanders might perhaps have rejected all whites; instead they identified themselves with the whites who did not look down upon them but adhered to the values respected in the islands. In this way, islanders modified the general identification with whites that had grown up during the war, becoming instead members of a sect.

PENTECOSTALISM IN THE ISLANDS

Island Pentecostalists returning home struck trouble. They were free to follow the new religion on Thursday Island, but at home they encountered bitter opposition from the councils. Most succumbed to the pressure and reverted to Anglicanism, but on Murray Island the assembly gained a permanent foothold.

This move into religious dissidence may be seen as a development from Murray's long-standing political dissidence. Failing to satisfy their economic and political aspirations through the government, they were looking for alternative allies in the white society. Not surprisingly, they looked first to the church, only to find that it would not become politically involved. Murray Island had been the center of the 1936 strike, and it was Murray's chairman who had unsuccessfully petitioned the bishop to take over the islands. By 1950, this same leader was the main antigovernment spokesman for all Torres Strait, and he had lately clashed with a senior official of the diocese over this matter. He had also quarreled with the family of the parish priest over political and private issues. At this point, a Murray Islander returned from the mainland with the declared intention of establishing an assembly in the community. The chairman did not join the sect, but gave his consent and a piece of land on which to build a meetinghouse. His actions caused a furor on Murray Island and throughout Torres Strait which resulted in his excommunication and removal from office. His main persecutors were progovernment island leaders.[7]

The Anglican synod resolved that religious dissent was unacceptable in the island reserves. The island councillors, many of whom were also members of the synod, echoed this resolve and gave it the force of sanctions, which they controlled through the island courts. No pastors would be allowed onto the reserves. No meetings would be permitted. And no Pentecostalist would be allowed to hold public office. This was enough to stifle dissent on every island except Murray, where it survived and, by 1960, amounted to some 29 percent of the population. Without pastor or meetinghouse, and allowed only to sing together once a week, they nevertheless held together and enjoyed, besides, a wide sympathy among rank-and-file Anglicans.

This development occurred in a context of economic impoverishment and political frustration. Murray's economic enterprises foundered; wages failed to keep pace with living costs; more and more young men were emigrating; and the long-promised "new deal" was still remote. Everyone was affected, but perhaps the veterans felt it most keenly. It is remarkable that 60 percent of the adult male Pentecostalists (fifteen out of twenty-five) were veterans, and that this age group had a much higher representation in the assembly than in the general population. Of the forty-eight adult female Pentecostalists, twenty were the wives or widows of veterans. Pentecostalist veterans described the assembly as being opposed to the Queensland government as well as to the Church of England, prophesying that it would come into its own when they were delivered from the government's control. The majority of Murray Island veterans remained Anglicans, but they sympathized sufficiently with the Pentecostalists to prevent total suppression.

Murray Island religion held up a mirror not only to Torres Strait political conflicts but to cultural conflicts as well. The Anglicans and the Pentecostalists represented different responses to the bicultural society in which they lived. The latter stressed modernity and Europeanism. They went to church wearing pants and shoes, whereas the Anglicans continued to wear waist cloths and go barefoot. They sang English-language choruses instead of vernacular hymns of Samoan origin. They eschewed—though with some difficulty—island dancing. Such things were "not civilized." In these terms, black Anglicans stood doubly condemned: not only did they belong to the wrong church, but they belonged to the uncivilized section of it! By contrast, black Pentecostalists were the same as white Pentecostalists. The Anglicans, for their part, were unimpressed by these pretensions to Europeanism, pointing out that in their tolerance of smoking, drinking, and entertainment they were more like ordinary white people than the puritanical Assembly of God.

The religious cleavage also reflected contradictions specific to the community, though reproduced in most other communities in the strait. As is often the way with groups situated at the bottom of the social scale, islanders evinced a strong egalitarianism in their dealings with one another (Jayawardena 1968). At the same time, there was a strong streak of competitiveness which revealed itself in eagerness for church and local government offices.[8] The people tried to play down this competitiveness at the ideological level by stressing the values of selflessness and service to church and community; at the practical level, they ensured that offices circulated. But with the heightening of aspirations after the war, islanders demanded more of their representatives than all but the ablest could provide. Consequently, circulation of the key offices was no longer possible and the communities came under increasing strain (Beckett 1967, 1971). The Pentecostalists consisted of people who had little hope of holding public office: women, for whom no offices were open; men with low educational achievement and defective English; and some failed theological students and teachers. One might see their religious choice as an opting out of a race they had no hope of winning. One could also see it as an inversion of the inequality that was emerging in the secular sphere, allowing those who counted for least to claim moral superiority. Anglicans found this moral superiority particularly irksome.

The Anglican response to the contradiction between egalitarianism and growing differentiation was to multiply the number of minor offices to which anyone might aspire. The church set a limit to the number of churchwardens, who made most of the important decisions, but none to the number of lesser offices, such as lay preacher, church councillor, Sunday school teacher, chorister, sideman, and so on. By 1960, there were so many that there were not enough duties to go round, even with careful rostering. Fortunately, many were content simply to have a title. Even so, on important festivals there were as many as twenty becassocked laymen at the high altar, to say nothing of the half-dozen altar boys.

Some 70 percent of Anglican men over the age of thirty—which one might call the age of responsibility in Torres Strait—held some kind of church office. It was less a matter of having a title than of not being without one. But people valued their titles, even when they were only empty honorifics. They were likely to join the Pentecostalists if deprived of a title, and several were drawn back into the fold with the promise of a position. It seems likely that the Anglicans inflated the number of positions as a means of stemming the drift.

With the exception of a few churchwardens, none of these officeholders thought of themselves as the exact equivalent of their opposite number in the white sector. Most were sensitive about defective English and some were barely literate. Theirs was local rank. But at least they were loyal workers for a church that was not only among the most important but had royal patronage also. If all went well, the next generation would be better equipped to perform its duties. Murray's Anglicans, then, recognized that they were different from, and perhaps in some respects inferior to, white people. They might hope for a change to come in time, but in the meanwhile they were ready to put up with the situation.

CONCLUSION

The Torres Strait Islands, unlike the other territories considered in this volume, are situated within the borders of a metropolitan power. This does not mean that they cannot be understood within the same colonial framework. However, the contradiction between the developed nation-state and its underdeveloped enclave is, perhaps, more intense than that between a state and its external colonies.

Torres Strait became a colony of Queensland when it proved to have valuable marine resources. The industry required a variable supply of cheap manpower, and so the islands became pools of captive labor under the control of the government. The LMS and later the Church of England worked within this framework and more or less consciously legitimated the new order. Thus wage labor was not just an alternative means of satisfying material needs—it brought cash which could be given to the church. Similarly, the law was to be obeyed not just out of fear of punishment but because it was God's law.

The whole missionary effort was not devoted to this end; nor was this its only function. Its support came from people in Britain and in the cities of Australia who knew nothing of pearling, although they might approve of teaching the natives to be industrious and law-abiding. But while hymn singing and Sabbath observances might irk the hard-living pearler, they did not threaten his interests.

The missionaries' main effort went in reconstructing the island communities. The petty theocracies that resulted were certainly inspired by Anglo-Saxon Christianity, but they could only have existed on a colonial frontier. The pietistic Christian native they produced was scarcely less exotic to ordinary whites than his savage forebears.

World War II in the Pacific brought islanders into direct contact with the outside world and caused many of them to look critically at the existing order. Growing discontent, coupled with an expanding labor force and a demand for manpower in northern Australia, prompted the government to let them emigrate.

On the mainland, islanders found a very different kind of life: free of the restrictions that irked them at home, full of novelty, but confusing and sometimes frightening. The government left them alone, but so did the church. The Anglicans did not try to transplant their Torres Strait regime; all they offered was a regular church adapted to the needs of comfortably settled whites. The uprooted and disoriented island worker found the help he expected from the church in the Assemblies of God. Simply by accepting conversion he could win white fellowship, a way of evaluating his surroundings, and guidance in coping with them.

Back home, Pentecostalism assumed a different significance. Conditions were not anomic and there were no white brothers and sisters to relate to. Instead, Pentecostalism became a religion of dissent, counterposing the restrictiveness of the government's regime in Torres Strait to the self-restraints to be derived from Pentecostalism on the mainland. Moreover, it lumped the Church of England, which had combated religious dissent through the secular administration, with the government.

In fact, although the church was integrated with secular authority at the village level, it was not higher up. It had little influence and for the most part left policymaking to the government. If one saw the church as politically neutral, as many islanders did, there was no inconsistency in remaining an Anglican while opposing the regime. Pentecostalists, on the other hand, were always radical.

I have suggested that the islanders' acceptance, in turn, of the LMS, the Church of England, and the Assemblies of God is to be understood in terms of concomitant socioeconomic developments. The mission form "fitted" the colonial situation in Torres Strait; the sect "fitted" conditions on the mainland. The Church of England started out as a church, as I have defined that term, but local conditions forced it into the mission mold. Events on the mainland indicated that as an ordinary church it had little to offer islanders. Those who have stayed with the Anglicans in Torres Strait may complete the transition from mission to church, but for those on the mainland the transition has been from mission to sect. Earlier I argued that the two forms were in many respects parallel, and in fact some older islanders recognized the similarity between the LMS and the Assemblies of God.

Unlike aborigines and most white workers, the islanders have continued to look to religious organizations for solutions to their problems. The quest has not yet ended. After the completion of my study, large numbers of emigrant islanders joined the World Church, a new sect formed explicitly to appeal to them and drawing extensively upon their folk Christianity. Its leader, however, is white. Evidently islanders still like to take their religion ready-made, rather than making their own synthesis.

NOTES

This chapter is based on twenty-four months' fieldwork in the Torres Strait, between 1958 and 1961, while the author was a research scholar of the Australian National

University.
1. I have been unable to find a reference for this formulation but recall that it was used by Archbishop Fisher on a visit to Rhodesia during the 1950s.
2. The pearling began by importing labor from the Pacific islands, ranging from sophisticated Rotumans to blackbirded New Hebrideans. Later in the century Malays and Filipinos predominated and during the last decade Japanese became the diving elite. Islanders, aborigines, and Papuans became increasingly numerous in the years preceding World War II in the Pacific, and after 1945 islanders and aborigines made up the entire labor force.
3. Early in the mission, some Loyalty Island teachers were killed in Papua. On discovering that they had been involved in adultery, the Reverend Mr. Murray commented that their fate would be a salutary warning to others.
4. Frustrated by this ordinance, Frederick and Charles Walker left the society to form the Papuan Industries Company (PIC). Based on Badu, the company provided islanders with boats, marketed their shell, and sold them cheap goods. This enterprise inspired the government to form a similar company which took over the PIC when the brothers retired in 1934.
5. It is interesting to note that most of the government officials in Torres Strait after 1930 were Roman Catholics.
6. Malcolm Calley reached similar conclusions in his study of aboriginal Pentecostalists (Calley 1955, 1964).
7. For a more detailed account of the politics of religion on Murray Island, see Beckett (1967).
8. For a detailed exploration of this problem, see Beckett (1971).

INTERCULTURAL COMMUNICATION IN THE WESTERN SOLOMONS: THE METHODIST MISSION AND THE EMERGENCE OF THE CHRISTIAN FELLOWSHIP CHURCH

Frances Harwood

The Christian Fellowship Church (CFC), a native separatist movement in the Western District of the British Solomon Islands Protectorate, broke away from the Methodist mission in 1961. The movement centers on the charismatic leadership of Silas Eto, the "Holy Mama," who has gained the allegiance of over 3,500 islanders in twenty-two villages and won recognition from the protectorate government for the CFC as a legally constituted church. The church administers its own school system and raises funds through cooperative efforts to support CFC projects and pay the government head tax for its members. Church services invite congregational participation which often leads to a *taturu* 'trance.' A large corpus of hymns celebrates the divine attributes of the Holy Mama and exhorts members to "be of one mind," "work together," and "love one another."

The CFC is a product of the policies of its parent organization, the Methodist mission of the Solomon Islands. The CFC has developed out of more than fifty years of sustained contact with Europeans. The Methodist missionaries have provided the most pervasive and influential form of intercultural contact—from the founding of the mission in 1902 until the breakaway in 1961, at which point government officers replaced the missionaries as the main source of contact with European society. Thus the breakaway movement has been organized by islanders whose education, concept of Christianity, and model of organization are derived in large measure from the Methodist mission. In fact, the controversies which culminated in the breakaway resulted in a claim on the part of the CFC to represent the *true* Methodist church in the Solomons.

In no sense, however, did sustained contact with the mission for the first half of the twentieth century result in a shared set of cognitions, motivations, and goals. Instead, interaction between the two cultural frameworks has led to the formation of a series of what Wallace (1970:36) has termed "partial equivalence structures." Shared cultural understandings, far from being a prerequisite for interaction, can in fact inhibit accommodation if the motivations and goals of the two groups are markedly discrepant. The minimal condition for accommodation requires merely a predictability in the behavior of others in relation to one's own actions. As Wallace (1970:35-36) points out:

> Reciprocal interactions between representatives of geographically separate groups as alien as American Indian tribes and colonial or state governments have proceeded for centuries, with only minimal sharing of motives or understanding, on the basis of carefully patterned equivalences. . . . In no case is it necessary that a basic personality or a basic cognitive framework be shared, but it is necessary that behaviors be mutually predictable and equivalent.

The history of interaction between missionaries and islanders and the subsequent emergence of the CFC can be viewed as a process of formulating and modifying a series of partial equivalence structures.[1] These structures have displayed a pulselike character of expansion and contraction of contexts for intercultural communication. An open and improvisational style over a broad but shallow spectrum of occasions for contact gives way, in the absence of shared motives and goals, to a progressively narrower band of restricted and formalized routines having the properties of rigidly choreographed tableaux. For participants on both sides of the encounter, the improvisational stage is highly unpredictable. Such an open give-and-take may point up glaring cultural misunderstandings. Ideally such misunderstandings can be acknowledged, discussed, and resolved in a mutually satisfying manner. In many intercultural situations, as in the present case, misperceptions are brought to manageable proportions by a narrowing of both the content and the occasions for contact to produce stylized routines which are predictable, redundant, and formalized. Both parties to the encounter know what to expect, but the price paid for such predictability is a restriction in the input of new or modified messages.

From the founding of the Methodist mission in 1902 to the attainment of organizational stability by the CFC during the 1960s, two such cycles of expansion and contraction of contexts for communication can be identified. The first opened with the Methodist drive for converts in the Western District and culminated in the stabilization of the mission in the 1920s. The second phase was initiated by the decline in mission influence after World War II. Increasing factionalism on the village level led to the breakaway of a number of Methodist villages which went on to form and then to regularize the CFC.

FIRST PHASE: THE DRIVE FOR CONVERTS

The Australian Methodists developed a serious interest in the Solomon Islands following a visit to the Roviana Lagoon in 1900 by the ubiquitous Reverend George Brown, then general secretary of the Australian Methodist Mission. Brown made three observations at the time which are worthy of note:

> Many of the villages were destroyed a few years ago by H.M.S. *Royalist* for some outrages against white men, and they do not yet seem to have recovered.
>
> The houses are not so large nor so well built as formerly, and I noticed a great apparent decrease in population to that which I saw twenty years ago.
>
> For some reason neither [chief Ingava] nor his people want missionaries to live there. This is not a notion of recent years, for I remember that they had the same objections when I was here twenty years ago (Luxton 1955:18).

These observations give an indication of conditions prior to the establishment of the mission: the use of gunboat diplomacy as a tactic for pacification by the newly established British protectorate government; depopulation from diseases introduced by the Europeans and perhaps from psychological factors (Rivers 1922:98); and the initial resistance by local big men to the founding of a mission. The Australian Mission Board, far from being daunted by these conditions, appears to have been stimulated by the difficulties inherent in the undertaking. The report of the annual meeting of the Methodist church for 1902 cites three official reasons for choosing the Western District as a promising field for evangelism:

> (1) It was the darkest area and had the greatest need for the gospel. (2) It was untouched by other Protestant work. (3) The nearest Protestant Mission (Melanesian Mission of the Church of England) had agreed to the opening, as they were unable to develop serious occupany of the area (Tippett 1967:55).

The choice of the Roviana Lagoon as the site for the proposed mission was a master stroke. Not only was considerable prestige to be gained in mission circles by the conversion of the "dread headhunters of the Roviana lagoon," but the venture also imparted a dramatic quality to appeals to the Australian Methodist Congress for the financial support of mission activities. Initial converts made among the Roviana headhunters were expected to produce a domino effect, leading to rapid expansion into surrounding areas.

The mission in the Western Solomons was conceived as an adventurous, difficult, and perhaps dangerous undertaking. In selecting John Francis Goldie to head the mission party to the Roviana Lagoon, Brown chose a man whose abilities were well suited to the job. Goldie was born in Hobart, Tasmania, in 1870, became a convert to evangelistic Christianity at the age of seventeen, and thereupon became an itinerant preacher. At the age of twenty-one he arrived in Sydney determined to find passage to the South African goldfields, but was persuaded to enter the Wesleyan church instead. He preached on the Queensland circuits for five years, advanced to the status of probationary minister, and was appointed in 1902, at the age of thirty-two, as leader of the Methodist venture in the Solomons (Luxton 1955:23-24).

The missionary party set sail from Sydney, Australia, in 1902. In addition to Goldie, the group included a second minister, the Reverend S. R. Rooney, and a Methodist layman, a builder by trade. With them went a contingent of thirteen Fijians and Samoans and Samuel Aqarau, a Solomon Islander from Guadalcanal who had been transported to Fiji to work on the sugar plantations. Aqarau had been part of a group of Solomon Islanders in Fiji who had petitioned the Methodists to establish a mission in the Solomons. The use of converts from established missions to spearhead the drive for conversion in a newly opened area was a common practice in the Pacific (see chapter 4). The appointment of Fijians, Samoans, and later Tongans by the Methodists in the Western Solomons as village pastors and teachers appears to have been effective in the early days of the mission. In later years, however, increasing demands by these people for greater participation and influence within the mission, and strained relations with local village leaders, led to a growing sense of their marginality and many opted for a return to their home islands.

From its inception, the mission developed as a station-oriented and missionary-controlled, rather than a village-oriented and islander-controlled, organization. Special effort was given to the development of the head station on and around Kokeqolo hill, a location on the coast of New Georgia at the intersection of the Roviana and Wana Wana lagoons. The strong station orientation of the mission in the Solomons was at variance with Methodist practice in other parts of the Pacific (Tippett 1967:56) and contrary to the policy of other Christian missions operating in the group (Hilliard 1966:347). The practice resulted in weak pastoral supervision in the villages, especially those distant from the head station in the Roviana Lagoon.

Early attempts to establish contact with the islanders in the Roviana Lagoon were frustrated by the hostility of the big men and the indifference of the people. The initial success of the elders in dissuading their people from converting began to break down between 1906 and 1910. By 1913, Goldie was able to inform the Mission Board of 511 baptized members, 524 members on trial awaiting baptism, and 6,625 adherents or regular church attenders, probably the total populations of those villages having resident preacher-teachers (Goldie 1914:585). This was the beginning of the numbers game. Statistics became the measure of church growth and influenced the allocation by the Mission Board of financial aid, increases in European staff appointments, and the building of substations.

With regard to the growing numbers of converts, Goldie wrote to Australia in 1910:

> I have never seen such evidence of the power of God, and of the efficacy of the Gospel of Jesus Christ, as I have seen in the last few months. All over the lagoon the people are definitely coming out for Christ, and taking a firm stand for him. The devil is raging very loudly, and his slaves are doing their worst to hinder the work, but God's people are "more than conquerors" through him that loved us, and not a single day passes that does not see some souls brought to Christ. Some of the very pick of the young men have definitely given themselves up to him, and are doing their best to lead others to him. Also . . . the one feature that strikes one about them is the total absence of any excitement, but the quiet steady determination to follow Christ (MC, CSID 1910).

Mabelle Davey, a missionary sister, wrote home to Australia in 1913, commenting on some aspects of the conversions:

> The change in their villages is soon apparent, they soon change their mode of living after they become Christians—they really do seem different men. In the Roviana it has not been as in some other places where the chiefs have embraced Christianity first, and their people have naturally followed—here, it has been the people, who have no standing at all, sometimes slave people, who have accepted Christianity first. The other people have looked on, perhaps persecuted them, but they took their stand, and so are the stronger Christians. Now, some of the chiefs see the right way, and they have to start now, whilst their own people are far ahead of them in Christian experience (MC, CSID 1913).

THE INDUSTRIAL MISSION

In 1908, six years after the founding of the mission and at the time of the first large-scale conversions, Goldie began implementing the policy of the "industrial mission," a concept then in vogue among Pacific missions in general as well as in Methodist mission circles (Fuller 1908:3-4).[2] According to Tippett (1967: 66), this plan "required the acquisition of two large tracts of land large enough for the establishment of [coconut] plantations and technical and industrial institutions, which were supposed to demonstrate the importance of industry and the reward of honest labor, and in so doing bring people under the influence of the Gospel."

The industrial mission concept meshed easily with the mission's emphasis on a social ethic which stressed works over beliefs and present morality over future salvation. For missionaries like Goldie, Christianity was envisioned as a total way of life for his converts which entailed a renunciation of traditional values. Christianity was to replace the old way, not augment it. The industrial mission, with its regimented life of labor and study, was designed to remove selected converts from the context of village life, at least for the period of their schooling, and to present a milieu in which a Christian way of life could replace traditional values. Upon completion of the training period at the mission head station, islanders were given the status of pastor-teachers and were then posted to outlying villages. It was mission policy never to post a man back to his natal village. For token wages of a few pounds a year, or a stock of trade goods, these people organized church services, taught the rudiments of reading, writing, and biblical lore, and encouraged the development of coconut plantations from which the village's annual "thanksgiving" payments to the mission were derived. "To get the best from these people," Goldie maintained, "we must teach them to be industrious, honest, clean, and self-reliant, and, if need be, self-sacrificing. We must show them how to apply the new standard of conduct and the moral code we have forced on them. We must teach them to translate Christian creed into Christian practice" (1914:583).

Goldie never envisioned the mission as a setting in which islanders could achieve a measure of equality with European missionaries, and, although many islanders were converted and some trained as preacher-teachers, no islander was ordained until well after Goldie's retirement in 1951. Goldie had nothing but scorn for islanders who attempted to emulate the life-style of the European missionaries. He objected to what he termed the

> religious loafer . . . the half-civilized native who loves to strut round quoting passages of the Bible, singing hymns, and shaking hands on the slightest provocation, but who has learned nothing of industry, honesty or cleanliness. . . . He has been taught a Christian creed divorced from Christian conduct. He, too, is ready to "preach the gospel, not to work,"

but, unlike our white friend, he is to be pitied more than blamed (1914: 583).

Such was the European Methodists' view of the founding of the mission. It was perceived as an adventurous and dangerous undertaking among savage headhunters. The initial resistance of the big men was replaced by a quite startling increase in the number of converts within ten years. The building of the head station and several substations under the control of European missionaries, the founding of the industrial mission, and the continued success of the numbers game all gave the missionaries a heady sense of accomplishment. They had achieved what they had set out to do. By 1922, the mission staff included 4 European missionaries, 5 European missionary sisters, 1 layman, 18 catechists (mostly Tongan), 52 native village preacher-teachers, and 3,520 baptized members. The mission, despite its inauspicious beginnings, had become a stable and properous concern.

By the 1920s, the mission was characterized by the paternalistic control and retention of authority by European missionaries, the domination of mission affairs by its chairman, John Francis Goldie, and a station-centered policy which resulted in weak pastoral supervision at the village level. Instruction of converts in scriptures and doctrines was subordinated to an overriding emphasis on "leading a Christian life" and the inculcation of such values as humility, service, and sacrifice, as well as cleanliness and hard work.

THE ISLANDERS' VIEW

So far I have described the founding and development of the mission as it appeared to the Europeans involved. The other half of the picture, the islanders' view, remains to be outlined. Why did so many islanders opt for conversion? And what stands behind Goldie's observation that the islanders joined up with a "total absence of any excitement, but the quiet steady determination to follow Christ"?

Islander Methodists credit not only Goldie but also Samuel Aqarau, the Guadalcanal petitioner, with being the dual founders of the mission. Large portions of the Solomons had already come under the influence of Christian missions, and it appeared to the islanders in the Western District that they too should have a mission and not be left behind in establishing this form of contact with Europeans whose power and knowledge appeared so much greater than that of their traditional leaders.

Local big men, who saw the mission as a competitor for the allegiance and material aid of their followers, sought to discourage their people from making contact with the mission. Several big men moved their villages away from the head station. The first handful of converts was marginal to local society—war captives, those under suspicion of witchcraft, and several men wanted by the British government for attacks on traders.

The land given to the missionaries at Kokeqolo was believed to be inhabited by evil spirits. In fact, the leaders hoped that these evil powers would force the missionaries to abandon their project. When the missionaries not only stayed but flourished, the belief in traditional powers was undermined. This was but one in a series of incidents in which missionaries, inadvertently or by design, broke down local custom: babies were delivered at the head station without the prescribed segregation of the sexes; Western medicine provided effective therapy despite the neglect of traditional formulas; and it became evident that native curers were powerless to save the lives of villagers infected by European-introduced diseases. These challenges to local custom led not to the renunciation of indigenous practices but to a belief that traditional powers were unequal to the force of the Europeans and their god. Missionaries were not obliged to challenge native doctrine head on and were never forced to argue the superiority of Christian doctrine. For most islanders, Christianity was augmenting rather than supplanting traditional beliefs.

There is, moreover, a pronounced pragmatic and eclectic tendency in Melanesian religious thought. The New Georgia Islanders were ever ready to adopt alien practices and imported charms and formulas believed effective from such island groups as Simbo and the Shortlands. This pragmatism was extended to the mission. Islanders witnessing the reduced powers of the big men turned to the mission in the hope of gaining access to the superior knowledge and power exercised by the Europeans. The mission's aim of conversion and its promise of education, both formal and informal, led islanders to believe that this sharing of group membership and knowledge would soon lead to equivalence with Europeans.

According to the traditional belief system, knowledge gave access to power which was itself derived from supernatural sources. Those with knowledge guarded it closely and, in old age, passed it on to a successor, usually a close kinsman. Islanders were amazed by what they regarded as an indiscriminate and profligate offer by the missionaries to dispense knowledge. Early converts eagerly sought schooling, underwent trial periods leading to church membership, offered their services as pastor-teachers, and adjusted their behavior and values, at least outwardly, in an attempt to gain this knowledge. Islanders were well aware of the differences between themselves and Europeans and were eager to acquire whatever it was that the Europeans knew and they did not. Thus conversion can be seen as a bid for access to knowledge and equality with Europeans rather than submission to Methodist Christianity as the missionaries interpreted it.

The mission's offer of conversion and the acceptance of that offer by large numbers of islanders resulted in a working relationship based on mutually contradictory premises—on the one hand a European form of paternalism which offered knowledge but precluded equality and on the other the islanders' belief that access to knowledge would lead to equality.

In addition to these attempts to gain equality through access to knowledge, the islanders sought to gain an equivalence in social relationships with the missionaries. Social equivalence is a dominant theme in Melanesian political thought. The hierarchical and bureaucratic form of mission organization was foreign to native practice, which was based on personal ties to big men who were raised up or brought low by the freely given or retracted support of their followers. This idiom of consensus politics was used by the islanders to portray their allegiance to the mission. The missionaries saw themselves as converting villages, whereas the islanders, in describing this process, are quick to assert that they sent local representatives to the head station to invite the mission into their respective villages. This distinction parallels that implied by their assertion that it was Samuel Aqarau, as well as Goldie, who brought the mission to the region in the first place.

The islanders' relationship to Goldie was couched in a similar idiom, that of freely given personal allegiance intended to raise him up as their acknowledged leader, an idiom which Goldie encouraged. This view dovetailed with Goldie's style of paternalism. He became their protector, championed their causes, and filled the leadership vacuum created by the demise of the traditional big men. His style was not dissimilar, in fact, to that of a Melanesian big man. He described himself as a "benevolent despot" (Hall n.d., personal communication) and jealously guarded his flock.

In the course of time, Goldie developed a large and strongly personal following. The elite was composed of men who served him in the capacity of cooks, boat crews, and personal servants. These were Goldie's "boys," and today many still speak of themselves as "sons of Goldie," a phrase he encouraged them to use. Most of these "sons" were drawn from *butubutu bangara* 'group of potential leaders.' Silas Eto, the islander who was to become the charismatic leader of the CFC, claims to have been one of these "sons of Goldie." These men constituted Goldie's main source of information on local affairs. They understood his rather eccentric use of the Roviana language, and, being powerful men in their own right, were able to mobilize supplementary labor forces, monetary "thanksgiving" offerings, and the quantities of food needed for head station festivities. These "sons of Goldie" were later to play a central part in the organization of the CFC, and it was the mission as it existed during the 1920s that they were to use as their organizational model.

A government officer touring the Western District in the early 1930s reported on the islanders' "general air of satisfaction with life—a certain smugness, and a successful adjustment to European contact and culture change" (Hilliard 1966:344). To the disinterested observer, this indeed may have appeared to have been the case. But the adjustment was not that of a shared culture, that is to say, a common fund of cognitions, motives, and goals. By the 1930s, a set of partial equivalence structures had been negotiated. A fairly high standard of predictability between these two groups had been achieved, based on restricted channels of communication and stylized encounters. These occasions consisted of highly formalized visits by missionaries to the villages, the

Christmas and Easter festivities at the head station, and the annual presentation of "thanksgiving," a ceremony for which leaders gathered at the head station and, as Goldie called the roll, moved forward in turn to present their village's cash offerings in special baskets provided for the occasion.

SECOND PHASE: DECLINE AND DISINTEGRATION

Misperceptions abounded on both sides, but occasions for conflict were largely avoided through the successful negotiation of structures of partial equivalence. This working relationship was placed under enormous strain and finally ripped apart by the worldwide depression, which greatly weakened the financial base of the mission. Even more disastrous was the Japanese invasion of the Solomons in 1942 and the arrival of allied troops on New Georgia in the following year. The battle for Munda leveled the head station and its surrounding plantations, but, more significantly, contact with allied troops and their unheard of riches, in the form of technology, weapons, and material comforts, convinced the islanders that the mission was but a poor and relatively powerless sector of the European world.

The postwar mission never recovered its former prestige in the eyes of the islanders. Their optimistic belief that cooperation with the missionaries would provide access to knowledge and equality deteriorated. However, mission organization based on the continued relationship between Goldie and the big men who were the "sons of Goldie" remained intact and provided a measure of coherence and predictability in the chaotic postwar period. This form of integration came to an end with Goldie's retirement in 1951. The chairmanship of the mission was held by a series of men whom the New Georgians regarded as ignorant of New Georgian custom and politics.[3] These chairmen sought to replace the paternalism of Goldie's mission with a bureaucratic administration. To this end, they recruited a group of bright young islanders to aid them in the construction of what was to be more of a local church than an overseas mission. However admirable a goal, this practice bypassed the local leaders, the "sons of Goldie." The newly recruited leaders had a limited following at the village level; the long-standing relationship, based on the freely given allegiance of villagers to missionaries who operated in a way that appeared to the islanders as consistent with big man politics, was abandoned. The mission, with its rapid circulation of chairmen and attempts at bureaucratic organization, had become highly unpredictable in the eyes of the Methodist islanders. Moreover, Goldie's retirement occurred at a time when the protectorate government was in the process of replacing appointed village headmen, some of whom numbered among the "sons of Goldie," by elected local councils, a move which further disrupted the established balance between islanders and Europeans.

FORMATION OF THE CHRISTIAN FELLOWSHIP CHURCH

During this period of uncertainty, Reverend Allen Hall, a New Zealand missionary in charge of the Roviana circuit, began implementing a program of evangelical preaching designed to increase the level of Christian commitment in the villages. Circuit preachers stressed the message of God's love over social ethics and emphasized Christ's promise at Pentecost that he would send a "comforter" in the form of the Holy Spirit. An outburst of religious enthusiasm swept through the Roviana area in the wake of this preaching. Villagers were caught up in trance states, visions, and speaking in tongues. The missionaries quickly lost control of the situation and roundly condemned what they considered to be the psychologically damaging excesses of this religious enthusiasm. The islanders claimed that they were unable to control such outbursts and were both puzzled and frightened by what they perceived to be violent and uncontrollable seizures.

A search for the meaning of this enthusiasm failed to lead to consensus in the Roviana region. The missionaries claimed it was a psychological aberration; loyal Methodist islanders believe it derived from traditional "devil-devils"; and the villagers affected were convinced of its religious significance but were unable to agree on its source. It was at this point that the search for meaning was replaced by the search for a man who could attribute meaning to the phenomenon. Silas Eto, the leader of a variant form of Methodism which had flourished on the far side of New Georgia, was called. Canoes were sent from the various affected villages inviting Eto to each village in turn to witness the outbursts and determine their source. Eto was able to assure the villagers that the religious fervor was indeed the work of the Holy Spirit, a sign indicating a special relationship with divinity which was described as a "short cut to God" that bypassed the mission (Harwood 1974).

Eto had long been regarded by the Roviana people and missionaries alike as an unacculturated, eccentric, and troublesome character from the backward Hoava region on the far eastern end of New Georgia. He had been recruited for training at the head station during the 1920s, but had proved a difficult and troublesome student. He had, for example, advocated prayer vigils in the bush and claimed a special relationship with God. Well before the completion of his training, he was sent home, a breach of the mission policy of never posting a man back to his own village. Soon after his return, he was able to unite the role of traditional big man with that of preacher-teacher. He and his followers developed in the isolated Hoava-Hoeze region a variant form of Methodism which flourished in the postwar period. Eto's Methodism stressed community participation both in worship services and in communal living. His notable success in welding together the villages under his influence for community enterprises was at first viewed as a threat by Roviana leaders whose own villages were riven by factionalism. As relations with the mission became strained, this perception of Eto changed and Eto's brand of strong religious and secular leadership was regarded as the means for uniting villages at odds with the mission into a separatist movement which would not only be independent of the mission but could also claim to be the true Methodist church in the Solomons. Independence was important at this point not because it meant freedom from the mission but because it provided relief from the conflicts and uncertainties involved in the mission policy of the post-Goldie period.

One of the founding myths of the CFC is an account of how Goldie's leadership and power were passed on to Silas Eto. The story is told by David Gobe, one of the "sons of Goldie," who had served as Goldie's cook in the postwar period. It begins with Goldie's return to the Solomons in 1952, from his retirement in Australia, for the jubilee celebration of the first fifty years of the mission's work:

THE EMERGENCE OF THE CHRISTIAN FELLOWSHIP CHURCH   245

God had meant for Goldie to stay in the Solomons until his death but the missionaries who took his place sent him home to Tasmania. God therefore sent Goldie back for the jubilee to complete his work, as he still had not found a successor. Goldie, his daughter Nellie, and his cook, David Gobe, a "son of Goldie," stayed alone in the house on top of Kokeqolo hill. During the celebration six thousand people gathered at the station and there was much feasting, singing and dancing. Goldie was very old and crippled so Gobe had to carry him in his arms to the veranda where he could watch the events at the bottom of the hill. While they were sitting there, Goldie remarked that "six thousand people have gathered together here but none of them has come to see the 'Father of the Solomons.' Sometime today a person chosen by God will come to me, and man will become the leader of the Solomons." Gobe did not know who Goldie was talking about and he asked if someone had been sent to fetch this man, but Goldie replied that God himself would send him, and Gobe thought Goldie knew exactly who it would be.

Soon a man came up the path and appeared at the door. He stopped there and prayed. He then came up the steps of the veranda, knelt before Goldie and prayed again—it was Silas Eto! While he was there praying there was a roar like an airplane, then a swirling sound, coldness and an explosion. It became dark and Gobe was unable to see. When the dark passed away Gobe found himself with Goldie and Eto in the midst of a void. Gobe had no idea where he was as all the things of this world had disappeared and the invisible things began to appear. He saw Goldie and Eto sitting before a table. On the table was a crown from which emanated a path of light extending endlessly up into the air. It was white in the middle and blue at the borders. On either side were gathered crowds of little children, white haired, with flowers in their hands. The children had small wings. Flying above the children were many angels moving up and down, but Gobe didn't know where they were going because he didn't know where he was. The angels came down to Goldie and Silas and flew round and round the table.

Then Gobe heard voices. Goldie and Eto were speaking a strange language neither Roviana nor English which Gobe couldn't understand. He looked again and his body became weak and he fainted away like a dead man. He soon recovered but the heavenly things had passed and he found himself back among the things of this world on the veranda with Goldie and Eto. Then Goldie stood up, as though there were nothing wrong with him, and he gave Eto this promise: "One man will come after me. He will be able to see those things which are hidden and reveal them to the people. My son, this is the day of the Solomons, what is mine I now give to you in the name of the Father, Son and Holy Spirit." In this way Goldie passed on the power of leadership to Silas. Goldie said that Silas should not despair if he at first was the only one, for in time there would be thousands. "Now that I have given you the power [*minana* or *mana*] I will go back to my home. Do not ask me who I will see and where I will go, but someday I shall come again either in flesh or in spirit, and bring to you the Holy Spirit."

Goldie returned to Tasmania after the jubilee and soon after he died. His body was burned and his ashes were collected and put in a glass jar. But Silas remembered Goldie's promise that he would return. Before dawn on the day that he died Goldie came to Eto and called, "Silas! Silas!" Twice he called before Eto awoke and saw Goldie standing before him as a young man, like Christ arisen from the dead. He called a third time. "Silas!" Eto answered, "Yes, sir," and went to him. Goldie said, "I have come back as I promised. I am here at Kolobagia, the home of Godliness in the Solomons, but soon I shall go away. Take this box in your hands Silas. It is the box of the Holy Spirit. I give it to you now. When I am gone open it and begin your work in the Holy Spirit. In return I shall take your small daughter to the place of eternal life. You are to remain to do the work of the Holy Spirit on this earth." Goldie placed a black shining box in Eto's hands. He then took the young child and started to leave, but Silas called to him and said, "Thank you my Father, but I want to go with you." So Eto accompanied them to Paradise and then returned. When he reached Kolobagia he went at once to find his wife to see if the baby was with her. A marvelous thing occurred: her flesh and bones were gone, and all that remained was her skin, like the shell which a snake or a crab sloughs off. It was as though there had been a transformation rather than a death. Goldie had taken her spirit and given her a new life; she had been transformed into an angel.

This is how Silas received the black box, which is not a real box but rather a sign of the Holy Spirit. The black box is now the body of Holy Mama. When Eto returned from accompanying Goldie to Paradise, his first work for the Holy Spirit was to rebuild the village of Menakasapa which he named Paradise. Goldie had told him that the power in the box would start at Paradise and go on for two thousand years.

Internally, the CFC has replaced the partial equivalence of the mission period between missionaries and islanders with structures of equivalence based on shared cognitions, motives, and goals, at least within the movement. Although a measure of equivalence has been established internally, the external relations of the CFC with the European presence in the form of courts, administrative agencies, and elective political bodies continues to be marked by relations of partial equivalence. Following its formation, the CFC entered a period of withdrawal and isolation from surrounding groups. The church turned in on itself and opted for self-sufficiency, often at the sacrifice of lowered standards of living. The "go-it-alone" policy is in part self-determined but in part forced upon the church by the perception, often justified, of hostility on the part of environing social groups.

This withdrawal resulted in a restriction of occasions for interaction with outsiders, notably the officers of the protectorate government. These encounters, when they do occur, have taken on a markedly stylized quality—when, for example, government officers visit CFC villages or when islanders go to the district headquarters at Gizo to celebrate the queen's birthday.

A good example of such an encounter based on partial equivalence was a meal provided by the village of Eden Renewed, a CFC village in the Roviana Lagoon, for a visiting district commissioner and his party of three Britishers in 1968 during the period of my fieldwork. This "feeding of Europeans" is a standard routine in the repertoire of intercultural contact in the region. The meal was staged on the small veranda of a house put at my disposal during a month-long stay in the village, and the encounter was played out in full sight of the villagers. A heavy wooden table was commandeered from the village school for the occasion and five rickety chairs were rounded up. Villagers searched their meager stores for suitable plates and cutlery. A nearby cook house became the scene of frenzied activity as local women under the supervision of the local big man, a former cook for Goldie, prepared the food. Holy Mama, who was in residence at the time, put on a spotless white *tivitivi* 'wrap-around,' carried the food to the veranda, and waited on the table. At the conclusion of the meal, Holy Mama delivered a short speech to the seated Europeans, stating that the CFC and the government would continue to work together. The district commissioner, still seated, replied by formally thanking Holy Mama for the meal and assuring him of the government's gratitude for the continued cooperation of the CFC.

The government party then boarded its ship and left the village, carrying away the impression that Holy Mama, although a powerful leader in his own right, was a man who knew his place and was willing to play a subservient role to government. After all, they had been waited on by the leader of the movement; he had not insisted on joining them at the table, nor did he affect European dress but remained standing in respectful deference to them, attending to their every need. The district commissioner, who was at that time new to the area, and who had harbored suspicions about the subversive and anti-European intentions of the CFC, now pronounced himself satisfied that such was not the case.

Meanwhile the villagers, who had watched the proceedings closely, gathered at the cook house to assess the event. In their eyes, Holy Mama, far from being subservient, had asserted his dominance over the Europeans in the course of the meal. To Melanesians the provision of food, especially cooked food, is an expression of dominance. The ostentatious preparation and presentation of such food further emphasizes this position. Another mark of status differentiation is the relative position of the participants' heads during an encounter, inferiors keeping their heads lower than those of acknowledged superiors. Furthermore, superiors would always initiate the exchange of formal speech and the rhetoric employed should be aggressive and self-assertive.

On the occasion described here, CFC villagers had provided the food, their resident big man had supervised its preparation, and Holy Mama himself had served it to the Europeans, who had consumed the entire meal while seated below Holy Mama's head. The formal speeches had been initiated by Holy Mama in the assertive Melanesian rhetorical style which is modified on such occasions by an islander interpreter to include more polite phrasing for the benefit of the Europeans.

This encounter, although perhaps insignificant in itself, well illustrates the partial equivalence structures which have been negotiated between islanders and Europeans. Misperceptions abound, but each side comes away from the encounter convinced of the good intentions of the other side. Both have behaved predictably during the encounter. The balance permitting such a high level of contradictory perceptions can only be maintained by strict adherence to heavily stylized routines.

A set of routines had been worked out during the early years of Goldie's mission and had become stabilized during the heyday of the mission during the 1920s and early 1930s. The disintegration of these routines following World War II led to a period of confusion and improvisation out of which the CFC emerged. The strong separatist and isolationist tendencies which mark its internal organization were balanced by the formation of a new set of intercultural routines based on partial equivalence with surrounding groups. It remains to be seen whether these narrow bands of intercultural communication can be maintained in the face of changes in the political environment of the Solomons. The British are eager to give the protectorate self-government within the next few years. In 1974, the protectorate government arranged the withdrawal of financial support for church-administered schools unless they agreed to surrender autonomy to the district school administration. As of 1975, the CFC chose to retain control of its schools despite the grave financial burden incurred. The leasing of native lands on New Georgia by foreign timber enterprises is anticipated, government cooperative stores have been established in a number of CFC villages, and CFC members are taking a more active part in protectorate politics. Such innovations have gone far toward weakening the initial "go-it-alone" policy of the CFC and are bringing about modifications in the partial equivalence structures established during the church's first ten years.

CONCLUSION

The CFC belongs to that category of Third World phenomena variously termed "revitalization movements" (Wallace 1956), "charismatic movements" (Fabian 1971), or "religions of the oppressed" (Lanternari 1965). Such movements often appear subversive to governing elites. The CFC was perceived as a radical break with prevailing forms of social integration by many in both the mission and the government. On closer inspection and with the passage of time, however, the CFC appears not as an outright rejection of the European presence but rather as a major redefinition in an ongoing series of accommodations of partial equivalence designed to achieve equality and recognition from Europeans. Being both a product of and a response to the policies of the Methodist mission, it combines radical innovations with certain elements of the mission as it existed under Goldie.

Many analysts of Third World movements are far too quick to assign such labels as "conservative," "radical," "reactionary," or "revolutionary" and often fail to take seriously the complex cultural and historical milieu in which such a movement arises. This is a simplistic practice which glosses over the conscious and creative efforts of individuals in a movement to construct a social life appropriate to the historical and cultural moment.

NOTES

This chapter is based on a field study of the Christian Fellowship Church carried out in the Solomon Islands from October 1966 to September 1967. The research was funded by the National Science Foundation under the direction of Harold Scheffler, Yale University. I benefited from comments by George Carter, Robert Conkling, James Draper, Shulamit Decktor Korn, Alan Tippett, and Willard Walker. My special thanks go to the Holy Mama and members of the CFC for their unfailing helpfulness and generosity.

1. The concept of partial equivalence structures has been borrowed from Anthony F. C. Wallace. This chapter seeks to extend this notion to include the dynamic aspects of the expansion and contraction of such structures over time.
2. The industrial mission concept was a major policy issue advanced in the period 1902-1914. Fuller's article was only one contribution to a lengthy debate on the value of the industrial mission. For additional material, see official statements by Goldie and others in the *Australasian Methodist Missionary Review,* on file in the Methodist Overseas Missions Archives (housed in the Mitchell Library), Sydney, Australia.
3. The men who held the office of chairman from Reverend J. Goldie's retirement to the founding of the CFC were Reverend J. Metcalfe from 1951 to 1958, Reverend S. Andrews from 1958 to 1959, and Reverend G. Carter from 1959 to 1966.

INDIGENIZATION AS A MISSIONARY GOAL IN THE CAROLINE AND MARSHALL ISLANDS

Francis X. Hezel

Christian missions have long been a controversial force in the colonial history of Oceania. To some observers, the missionary is the very personification of that spirit of cultural imperialism which has succeeded in wreaking its mindless changes on unsuspecting native peoples and in making their islands cultural wastelands. The very word "missionary" often conjures up the image of a religious frontiersman, usually ill-prepared to appreciate the beauty and logic of the culture within which he works, who pursues single-mindedly his goal of converting the heathen. With cross raised over the pagan land, he busies himself in baptizing babies, uprooting degrading superstitions, and preaching a new and better way of life to a people who are in his eyes at best children, at worst savages. However noble his intentions, the Christian missionary is an unwitting perpetrator of ethnocide among the very people he professes to help.

This stereotype of the missionary as imperialist is not without a measure of truth. And yet it is surely not the whole truth, for ever since the inception of foreign evangelization in Micronesia one of the chief goals of missionary activity has been the indigenization of the church in those islands. However indigenization may have been spelled out at different times and by different groups—and as we shall see, it has been subject to frequent redefinition—its basic meaning has always been the establishment of what might be called a native church. The term "native church" has been variously interpreted, of course. In the early Protestant era, a native church was a church whose resources, in terms of personnel and money, were generated from within the island communities themselves so that outside assistance was no longer necessary. Such a church was autonomous in that it did not have to rely on foreign churches for support. In recent years, however, a native church has come to mean much more than the ability of a local congregation to supply enough pastors and material for the continuation of the ecclesiastical structure. Today it is usually taken to mean a church whose religious content, as well as its formal structure, is rooted in the local community. Indigenization, then, is the process whereby missionary and people fashion a church in which religious symbols, ritual, and preaching grow from the cultural traditions of the people. A native church is one in which Christianity can be thought and lived in terms of the cultural milieu of the islanders themselves, not of the Bostonians or Basques who brought them the faith.

This chapter traces the evolution of the meaning of indigenization as a missionary goal in Micronesia since the middle of the nineteenth century. I shall examine some of the forces that were in direct conflict with the goal of indigenization at different stages in missionary activity in Micronesia. The most notable of these, of course, was the colonialist mentality that the missionary was usually unable to shed even as he worked to build up what he saw as a native church. Finally I intend to show how, in the period from 1970 to the present, the missionary charge to establish an indigenized church is seen as part of an even broader task—nothing less than the indigenization of society itself. This recent movement, which has been particularly associated with the Catholic church in the Caroline and Marshall Islands, has resulted in a major *volte face* on the part of the church. Those who were formerly regarded as among the vanguard of the colonizers have now become the champions of indigenous rather than foreign institutions. It is ironic that the same institution which advocated conversion to a foreign way of life and a foreign god for so many years should lately have acquired the reputation of singing the praises of traditional ways and issuing warnings against rapid modernization. But such is the interesting reversal evident in the Catholic church of the Caroline and Marshall Islands. It illustrates the evolution that has taken place in the definition by foreign missionaries of their goals within the last hundred years.

EARLY PROTESTANT GOALS

At the very outset of its missionary activity in Micronesia, the American Board of Commissioners for the Foreign Missions (ABCFM) professed as its goal the establishment of native churches which were "self-financing, self-governing, and self-propagating" (Anderson 1860:1). Its work in Micronesia began in 1852 with the arrival of three American and two Hawaiian couples who took up the task on the islands of Ponape and Kusaie. In accordance with the established policy of the day, there was no rush to make converts. It was not until six years after the coming of the missionaries that the first natives were received into the church on Kusaie and eight years before the first three Ponapeans were admitted. A decade after the start of evangelization there were no more than twenty-seven Kusaieans and thirty-six Ponapeans who had become full members of the church. Once church membership began to increase, however, it was not long before a few were selected to assume positions of leadership in the nascent church. By 1869 the first native deacon (the son of "Good King George" of Kusaie) was ordained, and two years later another was elevated to the ministry. By the early 1870s the training school on Ponape was already preparing native teachers, deacons, and pastors, several of whom would be the first to bring Christianity to the Mortlocks and Truk within the next few years. In the Marshalls, which received their first foreign missionary in 1857, progress toward establishment of a native church was just as swift. Already in 1880—by which time the training school for the Marshalls was relocated in Kusaie and the last of the American missionaries had been removed from Ebon—the entire Marshalls mission was left to the care of a small band of Hawaiian teachers together with a few Marshallese who had been trained in the local mission school.

The dispatch with which the first American Congregationalists sought to carry out their commission—to "set in order native churches, raise up a native ministry for them, ordain ministers in the important places and train the Christian community, thus organized, to the power and habit of self-government"—did not go unquestioned (Anderson 1860:1). Mission letters during the 1880s complain of a relapse into heathenism by many recent converts in the Mortlocks who had again taken up the use of turmeric and tobacco. Blame was usually laid upon the native teachers in these islands, and some were afterwards removed. One foreign missionary laid the fault to his confreres' "inadequate supervision" of the work of the native teachers in the Mortlocks, "resulting in the lowered character of preachers and teachers, the feeble life of the churches, the want of discipline, and [the poor] numbers in the schools" (ABCFM 1890:99). There were apparently others, missionaries and nonmissionaries alike, who shared his belief that the Protestant churches were being turned over to native ministers and teachers too quickly. Reverend Robert Logan, the first American missionary on Truk, wrote just a few months before his death in 1887 of his own misgivings in this respect: "What folly to expect that these races can take on pure morals and Christian civilization in a few years! Souls can be saved, morals and manners improved, the seeds of all progress planted and nourished, but the century plant grows quickly in comparison with true civilization" (Logan n.d.:18). And the great German ethnologist August Krämer, who visited the Marshalls shortly after the turn of the century, expressed surprise that the spiritual care of a "community of 13,500 natives" could be responsibly entrusted to "one or two dozen uneducated men" (Krämer 1906:215-216).

The intention of the American Board was clearly to set up native churches throughout the Micronesian mission and then withdraw outside support at the earliest opportunity. From the very beginning of its missionary activity in Micronesia, the ABCFM discouraged excessive dependence on local churches on funding from abroad. Each native congregation was required to contribute food and labor for the support of its church. Chiefs in Truk, who requested native teachers for their islands during the mission's boon years in the early 1880s, had to promise to build a suitable home for the teacher and his family, construct a church, and provide for the continual upkeep of both. Doctor Gulick, one of the first American missionaries on Ponape, wrote in 1854 that he was frequently compelled to refuse the request of chiefs on that island for small gifts lest he subvert the clearly stated goal of a self-supporting church (MH 1855:27). This policy, admirable though it may have been, was not without its difficulties. The insistence of Congregationalist missionaries that natives buy, rather than receive gratis, clothes from the mission led to the accusation in later years of avarice and mercantilism. This unfounded charge was given all the more credence because of the pastors' rigorous insistence that natives be modestly attired if they wished to attend church services. The first Catholic missionaries, by way of contrast, had no such scruples about the long-range effects their practice of distributing gifts might have. When they distributed trinkets to the people of Yap and Ponape in the early years of their work in the Carolines, they hoped that their liberality would win the affection of the natives and prepare the way for their conversion. The hard line of the early Congregationalist missionaries eventually did lead to the establishment of self-supporting churches, but according to one witness it was also responsible for the defection of a good many members for pecuniary reasons and the refusal of others to join the Protestant church in the first place. One visitor to Ponape at the turn of the century recorded what had become a cliche by that time: "I shall not become a Protestant for I am poor. I shall become a Catholic, for the Fathers do not ask me to pay anything" (Hambruch 1932 I:257).

Despite the difficulties inherent in its policies, the American Board accomplished the task it had set for itself. By the turn of the century there were 20 ordained native pastors, and 80 more native preachers and teachers serving a church membership of over 6,600 in Micronesia (ABCFM 1901:121). Contributions from local sources totaled about $7,000 a year. The Protestant church was well on its way to becoming fully autonomous.

EARLY CATHOLIC GOALS

Catholic missionary efforts in the Caroline and Marshall Islands, which were initiated in 1886 on Yap and a year later on Ponape, did not exhibit the same urgency for the establishment of a native church that marked the Protestant activity during the last century. Although the number of baptized Catholics in 1905—only twenty years after the founding of the mission—was recorded as ten thousand, there were no native pastors, no catechists, and no collections (*Analecta OMCap* 1905:205). The financing and leadership of the Catholic church in the Carolines remained securely in the hands of the Capuchin missionaries who were entrusted with this field. This control can be explained in good part by the theology of missions that prevailed in Catholic circles of that day. The task of the missionary was to save, through his direct apostolic intervention, as many souls as possible in the pagan land in which he labored. The charge of the Catholic missionary, as it was formulated in the encyclical of Pope Benedict XV in 1919, was "to open the way of heaven to those hurrying to destruction" (Benedict XV 1919:445). The personal salvation of pagans was no less an object of concern for the Protestant pastor, of course, but the external constraints imposed on him by his mission board had the effect of recalling him to the more distant goal of indigenization. It was not until the 1920s, under the influence of missiologists such as Father Pierre Charles, S. J., that the goal of establishing a native church in a mission land— like that which guided Protestant missionary work during the nineteenth century—won any wide acceptance at all among Catholics. Thereafter, "implanting the church" came to be canonized in ecclesiastical pronouncements as the primary aim of missionary activity.

Even if early Catholic missionaries to Micronesia had espoused the goal of creating a truly native church, the structures within which they were forced to operate would have put its attainment out of their reach. Although by comparison with their Protestant counterparts Catholic missionaries seem to have admitted new members with relative ease, there was an extraordinarily long process of acculturation required before a baptized Catholic could assume a position of leadership in the church. There did not exist in the Catholic church the intermediate ecclesiastical offices, such as preacher and teacher, that might provide a means of screening and selecting those who would become pastors. One was forced to leap from the pew to the pulpit, as it were, in one long, arduous bound that demanded commitment to the priesthood from the beginning, rather than making a series of modest steps forward. Ordination of Micronesians to the priesthood was the only means of achieving native church leadership at that time, and the obstacles to ordination were formidable. It meant long years of study abroad, the mastery of Latin in order to read theological texts and say mass, and a life of celibacy among a people for whom this was all but unthinkable. The training program for native Protestant leaders, conducted as it was in a boarding school institution, was deliberately intended to shield students from undesirable cultural influences—"the contaminating influence of their homes and the interference of their chiefs," as one missionary observed (Bliss 1906:97). But the training lasted only two or three years, and the school was located in an island environment. Seminary training for the Catholic priesthood demanded a complete severance of the candidate from his community and the psychological capacity to live as a stranger in his own land upon his return from the seminary.

All things considered, it is hardly surprising that it was not until 1940 that the first Micronesian priest, Father Paulino Cantero from Ponape, was ordained. At the present time, there are only two native priests in the Vicariate of the Caroline and Marshall Islands, although in recent years alternative forms of church leadership have been added, particularly through the restoration of the married diaconate in the Catholic church.

Despite the obvious differences in the professed goals of Catholic and Protestant missionaries during the last century with respect to the formation of a native church, the two approaches had a good deal in common. It could be said that both Catholics and Protestants sought to convert the heathen not just to a religion but to a form of civilization as well. A Spanish padre in Palau unabashedly proclaimed this goal when he boasted that he and his confreres, "flying two flags: the cross and the Spanish colors, have been working not only to convert the natives to the Catholic faith, but also to make Palau a real Spanish land" (Valencia n.d.: 40). Certainly the peculiar symbiosis of the church and state in the Spanish realm was unique. A union such as that which existed between *la espada y la cruz* during the Spanish administration was never to be experienced again in Micronesia. Nevertheless, a glance through missionary correspondence, no matter what the nationality, is enough to reveal that foreign missionaries have always thought of themselves as performing a civilizing function in

Micronesia. It does not matter much whether the missionary seeks to save the people from "degrading customs" and "ignorance and superstition" or from the dangers of malnutrition and the health hazard of a contaminated water supply; he is the harbinger of a new and better way in either case.

CULTURAL IMPERIALISM

It is understandable that the missionary should have been concerned with the human development of the people he served. The representatives of foreign churches have never been exclusively taken up with the care of souls, for they have recognized from the beginning the link that exists between the material and the spiritual. There has always been an instinctive awareness, however poorly it may have been articulated in their theologies, of the truth of Berdyaev's axiom that "care for the life of another, even material bodily care, is spiritual in essence." Still, it is not the readiness of the missionary then or now to work for the advancement of a native people that is at issue, but rather his presumptuous belief that his ways are necessarily the path to advancement for this people.

Missionary annals from Micronesia teem with examples of what has lately been termed cultural imperialism. The censure of Protestant missionaries against long hair, native dances, and the use of turmeric with which Carolinians traditionally adorned themselves comes to mind immediately. Then there is the tired old question of why missionary hackles should have been raised when natives entered the mission compound without pants and dresses! Certainly more than one missionary must have gloated over the fact that after 1884 "those who [did not have] enough clothing on for purposes of decency" were not to be admitted into church in Truk (Logan 1884); while two years later it was decided that no nude babies were to be accepted at the baptismal font in the Mortlocks (Wetmore 1886:14). Catholic missionaries, who were inclined to be more tolerant about such matters, drew the line at divination, belief in spirits, and the use of magic. Baptismal names were Spanish or German, depending on the period, and religious processions were exact copies of what one would have seen in Western Europe of the day. These illustrations may be rather trivial, but they help to underscore the point that the "true civilization" which Logan helped to nurture and the "new way of life diametrically opposed to the old way" which was the goal of the Spanish priest on Palau implied much more than the change of a few religious values. Missionary activity in Micronesia was geared to a sweeping program of social reforms; the model was the civilization from which the agents of this reform had come.

The blatant ethnocentrism of these early missionaries appears shocking to us in hindsight, but it was only representative of the conventional wisdom of the day. The Christian mission was conceived and carried out as a *civilizing* mission. The meaning of an indigenous church for these early missionaries fell far short of what we imagine it to be today. The phrase was understood to mean that once converted, the "heathen" were to perpetuate the church and the civilization that had been graciously brought to them from across the sea. The native pastors were to be the caretakers of an essentially foreign institution that had been bestowed on their people. The end product of this effort was, as the Filipino Jesuit Horacio de la Costa observed, "not a native church, but a church staffed by natives" (1972:119).

The church was not a young shoot planted in the strange soil of a foreign land to take root and grow as it might, but a greenhouse plant that could only thrive in the carefully regulated temperature and sheltered protection of the hothouse. If the conditions simulated those of the country to which the plant was endemic, it might flourish. Otherwise, it would shrivel and die. Thus, while it was partially the result of unconscious cultural biases, the missionaries' drive to instill "true civilization" was also prompted by the desire to do what they could to create the only type of environment in which they imagined Christianity would thrive.

Missionaries could hardly have been expected to make any serious attempts to reconcile their gospel message with the cultural tradition of the people when they looked upon the latter as basically inimical to Christian values. Even if the old missionary refrain about "native ways steeped in degradation and debasement" need not always be taken at face value, it is clear that the missionaries regarded a good many elements of Micronesian culture as being subversive of their evangelical work. Even the language itself came under attack on this score. "The native language and purity," one foreign missionary on Ponape wrote, "can never travel the same road." He went on to explain that the natives "have sounds to represent all the bad, but their vocabulary is as barren as are their hearts of all good" (MH 1855:101). The same point was made by another missionary when he wrote that the languages of Micronesia, which are "wonderfully prolific in unchaste and impure words and terms," are "destitute of words and phrases to convey correct ideas of God and moral subjects generally" (Damon 1861:485). If the very language was little more than a reflection of the "moral and spiritual nakedness and deformity of the people" in the eyes of many a missionary, then it is difficult to see how other parts of the culture could have been more highly regarded.

Communal land ownership was another traditional practice that often drew fire from missionaries. Lack of private property, they argued, prevented the development of individual initiative and responsibility: virtues that were generally thought of as indispensable to a genuine Christian morality. The conviction of one pastor was that:

> Humanity here is a soft and viscid mass, with just enough consistency to resist all separation into parts, but not enough to assume an independent shape and bearing. We are obliged to work upon the whole, the mass as such, because we cannot find an individual. In fact, there is no such thing here as an individual action or individual responsibility (MH 1855:101).

To combat this "socialism," as they called it, a few of the Protestant missionaries in the 1870s attempted to introduce gradual reforms in the landholding system on Ponape through the establishment of a homestead plan that gave each man full title to his own plot of land. However, to bring about this legislation the missionaries found that they had first to work out ways of democratizing the tribal government, the result being the founding of a kind of municipal legislature (Crawford and Crawford 1967: 190). In the end, their efforts to dispense with the communal ownership of land proved unsuccessful and they were driven to tinkering with a number of interlocking traditional institutions in the name of Christian morality.

In his study, *Political Factionalism in Palau,* Arthur Vidich shows the unforeseen social and economic consequences of a more successful attempt by a missionary group to alter traditional institutions. Interference by the German Capuchins in Palau, he maintains, eventually put a halt to institutionalized warfare and concubinage that had formerly served the important function of conferring wealth and prestige (1949:53-54). Like the Congregationalists on Ponape, the Capuchin priests saw these traditional features of the culture as baneful to Christian morality. They could not have understood the enormous effect that the cessation of both ritualized warfare and concubinage had on Palauan culture. But even if they had, they surely would have fought for the abolition of both on moral grounds.

These missionaries were suspicious not only of those elements of native culture which they perceived to be a direct threat to the gospel message, but also of rather neutral parts of the same culture. The presumption was that everything, no matter how slight, was liable to be contaminated in some way by pagan perversion. In the words of an anonymous missionary on Truk, "the whole life of the pagans is determined by their religious views, so that even a seemingly harmless custom is connected in some way or other with religion" ("Some Remarks" 1915:17). In the face of what they saw as a culture "steeped in degradation," it is understandable that missionaries should fear for the purity and integrity of the gospel message that they bore. Syncretism was a danger that had to be avoided at all costs, even at the risk of making Christianity appear a far more alien belief system than it might have been otherwise. The missionaries' response, then, was ordinarily flight from the culture rather than a proclamation through the culture.

This analysis, of course, does not do complete justice to the complexity of the situation. Not all missionaries were cut from the same cloth, to be sure. A survey of missionary literature reveals a rich variety of personalities with, as we might expect, widely differing opinions on many matters. And then, too, the attitudes of individual pastors toward the people and their ways could change to an astonishing degree as they gained deeper insight into the culture. The same missionary who judged the Ponapean language "as barren as the natives' hearts of all good" and who flailed the spirit of communalism for hindering individual responsibility wrote in a far different vein of Ponapean religious belief after twenty-five years in the field:

> The Ponapean heathen are very far from being irreligious. . . . It is to our great advantage that we recognize the religious faith of these people. Paganism is infinitely more cultivatable than atheism. The heathen who sees God in everything is a much more hopeful subject for the missionary than one who sees no need of God. We do well to study the religious thoughts and habits of these people. We ought never to attack their beliefs or worship. It will not compromise our religion to recognize them as our fellow religionists. . . . We gain nothing by weakening the heathen's veneration for diety (Crawford and Crawford 1967:74).

Statements like this serve to correct the mistaken impression that early missionaries as a genus were incapable of seeing any value in traditional cultures. Indeed, some of the best ethnographic studies in Micronesia were written by missionaries like Walleser, Erdland, and Salesius, who had more than a merely academic interest in the customs and beliefs they described.

Even if most missionaries did carry with them a pronounced sense of cultural superiority over the natives, this did not necessarily vitiate their effectiveness. It is clear from some of their writings that a genuine respect and affection existed between these men and women and the native peoples they served. Logan's distinctive trademark—the black umbrella he always carried with him into the middle of a fracas between hostile parties on Truk—guaranteed his safety and usually brought an end to the fight. He was much beloved by the Trukese, who shed tears of grief at his funeral in 1887. If the relationship of the missionary with his flock was decidedly paternalistic, this was not altogether the fault of the former. Most church members were only too well aware of the awesome prodigies the white man had created with his superior technology and were inclined to listen respectfully to his religious beliefs. They would have been as little likely to shout down a foreign preacher with charges of cultural imperialism as they would have been to do battle full tilt with a foreign man-of-war in their sailing canoes. They had, for the most part, acquired a healthy respect for the power of the foreigner.

We may suppose, in the absence of real documentary evidence, that the tendency of church members after some exposure to mission influence was to cling hard and fast to the foreign symbols of Christianity. Religious medals, short hair, white smocks, and the like would have been the badges of acceptance into the new (even if still somewhat unintelligible) society. They would have reassured natives of their membership therein, much as the black trousers and white shirt of the government employee accomplished the same purpose a few years ago in a different sphere. The convert syndrome is a widespread phenomenon among new Christians and naturalized citizens alike that produces a conservative set of attitudes toward the institutions of the social group they have just joined. It is easy to imagine that the majority of Christian converts would have earnestly desired to retain religious practices exactly as they received them from the hands of the foreign missionaries. Even the plans of the first churches, which were singularly ill-suited for a tropical climate with their small windows and boxlike construction, appear to have been rigorously imitated by native pastors in succeeding years. So, too, was the precise order of the service. The same could be said of religious hymns, which for many years were simply translations of such New England standards as "Never Be Afraid to Speak for Jesus" and "I Am So Glad that Jesus Loves Me." To depart from conventional models in favor of something better adapted to local needs requires that the innovator feel at home in the institution, have a firm understanding of its nature and purpose, and possess a good bit of self-confidence. These conditions were not met in the case of the native pastor or catechist.

Overall, we can conclude that for a number of reasons the attitudes of both missionaries and native Christians were not conducive to the cultural adaptation of religious practices and teachings to the local traditions. Indigenization meant, in the case of the Protestant churches, a native clergy supported by a native congregation; but it went no further than this. Catholics had not progressed nearly as far in promoting native church leadership or working toward self-support, although they tended to be somewhat more tolerant of native customs. Neither Catholics nor Protestants adopted any policy that might deliberately promote a synthesis between the Christian faith and the people's culture. As a consequence, Christian churches in Micronesia remained carbon copies of their Western models.

"NEW INDIGENIZATION"

The liberation of religious faith from its Western trappings requires nothing short of a revolution, and this did not take place until the last two decades. The rise of nationalism in Africa and parts of Asia, which followed the movement of many ex-colonies toward political independence, brought with it a new consciousness of the Third World and its aspirations. One theme that emerged strongly in every quarter was the quest for identity. The new states, once they had achieved political freedom, were bent on achieving selfhood and discovering what they really were and what they were to become. It was only to be expected that these aspirations should be reflected by religious leaders, as De la Costa points out, and that they find their echo in the churches (1972:122). Always influenced by the mood of the age, theological reflection focused on the importance of respect for a people's cultural identity during the course of missionary activity. While the faith must be brought to foreign lands, it was now held that evangelization could and must be done in such a way as to avoid the inadvertent colonialism of bygone missionary days. Christianization and Westernization were finally seen as two quite different things, and it was realized that care had to be taken by the missonary not to confuse them in his work among a non-Western people. The Christian message, although it is not shaped by the national aspirations of any people, should be able to accommodate these aspirations easily, for Christianity is not the possession of a single nation or culture but of the entire family of humankind. It should not, therefore, be represented as identifiable only with a particular cultural group.

These new theological currents were publicized and legitimized for Catholics during the 1960s in several documents issued by the Vatican II Council. One of these documents states expressly that the "Church is not bound exclusively and indissolubly to any race or nation, nor to any particular way of life or customary pattern of living, ancient or recent" (Abbott 1966:264-265). Missionaries, then, were called upon to be collaborators or partners in the establishment of the native church rather than the sole architects of this work. To put it in other metaphorical terms—those used by Ivan Illich in an essay on missionary work—

the missionary is a midwife who assists in the birth of a "new community in the world" (Illich 1970:105). To be sure, he must introduce new beliefs among the people to whom he is sent. He proclaims, as he has always done, that Jesus Christ is the lord of the universe and the unique manifestation of God to men, and that he lives on in his people through the Spirit. Moreover, the missionary message is a challenge to the people who receive it to reexamine and reorder their values and ideals, both collective and individual. The "new missionary" does not harbor illusions, any more than his predecessors did, that he is leaving the culture perfectly intact. Nor does he want to leave it unchanged. If he did, he would not have come overseas in the first place.

Unlike his predecessors, however, today's missionary is wary of taking it upon himself to determine the precise nature of the response to the message he bears. He is most loath to wield the ethical scalpel to excise those parts of the culture that he might regard as "diseased," for he is aware of his own limited understanding of his people's ways and the values that are implicit in them. Furthermore, recent theological movements have taught him that the final form of the church should not be the product of the missionary but of the local people working together with the missionary. In this setting, he is to work not so much on behalf of the people as *with* the people. If the missionary is called to preside over the church during its infancy, he must be extremely careful to allow it to develop in its own unique way. In time, the ritual and worship as well as the preaching and theology should grow out of the living culture and express the singular character of the people for whom the church exists. The task of the missionary, then, is to help the local people to whom he is sent fashion a church in which Christianity is thought and lived in terms of the people's cultural tradition.

New emphasis in post conciliar Catholic ecclesiology has been placed on the relative autonomy of the local churches to balance what had in the past been a one-sided stress on the unity of the universal Catholic church. Catholics have slowly regained sight of a truth that had always formed a basic tenet of Protestant missionary activity—that the church is in fact composed of churches. Only when this principle is paid its due can structures be developed that really meet the needs of the local church. Rites need not be conducted in a universal ecclesiastical language, seminary training need not meet a universal standard, worship need not follow a single pattern.

On the other hand, Protestant churches, which had tended, by and large, to limit mission activities to those of a more directly religious nature, have begun to embrace a broader vision of the missionary role in the Third World. A statement by the National Council of Churches of Christ of its goals for the mission in the 1970s reflects a deepening concern for human development, as do other documents of this period. Although the summons to religious faith is still very much seen as the express goal of missionary work, there appears to be a thrust toward a multiform type of ministry that takes greater account of the concrete human needs of different communities.

With the advent of a new national consciousness among former colonies (and the theological repercussions it has given rise to), the stage was set for a new era in the indigenization of churches. The ripples of this movement have been felt in Micronesia only since 1970.

CURRENT THRUST OF THE CATHOLIC MISSIONS

In the remainder of this chapter, I shall discuss this new thrust toward indigenization—or enculturation, as it might be called more properly—exclusively in terms of the Catholic Vicariate of the Caroline-Marshall Islands. Although it is not my intention to belittle recent Protestant missionary efforts in this direction, there is reason to believe that the Catholic mission has assumed a pioneering role of late. Just as it was the Protestant churches that took the lead in implementing a concept of indigenization in an earlier age, when the Catholic mission was not yet prepared either tactically or ideologically to carry out such a policy, so it appears now that the Catholic church has taken the lead in formulating policies for the realization of the new notion of indigenization. The reasons for this apparent reversal are not altogether clear. Perhaps the Catholic mission, which has had so much more ground to make up, has been swept forward by the revolutionary impact of the Vatican II Council and the call to church reform that it sounded. It is also possible that the very success of the Protestant drive to establish native pastors may have retarded further movement toward enculturation at this time. Just as it has been observed that African clergymen who have undergone Catholic seminary training frequently return to their land "more Roman than Romans," it may be that the foreign-trained Protestant ministers are habituated to think of the church they have received from the hands of their mentors as definitive. Whatever the reasons, we shall proceed on the assumption that the Catholic mission in Micronesia today has found itself in the position of the standard-bearer for the new indigenization.

The first meeting of the Vicariate Pastoral Planning Council (VPPC), in June 1971, was a watershed for the Catholic mission in Micronesia. This meeting of representatives from the entire vicariate charted a new course for Catholic missionary work in the islands. Three years earlier, at the first mission-wide meeting of Jesuits in Micronesia, plans were laid for a future pastoral congress at which the needs of present-day Micronesia would be assessed and programs shaped to answer these needs. In addition, the diaconate was discussed and approved as a suitable means of promoting native church leadership. However, the significance of the VPPC lay in other things than the programs that eventually resulted from it. The theme that dominated the first two-week session was the self-realization of the Micronesian people. The church of Micronesians must be truly a Micronesian church; it must be their own. But beyond this, it must reach out to serve the needs of the entire society. Moreover, the greatest service it could render to the Micronesian community at large, at this stage, is to assist people in acquiring a greater sense of power and control over their own society and to subordinate foreign elements in their society to Micronesian direction. Only in this way could the church contribute to the development of a genuine sense of pride and self-esteem: qualities that are perhaps the most badly needed now. At a time when Micronesians are subject to numerous pressures from without, caught in the teeth of cultural change and conflicting values, and confronted with problems that they have never had to face before, their self-confidence is bound to be weakened. Pride in themselves and their institutions is the inner resource on which everything else in the development of Micronesia depends.

What emerged from the VPPC discussions was a widespread appreciation among participants that one age had ended and another had begun in Micronesia. If at one time the greatest needs of the people of Micronesia were better housing, a more varied diet, roads and dock facilities, and the other paraphernalia of material development, an entirely new set of needs were surfacing now which would demand the churches' attention. Without denying the importance of these other things, members of the Vicariate Planning Council directed their attention to those social and psychological needs that often follow upon a period of rapid cultural change in a society. An individual and communitarian sense of self-respect was singled out as the most pressing of these. It was agreed that Micronesians had been told in hundreds of subtle and not-so-subtle ways that they were only second-class citizens in their own land. A foreign-born educational system, begun decades before by missionaries themselves, was imposing on the Micronesians the burden of having to meet alien standards and then condemning them to mediocrity when they failed to do so. Okinawans, Koreans, Filipinos, and Americans were building their schools, running their hotels, fishing their waters, and laying their water pipes. The effect of this was to make people ask whether there was not anything that they could do and do well. While planners, managers, and even churchmen pondered the quickest and cheapest way to get the job done—with thoughts focused only on the quality of the finished product—many Micronesians wondered aloud whether they would ever be real participants in the creation of their own society. Everywhere the problem seemed to be the same: a sense of powerlessness and futility in the face of a progress that was hurtling on with awesome speed.

As a consequence, the missionary thrust of the Catholic church in the Caroline and Marshall Islands has changed (if we may oversimplify a bit) from promoting material development as measured by Western standards—better houses and better schools—to helping people achieve a sense of self-confidence and mastery over their destiny. The ideal missionary is no longer the man who has erected edifices, whether concrete buildings or parish clubs. He is the man who has given of himself so that his people might learn who they are and what they can do. This is not to say, of course, that housing cooperatives and schools have been simply jettisoned. But there has been a perceptible shift in emphasis during the past five years or more, and if such institutions slowly fade away it will be owing less to their financial difficulties than to a reordering of priorities on the part of the churches. Missionaries have always seen themselves as jumping into the breach to meet the most urgent needs of the day as they perceived them, and in our time they are recognizing that a different set of problems has come to the fore. "The society, and with it the church, must be restored to the people" has become the rallying cry of the new missionary; not to gratify his own liberal political fancies nor to emulate what has become fashionable in other parts of the Third World, but to make persons whole once again in the conviction that they can be masters of at least their own corner of the globe.

The concern of Catholic missionaries has become more than indigenization of the church; it is indigenization of the society itself (if we may speak of such a thing) with all its political and economic structures. This new thrust has appeared in different forms, not all of which are explicitly church-related. It is not really surprising that the missionary concern for indigenization should carry beyond church matters to the secular sphere, for it was from what they observed there that Catholic priests and nuns first sensed its importance. As is usually the case, stirrings were first felt in the City of Man and only later were they related to what was afoot in the City of God.

Although it is difficult to generalize on such matters, one could say that the prevailing spirit among Catholic missionaries now is something resembling "power to the people." Not just ecclesiastical structures but all structures should somehow be brought under the control of the Micronesian people. After all, if the goal is to nativize the church, why should not the hotels, fishing industries, and even the government itself also be nativized? The same logic that has urged missionaries to turn the workings of their own churches over to Micronesians also urges that foreign investment be carefully controlled and that the government eventually belong as completely as possible to the Micronesian people. In contrast with former ages, missionaries have started recently to lean heavily in the direction of the traditional rather than the modern, the Micronesian rather than the foreign. This applies equally to clothes, foodstuffs, legal codes, and roofing materials. Although often mistaken for a type of cultural archaism that idealizes the past and downgrades the value of innovation from abroad, this new missionary attitude is based on a recognition of the fact that precisely those parts of the Micronesian cultures which are most unique are also the ones most capable of helping people affirm their individuality as a group. We might say that the distinctively Micronesian cultural elements are of more value than those they share with nations of the developed world, at least for the purpose of symbolizing an identity of their own. And certainly attainment of a corporate identity is one of the most critical problems facing Micronesia!

The consequence has been a spate of mission-sponsored conferences, workshops, and training programs whose aim is to inform people regarding the social, economic, and political realities of life in Micronesia today. Other conferences, held for a limited number of higher-level participants, have tried to promote discussion of political status and educational goals. Since 1970 the emphasis has been primarily on increasing the awareness of the populace and stimulating them to confront the major problems of their day. In most programs of this sort sponsored by the Catholic mission, there is a discernible bias toward what might be called "societal indigenization."

With respect to the creation of a native church, efforts at indigenization have been concentrated in three main areas: leadership training, financial responsibility, and the incorporation of meaningful cultural symbols into worship and preaching. The first of these, leadership training, was implemented with the first diaconate training program on Ponape in 1971 and on Truk and Yap in 1973. About the same time, teams of catechists were trained to visit the villages for a week or two at a time. The intent of these programs was to prepare Micronesians to take responsibility for communicating the religious message to other Micronesians rather than to have the foriegn missionary do it himself. Like the second element, financial responsibility, the emphasis on preparation of native leaders was late in coming to Catholic churches in Micronesia. The third element, founded in the obvious principle that what is religious is not necessarily Western, was implemented with the first adaptations of liturgy to include such traditional symbols as the bestowal of the *mwaramwar* 'head garland' at baptismal rites and the use of kava at penitential ceremonies on Ponape.

But neither brown-skinned men in the pulpit nor 'head garlands' at the baptismal font suffice to make a church truly indigenous, as many missionaries have accurately testified. One author, writing on African churches, points out that it is often the Westerner who picks and chooses those elements in the culture that he judges suitable for religious worship and compatible with Christian doctrine. Often such attempts lead to mere tokenism with its "superficial substitution of African songs for Western hymns and drums for organs" (Gilliland 1973:345). In such cases, the outsider finds later to his dismay that he has selected appealing but often meaningless cultural items for assimilation into what remains essentially a foreign system. Such benevolent cultural paternalism is at heart artificial and ornamental. So, too, is the cultural romanticism that sometimes inspires it, for an indigenous church must be a living part of today's culture, not yesterday's.

Likewise, the training of native pastors, while indispensable, will not of itself guarantee the indigenization of the church. What must also be communicated to the members—and future leaders—of the native church is the propriety and even urgency of using those things that are distinctive to the people in the religious response they make. They must know in a profound way that God bids them fashion their church out of whatever woods and metals are to be found in their land rather than slavishly following the specifications set down for the construction of the Temple of Jerusalem. They must know that their own culture is the stuff out of which religion is made and that the church must take on the shape of the unique culture in which it is situated. If this idea is not conveyed somehow, native pastors will be simply lackeys of their white teachers and do nothing more than imitate what the foreign missionary has taught them for years.

If the missionary avoids the pitfalls of sterile archaism, cultural romanticism, paternalism, and tokenism in his attempts to assist in the indigenization of the church, he still faces the most dreaded of them all—neo-colonialism. Yesterday the missionary stood before his congregation and told them of the glories of his culture; today he stands before them to proclaim the wonders of their own. But if the content of the message has been changed remarkably, one thing might all too often remain the same: the oracular tone of the missionary's pronouncements on cultural superiority. One of the greatest tactical problems that the churches in Micronesia face today is how to speak out in endorsement of the local cultures while avoiding the taint of neocolonialism in doing so. If indigenization of the entire society is of real importance as a goal in Micronesia today, how can restoration to Micronesians of the power of choice and self-determination be preached without the church appearing to take sides in political and economic issues that, strictly speaking, are outside its competence? The very fact that the Catholic church in the Caroline-Marshall Islands has been charged by many Americans and Micronesians with adopting a political stand in favor of independence—and, therefore, of yielding to the temptations of neocolonialist ways—points out quite simply how real the dilemma is for the contemporary missionary.

CONCLUSION

For all the risks the missionary faces of adopting the same paternalistic or colonialist stance that was all too evident in the past ages of mission history, the missionary goal of indigenization has run a far course since the coming of the first Congregationalists in 1852. Indigenization of the church, which one author described as a "new creation: a march into the future, and not a return to the past or mere adaptation of the present" (Gilliland 1973: 346), is quite an advance from the "self-financing, self-governing and self-propagating" church that was the goal of the early ABCFM missionaries, and even more of an advance from the European-bound church that the earliest Catholic missionaries envisioned. The indigenous church, as today's missionaries understand that term, implies a true cultural synthesis between the gospel message, even in its Western cultural form, and the living culture of the people who respond to this message. The resulting religious response, while maintaining some continuity with the traditions of churches of the East and West, should be a unique entity reflecting that which is singularly the culture's own.

Furthermore, in Catholic circles at least, the newfound emphasis on self-identity as one of the most urgent needs of the Micronesian people is bound to lead to continuing efforts on the part of foreign missionaries to extend indigenization to areas outside the church. It will mean missionary involvement in such secular areas as politics and economics, even if their involvement lays the missionaries open to charges of adopting partisan positions and meddling in areas that are not directly related to church work.

Indigenization has always been the proclaimed goal of missionary activity. Yet it is only in recent years that this term has come to mean more than the capacity of the local church to furnish sufficient human and material resources to perpetuate itself. A truly native church, as it is understood today, can only mean one that throbs to the pulse of the living culture. It is one that draws upon the life forms of the people. If such an understanding of "native church" was impossible for early Catholic and Protestant missionaries in the Caroline and Marshall Islands, it was because they professed to save the islanders from their culture. Today Catholic missionaries profess salvation for both the islanders and their culture. Even if the dangers of crypto-colonialism are every bit as great today as they were for Spanish Capuchins or American Congregationalists in the last century, due recognition has at least been granted to the principle that Christianity does not demand that Kusaie be made over into Boston or Yap into Madrid.

THE IMPACT OF VATICAN II ON THE MARISTS IN OCEANIA

Gerald A. Arbuckle

Early in his *Nicomachean Ethics,* Aristotle felt the need to stress the complexity of his subject. "It is a mark of the educated man and proof of his culture that in every subject he looks for only so much precision as its nature permits."An effort is made in this chapter to pinpoint the impact of the Vatican II Ecumenical Council (1962-1965) on attitudes of a religious congregation of men working in Oceania. Attitudinal change is rather difficult to assess but, with Aristotle, we take comfort in the thought that in studying this subject we must be content if we attain as high a degree of certainty as the matter of it admits. The main part of the chapter consists of an analysis of responses of missionaries to a series of theological orientations presented to them. The responses indicate just how far the new values in missionary activity have been internalized and what influence they have had on action.

The religious congregation, technically called the Society of Mary, known popularly as the Marist Fathers, is today the main clerical force of the Catholic church in Western and American Samoa, Tonga, Fiji, New Caledonia, New Hebrides, Wallis and Futuna, Solomon Islands, and Bougainville (Papua New Guinea). The congregation, which has 306 members in Oceania, has been very slow to localize since approximately 90 percent of its missionaries were born outside the area, mainly in France, Holland, Germany, Ireland, the United States, New Zealand, and Australia. Theological orientations were examined in two lengthy questionnaires on missionary life submitted to all members in the area in the first part of 1974. All the above regions, except Wallis and Futuna, were visited by the survey team over a seven-month period. The questionnaires, which required four or five hours for completion, were filled in individually and privately by respondents who remained anonymous. Cooperation from the missionaries was excellent: 98.4 percent filled in the questionnaires, although not all questions were necessarily answered by all respondents. To supplement material gathered from the questionnaire responses, interviews were held with missionaries, individually or in groups, and with various lay people and government officials.

HISTORICAL BACKGROUND

The Society of Mary was formally approved by Pope Gregory XVI in 1836 as a religious congregation of men within the Catholic church: "The principal aim proposed by this Society is that of increasing the glory of God and the honor of His most Blessed Mother, and of spreading the Church of Rome whether it be by the Christian education of boys or by missions even in the remotest parts of the world" (Gregory XVI 1836:875). Approbation of the new congregation had been hastened once Rome knew that the founding members were prepared to send personnel to distant Oceania (Wiltgen 1971:149). Since various Protestant churches had already begun to establish themselves in the area, Rome considered the sending of its own missionaries a matter of urgency. With the fervor of a new congregation to encourage them, but with little knowledge of the physical or cultural environment of the region, the first Marist missionaries left France for Oceania in 1836.

Until the Vatican II Council the purpose of evangelical activity for Marists, as for most other missionary congregations within the Catholic church, remained simple, uniform, and consistent: souls were to be saved by conversion to the Catholic faith from paganism and from Protestantism. Historically the church had been committed in theory to respect local cultures, or at least to tolerate them. The Twelfth Ecumenical Council of the Lateran (Canon IX), for example, insisted that national minorities be respected:

Whereas in many parts of the world peoples of different languages are mingled together within the same city or diocese, having one faith but a variety of rites and customs, we strictly command that the bishops of such cities or dioceses shall provide suitable men, who shall celebrate the Divine Office and minister the sacraments of the Church to them according to their diversities of rites and speech, instructing them both by word and example (Eppstein 1935:387).

In 1951, eleven years before Vatican II, Pope Pius XII reminded missionaries that "the Church from the beginning down to our own time has always followed this wise practice: let not the Gospel, on being introduced into any new land, destroy or extinguish whatever its people possess that is naturally good, just or beautiful" (Pius XII 1951). Despite these and many similar official statements down through the centuries that what "is naturally good, just or beautiful" among local cultures should be respected, in most mission lands, including Oceania, the expression of the church's teachings and its liturgy showed little regard in practice for "the local way of doing things." It is true that some Marist missionaries wrote at great length on local customs to Rome and elsewhere, but their interest was generally considered to be rather in the nature of a hobby. Evidence of the Marist missionary neglect of local cultures is vividly present in the style and structure of church buildings of the period. When Marists built solid church buildings in Oceania, they were fine copies of Gothic churches in rural France or Germany. Sometimes there was adaptation to climatic differences, but no adaptation to local art or architectural forms.

Since Marists came to Oceania as members of an international religious congregation, it is important here to outline what membership in the congregation demanded. In church law a religious congregation or institute is a society of men or women approved by legitimate ecclesiastical authority, the members of which commit themselves to strive after Christian perfection by the profession of public vows of poverty, celibacy, and obedience, and according to the laws proper to their society (Bouscaren and Ellis 1953:23). The approved rules of a congregation set out certain basic norms that members are expected to follow. The congregation's administrative structure exists to safeguard these basic norms, to remind members of their responsibility to follow the rules, and generally to help members achieve the purpose for which they entered the congregation. Although a religious congregation commits itself to work in a diocese headed by a bishop, church law sets out areas of autonomy for the congregation. While a bishop has full powers over works he has explicitly assigned to the congregation, he has no authority over the internal running of any congregation formally approved by Rome. Hence when Marists left for Oceania in the nineteenth century they left as members of a religious institute. They were therefore committed to follow definite norms and give allegiance in internal matters to an administrative head based in Europe.

But, almost immediately on arrival in the Pacific, Marist missionaries quickly found that rules made in Europe were often ineffective in the geographically isolated islands of Oceania. They found they were unable to develop an identity as a distinct religious congregation or to evolve missionary policies uniquely their own. While the rule demanded that Marists live together in communities, the conditions they found in Oceania made it generally impossible to follow such a regulation. The number of missionaries available was small, but the areas to be covered were immense. Moreover, missionary policy of the period dictated that the people be contracted as quickly as possible in order to be saved from the "darkness" of paganism or the "heresies" of Protestantism. Hence the practice developed of missionaries working and living alone. In addition, administrative difficulties quickly emerged that hindered the evolution of Marist identity right through to the 1960s. Bishops often interfered in areas of administration that legally pertained to the Marist superior. But the latter, based in Europe, despite vigorous efforts to stop the interference, was too distant from the scene of action to be effective. In 1858 an effort was made to solve the problem. Bishops in Oceania were formally made the official representatives of the Marist superior. But in practice the problem remained unsolved. Bishops, somewhat understandably since they were the official representatives of the mission policy of the period, tended to consider the needs of the missions first, showing little practical concern for the needs and rights of a religious congregation. For them, community life was a luxury that simply could not be afforded; personnel had to be scattered as widely as possible if souls were to be saved (J. Hosie 1971:223-224; Keys 1957:203-205; Roach 1963). In 1898, Marist missionaries in Oceania were grouped into an administrative unit called a province under the leadership of a superior or provincial. But the effort to provide a legal structure that would guarantee Marists the opportunity to develop their commitments to their religious congregations failed. This was inevitable since the structure was merely a legal fiction: the provincial could offer advice to bishops only on matters relating to Marists as religious, not as priests. Marist autonomy as a religious congregation in Oceania would not be achieved until 1969.

Marist missionaries certainly reflected the missionary zeal that characterized many new French congregations of the time. Though not necessarily reckless on the point, martyrdom was realistically considered a possibility and a personal blessing in their efforts to win converts to their message. On one occasion, Father Jean Claude Colin, founder of the congregation, addressed departing missionaries: "You are leaving your country, parents, friends—everything—to save souls and to suffer martyrdom. Yes, it is true, because, if not a martyrdom of blood, it will be a martyrdom of hunger, thirst, heat, problems, anxieties and tears" (Coste 1965:158).

By 1854, 117 missionaries had been sent to Oceania of whom 21 had died by that year, some violently at the hands of local people. One missionary wrote to a confrere in France in 1847:

> Tell young people . . . who are disposed to come to the missions but are, perhaps, afraid of the apparent sterility of our ministry, that the chance of martyrdom and the glory of being the first apostle of a country are well worth the pain of renouncing for a time at least the satisfaction of seeing the word of God flourish (Laracy 1970:130).

The ideal of personal sacrifice, if not actual martyrdom, remained strong in the minds of Marist missionaries in the century that followed.

VATICAN II ORIENTATIONS

In late 1962, the Vatican II Ecumenical Council opened in Rome, the church's twenty-first ecumenical council and the first since

Vatican I of 1869-1870. The assembled bishops stated their aims clearly in the "Message to Humanity": "We shall take pains so to present to the men of this age God's truth in its integrity and purity that they may understand it and gladly assent to it." The council, which ended in 1965, did in fact often make dramatic efforts to adapt the church's teaching and discipline to the needs of the contemporary world, including those of mission areas. Consequently, the council marks a definite turning point in the theology of mission within the Catholic church.

The council made a strong appeal to the essentially community dimension of church, moving away from what it considered the earlier overemphasis on the individual: "It has pleased God, however, to make men holy and save them not merely as individuals without any mutual bonds, but by making them into a single people, a people which acknowledges Him in truth and serves Him in holiness" (*"Lumen Gentium"*:9).[1] "Missionaries must raise up congregations of the faithful" (*"Ad Gentes"*:15), who "everyday must become increasingly aware and alive as communities of faith, liturgy and love" (ibid.:19). One study put the new stress (or rather the return to an ancient idea) in this way:

> Before Vatican II many priests considered that the Church was an instrument of individual salvation. Their pastoral activity was centered on the distribution of the sacraments, the instruction of the catechumens, and the care of the "lost sheep." With the coming of Vatican II, the Church is increasingly seen as a community. In this perspective the primary role of the priest is to build up the Christian community (Commission for Catechists 1972:7).

The council sought to restore a balance so that the concept and reality of local churches took their rightful place. Prior to the council, the concept of the universal church had been overstressed to the detriment of the local congregation or churches. The local church is now seen as the legitimate realization of the Universal Church at a particular time and place (*"Lumen Gentium"*:26). Vatican II affirmed the value of pluralism in the church. It portrayed the church not as a huge, uniform monolith but as a fraternity of local churches, each of which seeks to realize the gospel in accordance with the native genius and traditions of its own members. Particular stress was to be given to adapting the expression of belief to local cultures; worship had to be expressed in the art and the language understood by the people (*"Sacrosanctum Concilium"*:37). The emphasis is one of dialogue or interaction with local cultures, not domination or condescension. At one point the council refers to this interaction as a process of exchange. Customs not in conflict with basic Christian principles are to be seen as good in themselves and as living testimony to humanity's efforts to develop gifts given by God. The process of interaction must be the responsibility of local churches if authenticity is to be achieved (*"Ad Gentes"*:22). It was recognized that many isolated attempts at cultural adaptation had failed in the past, or remained the hobbies of a few, because many missionaries had entered alien societies without adequate preparation. Hence not only did the council make a dialogue with cultures obligatory, but it insisted that missionaries be trained in the required social sciences (ibid.:23-27).

As a consequence of the stress on dialogue, every effort had to be made to avoid physical or moral coercion in encouraging people into the church. Freedom of religion and belief had to be respected. Any move to conversion had to be based on the personal conviction of people themselves (*"Dignitatis Humanae"*: 2). The council also stressed the service dimension of the church. It is not sufficient to preach the message of justice. Action must follow: not directly for the sake of conversion, but because justice is to be seen in this world as the sign of the perfect justice in the world to come (*"Lumen Gentium"*:48).

Vatican II reflected on the role of religious congregations in mission areas. They were strongly encouraged to maintain and develop further their particular identities but in the service of the people. In the past, little attempt had been made to adapt the external forms of religious congregations to local conditions and customs. Too frequently they were seen as mere transplants from the Western world. Now forms of life and exercises of piety conditioned by their age and social milieu had to be adapted to local cultures or nations (*"Perfectae Caritatis"*:3).

In brief, the values stressed by Vatican II for missionary activity varied greatly from those that prevailed over the previous century or more. Most frequently the values underlined were not new. Rather they were a return to ancient tradition or to the logical consequences of such tradition. Since Vatican II, theologians have tended to emphasize progress and evolution on all levels—theological, political, social, and economic. The theological outlook on the world is optimistic with Christ at the peak of an unfolding human history. God and the world are viewed as interrelated: God reveals himself in men, things, and events and continues his creation in the development of the world. Vatican II stressed a dialogue with the world; post-Vatican II theology has rather emphasized the interrelationship of the church and the world. Hence the humanistic trend in Vatican II has now become more marked in theological reflections (see Gutierrez 1972).

CONTEMPORARY MARIST ORIENTATIONS

One anthropologist, Clyde Kluckhohn, defined a value as "a conception, explicit or implicit, distinctive of an individual or characteristic of a group, of the desirable which influences the selection from available modes, means, and ends of action" (Parsons and Shils 1951:395). We are here concerned with values in this sense. We aim to discover just how far the value system inherent in the teachings of Vatican II has been internalized by Marist missionaries. (Obviously we are not concerned about the objective validity of the value system.) We are also interested in discovering how far the Vatican II value system has effectively changed the actions of missionaries. After all, people can believe in an ideal without its influencing their behavior, although the contradiction may not be evident to those concerned.

Missionaries were presented with a series of statements on the concept of church, salvation, ministry, purpose of missionary activity, and involvement in socioeconomic activity. The three or four statements under each heading in actual fact could be fitted into three categories: pre-Vatican II, Vatican II, and post-Vatican II theological orientations. Respondents were not given these categories, but merely the statements from which they had to choose what appealed to them most.[2] In brief, the responses showed that in a number of crucial areas most respondents have a strongly Vatican II and post-Vatican II theological orientation. No significant differences in the pattern of response could be detected either between the two age-groups analyzed ("forty-four and below" and "forty-five and above") or among the various regions in which Marists work.

As regards the concept of church, 45.2 percent considered it as "the people of God, intimately related with Christ; the Church is a sacrament or sign of man's union with God and with each other." This is Vatican II orientation. A further 31 percent reflect post-Vatican II thinking, most considering the church as "the pilgrim in this world, a servant of mankind's total needs." A much smaller number (3.8 percent) opted for an extreme post-Vatican II position on the church as "the prophetic critic of society and culture." Only 20.1 percent showed pre-Vatican II orientation. For some of the latter (12.6 percent), the "Church, as mediator of God's grace and truth to men, is the *only* true way to salvation"; others (7.5 percent) took a more traditional view still: "The Church is a perfect religious society organized under the Pope and the Bishops."

As regards the concept of salvation, 58.6 percent have either a modern or very modern view: 31.6 percent accepted Vatican II thinking that "God's grace of salvation is equally at work within each man," 15.2 percent held to the post-Vatican II stress that "*all* Christian Churches are channels of God's saving grace for men," and 11.8 percent showed an ultramodern view in their belief that "all religions are channels of God's saving grace for men." However, 41.4 percent held to the pre-Vatican II stress that "the Catholic Church is *the* medium of God's saving grace for men."

Vatican II and post-Vatican II views on the purpose of missionary activity are readily accepted by the great majority of respondents. Fifty percent claim that the purpose of missionary activity is "to be witness of God's love, preach and form the Church among people who do not yet know about Christ," which is the Vatican II orientation. A further 41.6 percent accept the post-Vatican II orientation that the purpose of missionary activity is "to help man develop his own resources to fulfill total human needs, i.e., religious, economic, educational, political." Only 6.7 percent claim a pre-Vatican II orientation. For them the purpose of missionary activity is "to convert people to the Catholic Church through preaching, teaching, catechism, administering the sacraments."

On the theology of ministry a very high percentage reflect modern and contemporary thought. A reasonable minority (38.9 percent) hold to the Vatican II stress that "the minister is someone whose fundamental obligation is to spread Christ's Gospel and to administer the sacraments to the faithful." A small majority (50.6 percent) believe in the post-Vatican II theological thrust: "A Christian minister is someone who has been authorized by the people of God to build the Christian community, lead it to its celebration of the sacraments, and inspire it to share actively in the world's concerns." Only 10.5 percent favored the pre-Vatican II orientation: "The Christian minister is someone ordained to the priesthood and thereby authorized to celebrate the Eucharist and administer the sacraments of Penance and anointing of the sick."

A similar pattern is to be found regarding the relationship of mission to development or socioeconomic change. The post-Vatican II emphasis that "development is an essential part of mission work" is held by 35.8 percent, and 26.7 percent favored the Vatican II orientation that "development is useful to show people that the Church is relevant." On the other hand, 30.1 percent opted for pre-Vatican II views that "development work helps the missionary to make pastoral contact with people" or that "it has no direct connection with missionary work, but it can be useful." Only 7.3 percent would advocate an extremely pre-Vatican II opinion that "development work is dangerous, it distracts the missionary from his real work."[3]

There is further confirmation that a significant impact has been made by examining the responses to other questions relevant to the themes. Marists were asked to what extent stress, compared to the present level of effort and the needs of the church, should be given to the seeking of converts from other Christian churches. Only 13.7 percent considered there should be more stress on conversion; 50.2 percent favored the present emphasis and 36 percent thought there should be less stress or none at all. A good majority (69.1 percent) agreed that "the Church in Oceania has expanded far enough; our main task should be to deepen the quality of the people's faith." As regards missionary involvement in economic development with the people,

49.5 percent thought that more stress should be given to such activity, 34.6 percent the same, and only 15.8 percent less or none at all. There was also strong support for more involvement in agricultural education: 71.9 percent wanted involvement increased, 18.8 percent favored the present level of involvement, and only 9.3 percent favored less involvement or none at all. Marists have traditionally been committed to secondary education, but by comparison with involvement in agricultural education, only 30.9 percent would wish more emphasis on this type of work.

In view of responses to other questions, it is somewhat surprising to see that such high percentages reflect Vatican II or post-Vatican II theological orientations in crucial areas of missionary activity. While many thought that they themselves were quite up-to-date on Vatican II thinking, 74.7 percent confidently claimed that their colleagues were definitely not, or only partly, well informed. Moreover, 87.0 percent stated that their confreres were not, or only partly, well informed on modern theological trends. Since the Marist missions are generally very isolated from the centers of theological thought, it is difficult, despite the poor image Marists have of one another's theological thinking, to explain just why so many are oriented along modern theological lines. Despite a little skepticism on the part of this writer, many claim that they read good theological texts regularly. Many return to Europe or the United States on regular leave, but most do not undertake special updating studies while absent from Oceania. It is possible that in recent years some new missionaries trained particularly in Holland or Germany have influenced the thinking of their confreres. Discussions held with visiting preachers may also have contributed to the growth in theological thinking.

THE IDEAL VERSUS THE REAL

Despite the generally widespread internalization of modern theological values, the survey revealed serious divergences between the expressed ideal and its actual implementation—in the understanding and use of local customs and languages, for example, and in the relationship between missionary and lay people.

About two-thirds asserted that their colleagues were not reasonably well informed on local customs and culture. A significant minority (43.6 percent) claimed that the Marists in their area could not communicate well in local languages, and a small majority admitted that they themselves could not communicate well in local languages. It is understandable that difficulties are experienced in Melanesia, but significant minorities in Polynesia thought that their confreres and themselves had insufficient grasp of the languages.

Theology and liturgy can be adapted to local needs only if three requirements are fulfilled: first, understanding of local customs; second, fluency in the language of the area; and third, sensitivity to the fact that adaptation is not something to be imposed but must grow out of community dialogue and decision. By their own admission, a good percentage of Marists would find it difficult to fulfill these three requirements. As regards the third, 70.7 percent agreed that "too many priests consider their parish their own little kingdom, and do not share enough responsibility with local people." A significant minority (39.9 percent) agree that local people find European missionaries too domineering; a further 42.1 percent agree that "we are seen as foreigners, with little interest in adapting the faith to local cultures."[4] If these observations are accurate, then the right type of relationship, empathy, or atmosphere does not exist in many parishes that would permit the necessary dialogue upon which liturgical adaptation must be built. Over 83 percent felt that missionaries in the past did not make real efforts to adapt the liturgy to the needs of the people. Moreover, 59.6 percent believe that this is still the situation today. In the author's mind this latter response is still somewhat optimistic. Too frequently, the mere translation of official Roman liturgical texts into the local language is considered to be sufficient adaptation. In fact, this is really only touching the surface of the problem.

Prior to Vatican II, theology and tradition had so emphasized the role of the priest in his parish that he held power over all parochial affairs. Laity would be consulted or asked to assist in decision making only if the parish priest so desired. Vatican II theology changed the position of the laity within the church dramatically. According to the principle of shared responsibility, laity were to become involved in the conducting of parish activities (*"Lumen Gentium"* :37). To provide opportunities for laity to share responsibility with the parish priest, the formation of local administrative councils was vigorously recommended. In the period before Vatican II, Marist missionary activity at the parish level merely mirrored the pattern found commonly elsewhere in the church: it was heavily clerical. Parishioners were rarely consulted on matters relating to the running of their parishes. Many Marists recognize the problem, since 62.7 percent agreed that in their respective regions "the Church had been rather late in giving responsibility to local people" and 97.3 percent agreed that in consequence more, or at least the same, stress should be given to the formation of parish councils. Opinions differed as to how far the clergy should go in giving responsibility to lay people within these councils. One-third felt that the parish council should give advice "but also have a say in pastoral matters, such as decision making and finance." A further third would hold to a slightly more liberal view: for them the parish council should have a "great say in all matters, including pastoral and liturgical matters." About 20 percent went still further by saying that the "parish council should be the real governing body, and the priest should be prepared to step down as a personal director in charge." Such an opinion would effectively reduce the priest to the equivalent of an employee of a lay council. Only about 5 percent would hold to the pre-Vatican II view that "the parish council should help the priest by doing the work entrusted to it by him."

Despite protestations that the laity have been neglected as potential coworkers with the missionary and despite the admission by many missionaries that more stress should be given to involving lay people at various levels of decision making, the reality seems widely divergent from the ideal. The Vatican II Council ended in December 1965, but by 1974 only 55.4 percent of the missionaries had actually established parish councils. Of these, 10.8 percent claimed that the parish council was not very successful, 36.9 percent considered their councils were making some progress, and a further 7.7 percent felt their councils were doing well. On the other hand, 10.8 percent admitted that they did not have councils "for they did not think they were necessary"; 22.8 percent asserted that while councils were necessary they had not started them; and 11.5 percent said that they were starting councils "right now." Even if we allow for variables outside the control of missionaries, there is still a significant gap between the ideal stated and the actual implementation of that ideal.

OBSTACLES TO IMPLEMENTATION

The survey responses to a variety of questions offer some reasons for this evident discrepancy between the ready acceptance of new theological orientations and their apparent lack of influence in important areas of missionary action. According to Vatican II, "a diocese is that portion of God's people which is entrusted to a bishop to be shepherded by him with the cooperation of the presbytery" (*"Christus Dominus"*:11). The bishop in charge of a diocese has the authority and the obligation to lead in pastoral matters. It is assumed, therefore, that he will initiate, with the cooperation of priests and others in his diocese, definite planning to meet the needs of the people. But in Oceania, 61.5 percent of Marist missionaries felt that their bishops did not in fact provide the necessary long-range planning. Only 20.5 percent could definitely state that information about their bishop's plans for the diocese was readily available to them, and only 45.8 percent felt that they had a sufficient voice in diocesan planning.

There are possibly some very sound reasons for this obvious communication gap between the eight bishops in Oceania and their missionaries and explanations for the lack of leadership that missionaries expect from their bishops. Prior to Vatican II, political, social, and economic changes in Oceania were gradual. But at the same time the council was taking place, change in these areas became increasingly rapid. Formerly, missionaries knew exactly what was to be taught. They knew the needs of the people, who lived fairly static lives. But in the early 1960s the situation altered, sometimes dramatically. With the increase in urbanization, culture contact, and social disorganization, the missionary began to feel much less certain of the people's needs. New missionary methods were required to face the new challenges, but few Marists felt equipped to devise new missionary responses. Up to that stage, the role of bishops had been confined to fairly simple administrative concerns. Missionaries conducted their own parishes and stations with a minimum of supervision from their bishops. But with the changes on the local scene and with the decline in the number of volunteer priests and religious from overseas, a malaise began to develop in missionary policy. This inevitably placed bishops in an extremely difficult position. Missionaries began to turn to them for leadership they had never asked for in more secure times, and bishops themselves, having become used to the demands of day-to-day administration only, were ill-equipped for the new role.

Prior to Vatican II, bishops in the Catholic church tended to follow a traditional type of leadership. Though there were understandably exceptions, bishops commanded and the clergy obeyed with little expectation that the clergy had any right to be consulted on diocesan policy. The council requested that at all levels— parish and diocese—there had to be due consultation. Only then could authority proceed to decision making and planning. But for those accustomed to a different type of leadership adapted to a previous age, the transition to this modern systemic leadership method is fraught with all kinds of difficulties (Rudge 1968:21-36). Missionaries themselves were unaccustomed to consultation. Since they lived isolated lives, they had developed considerable independence in the management of their work and parishes. Thus they were not prepared to change suddenly to communication and cooperation among themselves and with ecclesiastical administrations.

Marists in Oceania work in eight small dioceses. Fiji, the largest, has a Catholic population of 47,000; the smallest, Wallis and Futuna, has 8,000. The survey aimed to discover if, in fact, missionaries considered themselves united within their respective dioceses. While 50.2 percent felt that they were united socially and 45.2 percent felt united in spirit, only 26.7 percent thought they were united in apostolic action. In Fiji only 32.1 percent definitely felt that Marists were united, while only 25 percent felt this way in Wallis and Futuna. As for the reasons for this lack of cooperation, 64.2 percent believed that "the lack of adequate communication and sharing at all levels has hindered the growth of true community" in their respective areas; 66.7 percent felt that "excessive individualism has caused a lack of proper concern and interest for colleagues and their work"; 55.4 percent agreed that "their colleagues do not want to work with others"; 74.8 percent felt that "colleagues are so used to living alone that to live with others would be impossible"; and 66.2 percent considered that "colleagues do not want to lose their independence." In the Diocese of New Caledonia, which is staffed by forty-five Marists, 81.8 percent claimed that their "colleagues do not want to lose their independence." One Marist from this diocese summarized the problem bluntly: "Too many of us have lived and worked too long by ourselves in our own little parish kingdoms. We are frightened to give up our independence which we have enjoyed for so long."[5]

Since Marists first arrived in Oceania in 1837, they have been severely handicapped by a lack of specific training for their work. It was taken for granted that the training in theology and in pastoral methods adapted to Western conditions was sufficient. Basic missionary sciences were either ignored or touched on only lightly. In the survey, for example, 93.8 percent admitted that linguistics was either not included or given insufficient stress in their formation program; 89.5 percent said the same about social anthropology, 85.4 percent about the principles of socioeconomic development, and 74.9 percent about the principles of mission adaptation. Only 23.9 percent definitely felt that their formation as Marists had adequately prepared them to be missionaries. Of the 306 Marists in Oceania today, only 3 have formal academic qualifications in social anthropology (Bachelor of Arts). Moreover, there has been no tradition of giving particular orientation within the dioceses to incoming missionaries.[6] As one elderly missionary in the New Hebrides observed: "The best way to learn about the people and the work is to be thrown as soon as possible on arrival into the villages." One missionary from Bougainville recounts his own initiation into missionary activity: "When I arrived in the 1940s, I went to an elderly confrere to seek advice on how to approach the people. He told me to kneel down. I did. He gave me his blessing and then pointed to a distant mission station. 'Go, you have my blessing. The boat leaves in thirty minutes.' I went feeling thoroughly inadequate for the job."

Many are clearly not at ease with the gap they perceive between the values they have internalized and their failure to alter long-established methods of approach. Visitation of parishioners and villages, even though the travel involved is often difficult and considerable, has always been regarded as a basic pastoral activity by missionaries in Oceania. But a high percentage believe that this visitation is no longer being done as often as it should be, or as it was done in the past. The reasons given for this decline are varied. But 87.6 percent agreed, though sometimes with reservation, that missionaries were simply caught up in nonessential activities on their stations or in their parishes, and 80.6 percent agreed at least partly with the view that they were being held back from visitation because they had failed to "train local people as managers of their station." Most felt that these obstacles had to be overcome, since 70.7 percent considered that far more stress should be given to visitation.

When they were asked what should be done constructively to face the challenges of rapid social change and the decline of the practice of religion among the people, 90.1 percent readily accepted the view that "there is an urgent need to improve apostolic methods." A small majority felt "that we are too concerned with traditional apostolates and methods, e.g., the maintaining of mission stations, because we are too conservative, [and] unwilling to try new, and even radical, apostolic methods of approach." Most did not consider that a mere increase in the number of priests in Oceania would solve the problems they faced. The real challenge to change lay within themselves. They generally recognized that they had to learn to work and plan common action together, even though this meant breaking down entrenched individualism and isolationism. Many, at all age levels, felt the need for expert guidance to help them achieve the desired changes in attitude and structure. Eighty percent (91.9 percent below the age of forty-five and 68.5 percent above) asked for in-service courses by specialists in such subjects as social anthropology, socioeconomics as adapted to village life, and mission adaptation.

VATICAN II AND MARIST LIFE

Sociologically, most religious congregations were founded by some charismatic figure whose insight into Christian life drew others to follow him. His particular insight was then shaped into laws and regulations. In time, routinization and institutionalization endanger the original spirit and reform movements are required to bring the congregation back to the insight of its founder. One of the important thrusts of Vatican II was directed to stimulating religious congregations to reform or renewal. This renewal was to consist of two simultaneous processes: firstly, a continuous return to the sources of all Christian life and to the original inspiration of the particular founder; and secondly, an adjustment to the changed conditions of the times (*"Perfectae Caritatis"*:2).

Partly as a result of this Vatican II emphasis, the Marist congregation in Oceania ceased to be very much a legal fiction. I noted above that circumstances of geography, and the necessity to spread resources as widely as possible to win converts, gave local bishops extensive powers over Marists, powers normally reserved to religious superiors. In these circumstances, there was little effective identity as a religious congregation or sense of overall cohesiveness. But by 1969 the congregation, through its localized administrative unit (provincial administration), was making contracts with the eight bishops which would permit it to act within limits as a normal religious congregation with legal rights and privileges. Hence religious superiors at last had effective powers over members and the authority to establish the congregation with an identity in its own right. In 1971, religious superiors and representatives of all Marist missionaries working in Oceania met in an assembly, called the provincial chapter, to clarify the values and establish the norms that must guide Marists as men belonging to a particular branch (province) of an international religious congregation.

In the survey, an effort was made to assess the degree of commitment by Marists to the values and norms of the now structurally reformed congregation. Membership in a religious congregation gave 92.7 percent of them a definite or partial sense of belonging and identity. A good majority did not regret their decision to join the Marist congregation, and 78.4 percent considered that "their religious life has been a major factor in their happiness and success in the priesthood." Many felt that to some degree or other their membership in the congregation had been of value and meaning to them. While 86.8 percent definitely or partly felt they were achieving "an increasing sense of fulfillment as Marists," only 13.2 percent thought this was not the case in their lives.

But in the light of other questions on the nature of religious life and its obligations, the overall impression given is that approximately a third are in varying degrees not oriented toward religious life. Certain basic values pertaining to religious life impinge little—if at all—on their day-to-day living. Of the three religious vows, poverty, celibacy, and obedience, the vow of obedience is of particular relevance to this chapter. The spirit of the vow, if adhered to, particularly directs members to work toward the common good and develop group cohesiveness. While the great majority of respondents conceded that the vow does have a positive meaning for them, there were some significant differences of opinion on the actual nature of the vow. Respondents could choose one of three definitions. A very small minority (8.5 percent) considered that obedience demanded "the sacrifice of their personal goals and activities for the goals and activities of the congregation." Taken to its logical conclusion, such obedience would reduce members to something akin to machines, with no will of their own. A higher percentage (26.4) accepted the definition that obedience required them "to coordinate their personal goals and activities with the goals and activities of the congregation." This would reduce a religious congregation to something akin to a "gentlemen's club." Members would cooperate with one another only as long as their personal aims were not interfered with. Real group cohesiveness would be impossible if such a concept prevailed in a religious congregation. Almost two-thirds (65.1 percent) accepted the systemic concept, which is the "coordination and, if necessary, the sacrifice of personal goals and activities for those of the congregation." This last concept of obedience commits members to work out together the aims of the group and the means to achieve them. The obligation rests on those in authority to see that this widespread participation by members is in no way discouraged. Once the final decision has been made by authority, in the light of the discussion on aims and means, members then have the responsibility to commit themselves effectively to what has been decided. Ultimately, therefore, the control within the group depends on the commitment of each member to the organization's goals. This assumes that the goals have been clearly worked out, for they are the magnets that not only cause the individual parts of the organization to move but also draw members together.

As noted, Marists in Oceania belong to a particular province of the international congregation—that is, to a definite administrative section of the congregation based in the Pacific. In 1971, at the Provincial Chapter of Marists in Oceania, this administrative section was further decentralized so that eight regions within the province became the basic religious communities for Marist missionaries. The head (regional superior) of each region, which normally consists of between ten and forty-five men, was assigned definite administrative powers and made answerable ultimately to the head (provincial) of the province based in Fiji. According to the legislation:

> The regional superior, assisted by his councillors, has the task of animating and unifying the members of his regional community, in order to promote the apostolic work entrusted to them as well as the personal fulfillment of the religious in his region. . . . He will strive to inspire a spirit of service and cooperation in order to promote the effective and harmonious collaboration of all (Oceania Province 1971:12-13).

The survey aimed to discover to what degree a sense of belonging to a definite region had been achieved and to what extent regional superiors within the regions were assuming effective systemic leadership.

Of the respondents, 63.2 percent claimed that they definitely felt a sense of belonging to their regional community, and a further 19.3 percent felt only partly this sense of belonging. Most thought that their colleagues in their respective regions were in fact developing "a sense of region-wide community." But, as already noted, many Marists admitted that there were serious obstacles to the development of effective teamwork. Social unity is valuable, but commitment to a missionary community demands thorough collaboration founded upon open communication. This is the social purpose of the obedience. Most felt that excessive individualism, the desire among members to maintain independence, and the historical problem of living too long by themselves had all inhibited cooperation.

But the survey also shows that Marists generally feel their regional superiors are not providing sufficient leadership. The pattern of dissatisfaction is similar to that found in relationship to the leadership in the dioceses by bishops. Approximately 40 percent felt closer ties to their bishop than to their regional superior. Significant percentages of Marists complained that there was a lack of dynamic leadership by their regional superiors and that the latter, with their assistants, were not trying sufficiently to unify the Marists in their region. There is, however, a strongly felt need for regional superiors to assert vigorous leadership in the development of community spirit. But the systemic consultation requested by Vatican II is seriously lacking in the minds of Marists. Many complained that they do not have sufficient information on what the Marist regional administration is planning for their region, despite the protestation that they are definitely interested in policy decisions. Approximately two-thirds felt they had little or no voice in the planning of Marist affairs in their region. A significant number claimed that even when they did make suggestions to their regional superiors for improving collaboration for apostolic activity, little serious consideration was accorded them. Given the obvious communication gap, it is not surprising to find that 73.3 percent were uncertain about the exact apostolic or missionary goals of their regional administrations. With group goals uncertain, cohesiveness becomes difficult, if not impossible.

For their part, regional superiors are in very much the same position as bishops. Missionaries have quite suddenly felt the need for leadership, owing to the malaise that has resulted from the rapid social changes among the Pacific peoples themselves and from the almost revolutionary changes in missionary thinking that have emerged as a consequence of Vatican II. Up to 1971, when the provincial chapter was held to restructure the province, regional superiors had practically no power at all. They were mere figureheads with only vague powers of supervision over the religious life of Marists. Suddenly everything was changed structurally. Having been given considerable powers, even for apostolic supervision, the superiors have no past models of leadership. They recognize the need to consult, but are not certain just how this is to be done. Some have tended on occasion to seek support in the authoritarianism of the past; others have drifted into laissez-faire leadership. When this had happened, dissatisfaction and individualism among missionaries have intensified. Their problems of leadership have been exacerbated by the development of theological pluralism among missionaries after Vatican II. Missionaries are no longer united on what should be taught to the people. Even when they do agree, they are divided on the methods of instruction. This is something quite new to the regional superiors and often impossible for them to handle in discussions. It also seems that in some instances Marists, owing to the lack of decisive leadership from their bishops, are turning to their regional superiors for guidance in areas of pastoral life that are well beyond their ecclesiastical authority.

CONCLUSION

According to a leading Vatican official, Pietro Sigismondi, the missions staffed by Marists in Oceania are in a sense "the most difficult in the Church" (Buckley 1961). They are confined to small islands scattered over a vast ocean. Transport and general communications are difficult. And the commitment to a strategy that tended to isolate missionaries quite naturally cultivated a rugged type of individual with a strong sense of independence. Yet as members of a religious congregation, they were committed to close collaboration and even to living together in small groups.

Recently, however, Vatican II reinforced the urgency of building Christian communities and moved away from the emphasis on salvation of individuals, a salvation largely unrelated to the communities in which they lived. This demanded a corresponding response from missionaries. To build communities among the faithful, the missionaries had to develop closer community bonds and cooperation with one another. This, in turn, demanded a new type of ecclesiastical and religious leadership.

This chapter has outlined a paradox: although many Marist missionaries have accepted the values of Vatican II, there is little indication that these values are in fact influencing behavior to any significant extent. In the first place, since collaboration on a region-wide basis scarcely exists, though social contact has increased, there is little detailed discussion among members on how

Vatican II values can be applied to the local situation. For the ideal to influence the concrete situation, thorough discussion is essential before any realistic planning and apostolic collaboration is possible. Marist missionaries never felt the need for this in the past. Now they do. Yet problems of individualism—a product of the past—and theological pluralism—a product of recent times—combine to inhibit such discussion. At root, it is a problem of attitude and will. Leadership is itself confused, reflecting the malaise within regions and dioceses. The expectations of missionaries are ambivalent. On the one hand, they look for firm, even authoritarian, direction; on the other hand, they refuse to accept authoritarian decisions when given.

Despite these difficulties, the survey revealed that definite strengths are emerging. Morale is generally good. The great majority still believe in the validity of their missionary work, though they are somewhat confused about what they should be doing. They recognize the urgency of closer collaboration, but they also see what they must give up to achieve it. The survey did not, however, indicate whether there is a strong will to make the necessary changes. Since 1971, administration of the Marist congregation has altered along systemic lines. There are signs in some regions that the new structures are being used for discussion and collaboration in effective planning. It is quite possible that these moves will develop still further and spread to other regions.

In mid-1975, the survey team returned to the regions (with the exception of the small and remote region of Wallis and Futuna) to explain the findings of the detailed survey reports which had been distributed for study several months previously. Attendance at the workshops was excellent, and it was immediately evident that in many instances the reports had been carefully studied.[7] The aims of the workshops were essentially twofold: first, to give missionaries the chance to question the accuracy of the survey findings; second, to provide Marists with the opportunity to make practical recommendations for action. Throughout the discussions, the accuracy of the survey was never called into serious doubt. The subjects for discussion at the workshops were decided upon by the participants themselves. In all cases, the problem of collaboration received priority. It was clear that this would demand a radical rethinking and a change of heart. In three regions plans were made to establish experimental team ministries; that is, three or four missionaries would share pastoral responsibility for a definite geographical area that had been divided into rigidly distinct parishes. Four regions decided to seek expert assistance to help them develop closer collaboration among themselves and with the people. In some regions Marists called for firmer leadership, insisting that regional superiors use their authority to guarantee collaboration in pastoral activity. This was particularly noticeable in two regions, the Solomon Islands and Bougainville, where individualism has especially characterized missionary activity. In view of the objectivity shown by the missionaries in the workshops in facing up to the problems disclosed by the survey findings, there are good grounds to expect that the gaps between Vatican II and reality will narrow in the future. But, with the poet Simonides, it can be said of the recommendations made in the workshops that "there is no better test of a man's work than time."

NOTES

I am particularly grateful to John Harhager, who acted throughout as my research assistant.

1. The references cited in the text refer to decrees issued by the Vatican II Ecumenical Council. The number references are to paragraphs, not pages. For a complete list of these decrees, see the entry "Vatican II Ecumenical Council, 1962-1965" in the References at the end of this volume.
2. I am grateful for the assistance provided by the Society of the Divine Word Self-Study Survey, Rome, in the formulation of some of the theological questions.
3. Marists before and after the Vatican II Council have involved themselves in educational activities and, to a lesser degree, in socioeconomic projects aimed at village development. But such involvement seems rarely to have been considered an essential part of missionary activity; it was regarded as secondary and viewed by the missionary as an aid to evangelical work (see Laracy 1969: 203-205, 312-335). Hence the pre-Vatican II response noted here is significantly small and indicates a notable shift toward contemporary theological thinking.
4. A different questionnaire was filled in by 350 religious Sisters of the Missionary Society of Mary who work in the same regions as the Marist Fathers. Among other things, they were asked to comment on the work of Marists: 54.6 percent felt that Marists were definitely, or in part, "domineering towards the people"; 90.4 percent considered that "the people tend to see Marists in general as paternal figures in the community"; 72.3 percent thought that "in general, there is a hesitancy on the part of Marists to encourage the people to accept more responsi-

bility for Church affairs."
5. Marist personnel are quoted several times in this chapter, but for reasons of confidentiality their names and other relevant information have been withheld.
6. Since 1968, new missionaries in the Solomon Islands and on Bougainville may receive short missionary orientation courses at the Melanesian Institute for Pastoral and Socio-Economic Service, Goroka, Papua New Guinea. In Fiji the diocese has language programs for new missionaries wishing to learn Fijian and Hindi.
7. The workshop in New Caledonia was the first known occasion that Marists had come together to discuss purely Marist affairs.

PART 4: INDIGENOUS RESPONSE

INTRODUCTION

Sharon W. Tiffany

Indigenous reaction to missionary enterprise in Pacific island societies has not been uniform. The chapters in this part consider varying responses to the missionary presence, with emphasis on the secular and ideological components of missionization, its influence on different aspects of island social systems, and the variety of contemporary indigenous adaptations to these events.

In chapter 12, Peter Black considers the response of an atoll population to the conversion efforts of an individual missionary. Black analyzes the processes of indigenous interpretation of the statements attributed to Father Marino, a Spanish Jesuit priest, during his short visit to Tobi Atoll in the Caroline Islands around 1933. Father Marino's visit was preceded by a series of critical events for the islanders: depopulation, the administrative takeover by the Japanese in 1918, and the collapse of the traditional politico-religious hierarchy of chieftainship. The priest's visit came at a time when Tobians were attempting to restructure their social and ideological order in response to these disruptive events. Father Marino's acts, such as his baptism of the people and efforts to legitimize monogamous unions, have been incorporated, along with indigenous interpretations of the priest's utterances, into a corpus of beliefs that reinforce important elements of the traditional Tobian sociocultural system.

Black's central thesis is that Tobian interpretations of Father

Marino's utterances constitute a closed and interconnected ideological system that "expresses Tobian truths about the nature of man, society, and the supernatural." Black argues, moreover, that this system has withstood attempts at restructuring by later Catholic missionaries. Black examines the differential transmission, dissemination, and revalidation of Father Marino's messages and how his verbal and physical acts presently serve as justifications for continuing those beliefs and behavior thought compatible with his word. Father Marino's acts and statements are viewed from the Tobian perspective, thus emphasizing the islanders as active mediators and translators of the ideological components of missionization.

Dorothy Ayers Counts' chapter on the Kaliai of Northwest New Britain is concerned with the relationship between ideology and socioeconomic change. Established in 1950, Kaliai mission is a major agent of both ideological and secular change. In addition to their religious duties, the mission staff runs a trade store, buys copra, and dispenses educational and medical services. Counts examines how the mission personnel view their role in Kaliai—and how they, in turn, are viewed by the patrol post officers, the local expatriate residents, and the Kaliai people. Differing expectations, perceptions, and interpretations of mission actions have resulted in antagonism and conflict. The patrol officers have seen the priests as unwanted meddlers in local affairs, while the establishment of the mission station on a disputed parcel of land has generated conflict among the Kaliai.

The success of the mission depends in large part on the compatibility of the mission's objectives and the people's values. Thus the mission's policy of discouraging polygyny and bridewealth is acceptable to those who are willing to abandon these practices as unnecessary economic burdens. Others who continue to pursue their goals through traditional means view the mission's attitudes differently, however. Among the Kaliai, variation in response to the mission is expressed in the Story, a local cargo movement. The syncretistic ideology of the Story movement reflects both Kaliai and Christian belief and ritual. The movement illustrates Story members' attempts to reconcile rising aspirations with the frustrations of attempting to obtain new goals through politico-religious ends. Indigenous response to the secular and doctrinal aspects of the mission enterprise in Kaliai is a process of continuing change.

In contrast to the recent introduction of missionary activity to Tobi Islanders and the Kaliai, Tongans and Samoans have been in contact with missions since the early 1800s. Tonga and Samoa are fully evangelized: approximately fourteen different denominations are represented in the archipelagoes, some of which, such as the Congregational Christian Church in Samoa, the Free Church of Tonga, and the Church of Tonga, are autonomous indigenous organizations. The church provides an important source of organized social activity in Tongan and Samoan villages. The week is filled with a round of scheduled events which include choir practice, women's fellowship, Bible discussion groups, and prayer services.

Denominational multiplicity in Tonga and Samoa is associated with the option of changing church affiliation that provides opportunities for obtaining a variety of political, economic, and personal goals. The reasons for denominational switching in Tonga and Samoa are broadly similar, although the social structural contexts and personnel involved in such changes differ in several respects.

Shulamit Decktor Korn is concerned, in chapter 14, with the considerations that support changes in denominational affiliation in Tonga. Church membership provides an important forum for individual status striving through active participation in congregational activities and lavish feasting, which often requires the economic assistance of kinsmen who may belong to different denominations. The optative elements of Tongan social organization support not only the proliferation of different denominations but also changes in affiliation. Individuals change their affiliation for a variety of reasons unrelated to doctrinal differences. Some denominations actively compete for adherents through vigorous proselytizing and offer members access to special services and advantages that are eagerly sought by Tongans, such as secondary education, employment, and emigration opportunities. Recently the Mormon church has been particularly successful in increasing its membership through such incentives. Congregational memberships cut across village boundaries, kin groups, and, not uncommonly, household memberships. On the village level, denominations do not compete. The relation of different congregations to each other is one of "tolerant avoidance" which, according to Decktor Korn, is a tension-reducing accommodation to the fact that local congregational memberships crosscut other ties.

The decision to change one's church membership in Tonga is largely an individual affair, whereas in Samoa denominational changes reflect shifts in political alignments of chiefs and their followers. Changes in denominational affiliation are frequently precipitated by chiefly antagonisms and descent group rivalries that follow traditional points of cleavage characteristic of intervillage and intravillage relationships. A change in church membership in Samoa is an important and highly effective medium for expressing discontent and tends to exacerbate already existing tensions between opponents. Denominational competition which reflects underlying conflicts may be intense. This theme is illustrated by my description, in chapter 15, of the antagonism between two coholders of a chiefly title who used church-related issues as a reason for opposing each other.

The politics of denominational affiliation in Samoa involve economic considerations as well. Village and congregational rivalries are partly expressed in recurrent constructions and dedications of new church edifices. Villagers take pride in the magnificence of their churches and their ability to provide lavishly for their pastors, who are accustomed to a high standard of living and enjoy considerable prestige and privileges comparable to those of high-ranking chiefs. A major portion of congregational activity is involved with allocating and distributing goods, money, and services to the local pastor and participating in a variety of church-sponsored projects and events.

From these chapters we gain some understanding of the complex variables involved in the study of local adaptation to missionary enterprises in the Pacific. This response has been influenced by the nature of indigenous social systems, the type and extent of Western contact prior to the missionaries' arrival, the circumstances of the initial mission-islander contact, the specific enterprises undertaken by the missionaries, and the duration of their contact. The arrival of Father Marino on Tobi Atoll, at a time when the inhabitants were demoralized by depopulation and the collapse of their traditional politico-religious order, had a profound impact on their interpretation of Christian doctrine and subsequent missionary visits. By contrast, the missionaries in Samoa encountered a vigorous sociopolitical system whose members readily acknowledged the powerful Christian God but retained supreme confidence in their own institutions. In Kaliai, the presence of other Western institutions and the nature of the island mission enterprises have been key variables in determining indigenous responses to the priests. The relationship between the mission and the Kaliai people is in large part structured by the islanders' frustrated economic aspirations resulting from prior experiences with Western and colonial institutions. The duration of contact with mission influences is a significant element in assessing islander response and adaptation to mission enterprises. The Samoan and Tongan Islands have been exposed to mission influence for almost 150 years and have proceeded beyond the "frontier" missionary situation that exists in Kaliai to the establishment of locally autonomous church organizations. Christian religion has been thoroughly indigenized during the transition from mission to church in Tonga and Samoa.

There has been a tendency among anthropologists to view missionization as an exogenous force unilaterally impinging upon passively recipient peoples. As these chapters demonstrate, this view is misleading. Mission enterprises in Pacific island societies have in fact consisted of continuing interactions of Western and indigenous religious beliefs, structures, and institutional arrangements. Guiart (1962:122) has argued that Christianity in Oceania is "in many ways an entirely new phenomenon: the reinterpretation of occidental traditional religious ideas and structures by people who have chosen to make use of them as their own." The chapters in this part are convincing evidence of the processes of choice, interpretation, modification, and creation of religious beliefs and institutions. Pacific islanders have indeed made Christianity their own in a complex variety of ways.

THE TEACHINGS OF FATHER MARINO: CHRISTIANITY ON TOBI ATOLL

Peter W. Black

The people of Tobi, a small remote atoll in the Western Carolines, became Roman Catholic in the 1930s. The conversion occurred en masse during the brief sojourn of a Spanish Jesuit priest named Father Marino, the first missionary known to have visited the island. Apparently Father Marino made only this one short but extremely successful visit from his mission headquarters in Koror, the capital of Palau District in which Tobi is located.

The Tobians are a religious people and faithfully adhere to the beliefs and practices of their new religion as they understand them. Each day at dawn and again at dusk they gather together in their church to say the rosary. Every three or four months a priest comes to their island for a few hours and they all earnestly confess sins committed in his absence and eagerly flock to the church to hear mass. All pre-Christian religious and magical rituals have been abandoned and the old sacred chants are heard no more. The Catholic rituals for birth, marriage, and death are thought to be of great importance and are performed with enthusiasm. The high festivals of Christmas and Easter are the focus of much preparation and enjoyment. A number of women belong to sodalities, special church organizations that require dietary restrictions and extra prayer. Prayer marks many kinds of behavior. Meetings are begun and ended with prayer, as are formal meals. Individuals can often be observed sitting apart with hands clasped and heads bowed in silent prayer. Sundays are marked by an absence of work and a more elaborate church service which is attended by the people in their best clothes.

If questioned about their beliefs most people are able to present reasonably intact versions of traditional Catholic thought. They are familiar with such concepts as the human soul, divine love, hell, purgatory, and heaven. Quite accurate explanations of the Trinity, the Virgin, the Fall of Man, and the nature of Christ's mission are also common knowledge. Young people who have attended mission school in Koror are the recognized local experts in these topics and the older people have learned much from them. Many episodes from the Bible have become part of the storyteller's repertoire, and the exploits of Adam and Eve, Noah, and various other Old and New Testament figures are often told. In short, the conversion of the islanders seem to have been strikingly successful. The perception shared by the Tobians and their priests of the island as a Christian place seems to be quite accurate.

These observations of current religion and religiosity on Tobi give rise to three questions. Why was Father Marino, in the absence of either force or prior missionary activity, so successful? Why are the people so conscientious in the practice of their new religion? Why is there no local variation in Catholic belief and ritual? These questions involve issues of importance to anthropology as well as to an understanding of missionary activity in the Pacific. They are closely related and all three stem from the assumption that the religion of a given people is seldom, if ever, an isolated phenomenon. It is instead a part of their culture and as such both a response and a way of responding to the exigencies of their situation. From this perspective, aboriginal Tobian religion was Tobi-specific and, like Tobian culture, can be seen as one of many local adaptations of a general, pan-Pacific pattern. Roman Catholicism, inasmuch as it can be said to be unitary, is one of several European adaptations of the Judaic-Christian pattern. Aboriginal Tobian religion probably traced its roots back to Neolithic Southeast Asia and was influenced in its development by the largely obscure events which can be summed up as "the peopling of the Pacific." Roman Catholicism is ultimately rooted in the ancient Near East and has been influenced in its development by events summed up as "European history." Aboriginal

Tobian religion reached its full development on a tiny atoll isolated from the political and economic centers of power far to the northeast in the so-called Yap empire.[1] Roman Catholicism is a worldwide religion, and its history is interwoven with the history of various European power centers and, more generally, with the development of Western culture over the last two thousand years. The differences between the two cultures and, in particular, between the two sets of religious forms are the result of two discrete cultural traditions lived in two very different environments.

The symbols of a religion are one way private psychological states and public social forms are united into a more or less coherent whole. In this sense, religious symbols are channels through which private meanings are invested into shared forms and, conversely, order is offered to the individual in assigning meaning to private states. Both the private and the public poles are, in part at least, determined by experience. Thus whatever the origin of the religious impulse, the symbols used in its expression must be shaped by the physical, social, and historical environment in which they were formed. Why then would a people exchange their indigenous set of religious symbols for a set that arose in radically different circumstances? Specifically, why did the Tobians replace the miniature canoe and wooden phalluses of their old religion with the crucifix and sacred heart? The same question could be asked about the Tobian acquisition of other aspects of Catholic religious life such as myth or ritual. The shallow acquaintance the islanders seem to have had with Roman Catholicism before they adopted it makes the Tobian case particularly interesting. The resistance to change which the adopted forms have shown also makes this case intriguing. The Tobians seem to have made an alien religion their own without significant modification. The frequency with which they engage in "Catholic" behaviors indicates that they maintain a close involvement with those unmodified forms.

When Father Marino stepped ashore on Tobi, he encountered a people who had recently embarked on an experiment in secularism. They had dropped the practice of all their communal religious ritual. Although scattered individuals may have continued to interact with supernatural forces, the islanders no longer acted as a community vis-a-vis the sacred. Even the buildings in which communal ritual had taken place were destroyed along with all the religious paraphernalia they contained. This attempt at secularism failed, and the Tobians became firm Catholics. It is necessary to understand the background of this attempt at seculaism for three reasons: failure to meet certain needs of the Tobian population was probably the most important reason for the speed and success of the original mass conversion; the feelings that people have about the experiment today are some of the most compelling reasons for their adherence to their new faith; and the complex of cultural beliefs, personality attributes, and sociological factors which triggered both the attempt and its failure is still operative today and gives the teachings of Father Marino their special Tobian meanings. Although the decision to make this radical break with the past was implemented literally overnight, the processes which led up to it had been set in motion years before. In act, if we are to understand the events of that night we must go back to the dawn of the modern age on Tobi.

BACKGROUND TO SECULARISM

There is no way to assess the impact of the first Western ship to visit Tobi. The first known sighting occurred in 1710 (Eilers 1936:1), and a clue to the impression it made can be found in the explanation which Tobians offer for *uafarug* 'ship'. This word, a compound formed of the nouns denoting 'canoe' and 'island,' has its origin traced to the first time a ship was seen. It is said that the islanders believed the ship to be an island which had been made into a gigantic canoe. They thought that huge sails had been attached to its trees (the masts) and that the crew observed entering and leaving the cabins were the island's inhabitants going in and out of their houses. This may or may not be an accurate derivation of the term for ship, but it does indicate the alien nature which the West first presented to the islanders.

Bartering soon sprang up between the gradually increasing ship traffic and the island. Tobi was never a port of call like other, better-endowed islands. Although an occasional ship stopped to take on coconuts or other provisions, the majority sailed by without stopping. If sea conditions were right and the ship passed close enough to the atoll, the men would give chase in their canoes. If they succeeded in overtaking it they would barter for metal, that most prized of goods. A class of men arose who claimed to possess magical incantations which had the power to force the ships to come about and wait for the canoes to catch them. These men exercised their power in return for a share in the proceeds of the bartering.

In 1832, a small jerry-built boat with nine Americans and three Palauan castaways aboard drifted into Tobian waters. These men, adrift for fourteen days, were in very bad condition. The Americans were survivors of a whaling ship which had gone aground on a reef in Northern Palau. With their Palauan friends and their homemade craft they were trying to reach Ternate in the Dutch East Indies. The events which followed were forgotten by the Tobians, but fortunately one of the survivors has left us a record of his stay on Tobi (Holden 1836). The Palauans and Americans were allotted to various families as slaves and forced to work in the taro gardens. After four months several shamans, who decided that these men were the cause of the sickness and starvation which had decimated the island, persuaded elements of the population to do away with the strangers. Most of the men who had not already died of ill treatment or malnutrition were killed, but a few were protected by the families which had taken them in. After two years on the atoll, the surviving Americans persuaded their owners to release them to a passing ship by promising that they would help them obtain a large amount of metal. The exchange was made and the sailors departed, leaving the one surviving Palauan to his fate. The following year a United States naval vessel put into Tobi, landed a force of marines, and conducted an unsuccessful house-to-house search for this man.

These events gave Tobi a certain notoriety and, following the publication of Holden's book, foreign vessels were less willing to put into the island or even stop for barter. As late as 1900, some captains felt that allowing Tobians on their ships was simply too dangerous.[2] Others, however, either ignorant of the supposedly savage islanders or confident of their ability to control them, began in the late nineteenth century to recruit men from the island as workers. The population, after an approximate decrease of 50 percent during the two years the castaways were on the island, had recovered its original size by this time and was still growing. Genealogical evidence shows that the men who were recruited by these captains all had many siblings. Most of them were young and single.

Some of these men worked for German functionaries on Yap, the administrative center of Wilhelmine possessions in Micronesia. Others worked for English and Australian shipmasters harvesting the bounty of Helen Reef, an uninhabited atoll 63 kilometers east of Tobi. There were probably no more than a dozen men away from the island at any one time and most of them never made it back to Tobi. A few did return, however, and stories of their adventures are told and retold with relish.

One of the captains who used Tobians for his crew was a man whose name was probably something like Borrie. Apparently Borrie was either English or Australian and was engaged in the bêche-de-mer trade between Helen Reef and Manila. The nickname given him by his Tobian crew was Botchor, which means 'gums'—the story is told that on the first day out from Tobi the captain went into his cabin and reappeared without his teeth. This was the period in which blackbirding or unofficial recruiting of forced labor was being suppressed. The Germans suspected Borrie of blackbirding and eventually tracked him down to Sydney. A trial was held and the Tobian crew, after admitting that they had not been paid by Borrie, were taken to Palau and forced to make rope for one year as "punishment." Afterward they were returned to Tobi to live out their days musing over the curious ways of the Europeans. By this time Europeans were known by a generic term which is still in use today and which translates as 'person of possessions' or 'rich man'.

In 1909, the Thilenius ethnological expedition arrived at Tobi (Eilers 1936). The scientists set up their headquarters in the main spirit house, the building where the chief performed rituals associated with his office. These rituals centered on the chief as spokesman for and, in some senses, as a personification of the entire Tobian community. It was here that people came to participate in the communal rites, and now it was here that they came to have their skulls measured by the anthropologists. A census was conducted and it was found that 968 people were living on the island. The area of Tobi is only 59 hectares; thus the population density at this time was 16.4 people per hectare, which even for the Pacific is quite high. This figure is even more striking when it is compared with Holden's estimate of two hundred Tobians when the castaways escaped from the island seventy-five years before. Even if we allow for a considerable margin of error in Holden's estimate, it is apparent that the island had experienced a dramatic rate of increase.

This upward trend was soon reversed. An epidemic broke out after the visit of the Thilenius expedition, and six months later, upon the arrival of a German government vessel, it was found that two hundred people had died. The doctor on the ship attempted to evacuate the island, but the people hid in the bush and he was able to convince only fifty-one men and one woman to go with him to Yap. Tobians remember the epidemic but do not recall the doctor's "rescue" of the fifty-two people. Possibly this is the same event that lies at the core of a story relating how the Germans took hundreds of men from the island to work in the phosphate mines on Anguar, a Palauan island. I have found no documents to substantiate this claim, although the mines were opened in 1909 (Grattan 1963:351). The need for mine workers is a possible explanation for the imbalance in the sex ratio of those "saved" by the Germans in the same year the Angaur mine opened. In any case, it is certain that some Tobians went to Angaur at this time because the report of the Thilenius expedition contains several photographs of Tobian men there.

The Tobians say that the Germans ordered the chief of Tobi to accompany the men to Angaur. The chief delegated some of his functions to a younger man who remained on the island. This assistant was forbidden by the departing chief from carrying out at least one of the important rites. The assistant disobeyed his instructions and performed the ritual, thus, it is believed, causing the death of the absent chief and making himself chief. This is a crucial event in the evolution of modern Tobian society. It precipitated political quarrels and gave rise to two parties, that of the descendants of the original chief and that of his assistant and his descendants. All agree that these events took place but disagree on the interpretation which should be placed upon them.

This factionalism is a key element in all that followed, including the attempt at secularism, the conversion to Roman Catholicism, and the interpretations of some of the missionary's teachings. The argument between the two parties hinges on the legitimacy of the assistant's links to the chiefly genealogy and the legitimacy of the present chief, the details of which are not relevant to the following discussion. The assistant occupied the office of chief for only a few years and his title then passed to his son. When the son died, the title did not go to his son but to a descendant of the chief who had died on Angaur. This person is the present chief of Tobi, and the passed-over grandson of the assistant is the contender for the title. The present chief and his followers attempt to blacken the memory of the assistant while the contender and his few remaining followers attempt to defend it. The chief presents the assistant as a usurper who committed acts which he knew would lead to the death of the "true" chief hundreds of miles away on Angaur. The contender claims that his grandfather knew that the chief was already dead at the time he took over the title.

The ritual performed against orders by the assistant involved the distribution of coconuts from a tabooed plot of land in the northern part of the island. This land was magically forbidden to all but the chief and a subdivision of one of the seven matrilineal clans which existed at that time. This subdivision was probably either a lineage or a lineage section, although today in less populous times there are no such units on the island. The men from this group were responsible for taking care of the land and harvesting its coconuts for an annual ritual. This is the ritual which the assistant performed against the wishes of the absent chief. The assistant somehow persuaded the caretakers to harvest the coconuts from the sacred land and float them down to the chief's spirit house. While performing the chiefly ritual, which always preceded the distribution of this annual harvest, he shouted out the names of all the chiefs of Tobi. He started with the name of the first chief, the son of the ancestress of the present population, and continued up to the name of the father of the man who had appointed him assistant. He did not stop there, as might have been expected, but proceeded to call out the name of the chief in Angaur. If he had stopped with the name of this man's father the ceremony would have been identical, in this respect at least, to that which the absent chief would have performed. By extending the list to include this man's name, he asserted his claim to the chieftaincy, and, in the present chief's version, caused the death of the man who had appointed him.

It should be noted that the calling out of the list of all previous chiefs was a key part of another ritual which traditionally took place when an appointed successor to a recently deceased chief assumed office. In the opinion of the current chief and a large part of the present population, the assistant not only violated the taboos on the northern land and disobeyed the man who had appointed him, but converted the ceremony of distribution into one of accession. Their primary objection is that the assistant was not of the chiefly line, although the manner by which he is thought to have obtained the title also disqualifies him in their minds. According to the rule covering succession to the chieftancy, the old chief should instruct his heir in both the sacred and the secular duties of office and pass on the ritual paraphernalia. It was most important that he should pass on the chants through which it was believed the chief could communicate with the spirits. Everyone except the contender and his few followers profess that the chief who went to Angaur had neither the time nor the inclination to provide such instruction to the man he asked to stand in for him. Therefore, they view the acquisition of the title by the assistant and the subsequent death of the "true" chief on Angaur as an irremediable break in the flow of sacred power through the chiefly line. This interruption is thought to have had disastrous consequences for Tobi.

The chief's story continues, recounting that the "true" chief found a coconut on Angaur beach. He examined it and identified it as Tobian in origin. Closer inspection revealed that it was a coconut from the tabooed northern plot. Studying it further the chief realized that it had not fallen naturally to the ground but had been cut from its tree. From these conclusions he correctly deduced that his assistant must have recently performed the distribution ceremony even though he had been told not to do so. He reasoned further and decided that the assistant had probably proclaimed himself chief. He announced to his Tobian companions that he would soon die. "It's too bad for Tobi now," he is supposed to have said. "The island will be covered by grass."

This sentence is a prediction that the population of the atoll was going to drop to a very low level, if not extinction. As house sites are abandoned on Tobi their neatly swept sand compounds are invaded by grass. As fewer and fewer people use the island's paths they also become grassy. Taro pits too become covered with grass as they are abandoned. The prediction was accurate; the population of Tobi today is a mere sixty people and grass covers much of the island. To visitors this lends a certain parklike charm to the atoll, but to its inhabitants it is a constant reminder of the tragic nature of their recent demographic history.

The contender's version of these events is much less elaborate. He and his followers simply say that when the assistant learned that the chief had died he took over the office even though he had not been taught the sacred chants.

There is no way at this point to reconcile the three versions offered of this one event: the Germans said that there was an epidemic and a rescue; the chief says that there was a usurpation of the title; the contender says that there was a legitimate but incomplete succession. Yet in certain fundamentals the versions agree or at least do not contradict one another. For some reason the Germans did remove a number of men from the island. The chief accompanied them and died off the island without passing on to his heir in the prescribed manner the esoteric lore attached to his office. The present chief's version seems to be correct in drawing a link between these facts and the atoll's depopulation. It is probable, however, that his sequence is the reverse of the actual ordering of these events. That is, the performance of the ritual by the assistant is likely to have been the result, rather than the cause, of the population collapse.

In the aboriginal order the chief performed a number of rituals through which the community related to the supernatural. The sacred and secular worlds were not discrete and separate categories. Most profane behavior had a "religious" aspect, and even the most arcane of rituals was thought to have important effects on the course of everyday events. This pragmatic aspect of ritual life is quite clear in the minds of the islanders. The overall function of religion both then and now is to protect the island and its inhabitants from disaster. This pragmatic stance toward their religion would have led the islanders to resort to ritual when faced with the epidemic reported by the Germans. Perhaps to them it appeared that it was better in that time of crisis to have an imperfect chief than no chief at all. This decision may have eased the psychic distress of the Tobians but it did nothing to halt the decline in the population which continued up until recent times. The nature of the decline did change, however, and this change played a certain role in the events which followed. There was never again a murderous epidemic. The next population crisis was much slower in becoming apparent.

The Germans lost control of Tobi during World War I when the island passed to the Japanese along with the rest of Micronesia. It did not take long for the new masters to contribute to the processes which were leading to secularism. Sometimes in the 1920s, Yoshino, an agent for a Japanese commercial company, came to live on Tobi. He was the first outsider to live on the island for an extended period of time since Holden and his companions nearly one hundred years before. The circumstances of his stay were quite different from Holden's. The Americans had arrived lost, friendless, and starving in the remnants of a crude, handmade lifeboat. Yoshino arrived on a Japanese government vessel with the full weight of the vigorously expanding Japanese imperial order behind him. Holden and his companions were under the authority of local household heads; Yoshino had at his disposal the labor of a number of men and women enrolled in a school where he had begun to teach literacy, carpentry, and copra production. Most important, of course, the Tobians had experienced a century of intermittent contact with the power of men who arrived on ships. Given these differences, it is not difficult to understand the profound discrepancy in the fates of the two parties. Holden and company underwent an ordeal from which few emerged alive, whereas Yoshino was treated with great respect and exerted considerable influence on the affairs of the island.

He exerted this influence to increase copra production and received cooperation from the chief, the son of the ex-assistant. Yoshino was also helped by a landless Tobian named Johannes, who had recently been returned to the island from Yap by his departing German master. With the support of the chief and Johannes, Yoshino forced a division of the sacred northern land into separately owned plots in order to place more land into copra production, despite opposition from the people of the clan subdivision who were guardians of that land. Johannes wished to acquire an estate, while the chief not only acquired more land and buttressed his power by gaining Japanese support, but also succeeded in ending the annual distribution ceremony which had allegedly turned into a time of dissension and an opportunity for his opposition to deny his legitimacy. Apparently the demographic decline had halted by this time. The epidemic of 1909 had run its course and the population had stabilized; however, probably unknown to the islanders, a new and equally dangerous threat had appeared.

Just as the Germans had brought a "plague" (probably influenza) the Japanese brought venereal disease, most likely gonorrhea. Though not fatal to those infected, this disease led to barrenness in the women. Thus the stability of the demographic structure in the early years of the Yoshino era was only illusory. From about 1925 onward the birth rate plummeted until only one woman was bearing children by the time Father Marino arrived. The illusion that further disasters had been averted also must have been shattered by then.

By the early 1930s, the Spanish Jesuit mission in Koror was successfully established among the Tobians there, who had taken advantage of the opportunities offered by the regularly scheduled ships which now plied between Tobi and Koror to leave the atoll for varying lengths of time. Opportunities for cash income and the intense factionalism over chiefly succession probably played a large part in the growth of the expatriate community. Its inhabitants probably found themselves to be politically and socially peripheral to both Tobian and Palauan societies and must have found psychological and social advantages in adopting the mission religion. Eventually, one family from Eang near Koror left this community and returned to Tobi. This family included a young man who was probably a communicant of the church (all church records of this period have been lost). The elders' recollections are vague, confused, and contradictory on this point. The chief on Tobi at this time was the son of the man who had performed the forbidden ritual. The young islander from Eang explained to him the power of the Jesuits. The factionalism surrounding the legitimacy of his father's accession to the title must have played some role in the chief's agreement to what followed, but the stories do not mention this. Instead they stress the purely religious nature of the young man's arguments and imply that these are what compelled the chief's agreement. Armed with the chief's blessing, the young man joined with the youths from Yoshino's school and Yoshino's friend, Johannes, and on a dark night they attacked the chief's spirit house, the women's menstrual house, and the sorcerers' canoe house and burned them all to the ground. This event, rather than the conversions which took place a year or two later, marks the end of the traditional Tobian order. The old rituals were scrapped, the chief abandoned his exclusive rights to certain foodstuffs, and the great majority of prohibitions associated with everyday life were no longer observed.

The motives of the people involved bear some examination because it is through them that we can distinguish the operation of the historical processes which had been gathering force for some time. Several of the young men who participated in the burning are still living, and I have talked with them about their activities on that night. What emerges from their accounts is that they, and others of their generation, had come to view the many restrictions or taboos which hedged their activites as onerous. This was especially true of the food and sexual avoidances associated with many types of fishing. These taboos were essentially religious, and by doing away with the structures which were the focus of religion on the island the young men hoped to liberate themselves from them.

The young man from Eang died during World War II, so we can only speculate about his motives. No doubt he also felt the taboos to be a burden. He had lived in Eang for a number of years, in the ferment and excitement of the creation of a new Southwest Island community.[3] The prohibitions upon his behavior which he found when he returned to Tobi must have seemed even more difficult and meaningless to him than to the other young men. Perhaps he hoped that destruction of the old order would allow him access to land and other resources. His genealogy shows that he was only marginally integrated into Tobian society. Finally, of course, there is the motivation mentioned in the story. Perhaps the religious practices of the island seemed especially futile to him after his exposure to the political and economic power of the Catholic mission in Palau.

We can only speculate about the motives which led the chief to give his blessing to the destruction of the sacred structures. Perhaps the same factors which led to his agreement to the division of the northern tract operated here. It may have been the case that all ritual activity was contested by his political opponents who denied him legitimacy. The chief's attempt to use the buildings was bound to be both clumsy and presumptuous; yet failing to use them while they still stood was a reminder of his irregular rise to power. It should be remembered that the chief and his opponents were all agreed that the flow of ritual power had been terminated with the death of the old chief of Angaur. The sacred buildings were unusuable because the ritual knowledge and power associated with them had been lost. On a more general level, the ongoing demographic crisis was inescapable evidence that traditional religious forms of behavior were no longer protecting the island and had become empty as well as burdensome. The withdrawal of confidence from them led to their abandonment and the destruction of the structures and equipment associated with them. This break was not accompanied by radical transformations of other areas of the Tobian order. Life apparently went on much as before but without the ritual underpinning which had given it meaning.

This secular experiment by the Tobians failed and led to great anxiety. The fortuitous arrival of Father Marino a year or so later offered the people a chance to relieve that anxiety by adopting a new religion. Tobians believe that communal religious behavior has consequences for society as a whole. The most important of these is the prevention of disaster. It has been shown how the failure of the rituals to prevent the disaster of depopulation was probably one reason for abandoning the aboriginal religion. Ritual is thought to function in the prevention of both physical disasters such as depopulation and tsunami and also supernatural disasters, especially the activities of ghosts, the most feared of supernatural manifestations. Ghosts are hated as the essence of malicious evil and they are feared as a constant threat. Tobi is thought to be infested with them, and more are thought to live in the seas surrounding the island. The power of these ghosts to do harm is dependent on human action; in particular, the correct performance of ritual is thought to render the ghosts powerless.

Tobian belief in ghosts serves the same functions of displacing antisocial aggression and focusing free-floating anxiety that belief in beings called by a cognate name serves on the distant but culturally and linguistically related atoll of Ifaluk (Spiro 1952). On Tobi these ghosts are called *yarus;* on Ifaluk they are called *alus.* Faced with an environment in which forced intimacy is unavoidable and in which the ethic of nonaggression and cooperation is very highly developed, the Tobians, like the people of Ifaluk, displace aggressive feelings onto supernatural beings. Ghosts offer both peoples an acceptable focus for anxieties which have as their actual cause consciously unacceptable drives. With complete approval by both the self and others, a Tobian can hate and fear ghosts. By abandoning the aboriginal rituals, however, the Tobians denied themselves power over those ghosts. They were caught in a trap of their own unconscious devising.

Social and intrapsychic tensions were almost surely at a high point during the year or so of the secular experiment on Tobi. The process of sorting out the consequences of the recent population decline seems to have given rise to a great deal of covert conflict. Genealogical evidence shows that not all landholding groups declined at the same rate. Some disappeared entirely, others declined to one or two members, still others came through intact. With the Japanese-induced drive to expand copra production, control over land resources became an important political issue. Each family tried to expand its holdings by moving into the vacuum left by extinct groups. Claims were made to lands of this type by reference to genealogical links. Many cases arose where two or more groups with equally tenuous grounds claimed the same estate. In some cases there were still one or two members of the original group whose title to the land was clear but who could not mobilize the support of a sufficient number of people to defend it. There were other sources of tension, too, making this an extremely uncomfortable period. The establishment of the Tobian settlement in Eang, the acquisition and retention of new forms of wealth, the continuing failure of the women to bear children—all were important factors. Because belief in ghosts had not been abandoned, the antagonisms and anxieties contributed to the perception of a high rate of ghostly activity and a great number of ghost sightings. And since the Tobians had lost faith in the ability of traditional religion to control these hated and feared apparitions, the sightings in turn gave rise to more anxiety. A vicious circle had developed which was not broken until Father Marino was able to offer an escape through new prophylactic ritual.

It is possible at this point to provide a rough answer to two of the questions posed at the beginning of this chapter. Father Marino's success derived from the alternative he offered to the frightening powerless state which the Tobians felt themselves to be in due to the absence of control mechanisms over ghosts. The conscientiousness with which the Tobians practice their religion is a result of their understanding of the connections between religious ritual and disaster. Father Marino gave them mechanisms for preventing disaster and they dared not abandon them lest they again be overwhelmed by either physical or supernatural catastrophe. Thus it is not surprising that, despite all the time they spend praying, the Tobians seem remarkably unconcerned about their ignorance of the literal meaning of their prayers.

Before turning to the events that are remembered about Marino's visit, it will be useful to summarize the chronology presented in this section. The series of events is offered not to abridge the last century or so of Tobian history but to illustrate the most significant theme which has marked that history: the response the Tobians have made to the West. The chronology is a graduated measuring device for estimating the rising tide of Western impact and the simultaneous decline of Tobian confidence in their own institutions. Six stages of response can be distinguished. First, the material power of the West elicited awe, as indicated by the word for ship. Second, an attempt was made to control the West in its local manifestations and ritual was evolved for this purpose. Third, an effort was made to deny the power of the aliens. Holden and his fellow castaways suffered the consequences of this attempt. Fourth, the islanders began to exploit the outsiders for the special rewards they seemed to control. By working for people such as Captain Borrie, Tobians learned at first hand the extent of alien power. The fifth response was submission. The events of the disputed ritual and the division of the sacred plot of land indicate the direct impact which the West was beginning to have on Tobian autonomy. Tobian society, as a system, accommodated itself to the German and Japanese presences by passive submission.

The final episode in the chronology shows the system once more actively coming to terms with the West. The burning of the sacred structures was, in a literal sense, a necessary clearing away of the debris of old and apparently inadequate forms so that the incorporation of Western forms could begin. The subsequent acquisition of Christianity was the first act in a process which continues to this day. This process can most usefully be thought of as the creation of neo-Tobian culture and involves the integration of Western forms into a Tobian setting. Viewed in this perspective, the apparent orthodoxy of Tobian Catholicism is even more striking.

THE NATURE OF TOBIAN ORTHODOXY

If cultures are functionally integrated, then the acquisition of an institution as fundamental as religion must be accompanied by transformations in that institution so that it fits with the rest of the borrowing culture. The ethnographic literature is rich with examples of precisely this process. The Islam of some sub-Saharan Africans (Greenberg 1946), the Catholicism of some of the Yucatecan Mayans (Vogt 1964), and the Protestantism of some of the Native American groups around Puget Sound (Barnett 1957) are end products of histories of transformations. Such examples exhibit local features which can be interpreted only as the syncretic results of local attempts to adapt the borrowed religion to local needs and understandings. Tobian religious behavior does not appear to exhibit this dimension. The great bulk of their specifically religious beliefs also appear to be quite orthodox. One of the key institutions in neo-Tobian culture appears to have almost no Tobian coloring. If, however, we do not examine the religious beliefs and practices of the Tobians per se, but rather inquire into the islanders' beliefs about religion, then "Tobianness" begins to emerge. The functional orientation toward Catholicism, for example, is clearly a carry-over from the pre-Christian past; religion must be practiced in order to keep ghosts and other disasters at bay.

The functional integration of Catholicism into neo-Tobian culture thus occurs on a more general level than that of specific Catholic beliefs or practices.[4] Catholicism itself is appropriated to play the role of the discredited old religion; therefore there is no need to transform or even to think very much about the elements which make up Catholic belief and practice. The beliefs are simply subscribed to and the practices simply followed. In fact the elements become resistant to transformation since their success in preventing disaster lies not in their inner meaning but in their correct performance. Change, generated either internally or externally, is potentially disastrous. Once the Tobians became convinced of the utility of Catholicism, their self-perceived task was to learn the correct rituals and practice them. How they were convinced, or perhaps how they convinced themselves, of the power of the new religion is, therefore, a topic worth investigating. To do this, it is necessary to examine what is remembered about Father Marino, the man who converted them.

Marino arrived at Tobi on a Japanese government steamer. At that time, Japanese imperial policy was to encourage, within strict limits, the Christian missionaries in Micronesia. The reasoning behind that policy is of no importance here except that the Micronesians were not considered fit material for the Japanese creed of Shinto. This meant that such people as Yoshino could not translate their personal influence into an institutionalized religious setting. If this had not been the case there is little doubt that the islanders would have converted to the religion of the powerful Japanese and not that of the long-departed Spanish administration. There is also little doubt that missionaries such as Father Marino benefited in their evangelical endeavors from the approval of the Japanese.

Marino was accompanied by a Spanish-speaking convert from Merir—an atoll 240 kilometers north of Tobi which has a similar language and culture—who acted as Marino's interpreter. Also accompanying the priest were several of his Tobian converts from Eang, the settlement in Koror.

Interviews about Marino's activities during his stay on the island, which is given as anywhere from a few days to a month, betray a great deal of confusion. All surviving witnesses agree that

Father Marino baptized all the people on the island; all agree that he attempted to bring all the marriage unions into line with Catholic law. These are the only acts that are universally attributed to him. It is generally held that Marino made four statements—a threat to raise the dead, a promise that he would be their judge in heaven, a warning that they should not give credence to any outsider who came to the island claiming to be a priest unless he was wearing the Roman collar, and a pronouncement that marriage within a clan was incestuous. The chief and his allies claim an additional statement was made, but other people profess to know nothing about it. This denial is the equivalent to a statement that the chief and his allies are lying. The contested statement involves the destroyed spirit house, which the priest is alleged to have said would have made a good church. This is virtually all that is remembered today about this crucial event some forty years ago. There are no traditions about the responses of the chief, Yoshino, the young men who had burned the sacred buildings, or any of the other people who had been so important in shaping the course of Tobian events up to this time. Some of the narratives telling of the acts and statements of Marino do contain hints of Tobian response. Here a sorcerer or shaman challenges the priest, there a woman tricks him into agreeing to her marriage to her lover. Yet these few scraps do not make possible a confident reconstruction of the full history of the conversion. Rather than speculate about the behavior of the various actors in the events of the conversion, it is more profitable to discuss the reasons for the preservation of the remembered teachings.

Father Marino as an evangelist must have said and done more than is remembered of him. Nor do the seven things which are remembered appear to reflect those elements he would have stressed as being fundamental. Christ, the Trinity, and the Virgin are all absent from the remembered teachings. Moreover, some of the teachings seem to be quite improbable. Finally, it is apparent from internal evidence that the baptism probably did not take place in the manner described today. In other words, the preservation of the seven teachings is a result of a process of selective retention in which some of the matter retained has been distorted. Perhaps, then, the transformation, which the theory of functional integration tells us to expect, took place not in the borrowed religion itself but in the words and deeds of the man who brought it. That is, the words and deeds of Father Marino may have been subjected to systematic pressure over the last forty years to make them congruent with Tobian culture. The most direct test of this statement would be to compare the actual deeds and words of Marino with what is remembered today. Since the only source for his deeds and words is the remembrances themselves, this procedure is impossible. Another approach is to examine carefully each of the remembered teachings for the meanings they convey to Tobians. If these meanings are congruent with other Tobian beliefs and values transformations will have most likely taken place. Such evidence, combined with the facts that distortion is evident from the wording of some of the statements and that statements reflecting concerns much more central to orthodox Catholicism have not been retained, will be considered conclusive. If it can then be established that the memories of Marino are not merely bits and pieces but form a coherent corpus, that corpus would lend itself to systematic analysis.

BAPTISM

Only the vaguest outlines of the mass baptism are recalled today, but it is possible to reconstruct a more detailed picture from other data. For example, it is evident from census data that two of the Merir converts from Koror, who accompanied the priest, stood as godparents to all the initiates.[5] However, this fact was confirmed in interviews only in response to direct questioning and was never part of the narrative itself. The initial baptism is usually simply recounted as follows: "He called the people together and they were baptized." Some of the younger people can explain this rite in orthodox Christian terms, but their knowledge is the result of exposure to postwar mission schools in Koror and is not an interpretation surviving from the time of Marino. More fundamental and for many people the only meanings involve the notion of the island as a whole becoming a Christian place with emphasis on the mass nature of the act. This is a case where some distortion probably has occurred. Marino sanctified marriages during his visit, a process which necessarily took place after the baptism of the partners. Baptism involved assigning new

Christian (that is, Spanish) names to each individual. Apparently in the interest of symmetry, married couples received similar names (Juan and Juana, Terso and Teresa, Marino and Marina). This symmetry in the Spanish names of the newlyweds can only be explained by assuming that Marino knew who was to wed whom before he baptized them. From this it follows that he must have done the genealogical research necessary for making "good" marriages before he christened them. It is difficult to imagine that the sequence Marino followed was investigation of all potential spouses, mass baptism, and then marriage. It makes more sense to posit an individual sequence for each couple, including individual baptism. The probable distortion involved in seeing the baptism as a single collective rite is most likely based on a smaller event in which all children and those few adults who, for one reason or another, did not wish to be married were baptized together. It is evidence for the hypothesis that a key component of the meaning of the original baptism lies in its total nature, including all those actors in the Tobian sociocultural system who call themselves Tobian, and thus, in a sense, the system itself. The fact that the christening of each convert with a new name is not stressed, and seldom even mentioned, indicates that the individual aspect of the initial rite is not important. If the baptism is viewed as speaking about the nature of the sociocultural order, then it is necessary to inquire into the content of the message as perceived by the present-day inhabitants of the island.

The word used in Tobian for "baptize" usually refers to bathing (both swimming and washing), but it also has two other meanings which describe both the traditional cure for insanity and a traditional disciplinary measure. Fathers punished their misbehaving sons in the following manner: they took them to the sea and held their heads under the water until they lost consciousness. Shamans chanting incantations used a similar technique to treat the insane. This convergence of treatments for insanity and misbehavior illustrates one of the fundamental tenets of Tobian concepts of behavior: the similarity between 'crazy' and 'bad' behavior. There is an additional element, 'ghost-like', which will be discussed below.

It is no accident, I think, that the word for these techniques has been extended to cover baptism. When people discuss the pre-Christian era, and especially the years immediately preceding the coming of the priest, it is commonly said that people were both crazy and bad. The times are perceived as having been out of joint and Father Marino is viewed as having acted to put things right.

The symbolism is striking. Combining the role of father, because he insisted that he be called by this term, with that of shaman, by reciting ritual formulas, Marino linked together in one rite the cure for insanity and the punishment for transgression. Obviously, there can be no correction without a previous malfunction. Therefore Tobians seem to see Marino as having said symbolically, by the act of mass baptism, that the system had been out of order. While this one rite certainly did not trigger the perception of pre-Christian Tobi as a bad, crazy place, it has reinforced that view so that today the brief attempt at secularism between the time the spirit house was burned and the arrival of the priest is viewed in an extremely negative light, even by the men who helped instigate it. An additional element in this interpretation is related to the fact that there are important differences between the two traditional techniques and baptism. The two traditional techniques involved rendering the subject unconscious through near drowning, whereas Tobians say the baptism involved merely tracing a watery cross on the penitent's forehead and pouring a little water over his head. The former experience was undoubtedly terrifying; the latter, especially by contrast, was not. From the contrast emerged the perception of Marino as the good father-shaman whose corrective abilities embraced a whole society but involved no unpleasantness.

The baptism emerges as a fundamental event, and its retention in the corpus of remembered teachings becomes understandable. As a communication it has two messages, one of which deals with the contrast between pre-Christian Tobi and the present and the other with the nature of Father Marino. In addition to intervention at the highly symbolic level of the baptism, priestly intervention is also remembered at the more focused level of marriage.

REMARRIAGE

Pre-Christian Tobian marriage patterns are characterized by a wide variety of arrangements. Men were permitted a number of wives, and women could have one or two husbands. Cross-cousin marriages were preferred, and serial polygamy with frequent divorces was the rule for both sexes. Since all these practices are frowned upon by the church, one would expect that Marino would have acted to eliminate unions resulting from them. All that is remembered, however, is that he forced each married person to go back to their earliest living spouse and then sanctified that marriage. A number of points of interest arise in this connection. It is only in stories surrounding this incident that the Tobians are seen as more than passive targets of some item of priestly behavior. This fact is due to the impossible nature of the task which Marino apparently set himself. While newly christened Roberto may have been Fausta's first husband, for example, she could very well have been his second, third, or even seventh wife. The opportunities this created for the type of manipulation at which the Tobians are so skilled were not lost. What emerges from these stories is that many people succeeded in marrying their lovers, who may not have been either a previous or current spouse. More important, no one was forced to marry someone he or she detested. This proved to be highly adaptive, since the marriage ceremonies performed by Father Marino wrote finis to the aboriginal pattern of frequent divorce and remarriage. Tobians typically say: "He made everyone who had been divorced go back to their first spouse." That this is the only interpretation of his behavior brings us to a seeming anomaly.

If the body of stories about Marino is in fact the locus of the processing which the borrowed institution of Catholicism has undergone at the hands of the Tobians, we would expect each story to speak to important issues facing the islanders. We would also expect that most serious sociocultural problems on the atoll would be reflected in the stories. It is this latter point which is at issue here. Why does the corpus of remembered teachings not deal with changes in such practices as cross-cousin marriage and polygamy? From Marino's point of view the unions that existed prior to his visit were not marriages at all. It is quite likely, therefore, that the recollections are accurate and he did not deal directly with these practices in the limited time at his disposal. However, if these changes were viewed today as significant one would expect them to be reflected in the stories, whether based on fact or not. From the observer's perspective these changes certainly seem to have contributed to a major dilemma facing Tobian society today.

A Tobian, especially a man, has a rather narrow range of options concerning marriage. The church prohibits the two possibilities of polygamy (especially polyandry), and divorce and remarriage contribute to this restriction. The fundamental problem is demographic. One of the consequences of severe underpopulation is that random reproductive asymmetries are not balanced by complementary asymmetries as they are in larger, more stable populations. Few women of recent generations have proved fertile. Moreover, most of these women have given birth to many more males than females. In a larger population, such a disparity in the sex ratio of the children of a few women would be more or less cancelled by an opposite disparity in the sex ratio of the offspring of other women. On Tobi, of course, there are no other women, and the fate of the predominately male children is to compete for the few available women. The situation is made worse by the fact that a male remains in the marriage market much longer than a female and so there are a number of widowers who also are searching for mates among the young women. The combination of church marriage regulations with the retention of pre-Christian rules forbidding clan endogamy exacerbates the problem by restricting the number of options open to the men. This is quite apparent to the Tobians who ponder these matters. To these people, however, the most significant of the church's marriage prohibitions would seem to be the one against divorce. This is particularly striking because divorce, in the usual sense of the term, does occur on the island.

Marriages do break up, and the spouses may set up or join separate households or even form semisecret liaisons with third parties. These liaisons cannot be sanctified, however, nor can they result in the joint households which are characteristic of church-sanctioned unions until the legitimate spouses of the lovers are deceased. The rule seems to operate as follows: no one can remarry until his previous spouse has died. The factors which led to the instability of marriage in the pre-Christian era are still operative, yet the expression of those tensions (frequent divorce and remarriage) is no longer a possibility. It is not surprising that this is reflected in the stories. Objectively, prohibiting remarriage while a previous spouse is still living creates the most difficulty in terms of numbers of people involved. This rule can also be seen as an indirect prohibition of polygamy. It stresses the strength and exclusive nature of the marriage tie between a man and woman. This bond is so exclusive that a third party cannot be included in the equation even when the man and the woman are no longer living together. A relationship of such strength and exclusiveness rules out polygamy. One cannot marry a second spouse until the first is dead. Cross-cousin marriage is not spoken of in the story of the remarriages. There are no people on Tobi at the present time who would be eligible mates if the rule against cross-cousin marriage were to be waived. Therefore, although it is true that a significant change has taken place with respect to the cross-cousin rule, that change is not, currently, an issue.[6] Not being an issue it is not reflected in any of the stories told about Marino. At this point it might be asked why a story is not invented which would revalidate the aboriginal practice of frequent divorce and remarriage. As we shall see, this is evidently what has happened with respect to clan exogamy. But the priests who have followed Marino have refused to preside at second marriages when the first spouse was still living. It is not possible for people simply to set up joint households without the church's blessing—by concerning himself with marriage in the way that he did, Father Marino firmly set the institution of marriage within the realm of the sacred. In marked contrast to aboriginal unions, a post conversion marriage is a sacred event.

To summarize, Father Marino baptized all the people and presided over a number of marriages. The baptism signals a change from the old, bad, and crazy society to a new, good, and sane one—a change accomplished by a good father-shaman, Father Marino. The marriages make matrimony a sacred concern and signify the prevention of various classes of people, particularly those seeking a second mate before the death of the first, from making legitimate matches.

POWER OVER GHOSTS

While walking through the cemetery Father Marino is supposed to have said, "My power is from Dios and it is true. Shall I call the dead people here in this ground to stand up?" The cemetery had only recently, under Japanese pressure, come into use. Previously the dead had been disposed of over the reef at the northern end of the island, within the bounds of the old sacred grounds. This continuity in the spiritual geography of the island may or may not be accidental, but the fearful attitude of the islanders toward this plot today is probably similar to that of their ancestors. At night the area is avoided if at all possible. If a visit is necessary, as during turtle hunting season, people only go there in parties of three or more. The area is dangerous and frightening because it is the haunt of ghosts, and there is no reason to suppose that the situation was different in Marino's time. The setting in which the words were spoken thus conveys to the minds of the islanders an aura of supernatural power.

Among the several versions of this story, the most widely accepted has the missionary uttering his words in response to a challenge from a shaman. There is unanimity on two points: the wording of the phrase quoted above and the response of the audience. Everyone took Marino's utterance as a threat, since in the Tobian view of things a resurrection of the dead would be an unmitigated disaster for the living. The newly risen would not be mortals bound by the physical and moral restraints of the normal world but Lazarus-like beings who had passed beyond that world and returned, eerie and frightening. Whatever Marino's intentions when he uttered these words, assuming that he did, they are felt today to have been a stratagem designed to impress the people with the missionary's power and the dire consequences in store for any who would not follow him. He did not, so the stories go, actually have to raise the dead since the people begged him not to do so. The very act of pleading with him, of course, concedes his power to carry out the threat.

This leads to an important message contained in the saying: the unique and liminal position of Father Marino. Clearly the resurrection of the dead is no task for an ordinary mortal; only a man in close touch with the supernatural could do that. The claim of power to raise the dead is a claim over the processes of life and death. The statement makes clear the source of that power. The emphasis is on the concrete and the immediate. It is not a vague statement about the omnipotence of Marino's god which is reported here but a claim to be a channel through which that power can enter the affairs of this world. The theme of Marino's special spiritual abilities is one which runs through most of the stories told of his visit. In this instance, what is reflected is his power to create ghosts. To a people accustomed to the idea of human-ghostly dialogue, which is how the pre-Christian trance states of the shamans are remembered, Marino's assertion of the power to call up a whole new population of ghosts does not appear as farfetched as it would to a more secularly oriented audience. The claim is plausible but awe-inspiring. It represents a level of spiritual power for which there is no parallel in Tobian thought. The claim is an innovation but, like all innovations, it is built of preexisting elements. The most important of these elements is the belief in ghosts, which is itself reinforced by the statement under consideration.

The second message contained in that statement, then, is that ghosts exist and, furthermore, that there is a close connection between ghosts and religion. The threat can be paraphrased: "Do what I say or there will many ghosts on the island." The first half of this warning can only refer to the necessity of conforming with Roman Catholicism as understood by the islanders; the second half refers not only to ghosts as such but, by inference, to all disasters that are likely to strike the fragile Tobian ecosystem. A final reading of the statement would emphasize its congruence with the traditional Tobian notion of religion as a set of techniques necessary to ward off disasters in general and ghosts in particular.

POWER TO JUDGE THE DEAD

Father Marino is said to have made the following statement as he was about to leave the island: "Don't forget that I am in charge of you and when you die I, and no one else, shall be the one to decide where you go." When questioned about its meaning informants argued that Marino was saying that he, and not Christ, was the one to decide whether heaven or hell will be each Tobian's ultimate destination. Obviously this statement strengthened Marino's unique cosmological position vis-a-vis the islanders. Of all Marino's acts and sayings that are remembered, this one speaks most directly to that point, and it does so via an idiom of power, that is, the concept of *hosuar* 'in charge'.

In the Tobian view of human nature the only true adults are men between middle age and senility. Only individuals of this class fully possess the prime virtues of self-restraint, competence, and independence. Females and all other males are thought to be capable of exhibiting these characteristics only in varying degrees. In other words, there is a single model of the good person and men of middle age and older are thought to be the best examples. People lacking the first two virtues of self-restraint and competence are deprived of the third virtue of independence by having someone, usually an adult male, placed 'in charge' of them. All major decisions are made only with this person's consent; he has the power of reward and punishment over his wards, especially if they are children. Ideally, all women, children, and young and senile men are supposed to have someone 'in charge' of them. Exceptions do not vitiate the rule, which can become quite complex in operation. For example, an adult male, Roberto, is 'in charge' of both another adult, Honaria, and her daughter, Tina, while Honaria is 'in charge' of Tina. The rule also applies to temporary arrangements so that a woman in mourning will have another woman placed 'in charge' of her for the duration of the mourning period.

Women, children, and young and senile men are thought to have imperfect impulse control. It is therefore necessary for the well-being of everyone that people who do have this virtue be permitted to intervene in their affairs.[7] Tobians say that in pre-Christian times the chief who wielded political power and acted on the island's behalf in exchanges with the spiritual world was 'in charge' of the whole island. Marino's claim to be 'in charge' is a similar metaphor. As a metaphor it implies that the population of the island as a whole is deficient in the three prime virtues and a superordinate must interfere in its affairs. Marino's claim is considerably more extensive than that attributed to pre-Christian chiefs because it is thought to transcend both his and his congregation's mortality. Father Marino was beheaded by the Japanese about ten years after he converted Tobi. Thirty years after his death, it is thought that he is still in charge of the island and is still watching from on high the behavior of its inhabitants. In addition, Marino is thought to have the responsibility for deciding the peoples' post mortal fate. The belief that Marino will judge the Tobian dead has firmly established his unique cosmological position. The islanders' belief that they will be judged and either rewarded or punished according to their earthly conduct is an important moral sanction that acquires its force from Tobian attitudes toward authority and, ultimately, the father.

The Tobian father is a remote and threatening figure in the life of the child. This relationship is now changing as other styles of childrearing are practiced, but for the old people and those raised by them the father was a figure to be treated with respect and fear. Stories told by other people of their childhood commonly include beatings by the father and stress the respect and fear in which the father was held. This attitude has been institutionalized in the custom of avoiding, where possible, the mention of one's dead father's name.[8] When this is not possible, as for example during some of my interviews with them, Tobians make a great show of whispering the name into the listener's ear.

Evidence that this attitude is extended, especially among the old people, to other authority figures is not hard to find. Traditional behavior toward the chief was also apparently marked by fear and respect, as is behavior toward Americans or Palauans invested with some power over the islanders. No human figure is more frightening to old people, especially old women, than the Palauan policemen who are occasionally called to Tobi to investigate some problem.

This fear of authority is seen as highly functional by the more thoughtful people on the island. It is conventional Tobian wisdom that only fear keeps people, particularly those who are not fully autonomous adults, from dangerous and antisocial acts. Anyone who performs such acts is thus regarded as fearless. This attitude is congruent with the notion that ghosts are fearlessly antisocial beings unless kept in check by religious ritual.

This conception of the basis of compliance was shown during

a meeting held to determine the culprit in a possible attempt on the life of one of the men. During the meeting the question arose as to whether the matter should be reported to the administration in Palau. An affirmative consensus was quickly reached on the basis that no one's life would be safe and the island would be uninhabitable unless the young people were given an immediate object lesson by seeing the criminal brought to justice and punished.

A policeman was sent to the island on the next field trip some months later but was unable to make any progress in his investigation. Commenting on this, one young man made a statement which clearly expresses the shared belief in the importance of Father Marino in sanctioning moral behavior. "Maybe that guy who did it," he said, referring to the person who attempted the murder, "is really proud and happy now, but when he dies and meets Father Marino I think he will be very sorry."

OTHER MISSIONARIES

Father Marino's person is firmly embedded within the structure of Tobian theology. The beliefs which endow him with this status have also made it extremely difficult for religious personnel to deal with the islanders. Roman Catholic priests have little chance to introduce religious and social innovations, and exponents of other versions of Christianity can make no headway at all. This is made particularly clear in the third statement Marino is alleged to have made: "If any person comes here and tries to say mass but is not wearing the same thing around his neck that I am, do not listen to him." This statement was not given to me as part of the stories about Marino, which include all the other material discussed here, but rather as the basis for an anecdote about the first priest to visit the island after World War II. He was a navy chaplain who was wearing a uniform without a Roman collar.

The fact that the statement is not contained in the usual narrative of the activities of Father Marino does not mean that it is not part of the corpus of remembered teachings. Everyone is aware of it and there is no disagreement about its authenticity. But I do think the statement has a separate status. It is as though it is preadapted to the possibility, of which the people are keenly aware, that a non-Catholic missionary might visit the island. Since this is not a current issue, however, the saying does not form part of the active narration. In a negative sense, though, it is of current importance. While this statement is felt to be a warning against falling away from the religion revealed by Marino, it is primarily a warning against non-Catholic missionaries and not a direct admonition to pay heed to other Catholic priests who over the years have followed Marino to the island. The lack of a forceful direct admonition accounts for the ease with which teachings of subsequent priests have been ignored when they contradicted Marino's word.

It is notable that the Marino corpus is structured in such a way that the process of ignoring more recent church teachings in order not to violate that corpus does not in itself contradict a teaching of Marino. This would not be the case if the statement under consideration here were amended to read as follows: "If any person comes here and tries to say mass but is not wearing the same thing around his neck that I am, do not listen to him; but if he is wearing the same thing that I am you must do what he says."

CLAN INCEST

The next saying attributed to Marino conveys a limited message. It forbids clan endogamy, but it does so in an elliptical manner. The actual wording is as follows: "It is as impossible to marry a clan sister as it is to marry an angel."

The wording of the statement is that given by Tobian English-speakers, some of whom have achieved a high degree of fluency in English. If one talks to an old person who was at the crucial meeting when Marino is thought to have said this, he will quote a statement which can be rendered: "Intercourse with a sibling of opposite sex is like intercourse with a ghost. You cannot." The problem of interpretation lies in the fact that the words translated by the English-speakers as 'marriage,' 'clan sister', and 'angel' can with equal accuracy be translated as 'intercourse', 'sibling of opposite sex', and 'ghost'.

Before discussing the import of this complex statement about clan incest it is necessary to describe Tobian clans. These are named, unranked, matrilineal, exogamous groups in which genealogical connections between all members are felt to exist even though they cannot be traced by any one individual.[9] At the present time clans are the only recognized structural unit between households on the one hand and the collectivity known as "the people of the island" on the other. The most populous of these clans were subdivided into lineages in the past. Currently there are five clans, one of which, consisting of a single male, is doomed to extinction. A similar fate has aleady overtaken two other clans within living memory.

Exogamous clans have apparently existed on Tobi since shortly after the initial settlement. They possess a mythological charter in the epic which tells of the island's discovery, having been constituted by the original ancestress. If we assume that the clan exogamy rule is felt to be so important or so problematical that it requires supernatural justification, it is not surprising, given the general attenuation in power of the aboriginal religious system, that the original pre-Christian charter has been reinforced by one bearing Marino's stamp. This is the only instance in which a pre-Christian rule has been revalidated in such an overt manner. On a more general level, of course, the entire corpus of Marino's teachings can be seen as revalidating the entire Tobian ethical and moral system. Acts ranging from hoarding to murder were all thought to be as evil in aboriginal times as they are today, and all are sins which the Tobians believe Father Marino will punish.

The simile expressed in the statement that marrying a clan sister is like marrying an angel acquires its force from the Tobian notion of an angel as a kind of benevolent ghost.[10] Ghosts are frightening because they can flout with impunity the laws governing the normal world. Angels share this characteristic and thus arouse the same reaction of horror in Tobians as do traditional ghosts. The use of the word "angel" instead of the usual word for ghost is primarily a device to give the statement a Christian cast; the benevolent aspect of angelic nature is beside the point here.

Part of the strangeness of the statement when viewed from a Christian perspective is that it does not speak directly of morality; marriage to a clan sister is not said to be evil but rather impossible. To a Tobian, however, the word "impossible" in the teaching speaks to a greater truth about men and morality—the notion that there is essentially no difference between certain moral and physical laws. In the West the two are clearly distinguished, primarily on the basis that violation of moral laws, although bad, is possible, whereas physical laws are such that their violation is impossible without supernatural intervention. In this sense moral laws are less absolute in the West than are physical laws. In the Tobian view of things the two are indistinguishable. We occasionally show traces of the same attitude toward morality as, for example, when we speak of "unnatural acts." The word "impossible" in Marino's teaching is congruent with the Tobian idea that men are as bound by incest regulations as, for example, they are by gravity; neither can be violated by a normal person.

Violation of the incest regulations, then, produces a rupture in the fabric of the normal universe as dramatic and shocking as the flouting of the laws of the physical world by a ghost. Both acts are beyond the capacity of normal men but well within the power of ghosts. Thus it is not surprising that in the only two instances of clan incest I know of, both men were described as ghosts. The fact that only the men were so described is a product of the Tobian view of adulthood discussed earlier. The belief that people are capable of anything and that only fear keeps them from behaving in immoral ways forms a counterpoint to this attitude. A normal man is one who is, among other things, sufficiently afraid of the consequences of immoral acts. Since people other than men are not thought to be sufficiently afraid, which is why they need someone 'in charge' of them to monitor their behavior, they are not normal or true adults and thus are not covered by statements about normal people.

If it is correct to say that marriage to a clan sister requires a man to act in a ghostly manner, what does this imply about the way that such a man is viewed? In the two attempts at endogamous clan marriage of which I am aware, the primary reaction of the people seemed to consist of a mixture of wonder and horror. Wonder seemed to arise from the perception that a fundamental law had been flouted; horror originated from the people's feelings about incest. They were aghast.

In both cases the men were treated, within limits, as ghosts.

People did not run shrieking from their presence, but they were avoided as much as was consistent with the obligations of civility which minimally require that one give a cheerful response to any social initiative of another. Eventually, they were pressured into leaving the island. The gossip that continues to swirl about the two marriages stresses the men's frightening boldness and their untrustworthiness. These men are referred to directly as ghosts. This is, of course, a metaphor; everyone recognizes that they are human. However, it is a metaphor that contains a strong element of truth for the people of Tobi since these two men did indeed act like ghosts. One of the consequences for those who break the incest rule, then, is that people treat them like ghosts. The other and more severe threat implied by Marino's statement relates ghostly behavior to insanity.

Acting like a ghost and being crazy are forms of behavior which share important attributes: both are dangerous, uncanny, unpredictable, and give rise to a great deal of fear. One important difference between ghostly and insane behavior is that the fear of the former is directed outward while fear connected with insanity is directed toward the self. This is summed up nicely in the conventional wisdom that ghosts are harmful to other people whereas the insane are prone to suicide. The unknown person who was thought to have attempted murder was said to be a ghost; a man who repeatedly tried to kill himself was said to be insane.

The fear of insanity and subsequent suicide are important components of the sanctions against clan incest, and Marino's teaching speaks to this point by drawing attention to the ghostly nature of such an act. To a Tobian, what seems ghostly in others must seem to be insanity in the self. Recognizing the immense social pressure which is brought to bear on anyone attempting an incestuous match, a Tobian is likely to feel that he would have to be crazy to try such ghostly behavior.

There is one final point to be made in connection with this statement. The word translated as 'marry' refers both to intercourse and to marriage, depending on the context in which it is used. The fact that the English-speakers choose the former and not the latter is significant. Sexual intercourse with a clan mate (providing that the genealogical connection is no closer than first cousin) is forbidden but arouses no great reaction when it becomes known. It is expected that young people will make love as often as possible and with very little regard for the amenities, and while it is bad for clan mates to sleep together, there is usually a good deal of resigned tolerance for what is perceived as weakness of the flesh. Parents or guardians will try to break up such liaisons and ensure that the act is not repeated. It is only when the parties try to formalize the union that the full complex of wonder and horror, ghosts and insanity, is triggered. The dramatic difference in the reaction to incestuous intercourse and endogamous clan marriage lies in the nature of Tobian marriages, which involve the establishment of long-term economic exchange relations between spouses and, to a lesser extent, among their families. Marriage involves the formation of a household, the fundamental unit in Tobian society, and it involves the filiation of children to the mother's and the father's kin in different ways and for different ends. Embarking on such a project with a woman of the same clan publicly flaunts one's immorality. It makes the statement that society's respect is held in no esteem. It places oneself outside the conventions which govern the conduct of normal men. These are the actions and statements of a ghost or a madman.

The teaching that marriage to a clan sister is as impossible as marriage to an angel may be transformed into the following statement: "Only a person like a ghost, unbound by moral laws, could marry a woman of the same clan. One who does such a thing will be treated with fear and loathing by his fellows and will die by his own hand."

CHIEF AND CHURCH

The final teaching of Father Marino which is remembered differs from the others because the Tobians are not unanimous about its authenticity. This fact provides an important clue to the workings of the entire Marino complex. Referring to the chief's spirit house, the priest is alleged by some to have said, "It is too bad you burned this place down. It would have made a good church." Prior to the collapse of the old order the chief exercised ultimate spiritual and political power. His spirit house was the site of most of the important rituals over which he presided. This statement is an attempt to charter a role for the chief in the new religion.

The chief and his allies began a campaign some time ago to infiltrate the church's activities both on the island and in Eang. They have achieved a degree of success in certain minor areas, but overall direction of the church remains firmly in the hands of the mission. The chief's objective is to be formally recognized as leader of the congregation. He means to achieve a position of leadership over the rituals (novenas for the dead, for instance, and twice daily *rosarios*) which constitute the religious life of the island, except for the services held by the priest on the four or five days a year that he visits the island. The chief also would like to be the sole intermediary between the people and the priest on all matters pertaining to church business and ritual. Although the mission treats the chief with great respect, it has refused to fall in with his plans. The American and Palauan priests are unimpressed with his appeal to the authority of Marino, but it is obvious that the islanders understand the implications of the statement which the chief and his partisans attribute to Father Marino.

Disagreement over the validity of the statement about the chief's spirit house follows the lines of cleavage over the chiefly succession. Those who accord the incumbent legitimacy believe that Marino actually made the statement; those who support his challenger do not. This denial can be taken as a measure of the lack of confidence which the contender and his allies have of success in the near future. If they believed themselves to be close to replacing the present chief with one of their own party, it would be in their interest to strengthen the office (as opposed to the person) of the chief. Marino's statement is viewed as a recognition that the chief's office has legitimate religious attributes which can be incorporated within the Christian system without harm to the church. For supporters of the chief the validity of this statement means that his effort to gain power within the church structure is entirely justified. For those who deny its validity that effort is simply another example of what they profess to view as his despotic and grasping nature.

This, then, is all the material remembered about Father Marino: out of a much wider range of potential memories the Tobians have chosen these seven items. There is no way to tell at this late date whether they are grounded in fact or fantasy, though it is certain that they all contain particularly Tobian meanings. In this sense the alien missionary's teachings have been processed by the islanders so that they have become congruent with indigenous ideas. Understandings have arisen about them that are remote from the understandings of orthodox Catholicism but fit with the rest of Tobian culture. Transformation has taken place not in the borrowed religious practices, but in the words and deeds of its conveyor.

Further analysis reveals that these seven items form a coherent ideological complex with definite properties. The complex is nonfalsifiable, possesses a certain dynamic, and has both positive and negative functions for the people who use it. It is also an idiom which expresses certain Tobian truths about man, society, and the supernatural.

The system contains two major precepts: first, religion is necessary; second, Tobian religion must be Father Marino's. The former concept is supported by the baptism which teaches that society is bad and crazy without religion as well as the threat to raise the dead, which confirms the Tobian notion that religion is necessary to prevent disasters. The concept that the religion of Tobi must be Marino's religion is supported by belief in his special powers over ghosts, over the individual soul, and over society. These beliefs derive, at least in a cognitive sense, from Father Marino's remembered teachings. His power over ghosts is spoken of in the threat to raise the dead; his power over individual souls is asserted in his claim to be their post mortal judge. His power over Tobian society is taught in the baptism, in the statement about being 'in charge', and in the threat to raise the dead.

The other four items—remarriage and statements about clan incest, other missionaries, and the chief's spirit house—perform a different function. They speak to specific issues which have been given a religious coloring. These issues are marriage (in particular clan marriage), the chief's power, and the contradiction of the system by other missionaries. There is unanimity about the authenticity of the three items dealing with marriage and other missionaries. Therefore the solutions to problems embodied in these items are adhered to since Marino's power to dictate them is validated by the precepts about religion and his place in it.

For both sides in the succession dispute the argument about whether Marino actually made the statement is, in an important sense, the only argument that matters. It is a property of this system, and perhaps of all ideological systems, that once an issue has been framed in its terms only those terms are relevant. Arguments based on other grounds, such as personal interest or pragmatism, simply do not apply. This does not mean that the solutions it offers are permanent, but it does mean that as long as the two general percepts are accepted, change in the solutions requires change in the Marino corpus. The solutions can be seen as adjustments made to cope with past realities. When the realities change, the solutions may become maladaptive. This leads to considerable tension and pressure to modify the system. A number of factors make this a difficult and slow process. These factors can be most clearly seen in the current disputes over clan endogamy. By examining this issue these factors can be isolated and the actual operation of the Marino system presented.

A young Tobian may wish to marry a clan sister. He can point out his present unhappy, wifeless situation. He can assure her and her guardians of his deep love for the girl. He can offer the guardians tobacco and money and tell them of the land he owns and the lands he stands to inherit. All these arguments based on his, the girl's, and her guardian's personal interest will tempt but not persuade those guardians to give their blessing to the match (a blessing which is absolutely necessary if the young man is to succeed). He can raise the argument to a more general level and point out the scarcity of eligible women on the island and the dearth of babies. He can also claim that he and his fellows will have to seek non-Tobian spouses if the rule is not waived. The guardians will agree that this is a shame and will even complete his argument for him, pointing out the relatively large number of such marriages that have already taken place, resulting in many children with no Tobian clan. At this point someone is sure to say that if this keeps up eventually there will be no more Tobians but only half-caste Palauans, since most non-Tobian wives are Palauan. This is not a compelling argument, however, and the guardians will still not agree to let their ward marry within the clan. Their refusal will be framed in terms of the Marino ideology: "It is as impossible to marry a clan sister as it is to marry an angel." The young man can counter this by telling how he was taught at the Catholic mission school that the church does not forbid clan endogamy. He can even remind his elders of the many sermons which the American priest has preached on just this topic during his visits to the island. The guardians would probably respond along the lines of the following: "You know what the Americans are like. They are very nice but they want everyone to like them. The priest just tells us that to make things easy for us. But we are strong enough to follow the true law, the one of Marino."[11]

A full understanding of the reasons for maintaining the clan exogamy rule requires consideration of the structural positions of both the elders and the young men. The old people, who are guardians of the few unmarried women of childbearing age, are the ones who insist on the rule. They are in a position to enforce their wishes for a number of reasons. They control many other resources beside the young women: land, for example, and secret knowledge of medicinal recipes and fishing techniques. Therefore, it is not in the young men's interest to alienate the old people. Individual cases vary, of course. Sometimes the only thing a young man wishes from a guardian is the hand of the ward. Even then the young man's chances of success are not very good, for old people are central to the gossip network and therefore in a position to disrupt most proposed matches. Finally, if the guardians cannot succeed in provoking jealousy and dissension between the lovers by the use of rumors, they still have one other technique for preventing the match. As trusted elders of the congregation, they can attempt to convince the priest that the proposed match is inappropriate. In recent years, as the priests have gained more familiarity with the islanders, guardians have resorted to camouflaging their efforts by using agents to explain why the priest should not marry their ward to her clan mate.

The young men are in a difficult position. They cannot form a coalition against the old people. Not only do they hope to gain future property from the elders, but the very nature of Tobian marriage makes it a particularly difficult subject around which to unify. The subject of clan exogamy always arises in reference to particular cases. Someone wants to marry a clan mate and her guardians forbid the match. He cannot find any allies to help him convince the guardians or at least to fight their rumors. The other single young men who might be his allies in a different context are his competitors. If he fails, then perhaps one of them can marry the girl; if the girl marries him, then there will be a permanent loss of one woman from the field in which all the young men operate. The rule against divorce and the imbalance in the sex ratio make the competition for a girl's hand an extreme example of a zero-sum game. Young married people have no stake in this contest. They have succeeded in winning their mates; the success of their unmarried brothers and sisters is of only academic interest to them. Seeing no benefit in helping the young man, they find it in their interest to remain neutral and thus preserve their status as moral persons following the way of Marino. The young man's elders are also of little help to him. It is the exceptional old person who will help a young man get married in any case—as long as he is single, his elders have no competitors for his labor and its fruits. Thus there is a natural tendency for a young man's elders to oppose his marriage and, in cases where it applies, the clan exogamy rule is a perfect peg on which to hang that opposition. The only assistance a young man can expect is from the girl herself, who is not likely to be of much help. Although she cannot be forced to marry someone against her will, neither can she marry someone against the will of her guardians. They have control of her person and can apply both verbal and physical pressure to keep her from marrying someone of whom they disapprove.

A young man needs a good deal of courage and self-confidence even to broach the topic of an endogamous marriage. Knowing that he will be called a ghost by his fellows and face eventual exile if he succeeds, he is most likely to search elsewhere for a wife. Even if he could outmaneuver the girl's guardians and convince the priest to perform the marriage, he would have to leave Tobi. Disowned by the girl's guardians and family and perhaps by his own as well he would have extreme difficulty in mobilizing the kinsmen upon whom a reasonable Tobian existence depends.

Tobians also operate in two other social systems besides that of their island. One of these is the community which has grown up in Eang composed of people from all four of the Southwest Islands. These people are but one or two generations removed from their natal islands of Sonsorol, Pulo Ana, Merir, and Tobi. They have created a village and a social system based on linguistic and cultural similarities, and like the people of Tobi they are all Catholic. The other social system in which Tobians operate is that of Palau. Although there is religious diversity in Palau, one of the strongest elements in Palauan social organization is the Catholic church, which has considerable economic and political power. Tobians use their Catholicism as a major dimension of identity in their interactions with both Palauans and other Southwest Islanders. As fellow communicants of a universal church, they have a basis for meeting with these people that is not founded on invidious distinctions. This is particularly true of their interactions with Palauans. Just as a reasonable existence on Tobi demands the cooperation of one's kinsmen, a reasonable existence in Palau depends on overcoming the prejudice which Palauans exhibit toward Southwest Islanders. Education, health care, and employment are concentrated in Palauan hands. The Catholic church is virtually the only institution in which people from the Southwest Islands can make meaningful contacts with the people who control the levers of power and service. The church also directly binds the Southwest Islanders to herself by providing employment and education and by helping them when they run into difficulties with Palauan institutions. All these factors mean that a young man wishing to marry a clan mate cannot simply take her to Eang and marry her outside the church. He needs his identity as a Catholic to function adequately in the greater society in which Eang is embedded.

In effect, then, young men have no option but to comply with the clan exogamy rule. The old people control both the women and the priests. That their control of the latter is slipping is evidenced by the recent completion of one of the two intraclan marriages attempted since Marino's visit. However, this is not really a very hopeful precedent for the young men; it took a number of contention-filled years for the two middle-aged clan mates to persuade the priest to marry them. They now live in Palau and have very little to do with any of their relatives. None of the specifics of this case is likely to be repeated soon. Indeed, the total dependency of this couple on the husband's meager cash income has become something of an object lesson for the young people. The problem of maintaining the clan exogamy rule thus hinges on the motives of the old. Why do they persist in enforcing this rule when by doing so they will cause the extinction of the very institution it is designed to perserve?

There is no great commitment on the part of any Tobian, young or old, to the integrity of Tobian society. People are interested in their own fate and, to a lesser extent, in the fate of their families. The future course of their society is a matter of little concern. Therefore, when the young men point out to a clan mate's guardians the number of Palauan women who have been brought into Tobian society and the fact that their children have no Tobian clan, their arguments carry no weight. A girl's guardians know that she will eventually marry someone, so commitment to family is not a factor either. Finally, as people already in control of the island's resources, there is not much that a girl's guardians would stand to gain personally from allowing their ward to marry a clan mate. Indeed, for these firm believers in Marino's word, they stand to lose paradise, the only reward which lies ahead of them. As people close to death they are naturally much concerned with their fate after death. And Marino not only ruled out clan exogamy but also proclaimed himself the judge of that fate. The young men are armed with statements from current, unmythologized missionaries, but these missionaries can offer no arguments powerful enough to counter those drawn from the Marino corpus. A change in the marriage rule would require a change in the Marino corpus, and, as survivors of the original conversion, the old people control that corpus. It is their memories upon which it is based. And these memories are a resource in the struggle between the generations just as surely as are the women, land, and specialized knowledge also controlled by the elders.

It should be pointed out that the preservation of the clan exogamy rule has certain unique characteristics. The observation that the clans will become extinct if foreign women are continually incorporated into the population has become a truism for the Tobians. This prediction does not appear to be well founded, however, at least with respect to the more populous clans. The continuity of a clan depends not on the social identity of the women married by its men but rather on the production of female children by its women, something which the current population of Tobian young women has managed to do quite successfully. Thus far they have married only their fellow Tobians and given birth to a number of female children. All these children are full members of their mother's clan, of course, as are the few children who have been born to these women out of wedlock. Therefore the biological continuity of most clans is assured for at least one more generation, regardless of the fact that a number of Palauan women have married into them. The other fear, expressed by the young men in their attempt to persuade the elders to waive the rule, appears equally unrealistic. The foreign women who have married into Tobi have so far been mainly from inferior-ranked Palauan clans. Having relatively little to lose in Palau, they have been rapidly assimilated into Tobian society. These women have mastered the fundamentals of their adopted culture, even the Marino system. Although there is some difference in the speed and thoroughness of their integration, all appear to be quite at home with the islanders. Children of these unions are fluent in both Tobian and Palauan and are quite bicultural. Their mastery of Palauan culture is the only thing that combines with their lack of Tobian clan to distinguish these children from others of their generation. Although they are genealogically half-Palauan, there is certainly no evidence that they will cause Tobian culture to undergo any dramatic changes. Their social links to Palau through their mothers may help them when they participate in district institutions, and there may be a higher rate of movement out of Tobian society and into Palauan society from this group than from full-blooded Tobians. The prediction that "soon there will be no more Tobians but only half-caste Palauans" may or may not be accurate. The inference that Tobi will eventually be a mere appendage of Palau appears unlikely.

Finally, it must be noted that even if all the clans were to become extinct there would be few if any repercussions. The clans function only in the regulation of marriage. As regulators of who may marry whom, they are complemented by Catholic incest regulations. Clans have no other function today, regardless of the role they may have played in the past. This statement must be qualified by the exception offered by some of the old people for whom clan affiliation provides a minor, though important, component of self-identity. For all except these two or three persons, who are, of course, the most adamant about the inviolable nature of the clans, these social units are simply groupings of people who may not marry one another. The clans have no estates and neither do they play a role in the ritual life of the island.

If clan exogamy was not unique in these ways, the dispute over its maintenance might have been considerably different. The incorporation of a number of Palauan women into Tobian society threatens neither the clans nor the society as a whole. If this were not so then the young men might be able to force an abandonment of the clan exogamy rule. However, the underlying factors, in particular the young people's need to remain Catholic and the old people's control of the Marino corpus, do mean that the outcome of this dispute will be dictated by the elders. This is true of all disputes between the two generations involving the teachings of Father Marino. The argument over the relationship of the chieftaincy to the church is an example of another type of dispute. Father Marino's teachings also are involved in this dispute, but the parties are not divided along generational lines. There can be no resolution of disputes of this sort because all parties have access to the Marino corpus through their older members.

Changes in the Marino system and the behavior it justifies depend on the survivors of the original conversion. If they decide, either consciously or unconsciously, to remember things differently, then the system can be adapted to meet changed circumstances. Failing that decision, change must wait upon their death.

CONCLUSION

The questions of why the Tobians converted so rapidly to Catholicism, why they appear so orthodox in their observance of Catholicism, and why they are so active in its practice are three aspects of but a single problem: Why is Tobian religion the way it is today?

Past events reveal the fundamental and increasing pressures to which the Tobians have been subjected. Their world view helps to explain their response to those pressures. Thus the religious nature of the reaction to depopulation follows from the islanders' definitions of both disasters and religious ritual and the connection assumed to exist between them. This combination of history and world view promoted rapid and unanimous conversion to Catholicism.

The apparent orthodoxy of current Tobian religious behavior can best be understood as an epiphenomenon. The meaning of these behavioral forms is to be found not in their content but in their status as validated procedures for preventing disasters and maintaining Catholic identity. Their validation is provided by the system of precepts the Tobians have constructed out of the remembered fragments of events surrounding the work of their evangelist, Father Marino. Each fragment conveys meanings to the Tobians. Unlike the Kaliai of New Britain (see chapter 13), the Tobians have not seized upon similarities in Christian and native myths and symbols to adapt the religion to its new context. Instead Tobians have created a system which justifies and even compels close adherence to the new religion in an unmodified form. This adherence extends to the frequency with which religious ritual is performed. This frequency is a result of a combination of ideas about the function of religion with faith in the Marino system.

Of course in both behavior and belief there have been some departures from the faith propagated by the Vatican. To clarify these differences it is necessary to distinguish between knowledge of religious beliefs, personal commitment to those beliefs, and beliefs about religion. Tobians have knowledge of most traditional Catholic beliefs. They know of the Virgin, the Trinity, papal infallibility, and other Roman Catholic dogmas. They have little personal involvement with those beliefs, and in this sense they are different from many other Catholics. Such involvement as they do show is as much an epiphenomenon of the Marino system as the constant attention to prayers, the words of which also convey no meaning to them. Tobians also have a set of beliefs about religion which are not shared by most other Catholics. These ideas about the nature and function of religion lead them to give great weight to those few beliefs they do not share with other Catholics. Their faith in Father Marino as personal savior with power over ghosts would certainly be rejected by current missionaries were they to learn of it; however, this belief is basic to the Catholicism of the islanders. The missionaries would have little success if they attempted to bring the Tobians into conformity on this point of doctrine and to eliminate Marino from his role as savior. The highly personalized view of the church taken by the islanders, which is so evident in the manner in which they dismiss the American priest's efforts to withdraw church sanctions from the clan exogamy rule, would make the attempt a contest between the present missionaries and the ever-present Marino. Refusal to grant the American priest equal status with Father Marino rests upon the islanders' failure to grasp the institutional nature of the church. To them a contradiction of the Marino system by a missionary can only be resolved by balancing one priest's words against another's. Even when missionaries have the support of a considerable segment of the Tobian population they may fail to modify behavior based on the Marino system. This is particularly striking because the use of the Marino system to validate the prohibition of marriage between clan mates perpetuates a rule which is felt to be a burden by some and a blessing by no one.

Father Marino was an agent of change for the Tobians. He converted them to Christianity by offering them an escape from the paradox of formal secularism without a concomitant secularization of world view. Yet by mythologizing him the islanders have become immersed in another difficulty. In constructing an ideology out of his teachings, the Tobians invented a system which responds only minimally to changes in its environment and makes of Father Marino an agent of conservation. The very institution that Marino served is powerless to adjust the system to changed realities. For the Tobians the missionary's stature does not derive from his status as a consecrated representative of the true faith. Rather, the stature of Catholicism is derived from its status as the religion of Father Marino.

NOTES

The research upon which this chapter is based was financed by a National Institute of Mental Health grant (MH 12766). Thirteen months were spent with the Tobians; of this, a little over three months were spent in Eang, the Tobi village in Palau, and the remainder on the atoll. An additional thirteen months were spent with the people as a Peace Corps volunteer from 1967 to 1969. All but one of these earlier months was spent on the atoll. Comments and suggestions on an earlier version of this chapter were made by Decktor Korn, D. K. Jordan, R. Levy, R. McKnight, T. Schwartz, M. Spiro, and S. Tiffany.

1. Although administratively part of Palau District since the early years of this century, Tobi is linguistically and culturally much closer to the other atolls of the Western Carolines than it is to the high islands of Palau.
2. Captain Fred K. Klebingat (personal communication) informed me that he passed by Tobi on the vessel *Anna* in 1907. The vessel's master refused to stop for the canoes which set out from the island because he feared the Tobians' hostile intentions.
3. Eang village is located on Arakabesan Island, which is connected to the island of Koror by a causeway. The inhabitants of the village are derived from the populations of Tobi and three other small atolls south of Palau proper—Sonsorol, Merir, and Pulo Ana—which together with Tobi make up the Southwest Islands. The four atolls exhibit a great deal of uniformity in their cultures. Their peoples speak mutually intelligible dialects, and both culture and language are remote from those of Palau. About one-half of the approximately 150 people of Eang are permanent residents; the remainder compose a mobile population which commutes between the Southwest Islands and Palau. The culture of Eang differs significantly from that of each of the four home islands. These differences reflect the village's integration into the Palauan cash economy, the structurally marginal position of its permanent inhabitants to the societies of both their home islands and Palau, and the village's complex history.
4. Mourning rites provide the single exception to this. They are Christian in that they are the occasion of endless prayer and at least three church services, but they do not follow orthodox Catholic practice. From the canoe in which the deceased is buried and the elaborate food presentations after his funeral to the rigorous year-long taboos placed upon his close female kin, these practices seem to be an amalgamation of aboriginal and Catholic ritual. It is not surprising, considering what we know about Tobian ghosts, that the one area of ritual activity where syncretistic forces have clearly been at work is that which is concerned with death.
5. The pattern set by the first baptism still holds to some extent; that is, many godparents of the present population are natives of the other three Southwest Islands. There is a competing pattern in which close relatives of one of the parents (usually the mother) stand as godparents. Tobians who are not closely related rarely act as godparents. Godparenthood is of no great importance in Tobian social life. The other church-introduced pseudo-kinship bonds—those of marriage parents, or people who stand surety for the two partners to a marriage—are occasionally activated when the priest seeks help in the reconciliation of a marital dispute.
6. This will not be the case fifteen or twenty years from now when children of recently married siblings come of age. It will be interesting to see what will happen then. The prediction, of course, is that a teaching which validates cross-cousin marriage will be remembered. As with all predictions of this sort, the caveat "all things being equal" applies. A much safer prediction is that all things will not be equal—that the Tobian universe will expand ever faster, that these children will have more exposure to the priests in Koror, and that unforeseen

events will occur.
7. This system of people being in charge of each other is much more complex than I have presented it here. Of importance is the high value placed on noninterference in other people's affairs. This is directly contrary to the ideology behind the 'in charge' system and leads to many contradictions. Some women, moreover, especially widows, occupy powerful political and economic positions with flair and vigor and are far from the incompetent creatures the system makes them out to be.
8. Shouting in public the name of a person's dead father is thought to drive that person insane. Even overhearing the name of one's dead father is thought to be dangerous and likely to lead to insanity. I take this to indicate highly ambivalent feelings toward the father.
9. The population as a whole, however, possesses the knowledge to trace the genealogies of most people in a given clan back to a common ancestress. This was demonstrated to me when I compared the various individual genealogies I had collected. It is possible for me, but for no individual Tobian who has not duplicated the work that I have done, to construct a series of clan genealogies.
10. This was graphically illustrated in the meeting held to find the perpetrator of the attempted homicide. The meeting was held on the front steps of the church so that the angels could help the people find the truth. The fact that only church services can be held within the church is all that prevented the meeting from being held inside. The realization that a class of ghosts is not necessarily closed for all time, and that additional types of beings can be added to it in the way that angels apparently were, was brought home to me at that same meeting when one of the younger women, a great fan of Classic Comics, bemoaned the remoteness of the island from America in the following words: "If only we weren't so far from the States probably those fairies and elves would help us now."
11. This is an actual quotation overheard in just this context. There is a certain element of truth here. The American priest, who periodically visits the island, told me that he considers life on the island difficult and will do anything he can to make it easier for the people. In the past this has led to his exercising a considerable degree of flexibility in permitting related people to marry. To this priest the clans are an interesting impediment in the path of the happiness of young lovers. To the occasional Palauan priest, raised in a culture which can almost be characterized as clan-ridden, the notion of clanship makes sense. A Palauan priest has told me that he would like to see the Tobi clans continue because they provide people with a bigger family than they ordinarily would have.

13

CHRISTIANITY IN KALIAI: RESPONSE TO MISSIONIZATION IN NORTHWEST NEW BRITAIN

Dorothy Ayers Counts

In this chapter I present an analysis of the effect of the Kaliai Roman Catholic Mission (Order of the Sacred Heart, MSC) on the people of Northwest New Britain, focusing on the relationship between ideological and socioeconomic change. The mission has attempted to be an agent of change on two fronts. It offers the Roman Catholic version of Christianity as an alternative to the pagan beliefs of the Kaliai people, and it provides a combination of social services and programs that are intended to facilitate social and economic change. I am particularly concerned here with understanding the Kaliai response to missionization. Some of the mission's programs and doctrines have been accepted, some have been rejected, and some have been transformed by the Kaliai into a cargo movement. I want to show how and why these various responses have taken the form they have.

The term "Kaliai" has two meanings. It is the name of a census subdivision in Northwest New Britain that includes about 2,000 people who speak five different languages and live in some twenty-three villages on the coast and in the interior of New Britain. It also refers to the approximately 750 people who speak the Kaliai language and live in five villages located along the coast of the Kaliai census subdivision. In this chapter "Kaliai" refers to these latter people.

The Kaliai are subsistence gardeners who maintain a way of life that is largely traditional. Although almost all adults produce some copra as a cash crop, the people are deeply involved in the exchange and distribution of shell money and other valuables that is a central focus of their ceremonial life. People still hold their customary beliefs in the existence and potency of ghosts, bush spirits, and ancestral spirits, and traditional myths are believed to explain the relationship of men to one another and to their physical and spiritual universe. *Singsings*—festivals of dancing and singing that include masked ancestral figures—are regularly performed during ceremonial cycles, and it is common for people to dress in the traditional costume of barkcloth loin cover or fiber skirt and dance and sing throughout the night.

The important unit of Kaliai social organization is the *kambu* 'patrisib'. Each patrisib is named for the tract of land in which the group holds rights of use, residence, and alienation. The members of a patrisib customarily live together in a village, or in one section of a village, where they share a man's house with various non-patrisib members, such as orphans, affines who have settled uxorilocally, and other kinsmen related through females who have been drawn by the group or its big man.

Although the people of the Kaliai census subdivision have been in contact with white people since the turn of this century, they had had little intensive contact with them until World War II, when the area was the scene of a series of battles and occupations by the Japanese, the Australians, and the Americans. Today their contact with whites is limited to an occasional visit by an administration official from the patrol post at Cape Gloucester, some 80 kilometers from the eastern boundary of Kaliai and to meetings with the manager of Iboki Plantation where a few people go to work, sell garden produce, or buy at the trade store. There is, moreover, some interaction with the personnel at the Kaliai mission. Until 1971, all the priests and nuns at the mission were of Australian or European background.

Roman Catholic missionaries first contacted Kaliai in 1908. At that time Bishop Louis Couppé, the first vicar apostolic of New Britain, bought approximately 10 hectares of land about 2 kilometers inland from the coastal village of Taveliai in exchange for some steel tools. Shortly after the land was sold, a raid on the bishop was led by a number of the Kaliai big men. The missionaries left Kaliai without setting up a permanent mission. Although there were a few catechists in the area, the Catholics made no further attempt to establish a mission until after World War II. In 1950, Father McSweeney came to Kaliai and the first mission was built.

MISSION SERVICES

The Kaliai mission engages in two types of activity. It teaches the Roman Catholic version of Christianity and it offers social services. The mission provides the people of the census subdivision with almost all their medical and educational facilities.[1] It also purchases locally produced copra, runs a trade store, and offers assistance to local entrepreneurs who want to establish similar businesses in their own villages. The social services draw local people into the mission. Villagers who accept the invitation to education or medical care are also encouraged to attend mass and become parishioners.

The social services are intended by church policy to operate within the boundaries of the economic system. Although health and educational programs were initially offered free to the Kaliai, the mission is under heavy pressure to become self-supporting. In 1971, the church headquarters at Vunapope had instructed the Kaliai mission to charge small fees for school and clinic services. The Catholic priest assigned to the Kaliai was frustrated by this policy, for he feared that it would limit the people who could take advantage of mission assistance and would restrict his ability to expand into the isolated villages of the Kaliai interior.

Although the mission offers social services not otherwise available to the people, its presence has been regarded as a mixed blessing by the whites at Iboki Plantation and the Cape Gloucester patrol post and by the Kaliai themselves. Specifically, the missionaries are resented when they attempt to mediate between the people and other whites or when they compete too successfully for resources, dollars, or political strength. There has, for instance, been considerable friction between the Kaliai and the mission over the alienation and use of land. The mission's economic ventures are generally viewed with hostility, and attempts by the priests to engage in political activities or to mediate between the patrol officer and the villagers have angered government officials.

When land for the Kaliai mission was purchased by Bishop Couppé in 1908, boundary markers were reportedly placed around the section that had been sold. When Father McSweeney arrived to establish the mission, however, the boundary markers could not be located. This placed the missionaries in a difficult situation. The people of Taveliai village, who had traditionally owned the land, expressed considerable dissatisfaction with the missionaries who came claiming a right to establish a permanent mission after so long a time. There was never a dispute over whether the mission had, in fact, purchased the land. At issue was the fact that the payment had gone to people who were dead rather than to the living claimants of the land. In 1971 the priest and the patrol officer at Cape Gloucester both told me that the land problem had been settled. The land purchased by Bishop Couppé lay at the bottom of a hill near the beach and the village of Taveliai. This property had been exchanged for land at the top of the hill where the mission buildings stand. Although this agreement was accepted by the mission and the elders of Taveliai, some villagers were still complaining in 1971 that they had not personally received compensation for the alienated land.

In 1975, dissatisfied Taveliai villagers again raised the issue with administration officials. As of November 1975, no compromise had been reached. Indeed, settlement seemed impossible as different groups claimed ownership of the two parcels of land in question. As a result, the priest, with the encouragement of the patrol officer, planned to suggest to his bishop that Kaliai be converted from mission to parish status. If this change occurs, land ownership will revert to the people and the church will lose its external funding. The school already receives government support, and mission clinics will soon also be government financed and staffed, according to the patrol officer. These services will continue, with government funding, if the landowners agree, but the continued church presence in the Kaliai area will rest on the support of the local people and the ability of the church to pay its own way.

Dissatisfaction over the alienation of the mission land was transferred to a dispute between some of the people of Taveliai and the parents of the children who attend the mission school but live in neighboring villages. As the mission itself has no dormitory facilities, the children live during the week in small houses built on the beach. Although the priest persuaded some of the Taveliai elders, who are also parishioners, to agree to the building of the children's houses, some villagers complained that the children were using the land without the permission of all the people who had a claim in it. As a result, some persons in Taveliai were suspicious that the children stole food from local gardens and vandalized property, while the children's parents were concerned that their offspring might be the victims of sorcery. The villagers' antagonism to the housing of schoolchildren on their land came to a head in 1972 when they expelled the children from the beach. I have been given various explanations for the expulsion. According to some informants, the villagers were angered by criticisms that their unfenced pigs left excrement around the children's dormitories, creating a health hazard. Taveliai villagers felt that the critics should fence the pigs in their own villages before pointing at those belonging to others. Another group of informants claimed that Taveliai villagers became enraged when Kandokan children took all the first prizes in an intramural contest sponsored by the mission school. At any rate, the Taveliai villagers ordered the Kandokan children off their land. In response, the priest established another primary school at the village site of Avelalu in Kaliai interior and encouraged the Kandokans to send their children there until tempers cooled down.

Gradually, most of the Kandokan children returned to Kaliai to school after their parents were invited by a Taveliai kinsman to join him in building a small settlement on the bank of the Aliawana River, about 3 kilometers from the mission. As of 1975, however, seven Kandokan households continued to send their children to Avelalu and maintained that they intended to have nothing more to do with Taveliai villagers or their land. Thus the problem of land alienation and use by the mission has been a source of irritation between the missionaries and some of the Kaliai, while the use of land on behalf of the mission has caused controversy between the people of Taveliai and their neighbors along the coast.

The mission's economic activities are primarily confined to the purchase of local copra and the management of a small trade store. Catholic priests working with the Kaliai have emphasized to me that while they do not object to making a small profit, they have established their business enterprise primarily to provide a source of cash for the villagers. Such cash permits the villagers to dress their children for school and buy needed tools, clothing, and food supplements. The missionaries' concern that the local people be encouraged to enter the cash economy has led them to assist local people to begin enterprises that are competitive with the mission's. In 1960, for instance, Father Anton Hayes of Kaliai and the patrol officer at Cape Gloucester helped the people of the villages of Kandoka and Lauvori to open the Kandoka-Lauvori Copra Society. The society was originally financed by a tax of $A2 levied on each household in the two villages.[2] When Father Hayes was transferred from Kaliai, funds were withdrawn from the society's bank account and the original $A2 investments were repaid. The society operated by purchasing locally produced copra which it shipped to Rabaul for sale to the Copra Marketing Board. Profits from the sale of the copra were used to buy trade goods which were sold in Kandoka by the society's store. Profits from the sale of these items were used to buy more local copra. After the society was established, the patrol officer left its supervision to the priest in the Kaliai area. When my husband and I arrived in Kaliai in October 1966, the society had a small inventory with prices which had been set by the priest and which were slightly out of date on some items. After we became involved in the operation of the society by helping with orders and price revision, we were told by the society managers, by the manager of Iboki Plantation, and by the administration officials at Cape Gloucester that our presence in the area and our assistance to the society had "cramped the father's style," as he was more interested in making profits in his own store than he was in helping the local people. Resentment against the priest was also expressed by the villagers in 1971 when we heard the repeated complaint that the mission store's prices were too high, its copra purchasing prices were too low, and it was offering unfair competition to the society store which was defunct when we arrived in Kaliai.

The villagers' resentment of the mission store came as a result of two incidents. First, in 1971, the wholesale price of rice rose sharply and, consequently, the priest raised the price of a 100-pound bag of rice from $A5 to $A6. Then the patrol officer posted an announcement of the price paid by the Copra Marketing Board in Rabaul in the local government council hall at Cape Gloucester. The Rabaul price was $A.0526 per pound, or $A8.42 for a 160-pound bag of smoke-dried copra. There was no statement of a recommended or fair price for local purchasers. When the announcement was seen by the Kaliai councillors, they returned to tell their constituents that the mission's price of $A.0450 per pound or $A6.20 for a 160-pound bag of copra was too low and to insist that the local people refuse to sell to the priest unless he offered $A.0500 per pound or $A8.05 for a 160-pound bag. People also stopped selling to Iboki Plantation and to the Kandoka-Lauvori Society, which offered $A.0300 and $A.0350 a pound respectively.

Before I can offer an analysis of this particular dispute over copra prices and the more general criticisms of the mission by the patrol officer and the plantation manager, I must clarify several points.

First, the Catholic priests in Kaliai willingly offered us assistance in working with the society in both 1966-1967 and 1971. We were cheerfully allowed to see the financial records of the society on both occasions, and no resentment of our activities was ever expressed to us by anyone at the mission.

Second, in addition to the price paid by the mission for local copra, there was a fixed expense of $A1.50 for each bag purchased: $A.5000 for the sack and $A1 freight to Rabaul. Thus, when the price in Rabaul was $A.0526 per pound, the priest made a profit of $A.7200 on each 160-pound bag of copra he bought.

I know from my examination of the mission store's financial records that the priest often lost money on the local copra he purchased. He lost money when the ship service was irregular, as it frequently is in Kaliai, and his copra rotted in the sheds. And when the prices paid by the Copra Marketing Board went down, he lost as much as $A.05 on each bag he purchased. Nevertheless, he continued buying the local copra, as Father Norbert Empen explained to me in 1971, so that the villagers would not become discouraged and give up their attempts at cash cropping.

Third, the trade store at Iboki Plantation was the affair of the plantation manager. Profits from it were his own and were not shared with the owner of the plantation. Any profits from the sale of locally produced copra bought with trade store profits also belonged to the manager.

Fourth, prices in the plantation trade store were uniformly higher than those at the mission store and were either higher or the same as prices at the society store. Prices paid by the plantation for locally produced copra were usually lower than prices paid either by the mission or the society.

Fifth, the plantation's social relations with the mission and the local people depended on the personality of the manager. One of the managers during 1966-1967 was an alcoholic who bragged of having killed two native workers. He verbally and physically abused his workers, acts which we witnessed, and on one occasion his behavior so enraged his laborers that they advanced on him with machetes and might well have killed him had we not been present as witnesses. This man was critical of the priest's economic enterprise and suspicious of his motives in helping the villagers.

In contrast, the manager of the plantation in 1971 shared neither the antagonism toward the mission nor the contempt for the local people that was expressed by his predecessors. Although he frankly stated that he was in business to make a profit, he was also willing to help the villagers share in his economic enterprises, an approach which he said benefited both himself and the local people. In 1971 he helped a group of Kandokans who were related to one of his foremen open a village development group that operated in the same way as the society (Counts 1973), and he assisted the same group in starting their own cocoa plantation. His attitude toward the mission was one of neutrality. He explained the difference in his prices and the priest's as being due to their different goals and opined that if the missionaries did not offer more realistic copra prices they would soon go broke.

The resentment by the local villagers and resident whites of the economic involvement of the missionaries can, I believe, be explained. Many villagers did not understand the relationship between prices in Rabaul and local prices. Furthermore, most village people do not have a dependable source of cash income though they do have a steady need for money. They must depend on their copra production to provide them with the cash required to pay taxes, school, and clinic fees and to buy goods. When copra prices fall or store prices rise, they see their money disappearing and become frustrated. The missionary is a visible target for their anger, for it seems that he hypocritically expresses his concern for their welfare and his commitment to their development while at the same time he raises prices and profits from their labor. This explanation was originally suggested to me by an informant who, because he had a pension and was thus less dependent on his cash crop than his neighbors, was less emotional about the problem and more sympathetic toward the missionaries than were many of his fellow villagers.

Furthermore, the whites who felt threatened by the missionaries focused their criticism on areas where the missionaries were ambiguous and thus more vulnerable. The Western norm that missionaries may legitimately compete for souls but not for either dollars or political strength, makes political and economic activities particularly susceptible to criticism. I cannot prove, of course, that the plantation manager's condemnation of the priest's economic activities was a displaced defense of his own attitudes and life-style, which were antithetical to that of the missionaries. Yet it is relevant to note that the other manager, whose attitudes toward the native population were not inconsistent with those of the missionaries, was not critical of the priest's economic activities.

The antagonism between the patrol officer and the priest, on the other hand, seemed to be based on the officer's concern that the priest would interpose himself between the patrol officer and the people, thus usurping political authority that legitimately belonged to him. Furthermore, the patrol officer seemed to feel that any power, economic or otherwise, held by the missionary might be used to further his political ambitions.

The friction between the priest and the administration officials at the Gloucester patrol post, friction which was apparently absent in 1971, seems to have grown out of a personality clash. This clash took the form of a covert struggle for authority in the Kaliai census subdivision and resulted in a confrontation in 1966 when a fight occured in an interior village as the result of an illicit affair between a local girl and a native medical assistant. Everyone involved in any way in the fight, including the Catholic catechist, was arrested and sentenced to jail for thirty days by the patrol officer. These people were then required to walk from interior Kaliai to Cape Gloucester, a distance of about 80 kilometers, much of it through trackless rain forest and mangrove swamp.

Apparently the patrol officer, who was on patrol in Kaliai, and the Catholic priest stationed there heard of the fight and arrived on the scene at about the same time. Versions of what then happened between the two men differ. According to the patrol officer, the priest attempted to get special treatment for his catechist, a self-admitted participant in the fight, by trying to talk the patrol officer into setting a fine for him which the priest would pay (the term used by the officer was "buy the court"). When this approach was unsuccessful, the priest urged the officer to allow him to bring the catechist to jail in the mission boat rather than requiring him to walk with the others. The patrol officer refused.

The priest's version of the dispute was that his catechist had become involved only in an attempt to stop the fight, and that the patrol officer, who acted as both judge and jury, was grossly unfair in assessing responsibility and assigning punishment. The priest had left for the interior village as soon as he heard of the fight, hoping to get there in time to settle the problem before the patrol officer arrived. He got there too late and could do nothing.

The tension between the two representatives of white authority was exacerbated by the fact that the mission personnel were on the scene whereas the administration personnel at Cape Gloucester were 80 kilometers away. No roads link the patrol post to the Bariai and Kaliai divisions of the administrative district. When an emergency arose, there was a temptation for the priest to deal with the matter himself without calling in the patrol officer with whom he was often in disagreement. The priest could, with reason, argue that the official might be unable to get to Kaliai and settle a dispute before it had time to develop. He could also argue reasonably that because he lived in Kaliai, he knew more about the problems and disputes there than did the patrol officer who visited infrequently. It is against this background that the priest might be expected to become involved in political affairs to protect his own against what he viewed as the arbitrary "judge and jury" approach of the administration officials.

The patrol officer, on the other hand, had the ultimate responsibility and authority for maintaining peace in Kaliai. He viewed with alarm what he saw as the priest's attempts to carry out the prerogatives of a patrol officer rather than notify him, particularly as he was convinced that the priest gave preferential treatment to mission converts. The patrol officer was convinced of the priest's insistence that the people of Kaliai vote for the mission's candidate for the House of Assembly, threatening those who did not with hellfire. He was certain, moreover, that the missionary levied fines on couples who did not have their babies at the mission, that he failed to report violence but rather levied "fines" which went into church coffers, and that he refused medical treatment to local people who were not regular church attenders. Against this background, it might be expected that the patrol officer would react angrily to the priest's attempt to settle quietly a dispute before the officer arrived, especially when the priest attempted to arrange more lenient treatment for his own catechist.

The previous accounts illustrate the dilemma of the Kaliai missionary. On the one hand, he is expected to provide social services as well as religious doctrine to the people of his parish, and he is encouraged by his superiors to help his parishioners enter the cash economy so that eventually the mission can become self-supporting. But if he opens a trade store and buys local cash crops, his motives are suspect and other local people, white and native, accuse him of being unfairly competitive with local enterprises and of attempting to gain an economic hold on potential converts. Other whites especially feel that the missionary should limit himself to providing eduational and medical services and preaching the gospel. Yet the missionary may be the only representative of white authority who has an intimate knowledge of local affairs, who is on the spot, and who has, furthermore, responsibility for a number of local people, such as catechists and teachers, who are under his direction. Given these circumstances, it is to be expected that an active priest will develop an interest in local political affairs. If, however, this interest is translated into action, other whites in the area may view his action as an inappropriate exercise of power and a challenge to the administration.

It is obvious from the accounts just given that the whites with whom the Kaliai come in contact do not present a united front; far from it. There are tensions between the representatives of white authority, the church and the administration, and this fact is not lost on the Kaliai. The people's response to the conflict has, so far, been subdued. I know of no local person who has attempted to manipulate white antagonisms to his own advantage. Active hostility has not, to my knowledge, existed between the missionaries and other whites in the area since the dispersal of the antagonists from the 1966-1967 period. Even then, direct contact between whites was limited. The missionaries and the plantation manager did not exchange visits; the patrol officer seldom came to the Kaliai area. When he did, except for the altercation mentioned, he and the missionary avoided each other. Their antagonism was limited to bitter complaining about one another, but never to the villagers themselves. Although the people were aware of antagonism, their remarks were restricted to the cynical comments that probably most of the criticisms of the patrol officer, manager, and missionary were based in fact and that the whole quarrel was just a white man's affair.

THE MISSION AND SOCIAL CHANGE

The social services dispensed by the mission have been accompanied by explicit attempts to change traditional practices and beliefs. Some of these attempts, such as offering a primary school education, have been successful, whereas mission efforts to change the marriage practices of the people have been only partially accomplished.

Those Kaliai who seem to be development-oriented—those, for instance, who have engaged in cash cropping while rejecting cargo activities and who have attempted to limit their participation in traditional exchanges (Counts 1971, 1972)—are determined that their children will receive as much education as possible. They accept the priest's assurances that education is the road to a better life and insist that their children attend the mission school regularly. They punish their children when they are truant and are proud when their children are chosen to attend the secondary school at Vunapope. When their children do not succeed—that is, when they are not among the top third of Kaliai children completing standard six who can be sent on to high school—their disappointment is tinged with bitterness at the mission and with feelings that their children have been unjustly denied the chance to become something other than simple villagers. The parents of these children have repeatedly asked the Gloucester Local Government Council to establish a high school for the local children, a project the council has been unable to finance. In 1971, the fathers of several boys who had not qualified for the Vunapope secondary school walked to Kandrian to enter their sons in the government school there. They brought the boys home after investigating the school, however, because they felt that it was designed more to provide local whites with inexpensive domestic and plantation labor than to give children the training that would enable them to earn more than the minimum wage of common laborers.

The feeling that formal education is, at best, only indirectly associated with any improvement in life-style is shared by many of the Kaliai. The white man's schools, together with his government, taxes, and religion, are roundly denounced by those who are convinced they are being exploited. In 1967 four villages in interior Kaliai refused to participate in the newly formed Gloucester Council (Counts 1971). These people, many of whom had been involved in a cargo movement, told the patrol officer that they had no use for any of the white man's things, including his schools, his church, and his taxes. Again, in 1971, an irate councillor and leader of the Story, a Kaliai-based cargo movement, informed me that the whites were willing to share worthless things but not the secrets of real value that enabled men to obtain goods and live a modern style of life.

The attempts of the mission to alter traditional marriage practices have been successful only with those people who seem to have concluded independently that customary patterns were unwise or at least incompatible with economic development.

According to tradition, marriages were arranged by the parents of the bride and groom about the time a girl reached puberty. The young couple was expected to have minimal contact before their marriage, and the wedding was the occasion for the distribution of large amounts of shell money and other bridewealth items. However, the Kaliai assume that a sexually mature male and female are alone together for only one purpose, and any intimate contact between a man and a woman usually resulted in the payment of an indemnity if the woman was married, in marriage if she was not. Most Kaliai marriages of which I have knowledge were in fact not arranged in the ideal manner but were acknowledgments of the fact that a man and woman had become sexually intimate or had actually set up housekeeping together. About 5 percent of all marriages (3/60 households in 1966-1967; 4/70 in 1975-1976) in the villages of Kandoka and Lauvori were polygynous. One man had five wives. A man might have as many wives as he was constitutionally able to endure and could afford, as only his first wife was provided for him by his elder paternal kinsmen. The acquisition of several wives provided visible proof of a man's economic and sexual prowess and gave him a wide range of affines on whom he might draw, as well as many who could also come to him for economic support. Kaliai genealogies and traditional histories indicate that big men were frequently polygynous. One big man, who I estimate lived around the 1870s, achieved legendary status when he gave away all but one of his ten wives to his rivals in a mortuary distribution that has never been equaled in Kaliai.

The mission attempted to change these customs by ending polygyny, discouraging the marriage of newly pubescent girls, and limiting the amount of goods that might be given as bridewealth. It has been successful in its attempts to change the customs regarding polygyny and early marriage, at least among those people who feel that their best interests and those of their children are not served by either tradition. Progressive Kaliai, in particular, seem to feel that the marriage of their children in their early teens limits their educational opportunities and thus prevents them from acquiring skills that would enable them to work outside the village as anything other than common laborers. In 1971, for example, a young Kandokan man and a girl in her early teens from another Kaliai village were caught together in the bushes. At the urging of the girl's family, the parents of the couple agreed that they would be married. When word of the planned wedding reached the girl's village, however, the local government councillor, together with some of the important men of the village, came to Kandoka demanding that she be returned home and a fine be paid. Their argument was that since the girl attended Kaliai mission school the priest would forbid the marriage. The boy's parents immediately agreed, saying they considered their son too young to support a wife. After some angry shouting by the girl's father, who had anticipated a generous bridewealth, she was taken home by the men from her village. Thus a planned marriage between teenagers was canceled, at least ostensibly because of the missionary.

The priest has also been successful in preventing polygynous unions. In 1967, for example, a young woman from Kandoka village became pregnant by a married man. The couple planned to marry, but the priest in Kaliai protested to her parents and her maternal uncle. Not only was the arrangement in violation of church teaching, he argued, but the young woman would be a second wife and subject to abuse by the man's first wife. The girl's parents and uncle agreed, and the man paid a cash settlement for the child, who remained with her mother. When we returned to Kaliai in 1971, the young woman, then in her early twenties, still had not married. As it is unusual for a woman to remain single for so long, we asked why she had not married. We were told that the young men viewed her as a poor risk, for she remained fond of the father of her child, and they feared that they would be cuckolded.

As these accounts illustrate, the teachings of the mission regarding changing marriage practices may be taken into consideration when decisions are made, especially if they support decisions that might be made anyway, but for other reasons. The mission's stand against polygyny, for example, supports the feeling that is widespread among Kaliai men that polygynous marriages are best avoided. In spite of the prestige they bring to the man, such marriages are notoriously unhappy. The bickering between multiple wives has, according to accounts of informants, led several Kaliai polygynists to commit suicide or leave home for long periods of time. The plight of an aspiring Kandokan big man who had his house torn apart by quarreling wives in 1966, and who in 1971 kicked down his walls and door during a marital spat, is pointed to as typical. Thus, according to my monogamous informants, only an ambitious man or a fool takes more than one wife, an attitude that accords with the mission's teaching.

In contrast to the mission's success in limiting polygynous marriages and the marriage of teenaged girls, it has had little effect on bridewealth payments, even though limitations are heartily endorsed by many progressive Kaliai.

The mission's attempts to limit bridewealth began in the 1950s when the Roman Catholic missions along the north coast of New Britain tried to set a brideprice limit of $A50 in goods and cash. The same limit was set by the Gloucester Local Government Council in the late 1960s. Although there have been marriages performed by the mission that involved no exchange of bridewealth, their legitimacy is disputed by the older Kaliai leaders who still sponsor traditional weddings at which the $A50 limit is ignored. The younger, development-oriented Kaliai are frustrated by the insistence of their elders on expensive marriages. This division between older, traditional leaders and young progressives is, in essence, a disagreement between generations over the goals of a changing society. Traditionally, Kaliai leaders achieved big man status by, among other things, their acts of conspicuous generosity during ceremonial distributions. A man who could provide his followers with wives for whom a large bridewealth was given brought honor to himself and his entire kin group. A niggardly bridewealth was a cause for shame. In contrast, the younger men see little future for either themselves or their children in large traditional distributions which divert their time and energy from cash cropping and development projects which bring in the money. An account of contrasting attitudes toward a traditional wedding held in Kandoka village in 1971 illustrates this dichotomy.

M, the grandson of a retired Kandokan big man and the son of a rising big man, met L when they were both teaching in Talasea. M and L were married in Talasea in a church ceremony at which no bridewealth was given. L is the daughter of a Bakove-speaking big man from the Valupai area, and when her kinsmen learned of the wedding they approached M's paternal kin demanding that a large bridewealth be given. M's mother's brothers, who knew they would be required to provide half the bridewealth, are progressive Kandokans—they protested that the time and effort required to raise a large bridewealth would interfere with their cash cropping and informed L's kin that the official bridewealth of $A50 was all they were willing to pay. L's kinsmen rejected the offer, and M's mother's brothers asked the Valupai Local Government Council whether that area did not also have an official bridewealth maximum of $A50. The council replied that it did, but since L's family was important and demanded a large bridewealth, the council would not interfere in the matter. In July 1971, L's kinsmen came to Kandoka for the traditional wedding. M's kinsmen gave a brideprice of $A810 in shell money, valuables, pigs, and cash.

The bitterness and frustration of M's maternal kinsmen over the expense of the wedding were expressed to me by one of his mother's brothers:

> When are these ways going to end? All of us young men wish that these old men would hurry up and die so that this foolishness with shell money would end. They ruin us to collect this large bridewealth and we can't do our own work. Who is working copra? The clerk will come through to collect taxes and we'll have to say, "Sorry, can't pay, but we had a big wedding"! Then we can all move to Gloucester to jail. And it will serve us right.
>
> You may be happy to see a traditional wedding but all of us here are sick to death of it.

As the wedding of M and L illustrates, the mission's efforts to initiate social change are ineffective without support from the traditional leaders of Kaliai society. The elders regard the exchange of shell money and other ceremonial distributions as the heart of the society, and so long as they have influence they will resist attempts to change the system. Eventually, however, these old men will die or become senile and then the mission and the young progressives will succeed. This is acknowledged by the old men, who view it as a tragedy for their culture. The pathos of this inevitable change was expressed in 1967 by M's grandfather, who was then an active big man:

> These young men want to put an end to the bridewealth and the initiation payments. They want to end the mortuary ceremonies. They want to turn to cash and away from shell money. But if we don't have our ceremonies, if we don't have our shell money, what will there be to live for?

Obviously, the mission's success in dispensing social services and inducing change is closely related to ideological agreement between the missionaries and the people. People whose values are harmonious with those of the mission accept it and its programs, as do the progressive Kaliai. People who hold conflicting goals or feel threatened by the missionaries may be openly antagonistic toward them, as were the patrol officer and the plantation manager in 1966 and 1967; or they may ignore mission teachings, as the traditional leaders have ignored the limitations on bridewealth.

The mission's program of social service and its dispensing of doctrine are related. I shall turn now to a comparison of Christian doctrine and traditional Kaliai belief and a discussion of how the people have dealt with the introduced religious system.

THE TEACHING OF THE MISSION

The doctrine taught by the Kaliai mission may be treated in two parts: that relating to the nonempirical universe and that relating to Christian precepts.

The church's teaching regarding the universe is primarily concerned with the nature of God and the relationship between God and man: the teaching of the biblical account of creation and the origin of man's sinful nature; God's covenant with man and the giving of the Ten Commandments to Moses; the birth and crucifixion of Jesus; and the promise of redemption and union with God to those who accept the Christian faith, join the church, participate in church rituals, and live by Christian precepts.

The Christian precepts reflect the moral code of the white man and are closely related to the biblical account of man's nature and his relationship to God. To overcome his sinful nature, a person must believe in the Christian faith and follow the law of the church as it is interpreted by the pope. The law is found in the Ten Commandments, the teachings of Christ, and the letters and sermons of the organizers of the early church. Papal interpretation is based on nearly two thousand years of European theological debate and is heavily laden with European ethical values, many of them alien to Kaliai thought. Thus the missionaries urge Kaliai women to cover their breasts, they discourage polygynous marriages for moral reasons, and they teach that the practice of infanticide in case of deformity is sinful. Church doctrine predicts that man will inevitably fail in his attempt to lead a blameless life. Moreover, as sin separates man from God, the church through the person of the priest offers intercession through the rituals of confession and penance.

TRADITIONAL KALIAI BELIEF

The teachings of the Christian mission are based on a different view of the universe than that held by the Kaliai. There is, for example, no notion in Kaliai philosophy of the sinful nature of man and no idea that behavior might cause ethical problems that are not directly related to its practical results. The difference in philosophy affects the way in which the Kaliai perceive the mission and its offerings, and it structures the way they respond to it. For example, the degree to which the Kaliai are willing to accept medical care, the conditions under which they go to the clinic for treatment, and the kinds of illness they seek treatment for are predicated on Kaliai assumptions about the nature of illness and its relationship to the world of sorcery and spirits.

In traditional Kaliai belief, the boundaries between the empirical and the nonempirical world are unstable and may be shifted by human rituals or by the spirits themselves. Man is essentially noncreative. The significant elements of his culture—the cooking fire, crops, wealth, canoes—were given to him by spirit heroes during the mythological age. This period ended some six or seven generations ago when human behavior offended the heroes and caused them either to flee or to withdraw from intercourse with men. This "fall from grace" is analogous to the Christian Fall of Man, except that man's behavior was offensive, not morally defiling or sinful. Kaliai mythology recounts these events, and much of modern Kaliai ritual is concerned with reestablishing relations with spirits that are believed to bestow material wealth on human beings.

Although the mythological age is over, the world is still occupied by spirit creatures who may interact with men—*antu* 'ghosts' of long-dead ancestors who live in villages on the mountain peaks; *pura* 'cannibalistic monsters' who are often snake-man changelings who live in the forest or sometimes white people; and *iriao* 'bush spirits' that live in rocks, trees, or plots of ground and may take the form of snakes. Although contact is still possible with these creatures, it is not often sought because it is seldom beneficial. It is also possible to manipulate the nonempirical world through the use of sorcery, charms, and fertility magic. In addition, ceremonies often feature masked representations of the ancestor spirits whose appearance implies harmony between the two planes. One goal of the ambitious Kaliai man is to manipulate both the empirical and the nonempirical worlds to his own benefit, and traditionally the Kaliai big man could accomplish this feat better than most.

The intrusion into this world by white people with their superior technology and their different cosmology presented the Kaliai with a situation for which their traditional beliefs could not account. The Kaliai are a pragmatic people: the ultimate test of something is whether it works and it appeared that the whites, with their wealth of goods and their knowledge of different gods, had control of the situation. From the questions the Kaliai ask about the white man's world, it is apparent they assume that during the mythological age his spirit heroes/deities gave him the superior cultural items—steel tools, machinery, ships, airplanes—he now enjoys. The Kaliai seem to think that whites are still in their age of miracles, for informants frequently asked if these things were still being created and whether their creation was initiated by men or by God.

Contact with the white world and the offerings of the mission have not invalidated traditional Kaliai belief, but they have necessitated a retrenchment while people make sense of new information. Although traditional wisdom does not explain white people and their wonders, the Christian cosmology is not entirely satisfactory either. Biblical stories do not, for example, account for the unique experiences of New Britain people, such as the destruction of the population in the late 1800s by smallpox rather than by flood, nor are they in accord with the traditional explanation of prehistorical events, such as the dispersal of languages in New Britain. The Kaliai's attempt to reconcile their contact experience and Christian cosmology with their traditional ideological system has resulted in an evolving syncretic philosophy that incorporates both Christian and Kaliai beliefs. Because Kaliai ideology is evolving, it can be expected to continue changing as people experiment with alternative explanations and their environment. the experimentation with ideology, ritual, and new forms of organization that whites often term "cargo cult" is, in Kaliai, simply the overt expression of this syncretic process.

Missionaries in Kaliai have not encouraged the people to develop a syncretic religious system. Indeed, in 1971 the priest was annoyed that the leader of the Story had incorporated elements of Catholic doctrine and ritual into the cargo movement. The missionaries have, however, been consistently mild in their attempts to convert the people and tolerant toward traditional religion. The emphasis has been on positive action rather than on negating the existing religious structure. Few direct attacks appear to have been made on local beliefs and rituals; in fact, the priests have even participated in local ceremonies, to the delight of the Kaliai. People talk with distinct pleasure, for instance, of one priest who became involved in a mortuary exchange cycle and was given a pig which he then had to find a way to reciprocate. During our stay in Kaliai in 1971 the priest acted as a bank for the Kaliai shell currency that is required for weddings, initiations, mortuary cycles, and virtually all formal gift exchanges (Counts and Counts 1970). He also accepted shell money occasionally as payment for items in his trade store and then resold it at cost to his parishioners when they needed it for ceremonial distributions.

The Kaliai people say that although the church has forbidden ceremonies during Advent and Lent and discourages *singsings* on Saturday night because the all-night dancing interferes with attendance at mass, the missionaries have specifically encouraged the continuation of festivals and ceremonies, including those that involve the participation of masked dancers representing the ancestors. After World War II, for instance, a Kilenge man, who was both a high-ranking village official and a big man, went from village to village along the coast from Kilenge to Kaliai, took the ritual paraphernalia, ancestor masks, and bullroarers from the men's houses, and showed them to the women. He argued that traditional ways were bad and that people could get the white man's goods only by abandoning custom. Exposing the ritual objects to the women was, he reasoned, a direct way to bring an end to traditional practices. After the Kilenge man had left, some of the Kaliai leaders asked Father Hayes if the ways of the ancestors were indeed bad and whether the masks and bullroarers should be destroyed. Father Hayes reportedly told the Kaliai that the ancestral ways were not evil and that the items should be kept and the ceremonies continued, even though many of the things were no longer secret from the women. When I attempted to verify this story in 1967, the priest then at Kaliai said he had heard the same story and was in full agreement with Father Hayes, reasoning that traditional festivals with masks and betel were preferable to the Rabaul version with guitars and liquor.

The tolerant attitude of the Catholic priests toward Kaliai customs and beliefs has allowed almost all of the Kaliai to become parishioners of the mission and at the same time retain their traditions virtually intact. Thus while professing Catholicism, the people maintain the traditional rituals and firmly believe in the world of spirits, ghosts, and sorcery they were taught by their fathers. The activities of the mission have, however, altered the content of these beliefs and rituals. The mission's medical program has led the Kaliai to modify their ideology of disease, for example, and the Story, a local cargo movement, has blended Christian and traditional myth, ritual, and ideology.

THE KALIAI IDEOLOGY OF DISEASE

The coastal Kaliai believed that most congenital deformity, disease, and death was caused by a malevolent agent: a spirit or a sorcerer. Natural death or serious illness was almost unknown, but there was a category of illness called *sik nating* 'sickness without cause' or 'mild illness'. 'Sickness without cause' might occur in the natural course of things and was recognizable by the patient's spontaneous remission from it. If the curing spell of a sorcerer was required, then the illness was believed to have been induced, probably by the sorcerer who knew which spells would be effective in driving it out. After the mission clinic was established, it became obvious that the medicine of the whites could cure some of the sickness that previously had been attributed to a malevolent agent. The coastal people responded to this new fact by incorporating illnesses curable by medication into their system of disease so that three kinds of sickness could be distinguished: *sik bilong mipela* 'our (native) illness', which could be attributed to a causative agent; 'sickness without cause'; and *sik bilong waitskin* 'white man's sickness'. 'White man's sickness' does not imply that the disease may be attributed to whites but indicates that it is among those illnesses with which whites are familiar and thus can cure—that is, illness which is not caused by sorcery and which responds to medical treatment. They think that whites are ignorant of sorcery and can neither induce nor cure illness caused by it. The test of the two categories, 'our illness' and 'white man's sickness', is empirical. If a person goes to the mission, is treated, and gets better, then his illness was a 'white man's sickness'. If he does not recover, he is the victim of sorcery and must seek a sorcery cure.

An illustration of the way this system operates is provided by the case of Penga's finger. During a storm Penga took shelter under a house that had been "locked" with a sorcery charm called *iha aimata* 'fish eye'. A sorcery sign posted over the door identified the 'fish eye' spell and warned that it would cause a trespasser to be finned by a fish and that the wound would become infected. The same day, Penga caught a fish which finned his thumb. The wound became infected, and although the women who placed the spell tried with a counterspell to remove the poison, Penga developed gangrene. He went to the mission for treatment, but eventually had to have his thumb amputated. The outcome confirmed the generally expressed prediction that medical treatment would do no good. Penga himself explained that although he felt he should try the mission's medicine, he expected it to fail.

Although wounds and injuries are usually thought to be responsive to medical treatment, internal illness, particularly if it is serious, is assumed to be the result of sorcery. This is especially true if a sick person has a known enemy who has either threatened sorcery or has access to a sorcerer (and almost everyone has offended someone), or if the effectiveness of the medical care is not immediately apparent. When this is the case, people are reluctant to spend time at the clinic where they feel they cannot be helped. Instead they are likely to seek a sorcery cure or to give up hope and prepare for death.

Congenital deformity, disease, and death are also thought to be the work of spirit creatures, particularly 'bush spirits (which may take snake form)'. Although they are usually indifferent to humans, 'bush spirits' may become malevolent if they are disturbed, and areas where snakes are plentiful or where 'bush spirits' are thought to live are usually avoided. This belief has been challenged by the mission priests, who argue that these spirits either do not exist or are devils and subject to the control of God and the church. Shortly after the mission was established, Father Hayes sprinkled holy water on a tract of land that the people of Kandoka village feared to use for gardens because it was thought to be occupied by a 'bush spirit'. Blessing the land made it safe for cultivation and it is now the site of a coconut grove. Impressed by this demonstration, a Kandokan proceeded to cut down a large tree that was shading his garden and preventing him from fully utilizing the space. The tree was believed to be the home of a 'bush spirit', and when his wife gave birth to a child with deformed legs a few months later this belief was confirmed. The villagers, and the father of the child, interpreted the deformity as being the work of the 'bush spirit' who had "cut the leg of the child" just as the father had cut the tree.

As these examples demonstrate, the Kaliai belief system has been modified to accommodate both Christian and traditional explanations. The result is a syncretic cosmology that is more consistent with Kaliai experience than either traditional or Christian ideology alone. Thus 'bush spirits' do exist and are potentially malevolent, but they may be rendered harmless by Christian ritual. Anyone who wants to trespass on the territory of a 'bush spirit' is wise to practice "preventive medicine" by arranging for the malevolent power of the spirit to be neutralized.

THE STORY

The Story, a cargo movement that was active in Kaliai from 1969 to 1974, blended Christian and Kaliai belief and ritual in an effort to bring about a new mythological age.

According to informants, the Story began when P, the leader of the movement, came into contact with the daughter of a 'snake-man spirit' named Amulmul. At first P resisted the girl, who was sent to seduce him, but he finally weakened. After they had sexual intercourse, Amulmul appeared and told P that if he had not yielded he would have been given cargo to distribute to the people of Kaliai. His weakness demonstrated that men were not yet ready for the new order, but as he had tried to resist the seduction he would be allowed to teach his people the proper way to live so that they could have cargo and live as whites do. P was then given the ability to predict the future and the company of spirit familiars named Sensue, Senklok, and Kilo who would whistle messages from Amulmul. P was promised that he would have revealed to him knowledge of the genealogies and songs of the Story and the rules for proper living, the "Law of the Story," which must be followed before the Story could be fulfilled.

P was reportedly told to look in the interior of Kaliai for a group of mountains whose names, as revealed by Amulmul, included Sinai, Galilia, Golgota, Betlehem, and Nazaret. At the foot of these mountains he would find a lake named Meitavale which is the origin place of man and coconuts and the dwelling place of the ancestral spirits of the people of Kaliai. Amulmul told P that the echoes at the lake were the voices of the ancestors and that in nearby small lakes he would find three stones with marks on them which were made by the ancestors. These marks were the three parts of the Story. Their meaning would be revealed to P by Amulmul in due time.

According to informants, the first stone contained the story of the ancestors. The marks on this stone could only be seen through mossy water and thus they could not be clearly understood. However, Amulmul revealed that the marks indicated that Meitavale was the place where Andam and Eva and coconuts were put on earth by God. The marks also told the genealogy of the Kaliai people back to Andam and Eva and placed the Kaliai in the direct line of succession for cargo and other benefits from God (see figure 1).

It was revealed that Andam and Eva had two daughters and a

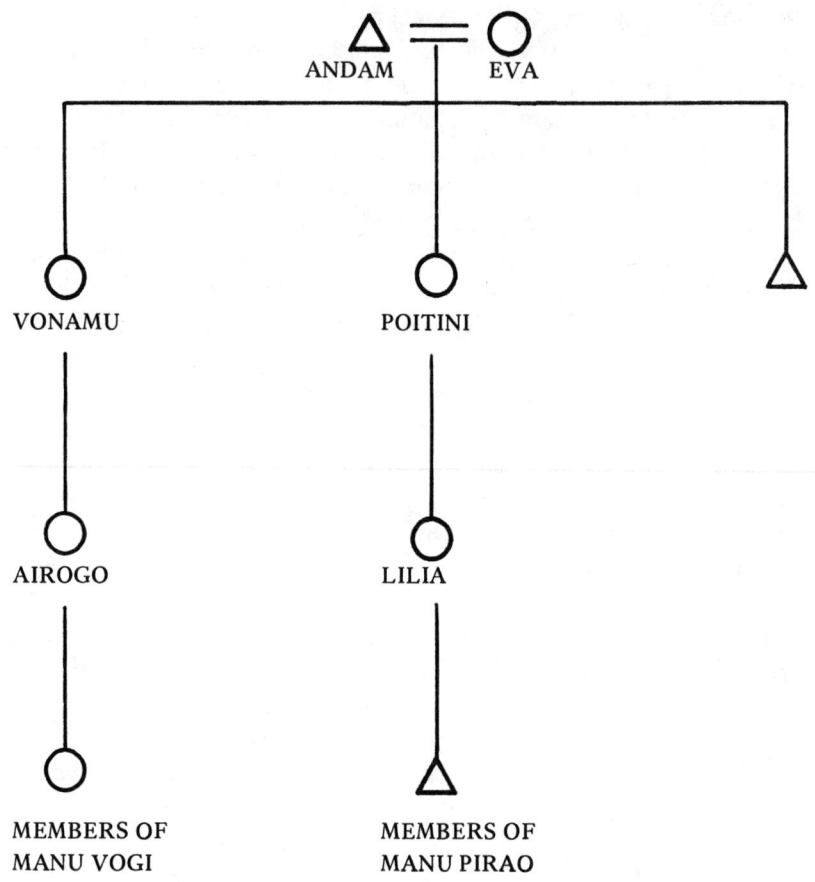

Figure 1. The Genealogy of the Story: Manu Pirao and Manu Vogi

son. The descendants through females of one daughter, Vonamu, were members of an exogamous group named Manu Vogi.[3] The members of Manu Vogi are distinguished by having three lines in their right palms. The descendants of the other daughter, Poitini, were members of the group named Manu Pirao ('swift') and were known by the four lines in their right palms. Manu Vogi is thought to be descended from a male great-grandchild of Andam and Eva and is thus considered the male group. Manu Pirao is descended from a female great-grandchild and is thus a female group.

The second stone reportedly revealed that two of the mountains,

Sinai and Galilia, are filled with cargo. The goods in Sinai are meant for members of Vogi while those in Galilia are meant for Pirao. The marks on this second stone were obscured by dirty water, but they were said to have directed P to gather the followers of the Story for a pilgrimage to Meitavale where they would decorate themselves and sing the songs of the Story until the meaning of the marks on the third stone was revealed to P. While attempting to recruit followers for the Story, P claimed that he had a vision in which he was warned by Sensue and Senklok that the people who joined the Story should leave the coast and return to their ancestral village sites in the Kaliai interior, as earthquakes, seismic waves, and storms would destroy the villages along the beach. There were, apparently, severe storms and seismic waves during the period of the northwest trade winds from January to April 1969, and a number of people followed P into the interior where the first Story villages were built on the slopes of Mount Andewa. More people joined them in late 1969 and 1970, and during this time P selected bosses to supervise each Story village and organize pilgrimages to Meitavale. My informants told me that there were a number of these pilgrimages, which required four or five days of walking and climbing over mountain ridges. During the walk, people were required to fast and sing Story songs to prepare themselves for the experiences they expected to have at the sacred site. Once they reached Meitavale, I was told, the people dressed in the traditional costume of barkcloth loin covering and fiber skirt, decorated their faces with white lime powder, and danced and sang the songs of the Story that were revealed to P by his spirit familiars. Then the people placed food in small caves at the foot of the mountains. When they returned the next day, my informants said, the food was gone and in its place they found small bits of cargo, primarily religious medals and coins of small denomination. These visits to Meitavale apparently lasted several weeks, and during the stay people believed they saw the ghosts of their ancestors dressed in white and floating above the lake.

The rules for the organization of the Story were revealed to P by Amulmul and his spirit familiars. These rules, "the Law of the Story," were told to me by P and members of the Story. The law required that all members of the Story behave as brothers toward one another, as all men are God's children. This brotherhood was to be expressed in each village by the community ownership and sharing of garden space and produce, pigs, wealth items, tobacco, and areca nuts under the supervision of the resident Story 'boss'. The villages were to be organized into long houses which would shelter as many as fifty people rather than into the nuclear family dwellings characteristic of ordinary Kaliai villages. The day was to begin and end with a *singsing*. This ritual, which I witnessed, began with the men facing the women across the village square. The people dressed in barkcloth and fiber skirts, would then sing Story songs and march around the square. During the ritual, which lasted two or three hours, a person wishing to confess behavior that violated the code of the Story, such as adultery, sorcery, lying, fighting, theft, slanderous gossip, selfishness, or stubbornness, would step forward and detail the transgression to P or the resident 'boss'. After hearing the confession, the leader would announce a penance, usually the payment of a fine or a session of singing Story songs through the night, and the group would resume singing.

The purpose of the *singsing* was to purge evil thoughts and bad practices of the Story members. It was also supposed to strengthen belief in the power of the Story. People who fainted from hunger or exhaustion during the pilgrimages to Meitavale were reportedly surrounded and sung to until they revived. People whose kinsmen or friends had died were supposed to sing their grief rather than keen. Those who refused to join the rituals were required to sing all night to remove their bad thoughts, and those who refused to do the penance were expelled from the Story village. It was believed that the cargo could not come until everyone had been purified and that the ritual would expedite this cleansing process.

The third story, the contents of the third stone, was reportedly revealed to P in 1971 after his return from a six-month jail sentence imposed for encouraging Story members to refuse to pay their taxes. This story, seen clearly as through clean water, predicted that snow will fall from heaven and the earth will quake and erupt with fire. When the snow melts, native people will live as white people do. Their villages will look like the towns of the whites, and the year will be divided into six months of hot weather and six months of cold, just as it is where white people originate. Differences in skin color will remain but will no longer be significant. If everyone believes, Amulmul told P, the Story will be fulfilled quickly; but if people laugh and refuse to believe, it will take many years.

The Story is obviously a syncretic creation. Elements from the Bible and the rituals of the Roman Catholic church have been combined with traditional Kaliai mythology, ritual, and social organization to produce a recreation of the mythological age. in the remainder of this chapter I shall analyze the Story by comparing certain elements in it with similar elements from Kaliai and Christian tradition. The three elements to be compared are the structural use of the snake, mountains, and water; the use of ritual; and the form of Story social organization derived from Kaliai tradition or church teaching. The purpose of this analysis is to reveal how traditional Kaliai ideology has influenced the selection and expression of those aspects of Christianity that have been borrowed by the Story.

Blythe (1975:8) has suggested that in Melanesian mythology the association of water and snakes is a common theme suggesting reproduction or rejuvenation. Men and snakes or the daughters of snakes may marry, and these new relationships allow men, who are not creative, to acquire new cultural items. Blythe's generalizations hold true for the Story. Amulmul, a snake spirit, lives near the Sul River and sends his daughter to have a sexual liaison with P. Their sexual congress does not bring about the acquisition of new cultural items for, as in the biblical story of the Fall of Man, intercourse between human and snake proves that man is unfit for the gifts of the gods. But, unlike Genesis, their relationship does not result in the utter removal of man from the age of miracles. Instead, Amulmul promises that in time a new mythological age will be established and the spirits will give men the items needed for the creation of a new culture. A brief description of three other Northwest New Britain myths illustrates that the theme relating snakes, water, and snake-human relationships with cultural creation is a traditional one which is readily adapted to cargo belief. I collected the myths of Moro II and Karonga Asosonga from Kaliai informants living in Kandoka village; the Moro I myth was told me by a Kilenge man who had kin ties with the Kaliai. Karonga Asosonga is said to be traditional to the Kaliai area. Moro I is the Kilenge version of a widespread myth whose variants are found at least from the Siassi Islands to the interior of Kaliai. Moro II is a recent adaptation of the older myth.

MORO I

A man, his wife, and their two sons, Moro and Aisapel, lived alone on a mountain in Bariai. The man learned that his wife's brothers were planning to give a feast and sent her to claim a large share of pork from a special pig. Her brothers tricked her and sent only a small piece of the special pork. Angered, the man attacked and was killed by his brother-in-law, who cut out his heart. The organ was cooked and fed to Moro who was told that it was a pig's heart.

The next morning Moro turned into a creature half human (the head) and half snake (the tail). The spirit of the father then came to kill the mother and sons, and they fled with Moro riding in a basket on his mother's head. Moro threw down, one by one, the pieces of the paraphernalia used for preparing betel mixture and each piece changed into a river that temporarily blocked the ghost's way. Finally Moro called up crocodile and shark. They killed and ate the ghost of the father as he tried to swim the last river.

They settled down to live and Moro created overnight a bountiful garden full of all the food that people now eat. Then he moved their former mountain home to Cape Gloucester, where it still stands, and caused pigs to appear for the first time. These pigs were wild, so Moro taught his mother and brother to feed and thus domesticate them.

Finally Moro married a woman from whom he hid his body, telling her that she should never try to see him but should go to his brother when she felt desire. The woman was curious, however, and broke into the house and felt Moro's body. Shamed, Moro caused a storm, earthquake, and seismic waves. During the commotion he fled over the sea away from the company of men.

MORO II

In this version of the myth, Moro was shut away by his mother after his marriage. His wife, who broke into the house to see Moro, was horrified by his appearance. Angered, Moro told her, "I had thought to remain here and give you all kinds of good food and things that you need, but now you'll have to work." He then fled to an island with his two sons. There had made a large canoe and placed in it many native foods, pigs, chickens, and a boat engine. These he sent to the people of Bariai, but they were foolish and took only native things, rejecting the machinery. Then Moro went to America, where he was greeted with kisses by white people. Pleased with his reception, he gave boats and motors, good houses with metal roofs, and ships full of cargo to the people.

KARONGA ASOSONGA

Karonga Asosonga, a snake-man changeling, was caught in his snake form by a group of men who were out hunting pigs. In spite of the warning of an old man who recognized Karonga Asosonga and urged his companions to let him go, he was cooked and eaten by the men. After the meal the men were forced by thirst to go to a river where they drank until they burst and were turned to stone. The pieces of Karonga Asosonga rejoined and he gave the old man a special song and a feather plume dance ornament, as well as the women and wealth of the slain villagers.

SYNTHESIS: TRADITION, THE STORY, AND THE BIBLE

The snake is a significant figure in Kaliai mythology and in cargo myth, as well as in the Story. It is frequently found in conjunction with water: with rivers (Karonga Asosonga, Moro, Amulmul) or with destructive rainstorms (Moro, Amulmul) that it either causes or predicts. When it appears in mythology the snake is usually portrayed as a spirit creature that takes the form of a snake or a snake-man, and it has the power to give or withhold cultural goods from human beings.

In each of the myths discussed, except Karonga Asosonga, the snake is offended by sexual violation or excess, and as a result it denies men further access to its cultural gifts. In Karonga Asosonga the hero is offended by alimentary violation; he is cooked and eaten. It may be argued that, structurally, the alimentary and the sexual aspects are universally linked and carry the same message (Lévi-Strauss 1969:269). Regardless of whether the offending behavior is alimentary or sexual, the Kaliai explanation for the loss of the mythological age has parallels with the Christian version of the Fall of Man. The sin of Adam and Eve in eating the fruit of the tree of knowledge resulted in their awareness of their nakedness and in sexual shame. In both the Story and in Genesis, the snake tempts man through a female agent, and the failure of man to resist temptation results in either his loss of paradise and the mythological age or in the indefinitely delayed return of the mythological age with its unlimited supply of material wealth.

The theme of the snake as culture hero responsible for the loss of the mythological age is found in three traditions: New Britain myth, the Story, and Genesis. In New Britain myth, the snake suffers through no fault of its own but rather from the offending intrusion of human beings. In the Story and in Genesis the snake is pictured as a tempter who urged man to sinful action which, although not in itself offensive or harmful to any being, results in man's loss of paradise. In New Britain tradition, man loses his advantageous relationship with the spirits because he offends the snake. In tradition influenced by Christian teaching, he loses paradise because he sins at the behest of the snake. When the three traditions are compared as in table 5, the transformation of themes is apparent.

Mountains, trees, and water are frequently found in Melanesian mythology to mediate between sky and earth, the world of spirits, and the world of men (Blythe 1975:6). These mediating elements both separate the two worlds and allow passage between them. Blythe's generalization is true for Kaliai myth. There are numerous examples of spirit beings who live on mountaintops and of spirits who are transformed into mountains, while water may either unite or separate men and spirits. In everyday life, the boundaries of named plots of land that are claimed by particular kin groups are often marked by rivers, while in mythology

TABLE 5   Synthesis: Kaliai Tradition, the Story, and Genesis

Kaliai Tradition	The Story	Genesis
Snake gives cultural items.	Snake gives song, ritual, Law of Story.	No tradition.
Snake is offended by violation or body or violation of sexual or alimentary taboo.	Snake tempts man through female agent; delays new mythological age because P's violation of sexual taboo proves man's sinful nature.	Snake tempts man through female agent. God is offended by man's violation of alimentary/sexual taboo proving his sinful nature.
Man's behavior is offensive to snake.	Man's behavior proves his sinful nature; he is unfit to receive cargo.	Man's nature is sinful; he is unfit for Paradise.
End of mythological age. No more intercourse with spirits, men must work, culture is static.	Delay of new mythological age and cargo.	Loss of Paradise. People must work, bear children in pain, die.
Mountains are home of spirits. Valuables appear in holes in mountain.	Mountains are origin place of man and coconuts and home of spirits.	God gives law to Moses on Mt. Sinai. Resurrected Jesus appears to disciples on a mountain in Galilee.
	Cargo has appeared in holes in mountain named Sinai, Golgota, Galilia.	Golgotha is where Jesus died, became spirit.
Water both separates and unites.	Lake where spirits appear to men, where stones with mark of Story are found.	Lake of Galilee where Jesus met disciples, walked on water, quieted storm.
End of mythological age. Departure of spirits accompanied by earthquakes, storms, seismic waves.	Reappearance of mythological age accompanied by earthquakes, snow. Quakes, seismic waves, destructive storms predicted.	End of mythological age. Adam and Eve are driven from Eden by fire; death of Jesus is accompanied by earthquakes, storm.

water serves as a contact point between humans and spirits. Almost every meeting or dramatic separation between man and spirit in Kaliai mythology occurs at a river, a spring, or the sea, during a rainstorm, or as a result of tears. Moro, it may be recalled, created rivers to separate himself from his malevolent ghost father, and when he fled he went over the sea during a violent storm.

Mountains, in biblical tradition as in Kaliai myth, occupy a position between the world of man and the world of spirits. It was on Mount Sinai that Moses talked with God and received the law. It was on Golgotha that Jesus was crucified and his death, like the departure of Moro, was marked by an earthquake and a storm (Matt. 27:45, 51). These two mountains are named in the Story together with Galilia (Galilee), the lake where Jesus walked, met his disciples, and controlled the storm, as well as the location of the mountain where Jesus appeared to his disciples after his death (Matt. 28:16-17).

RITUAL

The Kaliai believe in the efficacy of ritual and in its importance in maintaining favorable relationships between men and spirits.[4] Many rituals of the Story—the *singsing,* the feeding of the spirits, body decoration, and the recitation of genealogy back to the first ancestor (in this case Adam and Eve)—are consistent with traditional rituals still practiced outside the Story. There are also elements of Story ritual that are obviously consistent with the Roman Catholic rituals of confession and penance. It is my argument that the ritual of the Story, like its mythology, is a synthesis of Catholic rituals and those of traditional Kaliai. One example of the way in which the followers of the Story used ritual to settle a dispute and reaffirm the unity of the group will illustrate how rituals from these two traditions have been combined in the Story.

In 1971, I visited some of the Story villages accompanied by several Kandokans who were not members of the movement. One of these people, G, was an old woman who stayed with her kinswoman whose husband, L, was a member of the Story. N, who was G's son, overheard L comment that he could not stay in his own house as it was full of trash, referring to G and the fact that she was an outsider. According to N and my other informants, N angrily confronted L who refused to apologize. N discussed the confrontation with me that evening, and the next morning I heard him describe the insult to the Story members who had gathered for a *singsing*. He declared that he would not tolerate insults to his mother and that if the matter were not straightened out immediately he would return to Kandoka and bring his kinsmen to beat an apology out of L and anyone else who tried to interfere. Following this speech the people sang. Then L stepped forward to make a public confession and apology, and the people sang his wrong. N was not satisfied, and that evening the people met again to make further restitution for the slander against his mother, or so N thought. During the *singsing*, directed by the leader of the Story, the people of the village divided into their moieties and brought money which was placed on two pandanus mats in the center of the village. When all the money was collected, the mat containing the contribution of Manu Vogi contained $A10.20 and one fathom of shell money, while Manu Pirao had collected $A11.10 and one fathom of shell money.[5] People then sang the following song and the money was exchanged between the two groups.

Mon moni eeeeee	'Money money
Mon Moni i la i la	Money it goes, it goes
Mon moni eeeeee	Money money
Moni eee tangilo	Money we cry'

When it became obvious that none of the money was to go to G or her son, N remarked to me in disgust that he supposed that was all the satisfaction he could expect from a pack of idiots who had forgotten how to behave properly. I later asked one of the Story followers why the money had not been paid to G and N as compensation, as would have been done in a similar situation in a non-Story village. The man explained that the members of the Story felt that the confession and *singsing* had ended L's liability to N: the exchange was intended to pacify those kinsmen of G who were Story members. The exchange was also intended to atone for the laughter or talk during the *singsing* and to express the shame people felt for the sins they had committed before joining the Story.

Kaliai tradition suggests that the mythological age when spirits gave culture to humans ended because of the offensive behavior of man. There seems, however, to be nothing in Kaliai philosophy equivalent to the doctrine of original sin. Moral rules are not given to men by spirit beings, and the breach of moral rules is not ordinarily punished by spirits unless they themselves are the victims of man's bad behavior. I know of only one account of spirit intervention and punishment of men whose actions did not directly affect the spirits.

Most Kaliai myths contain the warning that breaking the rules of behavior, even out of ignorance, is dangerous for the individual and for society. There seems to be no concern with the moral dilemma of good versus evil, however, and there is no message that man is, by nature, morally defiled. Nor is there anything in Kaliai custom that is similar to the Christian traditions of confession and penance. These elements of the Story are clearly borrowed from the rituals of the Roman Catholic church. Other church rituals such as hymn singing and communion have their parallels in the Story, but they are also familiar to the traditional ritual practice of the Kaliai. A comparison of Kaliai custom, the Story, and Christian practice demonstrates that the ritual of the Story, like its mythology, is a synthesis of traditional rituals with those of the Christian mission.

SOCIAL ORGANIZATION

The Kaliai, like many other Melanesian people, express social relationships by sharing or exchanging wealth items. Wealth is shared among members of a group; wealth is exchanged between members of opposed groups or between the units themselves. People with whom a person neither shares nor exchanges are generally either hostile outsiders or neutral strangers. The action of the moieties in the Story village was consistent with this principle of social relations as well as the norms of brotherhood expressed in the Law of the Story. No wealth was given specifically to individuals; N and G were excluded because they were outsiders, while G's kinsmen inside the Story were expected to share wealth in accordance with the Law of the Story. Instead of going to individuals, the wealth was exchanged between groups in a ritual that reaffirmed their complementary relationship as well as the unity of the Story village.

The Law of the Story attempted to isolate members of the Story from outsiders and rearrange village life so that a new social order might be created that would be congenial with the anticipated new mythological age. Story members were encouraged to sever ties with their nonbelieving kinsmen. Debts to outsiders were no longer valid; ceremonial obligations to kinsmen outside the Story were not binding. Wealth was to be kept inside the Story and ceremonial exchanges, such as bridewealth, were to be kept to a minimum and circulated only within the Story.

The social organization of the Story villages blended traditional forms with those derived from church teaching. The exogamous matrilineal moieties, for example, were traditionally significant in interior Kaliai where they are still relevant, while the communal aspects of the Law of the Story, based on the notion that all men are the children of God, seem to owe much to the teachings of the missionaries.

CONCLUSION

Missionization in Kaliai, a complex and uneven process of change, has both ideological and secular components. The mission has attempted to offer social services, to institute social change, and to teach Christian doctrine. Response to these offerings has been mixed. Some offerings have been accepted, others have been rejected, and still others have been borrowed and transformed into the context of the Story. Before I can discuss the reasons behind this selective borrowing, I must clarify several points.

First, all the Kaliai of my acquaintance want a standard of living closer to white people's standards while retaining the values, rituals, and beliefs that give life meaning. These two goals are not necessarily consistent, nor do all people agree on which is the more important. The opposing views of the grandfather and the mother's brother of the groom whose wedding I recounted above exemplify this point.

Second, the Kaliai have a vital, ongoing mythology, cosmology, and world view. The missionaries have not tried to destroy the people's traditional religion. Roman Catholicism has augmented, not supplanted, the traditional belief system, and the new syncretic ideology is more consistent with Kaliai experience than either Kaliai tradition or the white man's ideology.

Third, the success or failure of the mission's programs can be understood in terms of the first two points. If a person's primary goal is economic development, and if the programs of the mission seem to be helpful in reaching this goal, they are accepted. Progressive Kaliai send their children to school, for example, argue for limited brideprices, and sell their copra to the mission. If the teaching of the church is consistent with existing belief, or if it offers an explanation that is consistent with experience, it is accepted and traditional belief is adjusted to accommodate it. Experience with the mission clinic has, for example, resulted in the Kaliai theory of disease being modified to take into account sickness that whites could cure. Kaliai who had independently arrived at the conclusion that polygyny and the early marriage of their children were bad ideas used the priest's stand on these subjects to support their arguments. If the teaching of the mission is inconsistent with or antithetical to a person's goals, it is ignored. Ambitious big men who wanted the prestige of multiple wives ignored the priest's attacks on polygyny as well as the restriction on the amounts of bridewealth that could be given. If the mission's activities seemed to threaten a person's goals, the response was criticism of the activities and the missionary himself. The activities of the missionary seemed to the patrol officer to be designed to give him excessive and illegitimate political power. It appeared to some that in spite of the missionary's words, the mission's activities were not designed to help them achieve a better standard of living. Anger with the mission's copra prices and higher store prices typified their response.

Fourth, the mission and its ideological offerings cannot be ignored by the Kaliai. Their belief that culture is primarily a spiritual gift, not the result of human ingenuity, places great emphasis on religion in manipulating the spirit world to achieve material success. It follows, then, that the religion of the technologically and materially wealthy whites must hold the secret of their success. Elements from Christan doctrine that had parallels in Kaliai myth were borrowed by the Story in a combination of traditional and Christian religion designed to restore the mythological age and release wealth to the Kaliai people. The synthesis of the two traditions into the Story seems to follow three principles.

Symbols that are cross-culturally similar or synonymous are emphasized in the Story, and biblical names are added to Kaliai names. Thus mountains which mediate between spirit and human worlds in both Kaliai myth and in the Bible hold cargo. Genealogy is used in the Story, as in Kaliai tradition and the Bible, to establish the link between the living, the ancestors, and God; it is also evidence of the people's claim to the cargo. The beginning and end of mythological ages in both traditions are accompanied by storms and seismic disturbances.

Elements with disparate qualities but common to both traditions are reconciled and combined in the Story. The snake is important as a culture giver in Kaliai mythology. In Genesis the snake is responsible for the temptation of man and his loss of paradise. According to Christian teaching, man loses paradise because of his sinful nature; in Kaliai myth, he loses it because his behavior is offensive and foolish. In the Story the two views of the snake and man's nature are consolidated. The snake is a culture giver who tempts man and then withholds cargo because P's violation of a sexual taboo proves that man is not yet fit for the return of the mythological age.

The Story is optimistic. P has borrowed from the mission's teachings the rituals of confession and penance that hopefully will enable his followers to become worthy to receive the cargo.

In summary, the Kaliai response to twenty-five years of missionization has been pragmatic. The Kaliai have borrowed from the mission those ideas which seem to explain Kaliai experiences and those programs which help them to achieve their own goals. These borrowed ideas are adapted to Kaliai beliefs and experience and are used to reach Kaliai ends. When the mission's offerings fill a clearly felt need, they are embraced. When the mission's programs do not meet Kaliai needs, they are ignored. And when they threaten the Kaliai view of progress, they are resented.

NOTES

The research on which this chapter is based was conducted in West New Britain in 1966-1967 and for three months in 1971. Funds for the research were made available by the National Science Foundation, Southern Illinois University, Wenner-Gren Foundation Grant 2809, and the University of Waterloo. I wish to thank the people of Kaliai, especially my friends in Kandoka village, for their patience, cooperation, and honesty. My thanks also to Fathers Norbert Birkmann and Norbert Empen and to Sisters Elisa, Felicitas, Hilaria, and Mary of the Kaliai mission, who were a source of medical care, good humor, moral support, and help of every kind.

1. In 1966 the mission clinic staff, which included a triple certificate nursing sister and several nurse's aids, saw 1,197 inpatients, gave 170,976 doses of medicine, and attended 107 births and 26 deaths.
2. In 1966-1967, $A1 was worth about $US1.14; in 1971 and 1975, $A1 was worth $US1.40.
3. *Manu* is a Kaliai word that may be translated as either 'moiety' or 'bird', while *vogi* is Kaliai for 'sea eagle'.
4. Anthropologists do not agree in their use of the term "ritual." I follow Leach (1966), who uses the word in a broad sense to denote occasional, repetitive, magical or communicative behavior expressed as speech or action. A ritual may be practiced by a single person or by a group, but its meaning (to fructify, to bewitch, to heal) is understood by the people who share a culture.
5. The shell money used in this exchange was made from brown to black bivalve shells and is called *vula asosonga* 'black money'. A fathom (6 feet) of black money was worth $A1 in 1975.

14

AFTER THE MISSIONARIES CAME: DENOMINATIONAL DIVERSITY IN THE TONGA ISLANDS

Shulamit R. Decktor Korn

The first Christian missionaries to Tonga were sponsored by the London Missionary Society (LMS) in 1797 as part of the society's earliest venture in the Pacific. Today, while the LMS is well established in many parts of the Pacific, it has no mission in Tonga. Instead, the Kingdom of Tonga hosts nearly a dozen missions of other denominations. As one census officer in Tonga expressed it: "The kingdom may not have any more religious bodies maintaining missions than its Pacific island neighbors but it certainly occupies the lead in the number of different religious denominations for the size of its population" (Tupouniua 1958:30).

The remarkable multiplicity of denominations in Tonga is regarded by some outsiders as something of a joke. The time-consuming involvement in church affairs that is also characteristically Tongan is treated similarly. Douglas Oliver (1961:185), for example, speaks of Tongans "returning [after a period of considerable political upheaval at the end of the nineteenth century] to the charming diversion of playing government and attending church." Oliver also remarks that "Tongans learned long ago that the easiest way to remain Tongan is to appear western" (1961: 179). This is a charming epigram, but it hardly explains the thorough indigenization of Christianity, the infusion of everyday life with religious elements, and Tongans' absorption with matters relating to church membership.[1] Far from Christianity being a Western facade for Tongan society, it is something that Tongans engage in with utter seriousness.

In considering the role of religion in Tonga almost two centuries after the arrival of the first missionaries, three questions must be asked: Why does religion have the position it has in contemporary Tongan society? What accounts for the multiplicity of denominations? And what are the local and national implications of the pervasiveness of religion and the multiplicity of denominations?

THE MULTIPLICITY OF DENOMINATIONS: AN OVERVIEW

Tonga lies east of Fiji and south of Samoa and is also known as the "Friendly Islands," a name bestowed by Captain Cook, who visited Tonga in the course of his voyages of 1773-1774 and 1777. About forty of the islands of Tonga are inhabited; in 1970 the total population was more than 80,000 persons, three-fifths of whom live on the main island of Tongatapu. The total land area of the country is about 660 square kilometers, of which Tongatapu comprises two-fifths of the total.

Tonga has only four centers of administration and commerce that can properly be called towns; however, about one-third of the total population is clustered in these areas, two of which are on Tongatapu. The remaining population lives in villages that are dotted throughout the islands in a nuclear pattern which developed during a period of civil war lasting from 1799 until the mid-nineteenth century. Most of the people who live in rural areas and many of those who live in towns depend for their livelihood on peasant agriculture.

Tonga was first contacted by Europeans in 1616, but sustained contact did not begin until almost the end of the eighteenth century, following the voyages of Captain Cook. Despite considerable European intervention since then, including the indigenization of Christianity, Tonga has always been formally independent. The LMS arrived in 1797, but lasted only three years. The second mission effort, sponsored by the British Wesleyan Conference, did not begin until 1822 and lasted only one year. Both these missions to Tonga are generally regarded as failures, but they provided Tongans and missionaries alike with important experiences in mission effort. Finally, what turned out to be a permanent mission was established by the Wesleyans in 1826.

I mention these historical events to emphasize that Christianity has existed for a long time in Tonga. The question for more than a century has been not whether Christianity would be accepted, but rather which denomination or denominations would prevail.[2] The Wesleyan missionaries who came in 1826 gained an early champion in the young chief Tāufa'āhau, who later became King George Tupou I (1845-1893). With Tāufa'āhau's support they managed for more than a decade to exclude other denominations that sought to establish a mission in Tonga. This monopoly came to an end in 1842 when Roman Catholic missionaries celebrated their first mass on Tongan soil.

The next denomination to be established came about because of a conflict between the King of Tonga and the Australian Wesleyan Conference (a situation with remarkable similarity to the breakaway of the Anglican church from the Church of Rome, although with different causes). The result was the founding in 1885 of an indigenous Wesleyan denomination: the *Siasi Tonga Tau'ataina* 'Free Church of Tonga'. Some thirty-eight years later, in the early 1920s, there was another upheaval among the Wesleyans in Tonga. One outcome was the founding of a third Wesleyan denomination: the *Siasi 'o Tonga* 'Church of Tonga'.[3] With the exception of the Anglican church, which entered the field before the end of the nineteenth century, all other denominations in Tonga have become established only within the past fifty years and the majority have been introduced since World War II.

The most recent government census, held in 1966, enumerated adherents of nineteen different denominations (Fiefia 1968: 70), but only seven of these had a membership of more than 1 percent of the total population. Members of these seven denominations together comprised 99 percent of the population in 1966 (see table 6).

The seven major denominations in Tonga, in order of size in the 1966 census, are the Free Wesleyan church (which is a member of the General Conference of the Wesleyan Church in Australia), the Roman Catholic church, the Free Church of Tonga, the Church of Tonga, the Mormon church (Church of Jesus Christ of the Latter-Day Saints), the Church of the Seventh-Day Adventists, and the Anglican church. Each of these denominations was

TABLE 6 Adherents of the Major Denominations in Tonga, 1931-1966

Denomination	Percentage of Total Population			
	1931[a]	1939[b]	1956[c]	1966[d]
Free Wesleyan	58	53.9	49.6	49.9
Free Church of Tonga	16	17.1	17.5	14.3
Roman Catholic	12	13.6	14.7	16.0
Church of Tonga	10	10.5	9.9	9.0
Mormon		2.9	5.1	7.1
Seventh-Day Adventist[e]		0.8	1.5	1.8
Anglican		0.8	0.9	1.0
All other	4	0.1	0.3	0.8
Unknown	0	0.3	0.5	0.1
Total	100	100.0	100.0	100.0

[a] Beaglehole and Beaglehole (1941:126).
[b] Tupouniua (1958:30-31).
[c] Tupouniua (1958:30-31). No census was taken between 1939 and 1956.
[d] Fiefia (1968:23).
[e] Separate figures were not given for these denominations; they were classified together as "other churches" (Beaglehole and Beaglehole 1941:126).

established in Tonga before World War II. Except for the three Wesleyan denominations, all are foreign missions in the sense that they are centrally administered in Tonga by senior personnel sent or appointed from abroad. The Free Wesleyan church, although linked to the Australian Wesleyan Conference, is internally autonomous, and the Free Church of Tonga and the Church of Tonga are indigenous organizations with no affiliations outside Tonga.[4]

The national census figures shown in table 6, however, are somewhat misleading with regard to the denominational distribution of the population. While there is no census breakdown of denominational affiliation among people living in the different parts of the country, the fact is that only the Free Wesleyan church has a substantial proportion of adherents throughout Tonga; away from the main island of Tongatapu, the other major denominations are unevenly distributed. It is impossible to estimate the distribution of denominational affiliation on the various islands, nor can the distribution in any one village be regarded as typical of that island. On the contrary, considerable variation in statistical patterns of denominational affiliation from one village to the next seems likely, reflecting patterns of intervillage migration, random differences in fertility, and the effects of personalities and events. The village of Pea on the island of Tongatapu was one of the early strongholds of Roman Catholicism and has remained a center of Catholicism to this day. Approximately half this village is Roman Catholic, in contrast to the much smaller proportion of Catholics in the total Tongan population. Thus the distribution of denominational affiliation in a village is the outcome of factors best understood in historical perspective.

DENOMINATIONAL ORGANIZATION IN THE VILLAGE

Despite statistical variation from one village to the next, a description of denominational organization in a single village can indicate the local features of denominational multiplicity. Such a description can also show what is involved in being a congregant, thereby illuminating what I mean by the pervasiveness of religion in Tongan society.

Tonga's characteristic diversity of denominations is manifest in the village of Motulahi (a fictitious name for the village where I was based).[5] Motulahi is one of the larger villages on Tongatapu. As in the case of most villages on the island (which is less than 30 kilometers across at its broadest point), there is easy access to the town of Nuku'alofa where the national centers of administration and commerce are located. Some people who live in Motulahi commute to work in Nuku'alofa, but Motulahi is no more a suburb of Nuku'alofa than are any of the other rural communities on Tongatapu.[6]

The denominational affiliation of the adult population of Motulahi in 1970 is shown in table 7. Each of the seven major denominations had adherents in Motulahi; however, only five had congregations in the village at the time of my fieldwork in 1969-1970. Neither the Anglicans nor the Seventh-Day Adventists had more than a handful of adherents in Motulahi. Indeed the Anglicans have only one congregation on all of Tongatapu, based in Nuku'alofa. The Seventh-Day Adventists in Motulahi occasionally conducted services at the home of one of their members; other-

TABLE 7 Denominational Affiliation of Adults in Motulahi

Denomination	Number	Percentage
Free Wesleyan	226	45.7
Mormon	92	18.6
Roman Catholic	70	14.2
Free Church of Tonga	56	11.3
Church of Tonga	35	7.1
Seventh-Day Adventist	10	2.0
Anglican	3	0.6
Unknown	2	0.4
Total	494	99.9

Source: Author's fieldwork survey in the early part of 1970. Adults are persons aged twenty and over.

wise they attended the Seventh-Day Adventist church in Nuku'alofa. Even if the Anglicans and Seventh-Day Adventists are set aside, congregations in Tonga are more correctly described as "local groups" than "village groups" since the boundaries of a congregation depend primarily upon the number of adherents. In most villages, the Free Wesleyan church is the only denomination whose congregation is village-based in the sense that all members of the congregation are residents of the same village. This stems from the fact that the Free Wesleyan church has many more adherents than any other in Tonga. Owing to their numbers, members of the Free Wesleyan church (including those in Motulahi) generally do not have to suffer the inconvenience of attending church away from home for they are able to support a church of their own in their village. Conversely, some of those who belong to the Motulahi-based congregations of the Free Church of Tonga and the Church of Tonga live about 3 kilometers away in the small village of Tatafa, for their denominations are not able to support a church in their own village. Similarly, the Roman Catholics in Motulahi, together with those from nearby villages, are members of a congregation that is based in Nukutau, the village immediately adjoining Motulahi. The Mormons, too, have a joint congregation with neighboring villages; their church is located on

DENOMINATIONAL DIVERSITY IN THE TONGA ISLANDS 401

the boundary between Motulahi and Nukutau.

Whatever the denomination, the local congregation is the focus of public activity in village Tonga. Everyone is nominally an adherent of some denomination, and there are few in the village who can withstand the pressure to attend church at least once a week. The Roman Catholic church in Nukutau has no regularly scheduled activities for the congregation beyond daily church services and three services on Sundays. Each of the other four denominations has a scheduled round of activities on a weekly basis.

In the Mormon church, there are two Sunday services for the entire congregation. In addition, on Monday evenings there is a family service which people attend in elementary family groups; on Tuesday afternoons there is a service for women (aged sixteen and up); and on Wednesday afternoons there is a children's service (up to about sixteen years of age). Besides services, there are a number of other church-related activities. Once a week members engage in genealogical research (an activity related to certain doctrines of the Mormon church). Twice a week choir practice is held. In addition to these weekly activities, a discussion group meets once a month for the three classes of adult members: men considered priests, men and youths who are not priests, and members of the women's auxiliary. About once a month there is a scheduled social event (dancing, costume party, movie, or other performance) on a Saturday evening.

In the Free Wesleyan church, there are services for the entire congregation three times on Sunday (although few members of the congregation attend all three services) and again on Monday afternoons and Tuesday and Friday mornings. On Wednesday afternoons there is a service for women only. On Sundays, there are a number of regularly scheduled activities in addition to services, Sunday school, and choir practice. About an hour before the mid-morning service, the men of the congregation gather informally to drink kava and discuss current events at the home of the steward of the congregation. After the mid-morning service, the men who have the status of *malanga* 'lay preacher' participate in a formal kava circle at the home of one of the members of the congregation.[7] This meeting is followed by the *fakaafe Sāpate* 'Sabbath feast', at which the preacher of the morning's sermon is the guest of honor. After the mid-afternoon service, the men of the congregation gather again at the home of a member, where they are served a festive tea called *fakaafe efiafi* 'afternoon feast'. Besides these weekly activities, there is a discussion session for adult members of the congregation that takes place once a month. Members of the congregation meet for about an hour before the Sunday afternoon service in groups of about fifteen people, men and women separately. Once a month, also, a special Sunday afternoon service is held late in the afternoon. On these occasions there is always some festive aspect to the service. The Sunday school might put on a play, for example, or there might be a joint service with another Free Wesleyan congregation, or a choir competition might be held. There are other special events in addition to this throughout the year. There is a special service to mark the beginning of the school year and another special service plus a feast for all members of the congregation to mark Mother's Day early in May. A special service is held on New Year's Eve and a week of feasting is celebrated in the first week of the new year.

The Motulahi congregations of the Free Church of Tonga and the Church of Tonga have a weekly schedule of services similar to that of the Free Wesleyan church and a similar routine on Sundays but without a congregational feast each week. There is less emphasis on communal feasting in these denominations, probably because the congregations are not large enough to support such activities on a regular basis. However, they do have feasts and other activities at Christmas, Easter, New Year, and special times of the year.

Participation in congregational and denominational activities is held to be a religious duty—public disapproval on earth and eternal damnation are sanctions for attendance. Beyond this, however, congregational activities are important social events that provide an arena for status striving.

CHURCH MEMBERSHIP AND PRESTIGE

In Tonga, kinship relations are the primary source of economic assistance and material benefits.[8] For prestige in the community, however, one must look beyond kinship. At the societal level, status is a function of rank by birth, wealth, occupation, and education. These criteria are also significant within the local community, but it is the rare villager who can hope to derive high status from one of these sources. For most adults in the community, and especially for men, status in the community depends largely on their standing in the congregation and their participation in its activities.

The majority of village women, of all denominations, spend most of their free time among kin, either at their own homes or visiting close kinswomen. If a woman organizes a day of tapa painting, for example, women of her local kin group will form the core of the work party. Similarly, young men do not necessarily associate with members of their own denomination; instead, they spend most of their leisure time in the company of others of their age. During the winter rugby season they are fully engaged in the activities of the village rugby club, and in the summer they serve as cheering sections for the girls' basketball teams. They also do a lot of visiting from one village to the next, seeking scope for their courting activities. Ordinarily, however, by his late twenties a young man has married and begun to settle down. From then on, the free time he spends outside his own household is in the company of other adult males of his congregation, often at a kava-drinking circle that meets at the home of one of the group.[9] This is especially true of members of Motulahi's Free Wesleyan congregation, which has enough members to sustain a kava group that meets almost daily at the home of the steward of the congregation.

This emphasis on associating with men of one's own congregation is due to the fact that the local congregation is the arena of prestige-acquisition for men. A man who wants to increase his status in the community cannot hope to do so without the participation and support of his fellow congregants. A feast-giver, for example, has to be associated with respectable people he can invite to his feasts if he is to gain the prestige that is derived from these displays. The higher the status of his guests, the greater the honor reflected upon him. In short, my argument is that Tongans' absorption with secular aspects of church membership is closely linked with the primary cultural theme in Tongan society—the process of continually reordering relationships.

In the discussion of congregational activities, reference was made to classes of membership within the Mormon church. The Wesleyan churches, too, place considerable emphasis on grades of membership. In the Free Wesleyan church, young men and women become full members at some point in their late teens or early twenties, after years of attendance at Sunday school and later participation in the young people's Methodist Christian Endeavor Society. The procedure is for them to ask a relative or some other adult to submit their request for admittance to the grade of communicant (*lotu fehu'i* 'enquiring prayer'). They are then appointed to junior membership in one of the discussion groups in the congregation. After some years, the leader of the group will inform the steward of the congregation that the person is ready to proceed to the highest grade of lay membership in the church. The steward then submits the person's name to the minister of the congregation and the minister registers the change of status with the central office of the church. Men become members of the *kau malanga* 'corps of lay preachers', and women join the *kau akonaki* 'corps of moral instructors'. There are similar grades of membership in the other Wesleyan denominations (although procedures of transition from one grade to the next are less formal). For women, there is little public display regarding the change to *akonaki* 'moral instructor' status in any of the Wesleyan denominations. The transition is evident, however, in the Free Church of Tonga and in the Church of Tonga: women of 'moral instructor' status in these denominations wear hats to church as a sign of their respectability (like the wives of the ministers who brought Christianity to Tonga). For men, the transition to lay preachers status is marked in all the Wesleyan denominations by their preaching their first sermon, usually ten minutes long, at a Sunday afternoon church service. The occasion is regarded as a matter of pride and congratulation for the new lay preacher and his family.

There was only one unmarried man under the age of thirty who was a lay preacher in Motulahi during the period of my fieldwork. This person had attained lay preacher status at the age of twenty-six and was known in the village for his piety. Generally, however, the standard of morality expected of a lay preacher is not consonant with the behavior attributed to young unmarried men.

I knew of an unmarried man in his late thirties who held a highly respected administrative position in government, was very active in denominational activities in his village, and yet was not a lay preacher. When I asked someone who knew him well why this was so, I was told rather huffily that membership in the corps of lay preachers is not automatic and the man had apparently chosen not to petition for membership. When I asked why not, I was told, *Fa'italiha pē ia*—"It's his prerogative." He got married a few months later, however, and not long afterward I heard that he gave his first sermon. Marriage, then, is taken to be related in some way to a person's moral fitness to belong to the corps of lay preachers.[10] This is also indicated by the case of a man who, shortly after he was divorced, requested that his name be removed from the register of lay preachers. I was told that he was not required to do this but may not have wanted his status as a divorced man to reflect upon his membership in the corps of lay preachers.

As far as I could tell, membership in the women's 'corps of moral instructors' makes little difference to one's behavior as a member of the congregation beyond the fact that it is a valued status that signifies decency and full womanhood. But only men of lay preacher status—of whom there were 78 out of a total of 104 adult males in the congregation of the Free Wesleyan church in Motulahi—may preach a sermon, and generally only a lay preacher may act as host at a congregational feast. Both are status-enhancing activities, for the very fact of a public performance of this nature is implicit affirmation of the person's moral worth. Indeed, any situation in which a person has been appointed to act publicly as a special member of the congregation is status-enhancing. Thus one indicator of whether a person is regarded highly beyond his own village is whether he has been asked to preach a sermon in another congregation. Admittedly, some situations are more prestigious than others: to deliver a sermon or host a feast on Christmas Day is more status-enhancing than to do so on the Sunday before Christmas; to serve as steward of a congregation is more prestigious than to be choirmaster or teach Sunday school.

The minister of the congregation, generally a full-time pastor appointed to the congregation by the national governing body of the church, decides who will be asked to prepare the sermon.[11] He makes this determination in consultation with the steward of the congregation, who is elected to the position for a year by his fellow lay preachers. The steward also makes up the annual roster of Sabbath and holy day feast-givers by himself. A minister may know the frequency and intensity of a person's participation in church services and other denominational activities, factors that are crucial in determining the roster of preachers, but usually he is insufficiently acquainted with members of the congregation to know their status in the village and what resources they can muster, factors that must be taken into account in determining the roster of feast-givers. (This is particularly true of the Free Wesleyan minister who serves Motulahi, but it is generally true because most Wesleyan ministers do not serve for more than a few years with any one congregation.) In making up the rosters, the steward judges the status of members, and the selection of feast-giver and preacher is one area in which the steward's social skill is crucial for the maintenance of good relations within the congregation.

It will be useful at this point to describe a feast, for its magnitude must be appreciated to understand the role of feast-giver and the significance of feasting in a Tongan community. Feasts are served on *pola* mats, about 2.5 meters long by 1 meter wide, at which eight to ten people can be seated. A feast is described in terms of the number of mats, which gives an indication of the number of guests, and mats are evaluated in terms of the number and size of the pigs that are presented—pigs being the primary criterion of lavishness. An adequate mat at a feast in Motulahi will include three or four suckling pigs and about the same number of large yams and bundles of steamed food, plus lesser items sufficient to cover the mat with food.[12] Most feasts in Motulahi have from two to four mats; a single mat is niggardly and five is munificent.

Given this description of what is required in hosting a feast, it is not surprising that there were only five men in the entire village of Motulahi who, according to my estimate, could afford to give a feast without assistance. Yet almost every household in the village finds itself called upon to host at least one feast a year on one ceremonial occasion or another (congregational feast, wedding feast, birthday feast, welcoming feast). They manage to make an adequate display because they are assisted by food and labor contributions from a wide range of relatives and other associates they have helped in the past. The greater a household's contribution at feasts, the more assistance it will receive when its time comes.

A feast-giver has the opportunity for a status-enhancing display and for having people acknowledge his status by the fact of their presence as guests at his feast. Nevertheless, there is no formal requirement to make a big display at a congregational feast. A feast may be as lavish or as modest as the feast-giver chooses. Feast-givers also have the option of inviting whomever they choose, including members of different denominations and people from other villages (although neither is common at a congregational feast). Some feast-givers invite the entire corps of lay preachers in their congregation, although not everyone who is invited necessarily chooses to attend. Other hosts, less interested in pursuing status through feastgiving or less able to do so, provide smaller feasts. This, in turn, affects who invites them. Thus congregational feasts provide occasions for ongoing exchanges between the hosts and their guests on the one hand and the feast-givers and those who contributed to their feasts on the other. People adjust their exchanges as their strategies for social recognition and their material needs and resources change. Every feast provides a new opportunity for redefining relationships.

TOLERANCE AT THE LOCAL LEVEL

In contrast to the activity within the congregation, there are no interdenominational events at the local level. In other words, the various congregations in the village do not interact with one another qua congregations. On the contrary, the mutual posture of the different congregations appears to be one of tolerant avoidance if not studied indifference. On the national level, the various denominations are sometimes bitterly if quietly antagonistic, but there are few signs of overt competition between denominations at the local level. On Sunday mornings people pass one another in the road and give the all-occasion Tongan greeting, *mālō e lelei* 'it is good that things are well', ignoring the fact that they are on their way to services at different churches. Similarly, proselytizing activites of the Mormon and Wesleyan churches are never carried out in a person's home village. Thus there is seldom an occasion to confront differences of denominational affiliation within the village.

Doctrinal differences among the denominations are seldom discussed in the village, not even among members of the same denomination. If asked, an informant would undoubtedly affirm the superiority of the doctrines of his or her own denomination, but comparisons of doctrine are seldom made and people do not seriously deprecate the beliefs of others. The only common exception to this is that Seventh-Day Adventists are occasionally called *kai-kosi* 'goat-eaters' because they do not eat pork, the primary status food in Tonga. In addition, snide remarks are sometimes made about Mormon activities such as full-time proselytizing, genealogical research, and costume parties, all of which are regarded as being most un-Tongan. Some members of the Free Wesleyan church in Motulahi claim that the Mormon church is not truly Protestant; a few go so far as to say that the Mormon religion is not a true Christian religion, a particularly shocking thing to say in Tonga. I suspect, however, that many of these remarks betray resentment at the Mormons' success in gaining new adherents. Moreover, while there is some ill-feeling toward the Mormon church as an institution, there is no condemnation of particular individuals merely because they belong to that church. People are far more critical of those who show little involvement at all in the activities of a congregation than they are of an adherent of a particular denomination.

INTERDENOMINATIONAL COMPETITION

The phenomenon of interdenominational tolerance within the village is in marked contrast to the relationship among the denominations beyond the local level. By this I mean not only that the leaders of the various denominations act as antagonists but also that ordinary congregants see their denominations as competing with one another.

The distinction between the acceptance of interdenominational differences within the village and opposition beyond is exemplified in proselytizing activities. I refer here not to the proselytizing of the newer missions, some of which engage in street-corner exhortation and the like on the pavements of Nuku'alofa, but to the activities of certain established denominations. The Mormon church, for example, encourages its members to serve a year of their lives as missionaries away from their home villages. Those who do this are allocated in pairs to live in a Mormon household. The host household supports them, assisted if necessary by other Mormons in the community, while the two missionaries engage in church work on a full-time basis. This work may include assisting the local congregation or teaching in a local Mormon school, but most of these native missionaries spend their time going from house to house and talking to people about their religion. What I find significant is that the missionaries are deliberately appointed to serve away from their home villages and thus work among strangers. In the context of Tongan society, this means they can have but little credibility.

Similarly, the Free Wesleyans do not work in their home villages when they conduct their missionary activities. A congregation is assigned at some time in the year to visit another community as guests of the local Free Wesleyan congregation. It is a matter of pride for the visiting congregation to have as many members as possible join in the expedition. They spend a day or two at the host village, going as a group from house to house, singing hymns, and in general making people aware that the Free Wesleyans are present. As in the case of the Mormons' proselytizing, it is doubtful whether any converts are won by these congregational visits; the Free Wesleyan participants themselves do not speak of it as an effective means of winning converts.[13] However, one important effect of these activities, among both Mormons and Wesleyans, is that they reinforce in the participants their identity as members of their own denomination.

Interdenominational competition is not limited to these activities, however. A far more powerful weapon in the competition for membership is the fact that each of the seven major denominations, with the exception of the Church of Tonga, has some control over access to secondary education. Primary school education, which is universal and compulsory in Tonga, is largely in the hands of the government, but 85 percent of all secondary school students are educated in the schools provided by the various denominations.[14] Higher education has become an important element of social differentiation in contemporary Tonga, and there is tremendous competition for admission to secondary schools.[15] Since the churches are the major source of this limited good, a means of control over their members is available. Not only does each denomination give preference in secondary school admission to children who have been brought up within the denomination, but priority also is given to those who attended a primary school run by the church, even though in general these schools are inferior to the government primary schools. When I asked a woman in Motulahi why her children were attending the Roman Catholic primary school in the next village though Motulahi has one of the best government primary schools in the country, she told me that her priest said she stood a better chance of getting her oldest son admitted to a Roman Catholic secondary school if the younger children were attending the denominational primary school. Another woman told me that the priest had urged her to send her child to the Roman Catholic primary school and at the same time assured her of his assistance when the time came for secondary school. Similarly, in 1970, I found that at Tupou High School, the chief secondary school run by the Free Wesleyan church, 50 percent of the students had spent their final year of primary education at a Free Wesleyan primary school. At the comparable government high school, only 7 percent of the students had spent their final year of primary education at a Free Wesleyan primary school.[16]

In considering the provision of education as an element in interdenominational competition, it is useful to distinguish between education's role in recruiting new members and its role in retaining those who are already within the church. The Mormon church, in particular, recruits many of its new members through the provision of education. To a lesser extent, this is also true of the Seventh-Day Adventists and the Anglican church. Among the other denominations, however, the provision of education serves nowadays more as a means of retaining those who are already adherents. Only the Mormons, Anglicans, and Seventh-Day Adventists are in a position to admit students who are not members of the church, thus attracting potential converts; the other denominations have insufficient secondary school facilities even to accommodate all of those who are already members.[17]

Besides missionary activities and the provision of education, there is another area that in some measure reflects interdenominational competition: the attitude of the churches toward family planning. For a number of decades, Tonga has experienced an annual rate of population increase of more than 3 percent. The population more than doubled in the thirty-five years between 1921 and 1956, and it is expected to double again in the twenty-five years between 1956 and 1981.[18] The results of the 1966 census give a clear indication that the country will face severe population pressure well before the end of this century if the rate of increase is not controlled.[19] Toward the end of the 1960s, therefore, a family planning program was instituted by the Department of Health and linked to the provision of maternity and pediatric services.

While I was in Tonga there was a weekly series of radio broadcasts in which important persons discussed the personal and national benefits of family planning. As I understand it, however, what was significant was not what was said, but who did and did not speak. Thus the premier of Tonga, who is the younger brother of the king, gave a talk; however, neither over the radio nor in any other forum did the king himself urge the people to join the family planning program. Similarly, none of the recognized leaders of the major denominations supported the program.

While directives from leadership are unlikely to persuade couples to practice birth control, the fact that national leaders have not endorsed family planning makes it all the more difficult for a couple to withstand the social pressures that favor large families. To the best of my knowledge, no national church leader spoke out in public against family planning, and it might be argued that the lack of church support for birth control should not be viewed as a reflection of interdenominational competition. Nevertheless, the message in their silence was clear. Some people in Motulahi explained to me that it would put their denomination at a disadvantage if its members practiced birth control while members of other denominations did not: the family with fewer children has fewer potential members of the church.

DENOMINATIONAL DIVERSITY AMONG KIN

The avoidance of interdenominational confrontation within the home village is perhaps best understood as an accommodation to the fact that the various denominations not only separate the village into a number of congregations but quite often cut across *fāmili* 'local stem kindred' membership. The core of that membership is usually made up of siblings or descendants of siblings who live in the same village.[20] Figure 2 depicts denominational differences among members of the sibling groups that constitute the core of two of the local stem kindreds in Motulahi.

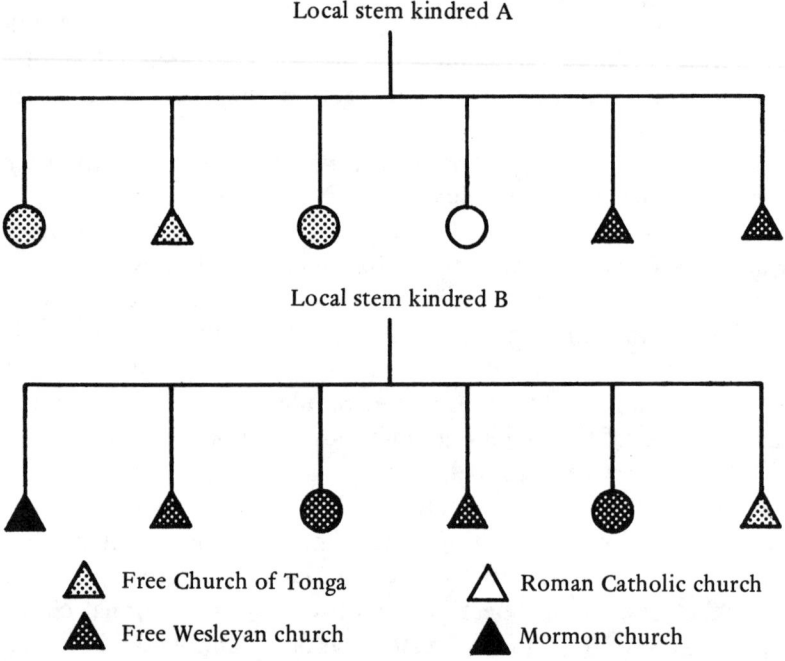

Figure 2. Denominational Differences among the Core Members of Two Stem Kindreds in Motulahi

As a result of the nonunilinear mode of reckoning membership in the local stem kindred, a household might be equally related to more than one local stem kindred in the village. When this is the case, the household as a unit will usually affiliate with the local stem kindred whose members are predominantly of their own denomination. If there is no such choice and members of different denominations find themselves associated in the same local stem kindred, then these people assist one another and contribute to one another's feasts, even if it is a congregational feast for a denomination other than their own. They may even be guests at such a feast without compromising their denominational affiliation in any way. Similarly, there is no difficulty if members of the same household belong to different denominations, which was the case in forty-three (30 percent) of the households in Motulahi.

CHANGING DENOMINATIONAL AFFILIATION

Switching to a different denomination is not uncommon in Tonga. Although I did not investigate this point directly, and my data are therefore incomplete, denominational changes apparently occur through schooling, through marriage, or through "personal retooling."

In speaking of switching denominational affiliation through schooling, I refer to children who attend a school run by a church other than that of their parents and later become members of that denomination. While children they usually belong to their parents' denomination, but once they reach their senior secondary school years, they may switch to the denomination that is providing them with their education. In other words, the recruitment of new adherents through the provision of education tends to be most successful when the student is just entering adulthood.[21] The fact that parents allow this is further evidence of the permissive attitude toward denominational differences among kin.

Interdenominational marriage reveals another aspect of the way in which denominational differences among kin are handled. Denomination is seldom a barrier to marriage in Tonga, and a husband and wife may well have been adherents of different denominations before they were married. In fact, there were 38 such cases in Motulahi of the 150 married couples living in the village.

As far as I could determine, there is no general opposition to marriage between people of different denominations; parents and close kin may be opposed to the marriage, but beyond this other people are seldom involved. Anyway, besides expressing their disapproval, there is little that anyone can do about the matter, and the couple usually deals with the situation by presenting the civil marriage certificate as a *fait accompli*. Refusal to have anything to do with the couple after this would almost certainly be condemned in the community as too extreme. I was told of how one formidable old woman of the Free Wesleyan church, incensed at her granddaughter's announced intention to marry a Roman Catholic, tore off her clothes and rolled naked on the floor to express her anger and contempt. However, I saw no sign of these objections in her present behavior toward her great-grandchildren, who are being raised as Roman Catholics.

In most interdenominational marriages, one member of the couple switches to the other's denomination.[22] There is no formal requirement that both members of the couple belong to the same denomination. Nevertheless, a person's status as a worthy member of the congregation is based in part on his or her spouse's participation in congregational activities and the children's induction into the church through Sunday school, and in this sense both members of the couple should belong to the same congregation. In almost all cases, it is the woman who switches to her husband's denomination rather than the other way around. Church membership is a more important status-defining attribute for men than for women, and it is more difficult for a man to establish his status as a full member of a church than it is for a woman. I know of only one case, not involving residents of Motulahi, where the couple did not get married because of denominational differences they could not reconcile.

Besides education and marriage, there is one more reason why people switch denominations in Tonga: "personal retooling." By "personal retooling" I refer to the fact that, irrespective of the sincerity of the religious conviction involved, conversion to a different denomination entails some examination of one's present circumstances and a comparison of these circumstances with the prospects that are possible within the new denomination. Whatever else it signifies, therefore, to change one's denomination implies a new set of commitments with a new set of congregants. Moreover, the transfer of denominational affiliation cannot be gradual; switching affiliation is abrupt and the person must immediately take up activity within the new denomination. Women are expected to do so at marriage and this is accepted in the community. Conversion as an adult in circumstances other than marriage is a different matter. It is generally regarded as a choice involving instrumental interests and is not, therefore, generally approved.

There can be little direct evidence of people's motivations for retooling: Tongans do not discuss motives. A Tongan explanation of why someone did something would probably not be regarded as satisfactory in our culture. When I asked people who had switched denomination why they had done so, they said they wanted to belong to the same denomination as their spouse or simply wished to belong to the denomination they had joined. (Matters of belief or doctrine were never put forward by way of explanation as they might be put in our own culture.) And when I asked why a certain person had switched denominational affiliation, I was told that it was done *fa'iteliha pē ia:* "It must have suited him to do so."

SWITCHING TO THE MORMON CHURCH

On the basis of my data from Motulahi, it appears that personal retooling is associated mainly with switching to the Mormon church. Table 8 depicts the circumstances under which adults now living in Motulahi changed their denominational affiliation. These data suggest that the circumstances associated with switching to the Mormon church may be different from those relating to other denominations. The table shows that a total of twenty people now living in Motulahi converted as adults to another denomination for reasons other than marriage. In some cases the person was an adult but not yet married; in other cases both husband and wife were affiliated with the same denomination and switched together to another denomination; in a few instances the husband converted first and the wife later; and in one case the man became a Roman Catholic and then a Mormon while his wife has always been a member of the Roman Catholic church. Each of these cases, in my view, falls under the heading of "personal retooling," and three-quarters of them involve switching to the Mormon church. Moreover, in those cases where there was a change of denominational affiliation at marriage, while there are thirty instances of women switching to their husbands' denominations, there are only six instances of a man converting to his wife's denomination and five of these cases involve switching to the Mormon church. Given what is involved in being a church member, a man's switching to his wife's denomination should also be viewed as a decision to retool.

TABLE 8 Circumstances of Adult Change in Denominational Affiliation, Classified by Sex, Motulahi

New Affiliation	Circumstances of Change			
	Marriage		Other than Marriage	
	Males	Females	Males	Females
Mormon church	5	7	12	3
All other denominations	1	23	2	3
Total	6	30	14	6

Source: Author's fieldwork survey taken over a number of weeks early in 1970.

Switching to the Mormon church may be viewed as a stratagem for gaining access to resources and opportunities otherwise unavailable nowadays. The Mormon church is a major employer in Tonga, second only to the government for employment outside teaching, and generally employs only Mormons. The Mormon church is also a major source of scholarships for study abroad, and these are allocated only to Mormons and graduates from Mormon schools in Tonga. Besides this, the Mormon church is a primary avenue of long-term emigration; indeed, almost all the Tongans who have emigrated to the United States mainland have done so under the auspices of the Mormon church. In short, membership in the Mormon church opens up prospects unavailable to most other Tongans.

In addition to employment, eduational, and emigration opportunities, membership in the Mormon church provides a legitimate basis for deviating from certain patterns of behavior that are part of *anga faka-Tonga* 'Tongan custom'. Mormon congregations, for example, do not have the feasts so characteristic of the Wesleyan churches. Thus members are relieved of the material burdens and social obligations of congregational feasting. Members of the Mormon church also tend not to engage in communal feasting on other occasions. Indeed, it is my impression that Mormons are less involved in kinship reciprocity than members of other denominations. It seems significant in this regard that Mormon doctrines and congregational practices place considerable emphasis on the elementary family. Certainly there are few multiple-family households among the Mormons in Motulahi. Either Mormon heads of household do not have the means of supporting more than their own families, or else having many dependents is not so prestigious for them as it is for other Tongans.[23] Mormons are also more open than other Tongans about asserting that traditional elements of status and privilege, based on a system of reckoning rank by birth, should be eliminated. In place of traditional criteria of status and customary forms of status behavior, material prosperity and individual achievement are emphasized.

In sum, membership in the Mormon church in Tonga seems to accord with the pursuit of an individualistic course of upward mobility. I am not arguing that people who convert to the Mormon religion do so only in order to pursue such a course. My point is simply that in Tonga an adult's switching affiliation from one denomination to another is an indication of personal retooling, just as a Tongan's moving to a different village would be an indication of retooling; each implies a decision to put oneself in contact with a new set of associates. That being the case, when denomination or residence is changed in circumstances other than marriage, some new strategy of achievement may reasonably be inferred.

DENOMINATIONAL MULTIPLICITY: A PROCESSUAL EXPLANATION

The notable success of the Mormon church in attracting converts is spoken of in Tonga as something unprecedented that is due entirely to the peculiarly aggressive proselytizing of the Mormons and the opportunities they offer. The fact is, however, that within a few years of the inception of the Church of Tonga in the 1920s, 10 percent of the population claimed to be adherents of that denomination (see table 6). For that matter, the first Roman Catholic missionaries in Tonga received an eager welcome among certain sectors of the population when they came on the scene in the 1840s, as did the Wesleyan missionaries some twenty years before that. These data from different periods of Tongan history call for examination of what appears to be a readiness in Tonga to welcome new denominations.

To begin with, it is my argument that the multiplicity of denominations is a well-integrated element of Tongan society. At the heart of this argument is the Tongan expression *fa'iteliha pē ia* 'to do as one pleases'. This idiom expresses a view of human conduct. According to this view, there are few prescriptions or prohibitions in Tongan society; in most matters, it is held, individuals have a range of alternatives and their choices are freely made.[24] The multiplicity of denominations and the freedom to switch affiliation are thus consistent with other optative elements of Tongan social organization: place of residence, household membership, kin-group membership, involvement in voluntary associations, and participation in status-striving activities. In each of these areas, and also in congregational and denominational matters, a person has considerable flexibility in determining with whom he will be associated and the extent of his involvement. Moreover, this is a dynamic process; as a person's needs and resources change, he shifts his alignments to accord with new stratagems. The process is clear in the organization of denominational affiliation; it is this shifting of alignments that I have called personal retooling. Retooling by switching denomination at once provides the convert with a new set of associates and makes it possible for him to restructure his commitments or even, in the case of some denominations, to take on wholly different commitments.

Understanding the adaptive functions of optation in denominational affiliation provides a basis for explaining how there has come to be a multiplicity of denominations in Tonga. In my view, consideration of the qualities, efforts, and conduct of the missionaries who came to Tonga is only one way of understanding their success. The acceptance of new denominations in Tonga cannot be explained simply as a matter of the material goods or spiritual values that the missionaries brought with them. I would argue, instead, that Tongans were—and are—attracted to new denominations because they make new stratagems possible; people choose a denomination at a time when they can use the opportunities it affords them.[25] The present success of the Mormon church in gaining converts is best understood in these terms. Moreover, the waves of shifting affiliation that followed the introduction of the indigenous Wesleyan denominations—the Free Church of Tonga in the 1880s and the Church of Tonga in the 1920s—are comprehensible only when viewed in these terms, for no expatriate missionaries were involved nor were goods or doctrines introduced.

CONCLUSION

It is easy for an outsider to be distracted by the multiplicity of denominations to be found in Tonga. What seems to me more important, however, is that the social system is conducive to the proliferation of denominations. In making this argument relating to the Tongan data, I have touched on a particularly significant aspect of missionization: the question whether local people are inclined to adopt the new denomination brought by the missionaries.

Implicit in much of the general treatment of missionization is a view of the natives as victims or, at best, persons merely responsive to initiatives taken by the missionaries. I suggest that we might more productively view missionization as a dynamic process in which local people themselves are active agents and manipulators. One way of operationalizing this approach is to focus on the relations and transactions between missionaries and natives. Which local people are attracted to the new denomination? What inclines them to welcome this particular denomination and these particular missionaries? Careful analysis of these elements may point the way toward understanding the processes by which a missionary-borne religion becomes indigenized.

It is clear from the materials that have been presented in this chapter that the domain of the churches affects most spheres and all levels of Tongan society. To speak of the Tongan practice of Christianity as being not really Christian is to imply that there exists somewhere a true Christian culture and society. By the same token, to suggest that Christianity is not really Tongan is to ignore the effects of missionary effort on Tongan history for the past hundred and fifty years—effects that today are more pervasive than ever.

NOTES

Fieldwork on Tongatapu was carried out from July 1969 to May 1970 with the support of an International Fellowship from the American Association of University Women. This support is gratefully acknowledged. I am also grateful to the government of Tonga for permitting me to conduct fieldwork and to many people in Tonga for their kind assistance. I shall not mention their names—not for lack of appreciation but to safeguard their privacy and that of their families. I wish to thank Fred Korn and Sharon Tiffany for their detailed comments and criticisms and Charles Forman, Sione Lātūkefu, and Alan Tippett for their helpful comments on an earlier draft.

1. Ernest and Pearl Beaglehole's study of village life in Tonga in the late 1930s includes a section on religion (1941:124-135) that clearly portrays the infusion of everyday life with religious elements and Tongans' absorption with matters relating to church membership. This portrayal remains valid today.
2. Two excellent studies of relations between church and state in Tonga encompass the history of missionization up to the end of the nineteenth century (Lātūkefu 1974; Rutherford 1971). Between them they cover the abortive early missions, the establishment of the Wesleyan and the Roman Catholic missions, and the establishment of the Free Church of Tonga.
3. The Beagleholes (1941:127) give a brief account of the circumstances associated with the inception of the Church of Tonga.
4. The Free Wesleyan church of Tonga has been completely autonomous only since 1972.
5. Details that would identify "Motulahi" have been omitted to preserve the anonymity of my informants.
6. See Walsh (1969) for an examination of rural-urban continuities on Tongatapu.
7. For a description of such an occasion, see Pratt (1922).
8. For a discussion of kinship relations among commoners, see Aoyagi (1966), Decktor Korn (1974, 1975), and Marcus (1974).
9. The Beagleholes (1941:112-113) give an excellent account of kava activities in village life.
10. The Beagleholes (1941:131) make a similar observation.
11. In each of the three Wesleyan denominations, pastors are ordained Tongan ministers. The Free Wesleyan church also has a few expatriate missionaries from Australia, most of whom occupy specialized positions such as principal of the Free Wesleyan high school. Village pastors are supported by a cash stipend from the church, supplemented by various nonmonetary contributions from members of

the local congregation. The Motulahi congregation of the Free Church of Tonga and the Church of Tonga each have a full-time minister appointed to Motulahi by the national governing body of their respective churches. The congregation of the Free Wesleyan church in Motulahi does not have a resident minister, primarily because the Free Wesleyan church does not have enough ordained ministers to appoint one to every congregation. About once a month the Free Wesleyan minister stationed in the adjacent village officiates at Motulahi; at other times Free Wesleyan services are solely in the charge of members of the Motulahi congregation.
12. This reflects the relatively high standard of living in Motulahi. People who live away from the main island and have less income have less lavish feasts.
13. The following anecdote indicates the importance attached to these visits. The Free Wesleyan congregation at Motulahi had been constructing a new school for three years, working in spurts to accomplish each stage of the building and then raising funds to finance the next stage of construction. In April 1970, the congregation was assigned to visit another congregation on the other side of Tongatapu. At that time they were ready to pour the concrete for the floor, a job that would require them to put aside all other activities for about a week. They therefore petitioned the central committee of the Free Wesleyan church to postpone their assignment and allow them to work on the construction project instead. The request was granted.
14. Statistical data on the role of the government and the churches in providing education are derived from the annual reports of the Department of Education of the Kingdom of Tonga, 1967-1969.
15. One indication of the competition for education is that in 1969 almost three thousand boys and girls under age twelve took the entrance examination that would admit no more than 70 students to the only government high school that prepared students for university entrance (Kingdom of Tonga, 1969:2).
16. These data are derived from a survey I took in the schools in May 1970.
17. As a sidelight on the churches' role in the provision of education, it should be noted that through church-building and school-building programs religious institutions account for as much construction as the Tongan government. Religion is comparable to big business in Tonga; outside the government, the churches are the largest investors, greatest employers, and biggest spenders in the country.
18. Kingdom of Tonga (1970:app. A.1).
19. For a discussion of the results of the census, see Rogers (1969).
20. See Decktor Korn (1974) for an account of the structure and organization of the *famili* 'local stem kindred'.
21. In this regard it is interesting to note that the Mormon church and the Anglican church have no primary schools, whereas three-quarters of the students in the Roman Catholic schools and one-half the students in the Free Wesleyan schools are at the primary school level.
22. There are only four couples in Motulahi in which the husband and wife are not of the same denomination; all involve marriages of long standing or older people or both. In each case the woman is prominent in the community, but it is not clear to me whether her prominence is a cause or consequence of her denominational independence. There is no clear pattern in the denominational affiliation of the children of these couples.
23. See Decktor Korn (1975) for a discussion of status in the structure and composition of Tongan households.
24. There is an important distinction to be noted between analytic recognition of a

set of various arrangements that are possible in the society and whether in fact there is a range of real alternatives. The distinction is not very significant in relation to denominational affiliation, but it may be critical with respect to elements such as kin-group affiliation or household membership (see Decktor Korn 1975).

25. The Beagleholes discuss a number of cases in which individuals changed denomination, all of which seem to support my analysis. Their conclusion is that "changing church affiliation provides a means of solving on a social plane interpersonal conflicts that might otherwise become strong enough to result in social disorganization and disintegration" (Beaglehole and Beaglehole 1941:129-130). Their approach differs from mine, but the analyses themselves are not incompatible.

THE POLITICS OF DENOMINATIONAL ORGANIZATION IN SAMOA

Sharon W. Tiffany

In the words of John Williams, leader of the first London Missionary Society (LMS) expedition to Samoa in 1830, "the Missionary enterprise is incomparably the most effective machinery that has ever been brought to operate upon the social, the civil, and the commercial, as well as the moral and spiritual interests of mankind" (1838:582). Williams had reason to be enthusiastic about the mission enterprise in the South Pacific, particularly Samoa. The missionaries were, for the most part, hospitably received by the Samoans, and within three decades of mission contact the Reverend George Turner, who spent eleven years in the islands, could write with justification that:

> On the reception of Christianity, temples were destroyed, the sacred groves left to be overrun by the bush, the shells and stones and divining cups were thrown away, and the fish and fowls which they had previously regarded as incarnations of their gods were eaten without suspicion or alarm. In a remarkably short time, under God's blessing, hardly a vestige of the entire system was to be seen (Turner 1861:243).

Many observers since Turner have remarked upon the success of the mission enterprise and the extent to which Christianity has been incorporated into the *fa'a Samoa* 'Samoan way'. An example of this view is provided by Douglas Oliver (1961:213):

> In Samoa, where religion was never so highly institutionalized as elsewhere in Polynesia, the mission teachers simply replaced native priests in the new system, and the *matais* ['chiefs'], formerly the families' intercessors with supernatural forces, simply became deacons in village churches. Ultimately the Protestant congregations developed into peculiarly Samoan native-church organizations, possessing many local twists in doctrine and practice.

Even the most casual observer is impressed with the religiosity and devoutness of the Samoans, who have transformed Christianity into a unique indigenous complex of beliefs and practices which led one missionary to lament that "Christianity, instead of bursting the bonds of the old life, has been eaten up by it" (quoted in Keesing 1934:410).

The LMS enterprise was successful in Samoa for many reasons, foremost among them its decentralized organization and local congregational approach to non-Christian peoples. In Samoa, the missionaries were confronted with a vigorous sociopolitical system which necessitated their adaptation to an indigenous organization of cognatic descent groups and chiefly hierarchies. The LMS missionaries concentrated their proselytizing efforts on the chiefs, recognizing that chiefly supporters could be persuaded to follow their leaders. In effect, the missionization process itself was politicized. Samoa became an arena in which political relations, consisting of labile alignments of chiefs, descent groups, villages, and districts, shaped the mission's administrative organization, procedures, affairs, and autonomy. In short, the missionaries' concern with their flock's spiritual welfare inevitably meant intervention in internal political affairs, which in turn influenced the structure and organization of the mission enterprise.

Samoa has been in contact with various missions for almost 150 years. Today virtually all Samoans consider themselves Christians, while the LMS, the first organized mission effort in the islands, remains the major denomination.[1] The transition from mission to church was officially recognized in May 1961, when the General Assembly of the LMS voted to change the organization's name to the Congregational Christian Church in Samoa (CCCS).[2] The CCCS is a politically and financially autonomous indigenous church to which 52.1 percent of the Western Samoan population and approximately 77 percent of American

Samoans belong.[3] Samoa, like Tonga, is characterized by denominational heterogeneity, and other denominations and sects have made significant inroads in "capturing" LMS adherents over the years. In addition to the LMS, the major denominations represented in Western Samoa are Roman Catholic (22.1 percent), Methodist (15.4 percent), and Mormon (7.2 percent). The remainder of the population is divided among the Seventh-Day Adventists (1.6 percent) and an assortment of religious groups and sects (1.5 percent),such as the Jehovah's Witnesses and Baha'i Faith.[4] Adherents of the four largest denominations are scattered throughout the Western Samoan Islands. Denominational heterogeneity is particularly evident at the village level; it is common for a village of a few hundred people to have two or three denominations, each represented by a resident pastor and a church building.

The phenomenon of changing religious affiliation represents a continuing process that began in the early 1800s with the introduction of alien religious ideas from a variety of sources, including castaway sailors, indigenous religious leaders, island teachers, and converts, as well as the missionaries themselves. The distribution of denominational affiliation during the period 1921-1966 for which census data are available indicates that denominational switching has been taking place for some time (see table 9).

The social structural contexts within which denominational affiliation and competition occur in Western Samoa are the subject of this chapter. A brief historical overview shows how the transition from mission to indigenous church was influenced by the organization of the early LMS enterprise and its adaptation to local sociopolitical institutions. The remainder of the chapter discusses the economics of congregational organization at the village level and the dynamics of chiefly rivalries and alliances entailed in denominational affiliation. I argue that denominational multiplicity results from competition for a variety of political, economic, and personal goals. This competition is structured in Samoa by cognatic descent groups and chiefly offices. The politics of denominational affiliation do not necessarily involve relations of conflict; however, when denominational competition occurs, it tends to reflect chiefly and descent group rivalries.[5]

Except for specific references to other missions and denomina-

TABLE 9 Denominational Affiliation, Western Samoa, 1921-1966[a]

Denomination	Percentage of Total Population						
	1921[b]	1926[c]	1945[d]	1951[e]	1956[f]	1961[g]	1966
LMS (CCCS)	63.9	63.8	56.3	56.5	55.2	54.0	52.1
Roman Catholic	16.1	16.1	20.3	20.7	21.5	21.6	22.1
Methodist	18.0	17.5	16.2	15.6	15.8	16.0	15.4
Mormon	2.0	2.5	4.2	4.3	4.6	6.3	7.2
Seventh-Day Adventist	0.0	0.0	0.9	1.1	1.1	1.3	1.6
Other	0.0	0.1	1.4	1.3	1.6	0.8	1.5
Not stated	0.0	0.0	0.6	0.5	0.2	0.0	0.1
Total	100.0	100.0	99.9	100.0	100.0	100.0	100.0

[a] Data on religious affiliation are not provided in the 1936 census.
[b] 1921 census, p. 76. "Native" Samoan population only.
[c] 1926 census, table 10, p. 14. "Native" Samoan population only.
[d] 1945 census, p. 13.
[e] 1951 census, table 15, p. 20. "Not stated" includes twenty-six non-Samoans who objected to stating their religious affiliation.
[f] Jupp (1958:40), table A.
[g] Figures for 1961 and 1966 are from the 1966 census, table B, p. 33; table 21, p. 133.

tions, discussion is concerned with the LMS and its indigenous offshoot, the CCCS. Field material is based on research conducted in a village on Savai'i where I lived for several months in 1969-1970 as well as my knowledge of CCCS congregations in other Western Samoan villages.

THE EARLY MISSION ENTERPRISE

John Williams' arrival on the *Messenger of Peace* off the coast of Savai'i in mid-July 1830 is usually cited as the beginning of formal missionary effort in the Samoan Islands. During his first visit, which lasted less than a week, Williams left a small contingent of island teachers under chiefly protection on Savai'i with promises to return with more teachers and missionaries as soon as possible, which was not until two years later. Williams' visits in

1830 and 1832 were not, however, the Samoans' first and only contact with Christianity. The frequency of contacts with outside influences accelerated a few years prior to Williams' initial visit and during his absence between July 1830 and October 1832. During this period Samoans were exposed to Christianity sporadically from a variety of sources, including Tongan Wesleyan (Methodist) adherents, an assortment of castaway sailors, and the Samoan leader of an indigenous millenarian movement.

The Wesleyan mission was established in Savai'i in 1828 by a Samoan who had been converted in Tonga (Danks 1914b:483). Several Tongan Wesleyan teachers married to Samoans were also known to be residing on Savai'i around 1828 (Garrett 1974: 65-67, 69; Gilson 1970:68-69; Keesing 1934:396), and a number of Methodist chapels had been established in Samoan villages prior to Williams' arrival in 1830. Castaways and deserters from European vessels were scattered throughout the islands and were also engaged in their own style of proselytizing during this early period. During a second brief visit to the islands in 1832, Williams described the following conversation he had with two English sailors on Upolu who claimed to have converted between 200 and 300 Samoans:

> "Why, Sir, I goes about and talks to the people, and tells 'em that our God is good, and theirs is bad; and when they listens to me, I makes 'em religion, and baptizes 'em . . . I takes water, and dips my hand in it, and crosses them in their foreheads and in their breasts, and then I reads a bit of a prayer to 'em in English." "Of course," I said, "they understand you." "No," he rejoined, "but they says they knows it does 'em good."
>
> In addition to this, I found that these two individuals had pretended to heal the sick by reading a "bit of a prayer" over them, for which they extorted property from the people (Williams 1838:421).

In addition to various sailor sects, it was the Joe Gimlet or Siovili cult, an indigenous millenarian movement, that introduced many Samoans to alien religious ideas. Siovili, the Samoan leader of this movement, is thought to have been influenced by Tongan Wesleyanism and by the Mamaia or "visionary heresy" movement that swept through the Society Islands in the late 1820s (Freeman 1959; Gilson 1970:87; Gunson 1962).[6] Williams, who apparently was not aware of the cult until his return to the islands in 1832, describes Siovili as follows: "This individual was a native of Upolu, and had visited Tahiti, where he had obtained a little knowledge of Christianity; and being an artful fellow, he had, like the run-away sailors, taken advantage of the general excitement, and had practiced much deceit upon the people" (Williams 1838: 428, fn.). The number of adherents of the Siovili cult increased rapidly throughout Upolu, Savai'i, and Tutuila in the early months of 1830, just before Williams' first visit (Freeman 1959:189).

In short, the LMS's first enterprise in Samoa was preceded by various interpretations of Christian doctrine and practice from several different sources. The stage had been prepared for an organized missionary effort. Moreover, Williams' first visit coincided with important political developments in Samoa: Lei'ataua Tonumaipe'a Tamafaigā of Manono Island had been assassinated only a few days earlier. Williams considered Tamafaigā, whom he described as the "king" of Samoa and a "devil chief," to be the main obstacle to the introduction of missionary activity (Gilson 1970:70-72). War ensued upon Tamafaigā's death, and forces loyal to the chief Malietoa Vai'inupō, an ally of Tamafaiga, were engaged in military operations against the parties responsible for the assassination. The smoke from burning plantations on Upolu could be seen by Williams as he prepared to send a contingent of eight Tahitian and Cook Island teachers, including five women and ten children, on shore at the village of Sapapali'i, to be placed under the protection of Malietoa (Williams 1838:334-335). Given the labile nature of Samoan politics, it is unlikely that Tamafaigā, despite his reputation for great political and supernatural powers, could have defeated the missionaries' early endeavors even had he wished to do so. In any event, political uncertainty following the assassination precluded the possibility of presenting a united front against the missionary presence.

A host of factors, including the nature of indigenous religious organization and the Samoan desire for Western goods, contributed to the acceptance of Christianity. Little is known about traditional religious institutions except that the highly organized priesthood and specialized temple centers associated with Eastern Polynesia did not exist in Samoa. Several writers (Gilson 1970:

73-74; Hanson 1973; Holmes 1974:59: Keesing 1934:399-402) have suggested that the absence of a priestly hierarchy and the localization of village and household deities under chiefly protection provided favorable conditions for the acceptance of Christianity, which was accompanied by little social disruption, as contrasted to the experiences of Hawaii and Tahiti. Religion in precontact Samoa was not everything, and the new opportunities for status enhancement and acquisition of material wealth made available through the missionary presence encouraged chiefly acceptance of new religious doctrines and practices.

The alacrity with which missionaries and teachers were accepted, and with which at least nominal conversions took place, was associated with the desire to obtain foreign goods which the missionaries seemed capable of dispensing. The stress on material wealth is evident, for example, in a speech by Faueā, a Samoan whom Williams had taken aboard his ship in Tonga. Faueā introduced the European visitors to his people in Samoa:

> "Can the religion of these wonderful *papalangis* [foreigners] be anything but wise and good?" said our friend to his naked countrymen, who by this time had filled the deck, and who, with out-stretched necks and gaping mouths, were eagerly catching the words as they fell from his lips: "Let us look at *them*, and then look at *ourselves*; their heads are covered, while ours are exposed to the heat of the sun and the wet of the rain; their bodies are clothed all over with beautiful cloth, while we have nothing but a bandage of leaves around our waist; they have clothes upon their very feet, while ours are like the dogs—and then look at their axes, their scissors, and their other property, how rich they are?" They all appeared to understand and appreciate this reasoning, and gazed on us with great interest and surprise (Williams 1838:329-330).

And in a later passage, Williams (1838:573) cites the speech of a Samoan chief exhorting his followers to accept the new religion: "Now I conclude that the God who has given to his white worshippers these valuable things must be wiser than our gods, for they have not given the like to us. We all want these articles; and my proposition is, that the God who gave them should be our God."

Williams (1838:571-572) was clearly aware that a variety of motives underlay the Samoans' acceptance of Christianity and that few people "had experienced a change of heart" as a result of their "knowledge of the spiritual character and supreme excellency of the Gospel." Regardless of the pragmatic concerns and individual motives involved in accepting the new *lotu* 'religion', the missionaries achieved considerable success in a relatively short time. Only twenty years after the arrival of the *Messenger of Peace,* "there were practically no self-confessed heathens left" in Samoa (Watters 1959:393).

Samoans responded positively to the missionary enterprise, which rapidly expanded its organization and activities with the arrival of six LMS missionaries in 1836. As many as 23,000 Samoans were receiving "instruction" by 1838, and by 1840 the islands of Upolu, Savai'i, and Tutuila were "covered with a network of mission stations" (Lovett 1899 I:375, 379). A printing press arrived in 1839 and in that same year five thousand copies of the first booklet *O le Tala i Lotu eseese* (A Talk about Different Religions), was published, the title an apparent reference to the missionaries' competition with the Methodist mission, sailor sects, and indigenous cult movements.[7] By the end of 1845, almost eight million "pages of useful reading matter" had been published and distributed throughout the archipelago (Lovett 1899 I:387). This outpouring of published materials was in response to the demands of an increasingly literate population.[8] Much of the adult population of Tutuila, for example, was literate as early as 1842 (Watters 1959:395). In 1844, the LMS established a seminary at Malua to instruct Samoan teachers for the work of evangelization.[9] Over the next twenty-five years, a total of 1,143 students and their wives were enrolled (Lovett 1899 I: 390-391), some of whom were eventually assigned to villages while others became members of a small but educated elite.[10]

The early mission enterprise was not without its obstacles and difficulties. The LMS missionaries found themselves competing with the Methodists and (later) the Catholic Mission, various sailor sects, and a proliferation of "native religious pretenders" (Turner 1861:109).[11] Wesleyanism had made considerable inroads by the mid-1830s, particularly on the islands of Savai'i, Manono, and Upolu, a point which led Gilson (1970: 85) to state that "for a short time the Methodists probably constituted the largest sect of all in those islands—perhaps outnumbering the *fa'atevolo,* or heathens, too." By around 1837 there were eighty Methodist chapels and approximately thirteen thousand Samoan adherents (Gilson 1970:85).[12] Heathenism was no longer a threat by the mid-1800s, however. According to the Reverend George Turner (1861:106), "it was all the *fashion* to have a foreign religion, and any worthless upstart, whether white, brown, or black, was sure to get a number of followers." By the mid-1830s, the Siovili movement commanded the allegiance of perhaps six thousand Samoans in spite of vigorous mission opposition. The movement declined by the 1850s, and many former cultists joined the Wesleyan or Roman Catholic missions, thereby maintaining their opposition to the London Missionary Society (Freeman 1959:197-198).

In addition to competition with other religious bodies, the rate of mission progress was also influenced by indigenous political considerations, notably the extent to which villages and districts were embroiled in political intrigues. Mission work progressed rapidly in Tutuila, "furthest removed from native politics and from contact with foreign vessels" (Lovett 1899 I:379), whereas the political scheming and warfare that seemed endemic to the islands of Upolu and Savai'i provided numerous opportunities for the political adversaries of a converted chief and his followers to oppose the LMS missionaries (see Watters 1959:393). Missionaries and island teachers were frequently involved in local politics because of their dependence upon the protection of individual titleholders.[13] By acquiring the allegiance of one chief, the missionaries risked alienating that chief's political opponents, who in turn extended their protection to the Wesleyan or Catholic missions or leaders of other sects. An illustration of religious affiliations following intravillage political cleavages is cited by Watters (1959:396): "Old factionalism was reflected in the division of the villages into three sects—one adhering to the LMS, another to 'Tangipo' [perhaps a Samoan cult leader], and a third following a runaway sailor." The arena of political intrigues and status rivalries provided fertile ground for the proliferation of religious groups and sectarian competition.

The politicizing of denominational affiliation was supported by two related factors: the general association of the LMS enterprise with chiefly hierarchies; and the local congregational orientation of mission organization. Administrative levels of the LMS largely coincided with traditional district and subdistrict levels of political organization, each district consisting of political alignments of local villages and titles. Mission stations tended to be located in political centers where district affairs were conducted, thus fostering the association between mission and high political status. The possibility of attracting people away from their villages and local political influences (as in Melanesia) was undermined by chiefly rivalries and local cleavages, thus precluding any chance of consolidating congregations and sharing the same teacher. Religious affiliation remained within the chiefly domain in Samoa. Chiefs jealously guarded their teachers, which led to administrative fragmentation and the establishment of small local congregations, each with its own teacher dependent upon his patron's political and economic support.[14] By 1850, more than 150 teachers were stationed in villages throughout the archipelago (Gilson 1970: 102); by 1895, there were "142 ordained native agents, and 184 native preachers" (Lovett 1899 I:397).[15] To keep teachers out of local politics, missions would assign them to villages other than their home villages and forbid them to take titles. However, the teachers, who were subject only to intermittent missionary supervision, depended on their congregations and chiefly patronage for their maintenance. Thus the established tradition of village autonomy, combined with the teachers' dependence on chiefly goodwill, supported the development of locally autonomous congregations led by teachers willing to modify formal mission policies to meet local political circumstances. This pattern of local congregational organization is still evident in contemporary Samoa.

The mid-1800s began a significant period for LMS policy and organization in Samoa. Religous indifference and backsliding had set in during the 1850s, a matter of deep concern to the missionaries.[16] Due to financial constraints from London, the number of missionaries in Samoa was reduced, thus giving the Samoan teachers increased independence over religious affairs. In 1850, the Samoan teachers' revolt in Tutuila, precipitated by dissatisfaction over their subordinate economic and religious status to that of the missionaries, marked the beginning of persistent teacher agitation for increased participation in mission affairs. In 1854, a system of annual contributions that called for separate congregational collections for the teachers' maintenance was established. Shortly thereafter, selected teachers were permitted "to administer the sacraments and to act as the missionaries' chief agents and advisers in other matters of church business" (Gilson 1970:131). The missionaries gave in to the demand that all Samoan teachers "be ordained and permitted to exercise full pastoral powers" in 1875 (Gilson 1970:135). Deacon-chiefs and other members of the laity were allowed greater participation at all levels of mission organization. The result of these events was a devolution of religious autonomy to the village where the pastors, assisted by their deacon-chiefs, regulated the spiritual affairs of their congregations. Thus "the life of the Christian Church tended to reproduce, with the native pastor or teacher as the equivalent of the old family head or chief, many of the features and qualities of the old village life" (Lovett 1899 I:396).

In summary, religious sects and cults proliferated during Samoa's early period of contact with the outside world. Religious diversity was encouraged by competition of different groups for adherents against the backdrop of chiefly rivalries. Sailor sects and indigenous religious groups eventually declined as the mission's version of Christianity was increasingly accepted, transformed, and incorporated into Samoan culture. The transition from mission to church had begun. The remainder of this chapter discusses present-day congregational organization and the social-structural contexts of denominational affiliation in Western Samoa.

A VILLAGE CONGREGATION

As has been suggested above, denominational affiliation correlates with descent group membership and political relations based on chiefly alliances. The decision to affiliate with a particular denomination is more than a choice to join a particular church. It is a manifestation of the desire to participate in the political and economic affairs of the descent groups of the chiefs who belong to that church. Patterns of denominational affiliation cannot be understood apart from the structure of cognatic descent groups and the principles of optation which govern membership in those groups. Before discussing the membership of a specific village congregation, it will be helpful to consider the structure of Samoan descent groups and chiefly offices.

Samoan social relations are structured by membership in *'āiga* 'cognatic descent groups' (see Tiffany 1975b). An individual claims simultaneous membership in a number of descent groups by demonstrating consanguinity to a recognized descendant of the group's apical founder. Samoans maintain as many group memberships as their time and resources permit, so that the number of memberships for which one is potentially eligible is restricted by the ability to sustain the obligations of membership. In other words, a claim to membership must be validated by active participation in group affairs. Descent group memberships consist of a local core of codescendants who occupy their group's named estate associated with a particular village in addition to nonresident members scattered on estates throughout the archipelago or residing abroad (primarily in New Zealand, Hawaii, or California). Residential cores also include persons who are not members of the descent group, such as spouses of members and some cognates of affines. Coresidents of an estate occupy nuclear, extended, or stem family households in which at least one member can trace a consanguineal connection to the group's apical ancestor. Villages typically consist of the residential cores of several descent groups. The residential cores of ten cognatic descent groups are associated with Fiafia village, the fictitious name of a village on Savai'i where I resided. Each descent group is represented by its senior ranking chief and by a varying number of junior titleholders. There are ten senior and twenty-five junior titles in Fiafia. All incumbents of senior and junior ranking titles represent their respective descent groups by sitting on the village *fono* 'council of chiefs'.

Chiefs are elected to office by descent group members and are expected to protect their group's corporate interests. Chiefs administer a variety of important descent group affairs: allocating land for residence and cultivation, maintaining peaceable relations among coresidents of the estate, protecting corporate property, and assessing goods and services for group participation in ceremonial redistributions, village projects, and congregational activities.

Villages, which consist of collectivities of chiefs representing their descent groups, jealously maintain their autonomy vis-a-vis other villages and are quick to note any infringement of their chiefly dignities and prerogatives. Chiefly alliances and rivalries develop between different villages and also within villages. Rivalry tends to cut across village boundaries as opposing alignments of titleholders in one village seek to extend their networks to chiefs in other villages through marital and political alliances (and in the past through military alliances), as well as by maintaining extensive economic ties by participating in ceremonial redistributions.[17] Political alignments and rivalries are fluid, as chiefs and their descent group members shift their allegiance to other chiefs. The labile nature of Samoan politics is reflected in the optative element of cognatic descent group organization. An individual chooses those descent group memberships which he or she wishes to maintain. This is to say that cognatic descent group organization entails multiple overlapping memberships. Samoans activate some memberships by supporting their groups' chiefs with goods and labor while permitting other potential group memberships to remain dormant. Samoans may prefer affiliating with particular descent groups over others, but individuals do not exclusively affiliate with one one descent group at a time. In short, the ability to maintain affiliative options with several descent groups is an essential component of Samoan social organization. As we shall see, options in choosing descent group membership are carried over to options in choosing denominational affiliation as well.

Residents of Fiafia village take pride in the fact that they have for the most part resisted the proselytizing efforts of other denominations. In 1970, 91.8 percent of the village's 561 inhabitants were adherents of the Congregational Christian Church in Samoa (CCCS), the only denomination which has a church building and resident pastor in the village.[18] According to elderly informants, the CCCS has been the major denomination in the village within living memory. This is borne out by the 1926 census, which provides the earliest available published data on denominational affiliation by village. According to the 1926 census, 91.3 percent of Fiafia villagers were adherents of the (then) London Missionary Society, while the remaining 8.7 percent of the population was divided between the Methodist and Catholic missions.[19] In 1970, only forty-six residents claimed to be adherents of other denominations; thirty-eight persons (6.8 percent) belonged to the Mormon church while eight (1.4 percent) were Roman Catholic. These persons occupy four of the fifty-three households associated with the village; one household is Roman Catholic and the other three are Mormon. Non-CCCS households are located in bush areas beyond the residential confines of the village proper, along with a few other villagers who have also moved their households into the bush to be close to their plantations. The Catholics and Mormons, however, are rarely seen in the village and participate irregularly or not at all in village activities such as the Women's Health Committee and the *'aumāga* 'untitled men's organization'. Members of the Catholic household have almost entirely withdrawn from village affairs with the exception of their titled head who occasionally attends meetings of the council of chiefs. This household attends Catholic services in an adjacent village. Of the three Mormon households, two are headed by untitled males who are supporters of the third Mormon household headed by a junior ranking chief. Members of the untitled Mormon households have completely withdrawn from village affairs. In contrast, the Mormon household head who holds a junior title limits his participation in village affairs to silent attendance at the meetings of the village council of chiefs, while his wife is an active member of the Women's Health Committee. Mormon families hold religious services in their homes or walk about 5 kilometers to a village where services are conducted in the guest house of a resident chief.

Congregational organization in Fiafia village consists of the Samoan pastor, lay pastors, deacons, the official membership, and adherents who are not formal church members. The CCCS congregation selects its own Samoan *faife'au* 'pastor' from the graduates of the Malua Seminary or from the pool of pastors who are not currently serving a congregation. The village congregation enters a *feagaiga*, a lifelong 'kinship relationship', with their pastor, who serves the spiritual needs of the congregation in return for which the congregation attends to the pastor's material needs. Pastors are usually members of high-ranking descent groups and marry well-educated women of good families. Indeed, the pastorate constitutes an educated elite in Samoan society comparable in prestige and status to holding a high-ranking title. Pastors may not hold chiefly titles or become involved in local politics, but they are highly respected and actively participate in village affairs that affect the church. Lay pastors are chiefs who have not completed formal theological training but through private study have passed a special examination administered annually by the CCCS, which permits them to preach in their village congregations. After ten years in their congregation, they may preach in any village in the islands. Many chiefs take pride in their verbal facility, and speaking from the pulpit is a prestigious way of displaying oratorical skills. There are three lay pastors in Fiafia, two of whom are also deacons in the village congregation. Deacons are invariably senior ranking chiefs who are formally recognized church members. The deacons are well-respected men who actively participate in church affairs and decision making at all levels of church administration. Their most important responsibilities involve the financial affairs of their congregation. The village pastor works closely with his deacons in raising and administering funds for the village church, the national church organization, and the pastor's personal upkeep. Other duties include visiting sick members of the congregation, serving the bread and wine during communion, passing the collection plates during services, and closing the doors of the church during prayers.

The *'ekālesia* 'ecclesiastical membership' consists of those persons who are baptized, have taken communion, and are formally recognized as full-fledged members of the church. An adherent who wishes to become a member must attend Bible classes for about six months and then be examined by the pastor. If he passes, and if his behavior has been satisfactory, the new member is accepted into the church and receives communion, which is held the first Sunday of every month. To remain in good standing, a member is expected to maintain an acceptable standard of moral behavior and meet his obligations toward the church. Adherents who are not formal members may attend church services and participate in church activities, and they usually contribute to the pastor's maintenance and offertories taken up for church projects.

The church is a center of social life in village Samoa, and the schedule of weekly church activities is full indeed. On Monday mornings the Women's Fellowship meets in the church: the pastor's wife, wives of the deacons, and any other woman in the congregation who wishes to attend. (In some congregations the Women's Fellowship meets twice a week; the wives of the pastor and deacons conduct a fellowship service on Mondays, and on Wednesdays they meet with any woman in the congregation who wishes to join them.) The choir meets for evening practice two or three times a week at the church or at the home of a member, beginning on Monday. In 1970, there were forty-three choir members (thirty-one males and twelve females) in Fiafia. The pastor conducts an evening prayer service for adults on Tuesdays, and on Wednesday evenings he meets with the young adults for a short prayer service. Friday evenings the pastor meets with the Sunday school teachers to discuss their lesson for the coming week. Sunday school teachers also conduct Bible reading classes for older children two or three times a week in the early evening. These classes are held at the church or the home of a teacher. Other activities include the participation of appointed congregational members in a daily prayer service. Members of one or two households are chosen on a rotating basis by the deacons to conduct a special prayer service every day (except Sunday) for one week—they are expected to come to the church every evening and pray for the welfare of the church and any ill members of the congregation. These activities are in addition to the evening prayer services for the entire village that are announced each day at dusk when the church bell (an empty metal cylinder) is struck. Villagers assemble in their homes for a short family service consisting of a hymn, the reading of a Bible passage, and a prayer conducted by the household head.

Organized sports are often sponsored by the village pastor and his wife. In one village on Upolu the young people of the congregation gather every Monday afternoon for cricket, basketball, and volleyball games supervised by the Sunday school teachers and other adult volunteers. Each team member is expected to bring one or two ripe coconuts which the pastor collects and sells to the Agriculture Department. These funds (about $US80 was collected during 1969 in this fashion) are used for uniforms and other team expenses. This village also has an active Girl's Brigade (similar to the Girl Scouts) led by the pastor's wife and female Sunday school teachers. Any girl in the village between the ages of six and twenty may join the Girl's Brigade, although in practice only those girls of the CCCS congregation are members.[20] In contrast, Fiafia village has no Girl's Brigade or organized sports except for a volleyball net which the pastor sets up outside his house for the young adults every evening. Since sports are not a part of a pastor's formal duties, the extent of involvement is up to the pastor.

Saturday is a busy day for the pastor, who makes his weekly tour through the village and visits his parishioners to check their general state of health. The village round usually consumes several hours, as members of each household implore the pastor to stay and visit while they prepare some food or drink for him. The pastor may divide an especially large village into sections and allot them to his deacons, who are responsible for making the health rounds of every household in their section. This method is also used when some members of the congregation live in adjacent villages which do not have their own resident pastor and church building. The afternoon is spent completing the village rounds and visiting hospitalized members of the congregation. Afterward the pastor, with the assistance of his deacons, holds a short service in the church to pray for recovery of the ill.

Sunday begins before dawn in the village, and by early morning the air is thick with smoke emanating from earth ovens in which bananas, fish, taro, and other foods are steaming. A short sunrise service for chiefs, deacons, and their wives takes place around 6:00 A.M., and the children's Sunday school follows at seven o'clock. the first regular church service begins around 8:00 A.M. and lasts about an hour. The children sit together in the middle section of pews toward the front where they are supervised by the Sundary school teachers, who occasionally deliver a rap on the head with a yardstick to maintain discipline. Young adults are segregated by sex, while chiefs and their wives usually sit in pews reserved for them at the front. The service consists of several hymns, prayers, a collection, and a lengthy sermon. After the service, people return to their homes to eat the special meal of the day, while the senior ranking chiefs of the village and their wives stay behind to eat their Sunday meal with the pastor and his wife in their home. Everyone is expected to bring a basket of food to share with the others during the pastor's meal. The rest of the day is spent in Bible study and resting until 3:00 P.M. when the second regular service begins. The afternoon service, usually less well attended than the first, is often conducted by a visiting pastor, a "resting" pastor (one with no congregation of his own), or a lay pastor. Sunday ends with evening Bible school from about 6:00 to 7:30 P.M. for students preparing for "ecclesiastical membership."

The pastor's schedule also includes daily instruction for the children of his congregation. The pastor's school is voluntary, and children of any age up to about eighteen may attend. The pastor's school meets for one or two hours in the afternoon four or five times a week at the pastor's residence, where the children are taught Bible stories, arithmetic, reading, and Samoan grammar. In some villages, the children attend the pastor's school four days a week and work on the pastor's plantation one day. For the few children with no birth certificate, a requirement for entrance into government schools in Western Samoa, the pastor's school constitutes the only formal education they will ever receive. The culmination of the pastor's work with the children of his congregation is White Sunday, or Children's Day, which falls on the second Sunday of October. This was a minor occasion for the Congregational church in England, but in Samoa it has become almost as important as Christmas. The entire day is devoted to children who conduct church services. Every child of the congregation presents what he or she has learned in the pastor's school through brief oral recitations and participation in religious plays. Parents spend considerable money on new white clothes for their children. They spend considerable time, moreover, in preparing for the huge feast during which the children are served first instead of last (or last least eat in separate quarters while the chief of the household eats). After the White Sunday ceremonies, the pastor's school closes until early January of the following year.

In addition to his daily schedule of activities, the pastor records the births and deaths in his congregation and conducts prayer services in households where there has been a birth or death. He also conducts prayer services at church dedications, title installations, funerals, and marriages. He meets regularly with the deacons and lay pastors to discuss financial and administrative matters of the congregation and with members of the laity who are studying for lay pastor status. The pastor also meets with the pastors and deacons of villages within the CCCS subdistrict and attends the annual CCCS conference held at the Malua Seminary compound in May.

MAINTENANCE OF THE VILLAGE PASTOR

Congregations have been responsible for voluntarily contributing to their teachers' upkeep since the establishment of the mission enterprise in Samoa. Village contributions were supplemented by a small clothing allowance provided by the London Missionary Society for every teacher and his family (Turner 1861:158-159). The decision in 1852 to organize contributions into an annual congregational subscription was a result of increasing economic discontent among the Samoan teachers, who up to that time received no regular salary or stipend. In spite of some chiefly objections, the new scheme was implemented in January 1853:

> We, therefore, decided that we should call upon the people simultaneously all over the group, to fix upon the first month of every year for making a voluntary contribution for the support of their village teacher. The people had all along been in the habit of building him a house, and of supplying him with the most of the food which he required, but they left him to his own resources, or the allowances from the Missionary Society, for everything else....
>
> Still, however, some grumbled, "Why not pay the teachers out of the May collection?" "If we subscribe for the teachers in January, there will be nothing for the Missionary Society in May." "If we yield to this, and pay the teachers, we shall be called upon to pay the missionaries next." These were the sayings of a few of the croaking, close-fisted, and unprincipled (Turner 1861:159-160).

Pastoral support has greatly increased since then. Today every household in the congregation, and particularly those individuals who are official members of the church, is responsible for supplying the pastor with food, contributing monthly for his personal expenses, and donating annually for the upkeep of his house.

Each household in the congregation is expected to provide at least one basket of food for the pastor every Sunday. In addition to the staples of taro and bananas, special items not ordinarily eaten during the week are included, such as chop suey, pigeon, chicken, or pork. Sunday food baskets are usually delivered by children to the pastor after the morning service. The Sunday food contributions supplement the pastor's regular daily food supply, which is contributed by two households on a day specified by the deacons. The pastor receives additional food contributions during the week from people wishing to share a particularly large catch of fish or a successful pigeon hunt in the bush. Another source of food and income for the pastor of Fiafia, one which is not provided to all CCCS pastors in Samoa, is the taro, banana, and cacao plantations on village land allocated by the council of chiefs. Fiafia is located in a rich cacao-producing area of Savai'i where cash cropping is the main source of income. Members of the Women's Health Committee, composed of all women of the village, work on the pastor's plantations once or twice a month and are responsible for planting and weeding and for drying his cocoa beans, which he sells to the local trade store. The money obtained from cacao is considered part of the pastor's personal stipend. Committee members also clean and maintain the pastor's house and grounds, clean the church and grounds, and prepare the church for Sunday services. Most members of the Women's Health Committee in Fiafia belong to the CCCS, since the Catholic and Mormon women have almost all withdrawn from village activities. The two active Mormon members of the committee do not participate in affairs involving the CCCS pastor and church. Women's Health Committees in villages with greater denominational variation than Fiafia confine their activities to public health: maintaining village sanitation, raising funds for the local hospital, assisting in maternal and child health services.

In addition to cacao cash cropping, an important source of personal income for the pastor in Fiafia is derived from church collections on the first Sunday of every month. One deacon is elected annually by the other deacons, to collect, record, and distribute monthly donations for the pastor. Contributions are voluntary; however, it is expected that everyone, especially church members, will contribute an amount commensurate with their rank and economic position. Generous contributions are encouraged by announcing in church the amount of money given by each household. The CCCS congregation in Fiafia contributed approximately $US552 to its pastor during 1969.

The annual contribution for the pastor is organized by the Women's Health Committee's officers, who are the wives of the highest-ranking chiefs of the village. These women, in consultation with the pastor and his wife, determine the amount of goods and money to be contributed, organize the collection, and ensure that each member donates her share. During a committee meeting held in February 1970, the officers announced that the congregation's annual contribution to the pastor should consist of 50 sleeping mats, 75 floor mats, 100 woven food trays, and $US27 in cash for dishes and cooking utensils. To meet this quota, single and widowed women and wives of untitled men were each to contribute one food tray, one floor mat, and 15 cents each; wives of chiefs were to contribute two sleeping mats, one food tray, one floor mat, 30 cents each. A day in early March was scheduled for the collection at the committee's building, the former village schoolhouse. On the appointed day, each member brought her contributions, which were recorded by one of the officers and turned over to the pastor and his wife after the collection.

OFFERTORIES AND CONTRIBUTIONS

Every household in the village congregation contributes once a month to a fund for the national CCCS organization. The money is collected and recorded by one of the deacons elected annually for this task, and the funds are eventually forwarded to CCCS headquarters at Apia. The offertory is announced in church once a month by the deacon-treasurer, who reads off the name of each contributor and the amount donated. The deacon and pastor then exhort the congregation to try harder for the following month's collection. In 1969, the congregation in Fiafia contributed a total of about $US755 for the national church organization.

Members of the village congregation may be asked for additional contributions of food and money during the year for special church projects. Church construction programs and dedications are significant economic events for villagers, who take pride in the size and magnificence of their church edifices. Indeed, tearing down old churches and dedicating new ones is a recurrent congregational activity throughout the islands that requires considerable descent group resources. Villagers depend upon their networks of kinsmen and affines to help them meet their economic obligations for large-scale projects of this kind (see Holmes 1974:72-74; Tiffany 1975a:276-279). In addition to church construction programs, congregations contribute to a variety of other projects. Matters related to the church are discussed at the congregational level, and since all but two titleholders in Fiafia are members of the CCCS, it is common for church affairs to be discussed at meetings of the village council of chiefs. Directives requesting food and money, and possibly labor, may be initiated at any level of church organization—from local congregation to national administration. When, for instance, the pastor in Fiafia receives a request for assistance from the CCCS district to which the village belongs, he first discusses the matter with the deacons and, in consultation with them, decides who will be responsible for turning the requested contribution over to the appropriate party. The pastor announces the nature of the project and the required amount of money, food, and labor during the morning church service. The chiefs decide at a subsequent council meeting how funds for the project are to be collected, how much will be contributed by each household, who will record and collect the contributions, and who will give the money and food to the pastor.[21] The pastor does not attend village council meetings except by invitation; thus he was asked to come to a meeting (which I attended) when the main topic of discussion was whether a new house should be built for him and how it would be financed.

The manner by which the village council of chiefs in Fiafia implements decisions made at different levels of church organization is illustrated by two examples which I observed. On one occasion, the congregation was informed by the pastor that eight cents should be collected from everyone, including children, in order to repair a pastor's residence in another village belonging to the same CCCS district as Fiafia. The village council decided that the senior ranking chief of each descent group would be responsible for collecting the money from all the members of households attached to his group and for turning it over to the pastor. On another occasion, the CCCS headquarters requested every village congregation throughout the archipelago (including American Samoa) to contribute approximately \$US32 and five pieces of taro in order to maintain pastors and church members engaged in a special construction project at the Malua Seminary compound. The village council determined the amount to be contributed from every household and allocated the responsibility of collecting contributions to the senior chiefs, who presented the money to the pastor. One chief volunteered to give the required taro.

We have seen that a significant portion of congregational activity is involved with allocating and distributing goods, money, and services to the local pastor and supporting projects initiated at all levels of church organization. Pastoral support is contingent upon the economic assistance of chiefs, who also hold administrative offices in the congregation and actively participate in subdistrict, district, and national church affairs as well. Having examined the economic components of the village congregation, we turn now to the political context.

DENOMINATION AND VILLAGE POLITICS

Church membership and changes in denominational affiliation are manifestations of shifting political alignments within descent group and village units. Hence political rather than doctrinal differences are most useful for explaining denominational affiliations and rivalries in a village. The social-structural contexts of denominational affiliation are illustrated here by two examples of conflict. The first case involves chiefly opposition to the Mormon presence in Fiafia, where the actions of three Mormon households reflect the decrease in chiefly power over religious conformity. The second case concerns a village on Upolu where the political rivalries of two coholders of the same senior title have produced two denominations.

Motives behind the decision to change denomination are difficult, if not impossible, to determine. Samoans do not usually speculate about motives for peoples' behavior in such matters except in vague generalities. Moreover, a change in denominational affiliation is a sensitive topic because status rivalries as well as interpersonal and intergroup conflicts frequently underlie such decisions to change. The presence of non-CCCS adherents in Fiafia village is, therefore, a source of embarrassment to other residents and is not freely discussed.[22] The general attitude is one of tolerant disinterest, as long as the converts cause no trouble. For these reasons I was unable to collect detailed information on members of the three Mormon households in Fiafia. I was, however, able to reconstruct some events subsequent to the conversion of one household which apparently occurred around 1963. This household consists of the untitled male head, who was born in Apia and lives in Fiafia with his wife, the daughter of a junior ranking titleholder attached to an important descent group in the village, along with their six school-age children. Members of the other two Mormon households apparently converted a few years prior to this, although I was unable to confirm this point. Both heads of these households were born in a subvillage of Fiafia located about a kilometer away.[23] The second Mormon household is headed by an untitled male whose father holds an important title associated with this subvillage. Both father and son moved to Fiafia in the early 1960s; the father eventually returned to the subvillage while an unmarried daughter and married son, along with the son's wife and six children, remained in Fiafia. The third Mormon household is headed by a junior ranking chief, whose title is also associated with Fiafia's subvillage, and consists of his wife, an unmarried son and daughter, two married sons, their wives (one of whom is the daughter of a Fiafia chief), and their seven and six children respectively.

Fiafia's subvillage is located about 1.5 kilometers from another village where the Mormon church has made considerable inroads in the last ten to fifteen years. Mormon residents in Fiafia support a high-ranking Mormon titleholder in that other village by contributing to ceremonial redistributions involving this chief and his descent group, while cultivating village land administered by Fiafia chiefs. Of course, it is not uncommon for Samoans to maintain several allegiances to different descent groups and chiefs at the same time, given the optative nature of the Samoan descent system. It would seem, however, that the Mormons' withdrawal from secular village affairs in Fiafia (with the minor exception of the junior titleholder mentioned earlier) was necessary from a religious standpoint, since village groups such as the council of chiefs and Women's Committee are heavily involved in matters relating to the CCCS denomination.

According to informants, the village council of chiefs declared around 1968 that only the CCCS could hold services in Fiafia, which meant that non-CCCS adherents would have to attend services elsewhere. This decision was in response to the Mormon residents who invited a Mormon missionary to conduct religious services in their homes on occasion. The Mormons protested the village council's decision by filing a petition at the Savai'i branch of the Land and Titles Court, a petition which was eventually dropped. The chiefs of Fiafia were apparently persuaded by court officials to rescind their council decision on the grounds that religious freedom was guaranteed all citizens under the constitution and denominational affiliation was not a matter of village and chiefly jurisdiction. The dispute over Mormon services in the village did not end there, however. A few weeks later, the village council of chiefs declared that Mormon households would not be permitted to ring a bell to summon worshippers because it conflicted with the pealing of the CCCS bell. The Mormons refused to accept the council's decision. A few days later, some untitled men attempted to silence the Mormon bell, which resulted in fisticuffs but no serious injuries. This incident prompted several chiefs to try to pass a council resolution banishing the Mormon families from the village. The issue was hotly debated. Some members of the village council of chiefs refused to support the resolution. They argued that the Mormons were unlikely to comply with the banishment decision and would take the case to the Land and Titles Court, which would in all probability support the Mormons since changing denominational affiliation is insufficient grounds for banishment. Thus, so the argument went, the village chiefs would be publicly humiliated by an unfavorable court decision. The matter was dropped, but most chiefs of Fiafia clearly resent the present situation.

The three Mormon households of Fiafia have challenged the authority of the village's senior ranking chiefs, all of whom are staunch supporters of the CCCS. Chiefly resentment is high because a change in denomination translates into a change of political allegiance as well. The Mormon residents have added insult to injury by attending services in a village that has been a political adversary of Fiafia for many years. Indeed, village resentment has been exacerbated by the fact that Mormon services are held in the guest house of a chief in that village who, in the opinion of many Fiafia chiefs, has instigated considerable trouble for them.[24] In sum, the senior chiefs of Fiafia have lost the allegiance and economic services of these dissident households to a political rival in another village.

While denominational switching reveals existing conflict, it may also exacerbate antagonisms between opposing parties.[25] This is illustrated by the long history of conflict between two men, both of them contenders for their descent group's senior ranking title. Members of this important descent group, which is associated with a village on Upolu, were unable to agree on one person to hold the group's senior title. The dispute was eventually taken to the Land and Titles Court for adjudication in 1938.[26] The court appointed both contestants to hold the title jointly with the condition that upon the death of both appointees, the descent group would revert to the practice of electing only one incumbent to the title. In cases of this type, coholders of the same title jointly exercise the *pule* 'power and authority' which pertains to the title and are expected to confer with each other in decisions affecting the descent group as a whole. Both contenders were appointed in the hope of restoring peaceable relations between the two men and among the supporters of each candidate. However, conflict between the men flared a few weeks after the court's decision when one of the appointees (Chief A) refused to attend the official title installation ceremony of the other appointee (Chief B). His refusal was considered a serious act, for it implied that conferring the title on Chief B was illegitimate and should not be publicly acknowledged. The matter was eventually settled out of court and the installation ceremony proceeded as planned. Three years later, Chief B retaliated for this affront to his dignity by threatening to withdraw from the LMS church, which at the time was the only denomination represented in his village. Chief B's threat was occasioned by a series of developments involving the LMS pastor of the village. In 1941, the LMS district council decided to remove the pastor from office for alleged involvement in local politics. According to informants, the district's decision angered village chiefs who claimed they were not notified in advance of a meeting and were not permitted to participate. Several chiefs, including Chiefs A and B, felt that the pastor's dismissal infringed upon congregational autonomy and in protest withdrew from the LMS congregation in their own village. These chiefs and their supporters began to attend LMS services in a nearby village while negotiating with church officials over the dismissal. The district council refused to rescind its decision, however, and after several months the dissident chiefs, fearful of provoking further schisms within the village over the issue, dropped their boycott and returned to the LMS congregation in their own village. Chief B, however, insisted upon total withdrawal from the LMS and wanted to invite another denomination into the village, to be headed by the former LMS pastor who had been dismissed. In spite of opposition from the village chiefs, including his coholder, Chief B proceeded with his plans.[27]

Chief B, along with supporters from his descent group, withdrew from the LMS and joined a denomination originally founded in American Samoa by a small group of dissidents who had broken with the LMS earlier. In 1943, this denomination claimed to have approximately 1,400 adherents in six villages on Tutuila and Upolu, although it has not been successful in increasing its membership which, according to the latest available figures, had only 557 adherents in Western Samoa in 1961.[28] The former LMS pastor who was removed from office was chosen pastor of Chief B's new congregation; Chief B himself was elected financial chairman of the entire church organization. Religious services were held in Chief B's residence. This arrangement was considered unsatisfactory, though, and after a series of lengthy consultations with the newly appointed LMS pastor and other village chiefs, Chief B was permitted to use the village LMS church for his denomination's services and activities. Attempts to share the church building between the two denominations soon resulted in conflicting schedules and confrontations between adherents which developed into fisticuffs on two or three occasions. These events prompted Chief B to submit a petition with the Land and Titles Court requesting that members of the LMS congregation be prohibited from using the contested church building and that the

LMS pastor vacate the residence site adjacent to the church. Chief B claimed that the LMS church and pastor's residence were located on descent group land attached to his title and that he could rightfully demand the withdrawal of the LMS congregation from use of these structures so that they would be available exclusively for his own denomination. But according to land registration records, the church was located on registered freehold land owned by the LMS and not on descent group land. The court ordered Chief B to build his own church elsewhere on descent group land and stop interfering with LMS activities, especially those involving the pastor's residence (Tiffany 1974: 49).

This was not the end of the matter. Chief B steadfastly refused to acknowledge the right of the LMS congregation to use the pastor's residence and church building, thus beginning a series of court adjudicated disputes between the chiefs of the LMS congregation (including Chief A) and Chief B over the latter's continued obstruction of attempted improvements to the contested buildings. At the same time, personal rivalries between Chiefs A and B were intensified by the church-related conflicts and their repeated but unsuccessful attempts to have each other removed from office. Tensions eased somewhat in 1963 upon the death of Chief A, which left Chief B the senior representative of the entire descent group. In 1967, Chief B filed a petition with the court claiming that the official change of name from the LMS to the CCCS invalidated the CCCS congregation's rights to the contested church building and residence site. The petition was rejected by the court on the grounds that the CCCS assumed full rights and obligations of the LMS and was therefore entitled to use the land. According to the court's decision, Chief B may not "arbitrarily or unreasonably" withhold his consent from CCCS members who wish to make improvements to the church building and the pastor's house. Access to the disputed buildings is not an issue at the present time; however, the legacy of some thirty years' contention has influenced the quality of relations that obtain between Chief B and other titleholders of the village. Moreover, the members of Chief B's descent group remain polarized. Supporters of the deceased Chief A remain fiercely loyal to the CCCS and resent B's court actions against their church and pastor, while B views the alliance of A's supporters with village chiefs belonging to the CCCS as disloyal high-handedness. It is unlikely that internal descent group relations can be normalized until Chief B dies and the title remains vacant for several years.

CONCLUSION

The early mission enterprise in Samoa changed over a period of two decades from initial contact and conversion to concerns of backsliding and lack of interest among converts as well as the problem of bureaucratization. By 1850, the London Missionary Society was maintaining a network of mission stations, dispensing medical services, publishing, providing village education, and training island teachers at its seminary. Students were trained as teachers and, later, as ordained pastors; some seminary graduates became members of a rising political and entrepreneurial elite. Samoan teachers were important mediative agents between their congregations, the mission, and a new world of challenges opened by the traders, merchants, consular agents, and political adventurers who soon followed in the wake of the missionaries. The teachers assumed greater status and responsibilities as missions became increasingly involved with administrative concerns. Teacher discontent surfaced over economic conditions. Due to financial constraints and decreased numbers, the missionaries eventually acceded to teacher demands for greater congregational autonomy and participation in mission policymaking. The teachers' economic and political status thus increased at the expense of mission control. Today village pastors are accustomed to a high standard of living and enjoy considerable prestige and privileges comparable to those of high-ranking chiefs, who in turn play important roles at all levels of church administration.

Both economic and political relations are components of denominational organization in Samoa. A major portion of congregational activity is involved with allocating and distributing goods, money, and services to the local pastor and participating in projects sponsored by the church. Status rivalries are reflected in recurrent construction of larger and more magnificent churches as well as congregational efforts to provide lavishly for their pastors. Although pastors depend on their congregations for economic maintenance, they are expected to remain aloof from local politics. This is a difficult stance, since economic support is predicated upon chiefly support. More than one pastor, like the pastor dismissed by the LMS district council, has run afoul of the political intrigues of his chiefly parishioners.

Denominational affiliation coincides with points of cleavage in the Samoan social structure. That is, denominational differences highlight the labile arrangements of alliance and cleavage that obtain among descent group memberships, chiefly alignments, and villages. A denominational change is an excellent means of expressing discontent. It provides an opportunity for switching allegiance to another chief or coalition of chiefs, and it is a means of avoiding what some dissenters view as the onerous economic obligations involved in maintaining descent group ties. Denominational changes entail conflict, as such changes tend to exacerbate existing tensions and underscore the dissenter's ability to make decisions contrary to the desires of other chiefs. Those who change their denominational affiliation in the face of chiefly opposition are testimony to the decrease in chiefly power over group members. Religious freedom is guaranteed by the constitution so that formal sanctions against religious nonconformists are neutralized and denominational differences must be tolerated. Banishment from the village is no longer an effective chiefly sanction in these situations. A troublemaker cannot be forcibly removed from the village except by court order, and the Land and Titles Court will not permit a person to be banished simply because he has changed his denomination. Thus the dissenter remains a persistent reminder of chiefly inability to sanction nonconformists and may even mobilize future opposition to the chiefs. The chiefs of Fiafia take considerable pride in the fact that the London Missionary Society was the first mission introduced into their village; out of loyalty to this tradition, they have tried to maintain denominational uniformity by resisting the proselytizing efforts of other missions and denominations. Few villages in Samoa have been able to resist such efforts successfully. Fiafia is of special interest in this regard because the Mormon presence in the village indicates a breach in denominational uniformity which may widen in time.

A denominational change is a serious action with both economic and political consequences because it commonly involves withdrawal from secular village affairs as well. Residents who adhere to another denomination, such as the Mormon households in Fiafia, simply move to their plantations in the bush and ignore village affairs.

Denominational switching is a particularly effective means of expressing opposition to policies, decisions, and personnel that may not be directly related to religious or doctrinal issues. Moreover, a change in denomination implies more than losing some members of a congregation. It constitutes a loss of village manpower and resources, which has considerable implications for the structure of descent group and chiefly relations.

Samoans responded to the mission enterprise by incorporating features compatible with their own interests and institutional structures. The result is an indigenized church whose organization, procedures, personnel, and affairs articulate with institutionalized alignments of chiefly power and authority. Religion has been incorporated into the domain of descent group activities administered and supervised by chiefly titleholders.

NOTES

The material presented in this chapter is based upon fieldwork in Samoa during 1969-1971 and the summer of 1973. I wish to acknowledge the Wenner-Gren Foundation for Anthropological Research, the UCLA Department of Anthropology, and the American Philosophical Society for their support of this research. I am grateful to the government of Western Samoa for permission to conduct fieldwork and to the many Samoans who generously contributed to my research efforts. The chapter has benefited from extensive criticisms by Shulamit Decktor Korn and Walter Tiffany. I also wish to thank Peter Black, Lowell Holmes, Reverend David Inglis, and Paul Shankman for their comments on earlier drafts of this chapter.

1. I follow Beckett's (chapter 8) definition of mission as "a specialized agency of church or sect having the task of attracting, instructing, and directing people who are ineligible for immediate membership of the parent body." A denomination, or "class church," is a formal organization characterized by a trained ministry, formalized services, and lack of dogma. Expulsion is uncommon, and education of the young is emphasized instead of evangelism. Above all, the denomination "accepts the standards and values of the prevailing culture and conventional morality, though the conceptions it entertains of these may be those of a particular social class" (Wilson 1967:25). On the other hand, a sect is a voluntary organization characterized by a high level of lay participation which emphasizes group and doctrinal exclusivity and rigorous expulsion of members who "contra-

vene doctrinal, moral or organizational precepts" (Wilson 1967:23-24). According to Wilson (1967:24), "the sect is hostile or indifferent to the secular society and to the state." See also Beckett (chapter 8).

2. See the CCCS constitution (CCCS 1962). The CCCS includes all village congregations in the Samoan archipelago, in addition to Swains Island, the Tokelau Islands, and overseas congregations in Hawaii, the mainland United States, New Zealand, and elsewhere. In this chapter the LMS after 1961 is referred to as the CCCS.

3. The most recent figures available for denominational affiliation in Western Samoa are from the 1966 government census (table B, p. 33). The figure for American Samoa is cited in Holmes (1974:68).

4. Government of Western Samoa (1968:33). The distribution of denominational affiliation for American Samoa is Roman Catholics 13 percent, Mormons 6 percent, Methodists 3 percent, and all others 1 percent (Holmes 1974:68).

5. Political behavior refers to the regulation of public affairs. This regulation is conducted by corporate units, whose form must be empirically determined. In Samoa, corporate units with political regulatory functions include cognatic descent groups and titled offices. For a detailed discussion of approaches to political organization, see Smith (1974).

6. Gilson (1970:87, fn.) states that Peter Turner, a Methodist missionary from Tonga who began work in Samoa in 1835, "was told by some Sio Vili people that their religion was also Tongan and therefore the same as Methodism, whereas the L.M.S. was quite alien." Moreover, "Sio Vili had visited Tonga before going to Tahiti and . . . had travelled in the company of a Samoan chief who became one of the earliest Methodist leaders in Upolu."

7. Lovett (1899 I:386) describes the pamphlet as "a short treatise, designed to give help to the Samoans in their troubles and perplexities, caused by the contentions of the different religious bodies, and the confusions arising out of this unfortunate invasion of previous unity and peace."

8. Owens' (1968:34-35) interesting discussion of Maori conversion emphasizes the importance of literacy in diffusing missionary influence.

9. Actually, Samoan teachers were active before the seminary was established. The first Samoan teacher was stationed on Tutuila in June 1837 (Daws 1961:328).

10. Davidson (1967:37) believes that "the church added an aristocracy of education to the Samoan social structure." See Oram's (1971) discussion of a similar pattern whereby the LMS pastorate contributed to the emergence of an indigenous elite in Papua.

11. Island teachers belonging to the Latter-Day Saints arrived in American Samoa from Hawaii in 1863 and, sometime between 1863 and 1868, extended their work to Western Samoa. The first Mormon missionaries arrived in American Samoa in 1888 and soon thereafter extended their activities to the islands of Western Samoa. The Seventh-Day Adventists are thought to have arrived in 1890 (Jupp 1958:41).

12. Garrett (1974) and Gilson (1970:81-94) discuss the comity arrangement between the London Missionary Society and the Wesleyan Society in London which led to the withdrawal of the Wesleyan missionary, Peter Turner, from Samoa in 1839. The Wesleyan mission was disbanded, but Samoans continued to receive Tongan Wesleyan teachers. The number of Samoan adherents declined, however, and by 1855 there were only about three thousand Methodists in the islands. The Australasian Conference of the Wesleyan Methodist church, which took over the South Seas missions of the Wesleyan Methodist Missionary Society in 1855, did

not recognize the comity agreement with the London Missionary Society. In 1857, the Wesleyans therefore reestablished a mission staffed by Europeans and Tongans in Samoa but did not succeed in regaining their former adherents, most of whom had joined the London Missionary Society, while about a thousand former Methodists joined the Marists who arrived in the islands in 1845 (Davidson 1967:34-35; Gilson 1970:126).

13. The same thing happened in Tonga (see Lātūkefu 1974).
14. Chiefs tended to view individual teachers as their exclusive possessions. An early instance of this is illustrated by Malietoa, who received William's contingent of island teachers in 1830. Upon his return in 1832, Williams was chagrined to learn that Malietoa had constructed a fence around the teachers, refused their requests to travel, and carefully controlled who had access to them (see Gilson 1970:76).
15. In 1970 there were 241 active Samoan pastors and about 100 "resting" pastors in the CCCS (Reverend David J. Inglis 1975, personal communication).
16. The reasons for this are not entirely clear but involve the resurgence of warfare on some of the islands and the waning novelty of the new religion. Religious indifference was widespread by 1850 in Tutuila, for example, which had experienced a period of intense revivalistic fervor beginning around 1839 (Daws 1961). Tonga also experienced a period of revivalism, known as the "religious revival" or "the Pentecost of Tonga," which began in 1834 and lasted several years during the islanders' early stages of contact with the Wesleyans (Lātūkefu 1974:69-72).
17. The multiplicity of chiefly and descent group ties acknowledged through participation in ceremonial redistributions is discussed in Tiffany (1975a).
18. Except where noted otherwise, all figures are based upon my village fieldwork census. The time period referred to is 1969-1970.
19. The total population of Fiafia village in 1926 was 103, of whom 94 (91.3 percent) were adherents of the London Missionary Society, 7 (6.8 percent) were Methodists, and 2 (1.9 percent) were Catholic (Dominion of New Zealand 1927: 12-14).
20. According to the CCCS pastor's records, the total population of this village in 1968 was 655, of whom 441 (67.3 percent) belonged to the CCCS, 166 (25.3 percent) to the Catholic church, and 48 (7.3 percent) to the Mormon church.
21. The extent to which the chiefs determine individual or household contributions depends on the project and the directive. Usually, requests state only the total amount of money and food required from the entire congregation, so that the village chiefs must decide who contributes and how much. In general, the total amount required is divided by the number of households in the congregation. Households headed by chiefs usually contribute twice as much as those headed by untitled persons.
22. It should be noted that members of the single Catholic household in Fiafia were long-standing adherents of the Catholic church before they were permitted, for reasons too complex to be outlined here, to cultivate land belonging to Fiafia. The discussion of denominational switching in Fiafia refers only to the Mormon residents.
23. This subvillage has been exercising increased autonomy over its own affairs. The subvillage now holds its own council of chiefs meetings and has its own women's committee and untitled men's organization, as well as its own CCCS church and pastor. However, subvillage chiefs periodically attend Fiafia council meetings to discuss matters of mutual concern.

24. The details of this intervillage rivalry are too complex to be outlined here.
25. Conflict may be defined for our purposes as "breaches of normally expected behavior that lead to a dialogue recognized as an exchange of oppositions" (Beals and Siegel 1966:26).
26. See Tiffany (1974:47-50) for details of this descent group's history of internal conflicts.
27. It is likely that other factors not described in the court files or remembered by informants were behind Chief B's action. The important point is that thirty-two years after the installation ceremony incident Chief B recounted this story to me with great bitterness, indicating that this event, perhaps more than anything else, encouraged him to pull his supporters out of the London Missionary Society, his coholder's denomination. In other words, the church issue was a convenient reason for Chief B to oppose his coholder.
28. Government of Western Samoa (1962:35).

16

CONCLUSION: RETROSPECT AND PROSPECT

Sione Lātūkefu

A number of important issues emerge from the chapters in this volume: firstly, that the impact of missionary activity on Oceania was not only inevitable but also highly significant and, therefore, ought to be studied as objectively as possible; secondly, that this impact should be viewed primarily as part of the story of Oceania and not merely as part of the history of European expansion in the Pacific; thirdly, that these societies were never the passive recipients of European impact; and fourthly, that missionaries were not always inflexible in their approach but adapted themselves to the varied situations which confronted them, even though the process of adaptation was painfully slow at times.

Many anthropologists and, to a lesser extent, historians have lamented the fact that missionaries came to Oceania to change island cultures. They believe that this should never have been allowed to happen. They assume that without missionary influence these cultures would have remained largely intact. But their assumption is erroneous. Missionary influence was an integral part of European expansion and as such was inevitable, whether formally instituted or not. Likewise, culture change stimulated by European contact was inevitable, irrespective of the presence of missionaries. There are, for example, anthropologists who do not seem to realize that they themselves are agents of change and that their very presence has an effect upon the islanders' outlook no matter how much they try to prevent or deny this. The principal difference, of course, is that missionaries set out deliberately to change a people's way of life and make no attempt to disguise their intentions. Moreover, because they usually live with their parishioners for many years and often identify with them closely, their impact is generally more extensive than that of other Europeans.

The islanders appreciated the usefulness of European goods, technology, and power. Steel tools, iron pots, kerosene lamps, corrugated iron, and cotton cloth replaced traditional counterparts. Clubs, spears, and the bow and arrow gave way to tomahawks and firearms. In addition to rapid depopulation caused by European-introduced diseases, more efficient weapons and alcohol resulted in widespread confusion among the people. Traditional cosmologies were inadequate to explain these phenomena. New cosmologies had to be developed, and the missionaries offered alternative value systems which explained these changes. Once this process of adaptation was set in train, the whole fabric of island societies was transformed. As an early nineteenth-century student of Africa observed: "Man in his individual and collective capacity is so constituted that no improvement can take place in any part of one or the other without diffusing its influence over the whole man, and over the whole frame of society" (Philip 1828:vii). Concepts of monotheism, the fatherhood of God, and divine love and forgiveness were accepted or even came to replace traditional notions of polytheism, animism, hatred, and revenge. In the same way, the concept of man's brotherhood challenged the traditional Oceanic attitudes toward outsiders: suspicion and hostility. This concept also helped break down class distinctions in rigid chiefly systems, giving commoners a place in the sun and hope of a future.

In many cases the missionaries identified Christianity with their own cultural backgrounds, adopting extremely ethnocentric attitudes and believing they had been called upon by God to wage continous and uncompromising holy war against the devil and the devil's instrument, heathenism. This introduced their converts to new forms of dogmatism and intolerance which resulted in the destruction of invaluable aspects of traditional cultures. Moreover, it was common for missionaries to be jealous of the influence of missionaries associated with other denominations or of nonmission personnel such as European planters and administrators. This antagonism was particularly bitter when it occurred between Roman Catholics and Protestants, for missionaries on both sides conveyed metropolitan rivalries to the islands. The islanders did not hesitate to exploit this hostility to reinforce their own political rivalries in such island groups as Tahiti, Samoa, and Tonga.

Not all aspects of missionization were negative, of course. Although missionaries were primarily concerned with saving souls, they also cared about the islanders' full development. As a missionary pioneer, the Reverend John F. Goldie, observed: "The Gospel of Christ is not merely a way of escape from some future hell for that mysterious entity called the soul, but it is God's message declaring Salvation embracing the whole man—body, mind and spirit—here and now" (quoted in Luxton 1955:161). In another context Goldie opined that "to get the best from [the islanders], we must teach them to be industrious, honest, clean and self-reliant, and if need be self-sacrificing" (1914: 583).

As the foregoing chapters have shown, the missions were the only agencies during the last century, and even up to World War II, that were seriously concerned with the provision of medical services in the islands. This concern came at a time when depopulation was such a serious problem on some islands that most Europeans, including some missionaries, believed that the islanders were doomed to disappear completely from the face of the earth. The missions were preeminent in education, too, as Boutilier has shown in his informative study of education in the Solomon Islands (chapter 6). He observes rightly (and this observation applies to most of Oceania) that the standard of mission education was low. It did, however, provide literacy in the vernacular to a great many, and in English to a few. It also produced skilled tradesmen. Most of these came to be employed by the missions themselves, but some were engaged by governments or private firms as clerks, carpenters, mechanics, and even radio telegraphers.

Mission education also provided trained personnel who served in government educational systems. Local teachers, for example, were for a long time invariably trained in mission schools. More important, mission education, inadequate though it may have been, broadened many students' horizons, giving them a thirst for more knowledge and a determination to see that their own children gained a strong education. As a consequence, the present leaders in Oceania, men and women alike, almost invariably come from families with strong mission backgrounds (Davidson 1967:37; Lātūkefu 1974:76-77). Others have received high-level training from Anglican or Roman Catholic seminaries and are either priests or ex-priests.

Contrary, then, to the views of those who dismiss missionary influence in the Pacific islands as undesirable and welcome its passing, the foregoing chapters and Burridge's introduction reveal that missions have made a substantial contribution to development in Oceania and will continue to do so through the growing number of autonomous churches in the region.

The authors in this volume have recognized that indigenous cultures never remained the passive victims of their colonizers. Their accounts highlight the dynamic and active response of the islanders, who were always selective in their acceptance of new ways and managed to manipulate situations to serve their own purposes. In some places, the response took the form of unsophisticated cargo cultism; in others, it entailed a remarkably rapid adoption of new ideas which they interpreted to accord with their existing cultures, thereby transforming those cultures to meet their changing needs.

In her account of the Story cargo cult among the Kaliai people of Northwest New Britain (chapter 13), Counts has described their attempts to reconcile mission teachings with their traditional philosophical system. The result was a syncretic philosophy that incorporated both Christian and Kaliai beliefs. This system proved flexible enough to permit the continued incorporation of new experiences without apparent difficulty or contradiction. In chapter 12, Black has outlined vividly the Tobian veneration of Father Marino and the corpus of beliefs attributed to him by these Micronesian people, illustrating how the islanders manipulate situations to suit what they want. In this case, interestingly enough, the imported belief system is used to prevent any further change either by their own educated young, the Americans, their own Roman Catholic church, or any other religious denomination.

In his study of missionary impact on the Mortlock Islands (chapter 5), Nason concludes that members of the Etal community had always sought to retain their autonomy and identity in transactions with outsiders and that even their conversion to Christianity occurred only because it seemed advantageous to them. Similarly, the positive Melanesian reponse to Fijian, Samoan, and Tongan missionaries, which I discussed in chapter 4 stemmed from a clear recognition of the advantages of the many cultural innovations.

Tiffany's chapter on Christianity in Samoa (chapter 15) provides an excellent illustration of how Christianity was incorporated rapidly into indigenous institutions and how the Samoans have continued to use denominational differences to pursue traditional political goals. In his study of mission rivalry in Malaita (chapter 7), Ross found that the Baegu exploited sectarian differences as a strategy for maintaining social integration and giving the lineage multiple sources of power. Similarly, Beckett's analysis of the transition from mission through church to sect (chapter 8) reveals how the Torres Strait Islanders rejected or adopted one form of religious organization or another to suit their own needs. This theme also figures in Decktor Korn's discussion of changing church affiliation among Tongans (chapter 14). She attributes denominational changes primarily to the Tongans' desire to achieve social status or secure educational or economic advantage.

The development of independent and indigenous sects and churches does not appear to have occurred as commonly in Oceania as in Africa, and well-documented accounts of them are very rare. Harwood's study (chapter 9) of the establishment of the Christian Fellowship church by a breakaway group from the Methodist mission is, therefore, of special interest and demonstrates once again how active the islanders have been in deciding the shape and direction of their own cultural development.

One cannot neglect the significant part played by missionaries in this process, however, for they frequently provided much of the stimulus for change, as well as the materials and, in many cases, the professional guidance. Forman in chapter 2 and Arbuckle in chapter 11 look closely at how missionaries adapted themselves to changing situations brought about by the influence of anthropology, new attitudes to native cultures, and changing philosophies of missionary work. The latest example of these changes is the Vatican II theological orientation which, interestingly enough, is a return to those policies adopted by the Jesuits in China during the eighteenth century which led to the dissolution of the order by Rome. Both authors describe the painfully slow pace at which these adjustments were made because missionaries, like all people, are products of their time and training. Their reluctance to accept change and delegate authority to the islanders was due to their sincere belief that the people were not yet ready for more responsibility and also (in some cases) to an unwillingness to accept less privileged positions. On the other hand, there have been exciting new developments in the indigenization of the church along the lines advocated by Vatican II, as Hezel has shown in his account (chapter 10) of the progress being made now by the Jesuits in Micronesia.

One of the highlights of the ASAO symposium in Florida in March 1975 (from which this volume evolved) was the coming together of anthropologists, missionaries, and historians to exchange views in a friendly atmosphere and examine the problems associated with missionary activity in Oceania. Relations between missionaries and anthropologists have occasionally been strained and even hostile in times past. The symposium therefore made an important contribution to the mutual understanding which Hughes pleads for in chapter 3, where he deals with the causes of the unfortunate relationship and warns that if this continues as before it will seriously retard the development of objective mission studies.

Speaking as the only native Pacific island participant at the symposium, I found it a remarkable experience and easily the best academic conference I have had the privilege to participate in. The venue was ideal. The comfortable isolation of the setting and the small size of the group facilitated the development of personal relationships which seemed to stimulate rather than hinder frankness and objectivity of discussion. The point which I tried to emphasize during the symposium was that the islanders were not passive spectators in the process of acculturation in Oceania. I only hope that other native Pacific island scholars will be encouraged to participate in such memorable occasions in the future.

As both insiders and trained observers, they will be in a unique position to discuss culture change in Oceania. I am not an adherent of the view, commonly expressed nowadays by some expatriates and by some of my fellow Pacific islanders, that outsiders can never fully understand our cultures. I believe it is possible for an outsider with ability, inclination, and time to gain a very full understanding of how islanders think and feel. It does, however, require a very real effort to rid oneself of preconceptions and prejudice. The islander faces a different problem: he must detach himself sufficiently from his own culture to see it objectively. The best research will probably result from collaboration between outside academics and educated islanders and is already under way.

Most of the discussion in this volume has been concerned with the nonreligious factors which prompted islanders to convert. No one has attempted to discuss the religious aspects of conversion in depth, and this is quite understandable, for the former aspects can be more readily observed whereas religious conviction is subjective and difficult for even the professional researcher to investigate. It should not be neglected, however, and it is to be hoped that future workers will focus more directly on this phenomenon and perhaps devise some techniques for determining what Christian belief really means to adherents of Christianity in Oceania. This might be a field of investigation for Pacific island scholars, particularly those who have been the subjects of proselytization.

Another focus of this volume has been the role of missionaries in culture change in Oceania. The factors which brought about changes in the attitudes and activities of the missionaries, as outlined in some of the earlier chapters, have been external ones: improved communications, the impact of anthropology, directives from the mission's home society. I suggest that it would be worthwhile to examine the degree to which events in the Pacific islands also contributed to changes in the attitudes and thinking of missionaries in Oceania.

There has been a strong upsurge of antimission feeling among many young, educated Pacific islanders, particularly in Melanesia, where there has been an awakening of interest and national pride in traditional cultures. This antimission feeling is based on the erroneous belief that mission influence was an entirely negative force which was primarily responsible for the destruction of traditional art forms, religion, and other aspects of culture. This volume, with its balanced discussion of missionary activity in Oceania, may help to correct such extreme and ill-informed views. It is also to be hoped that this volume will gain wide acceptance not only among academics but among the younger generations of Pacific islanders as well.

REFERENCES

Abbott, Walter M.
   1966   *The Documents of Vatican II.* Edited by Walter Abbott. New York: America Press.

Adams, Henry
   1930   *Letters of Henry Adams (1858-1891).* Edited by Worthington Chauncey Ford. Boston: Houghton Mifflin.

Ahnne, Edouard
   1931   *Dans les Isles du Pacifique.* Paris: Société des Missions Évangéliques.

Alexander, James M.
   1895   *The Islands of the Pacific (from Old to New).* New York: American Tract Society.

Allan, Alexander M.
   1968   "Before the mast and behind the pulpit." MSS. On file in the Yale University Library, New Haven.

American Board of Commissioners for Foreign Missions (ABCFM)
   1827   *Eighteenth Annual Report.* Boston: ABCFM.
   1890   *Eightieth Annual Report.* Boston: Press of Samuel Usher.
   1901   *Ninety-first Annual Report.* Boston: Press of Samuel Usher.

Analecta O(rdinis) M(inoris) Cap(puchinorum)
   1905   Vol. 21. Rome: Capuchin Order.

REFERENCES

Anderson, Rufus
   1860   "Circular to the Hawaiian Evangelical Association, 1 February." Honolulu: Hawaiian Children Missionary Society.

Annales de Notre Dame du Sacré Coeur
   1963   Issoudan, France: Sacred Heart Missions.

Aoyagi, Machiko
   1966   "Kinship organization and behaviour in a contemporary Tongan village." *Journal of the Polynesian Society* 75:141-176.

Armstrong, E. S.
   1900   *History of the Melanesian Mission.* London: Isbister and Co.

Australian Board of Missions (ABM). Papers on file in the Australian Board of Missions (Anglican Church of Australia) Archives, Stanmore, New South Wales, Australia.
   1964   "Chairman's Report." 7-9 April. MS.
   1966   "New Guinea Report." October. MS.

Australian Council of Churches (ACC)
   1966   *Australian Missions: A Statistical Survey.* 2nd ed. Sydney: Division of Missions of Australian Council of Churches.

Baldwin, Elizabeth
   1913   E. Baldwin to E. Bell. Letter in the collection of the American Board of Commissioners for Foreign Missions. On file in Harvard University Library, Boston.

Barnett, Homer G.
   1957   *Indian Shakers: A Messianic Cult of the Pacific Northwest.* Carbondale: University of Southern Illinois Press.

Bartlett, S. C.
   1869   *Historical Sketch of the Hawaiian Mission, and the Missions to Micronesia and the Marquesas Islands.* Boston: American Board of Commissioners for Foreign Missions.

Beach, Harlan P.
   1906   *A Geography and Atlas of Protestant Missions.* Vol. 2. Statistics and Atlas. New York: Student Volunteer Movement for Foreign Missions.

Beaglehole, Ernest
   1957   *Social Change in the South Pacific.* London: G. Allen.

Beaglehole, Ernest and Pearl Beaglehole
   1941   *Pangai, a Village in Tonga.* Memoirs of the Polynesian Society, vol. 18. Wellington: Polynesian Society.

Beals, Alan R. and Bernard J. Siegel
   1966   *Divisiveness and Social Conflict: An Anthropological Approach.* Stanford: Stanford University Press.

Beckett, Jeremy
   1967   "Elections in a small Melanesian community." *Ethnology* 6:332-344.
   1971   "Rivalry, competition and conflict among Christian Melanesians." In *Anthropology in Oceania,* edited by L. R. Hiatt and C. Jayawardena. San Francisco: Chandler.

Beidelman, T. O.
   1974   "Social theory and the study of Christian missions in Africa." *Africa* 44(3):235-249.

Benedict XV
   1919   *"Maximum Illud."* 30 November. In *Acta Apostolicae Sedis.* Vol. 11. Rome.

Benedict, Ruth
   1934   *Patterns of Culture.* New York: Houghton Mifflin.

Berkhofer, Robert F., Jr.
   1965   *Salvation and the Savage: An Analysis of Protestant Missions and American Indian Response, 1787-1862.* Lexington: University of Kentucky Press.

Birnbaum, N.
   1969   "The crisis in Marxist sociology." In *Recent Sociology No. 1: On the Social Basis of Politics,* edited by H. P. Dreitzel. London: Collier Macmillan Ltd.

Bleakley, J. W.
   1961   *The Aborigines of Australia.* Brisbane: Jacaranda Press.

Bliss, Theodora Crosby
   1906   *Micronesia: Fifty Years in the Island World.* Boston: American Board of Commissioners for Foreign Missions.

Blythe, Jennifer
   1975   "Myth and millennium in Melanesia." MS. Copy on file in the Department of Anthropology, McMaster University, Hamilton, Ontario, Canada.

Bouscaren, T.L. and A.C. Ellis
    1953   *Canon Law: A Text and Commentary.* Milwaukee: Bruce.

Brash, Alan
    1948   *How Did the Church Get There?* Christchurch: Presbyterian Bookroom.

Bromilow, W. E.
    1914   "New Guinea." In *A Century in the Pacific,* edited by J. Colwell. Sydney: Beale, Methodist Book Room.
    1929   *Twenty Years among Primitive Papuans.* London: Epworth Press.

Brown, George
    1908   *George Brown, D. D.: Pioneer-Missionary and Explorer: An Autobiography.* London: Hodder and Stoughton.
    1910   *Melanesians and Polynesians: Their Life-Histories Described and Compared.* London: Macmillan.
    1913   "Address." MS. On file in the Methodist Overseas Missions Archives (housed in the Mitchell Library), Sydney, Australia.

Buckley, J.
    1961   Circular letter, N. 133-VII, 1, located in the archives of the General Administration, Marist Fathers, Rome.

Burnett, Frank
    1910   *Through Tropic Seas.* London: Francis Griffiths.
    1911   *Through Polynesia and Papua, Wanderings with a Camera in the Southern Seas.* London: Francis Griffiths.

Burridge, Kenelm O. L.
    1960   *Mambu: A Melanesian Millennium.* London: Methuen.
    1969   *New Heaven, New Earth.* Oxford: Basil Blackwell.
    1973   *Encountering Aborigines.* London: Pergamon Press.

Burrows, Edwin Grant
    1963   *Flower in My Ear: Art and Ethos of Ifaluk Atoll.* University of Washington Publications in Anthropology, vol. 6. Seattle: University of Washington Press.

Burton, John W.
    1930   *A Missionary Survey of the Pacific Islands.* London: World Dominion Press.
    1949   *Modern Missions in the South Pacific.* London: Livingstone Press.

Butcher, Benjamin T.
    1937   "Annual Report." MS. On file in the Council on World Mission (formerly London Missionary Society) Archives, London.
    1963   *We Lived with Headhunters.* London: Hodder and Stoughton.

Cadoux, Thomas
    1953   "Evolution de la Chrétienite papoue." *Missions Catholiques* 85:260-268.

Cairncross, John
    1974   *After Polygamy Was Made a Sin.* London: Routledge.

Calley, M. J.
    1955   "Aboriginal Pentecostalists: a study of change in religion, north coast, New South Wales." Master's thesis, University of Sydney.
    1964   "Aboriginal Pentecostalism." In *Aborigines Now,* edited by Marie Reay. Sydney: Angus and Robertson.

Cato, A. C.
    1947   "A new religious cult in Fiji." *Oceania* 18:146-156.

Clark, Elmer T.
    1949   *Small Protestant Sects in America.* New York: Abingdon Press.)

Clarke, Nancy
    n.d.   "New Guinea." MS. On file in the Australian Board of Missions (Anglican Church of Australia) Archives, Stanmore, New South Wales, Australia.

Cochrane, Glynn
    1970   *Big Men and Cargo Cults.* Oxford: Clarendon Press.

Codrington, R. H.
    1885   *The Melanesian Languages.* Oxford: Clarendon Press.
    1891   *The Melanesians: Studies in Their Anthropology and Folklore.* Oxford: Clarendon Press. (Reprinted 1957. New Haven: Human Relations Area Files Press)

Commission for Catechesis and Catechists
    1972   *Catechists in Africa, Asia and Oceania: Synthetic Study.* Rome: Sacra Congregatio pro Gentium Evangelisatione.

Congregational Christian Church in Samoa (CCCS)
    1962   *The Constitution of the Congregational Christian Church in Samoa.* 4th rev. ed. Malua: Samoan Church

(CCCS) Press.
Cormack, J. E.
   1944   *Isles of Solomon.* Washington: Review and Herald Publishing Association.
Costantini, Celso
   1949   *L'Art Chrétien dans les Missions: Manual d'Art pour les Missionnaires.* Translated by Edmond Leclef. Paris: Desclee de Brouwer.
Coste, J.
   1965   *Lectures on Society of Mary History (Marist Fathers).* Rome: Society of Mary.
Counts, David
   1973   "Apprehension in the backwaters: part I, the progressives." Paper presented at the 2nd Annual Meeting of the Association for Social Anthropology in Oceania, 21-25 March, Orcas Island, Washington.
Counts, David and Dorothy Counts
   1970   "The *vula* of Kaliai: a primitive currency with commercial use." *Oceania* 41:90-105.
Counts, Dorothy
   1971   "Cargo or council: two approaches to development in Northwest New Britain." *Oceania* 41:288-297.
   1972   "The Kaliai and the Story: development and frustration in New Britain." *Human Organization* 31:373-383.
Crawford, David and Leona Crawford
   1967   *Missionary Adventures in the South Pacific.* Rutland, Vt: Tuttle.
Cronin, Vincent
   1955   *The Wise Man from the West.* New York: Dutton.
Damon, Samuel
   1861   "Morning Star papers, or glimpses and glances at the sights, scenes and people of Micronesia." In *American Activities in the Central Pacific, 1790-1870,* Vol. 4, edited by R. Gerard Ward. Ridgewood, N.J.: Gregg Press, 1967.
Danks, Benjamin
   1912   "Missions and the labor problem." *Missionary Review of the Methodist Church of Australasia* 22(2):1-3.
   1914a "New Britain." In *A Century in the Pacific,* edited by

J. Colwell. Sydney: Beale, Methodist Book Room.
1914b "Samoa." In *A Century in the Pacific*, edited by J. Colwell. Sydney: Beale, Methodist Book Room.

Darnand, Joseph
1920- "Diary." 14 booklets. MSS. On file in the Catholic
1943   Church Archives, Apia, Western Samoa.

Davidson, James W.
1967 *Samoa Mo Samoa*. Melbourne: Oxford University Press.

Davis, Hassoldt
1935 "Auctioneers of Paradise." *American Mercury* 36: 216-227.

Daws, Alan Gavan
1961 "The great Samoan awakening of 1839." *Journal of the Polynesian Society* 70:326-337.

De Bigault, Guy
1947 *Dramas de la Vie Solomonaise*. Namur: Grands Lacs.

De la Costa, Horacio
1972 "The missionary apostolate in east and southeast Asia." *Studies in the International Apostolate of Jesuits* 1:111-128.

Deck, Norman
1970 N. Deck to J. Boutilier, taped interview in J. Boutilier's possession. 1 March.

Decktor Korn, Shulamit R.
1974 "Tongan kin groups: the noble and the common view." *Journal of the Polynesian Society* 83:5-13.
1975 "Household composition in the Tonga Islands: a question of options and alternatives." *Journal of Anthropological Research* 31:235-259.

Doane, Edward T.
1873 "Letters from Micronesia." *Missionary Herald* 69(7): 228-229.

Dominion of New Zealand
1925 *Results of a Census of the Dominion of New Zealand Taken for the Night of the 17th April, 1921. General Report*. Wellington: Government Printer.
1927 *Population Census, 1926. Vol. 2, Dependencies: Cook Islands and Niue, Tokelau Islands, Western Samoa*. Wellington: Government Printer.

1947 *Population Census, 1945. Vol. 2, Island Territories: Cook Islands and Niue, Tokelau Islands, Western Samoa.* Auckland: Leightons Ltd.

Don, Alexander
1927 *Peter Milne (1834-1924): Missionary to Nguna, New Hebrides 1870-1924 from the Presbyterian Church of New Zealand.* Dunedin: Foreign Missions Committee of the Presbyterian Church of New Zealand.

Douceré, Victor
1934 *La Mission Catholique aux Nouvelles-Hebrides: D'après des Documents Écrits et les Vieux Souvenirs de l'Auteur.* Lyon: E. Vitte.

Dubois, L. L.
1928 "Activité Protestante en Polynésie Occidental et Mélanésie: Reactions et Espoirs Catholiques." *Revue d'Histoire des Missions* 5:369-406.

Dupeyrat, André
1935 *Papouasie, Histoire de la Mission (1885-1935).* Paris: Editions Dillen.

Eilers, Anneliese
1936 *Westkarolinen: Tobi und Ngulu. Ergebnisse der Südsee-Expedition 1908-1910* (II B9, part 1). Edited by G. Thilenius. Hamburg: Friedrichsen, De Gruyter & Co.

Eilers, Franz-Joseph
1967 *Zur Publizistik schriftloser Kulturen in Nordost-Neuguinea.* Kaldenkirchen: Steyler Verlag.

Elbert, Samuel H. and Torben Monberg
1965 *From the Two Canoes: Oral Traditions of Rennell and Bellona Islands.* Copenhagen: Danish National Museum.

Elkin, A. P.
1953 *Social Anthropology in Melanesia: A Review of Research.* London: Oxford University Press.

Eppstein, J.
1935 *The Catholic Tradition of the Law of Nations.* London: Burns Oates.

Fabian, Johannes
1971 *Jamaa: A Charismatic Movement in Katanga.* Evanston, Ill.: Northwestern University Press.

Fiefa, Sione N.
   1968   *Report on the Results of the 1966 Census, Kingdom of Tonga.* Nuku'alofa: Government Printing Office.

Finney, Ben R.
   1968   "A successful French Polynesian co-operative?" *Journal of Pacific History* 3:65-84.

Firth, Raymond
   1951   *Elements of Social Organization.* London: Watts.
   1975   "Prejudice in interpretation of Christianity." *American Anthropologist* 77:77-78.

Flierl, Johann and Arthur I. Hopkins
   1928   "Native life in the south west Pacific; from two points of view." *International Review of Missions* 17:538-549.

Forman, Charles W.
   1969a   "The wanted missionary—Pacific Island style." *Frontier* 12:267-273.
   1969b   "Theological education in the South Pacific Islands: a quiet revolution." *Journal de la Société des Océanistes* 25:151-166.
   1970   "The missionary force of the Pacific Island churches." *International Review of Missions* 59:215-226.
   1972   "Missionaries and colonialism: the case of the New Hebrides in the twentieth century." *Journal of Church and State* 14:75-92.

Fox, Charles E
   1925   *Threshold of the Pacific.* New York: Knopf.
   1958   *Lord of the Southern Isles.* London: A. R. Mowbray and Co.
   1962   *Kakamora.* London: Hodder and Stoughton.
   1967   *The Story of the Solomons.* Taroaniara, Nggela, British Solomon Islands Protectorate: Diocese of Melanesia Press.

Freeman, J. D.
   1959   "The Joe Gimlet or Siovili cult: an episode in the religious history of early Samoa." In *Anthropology in the South Seas: Essays Presented to H. D. Skinner,* edited by J. D. Freeman and W. R. Geddes. New Plymouth, New Zealand: Thomas Avery and Sons, Ltd.

Frerichs, A.C.
　1957　*Anutu Conquers in New Guinea: The Story of Seventy Years of Mission Work in New Guinea.* Columbus, Ohio: Wartburg Press.

Freytag, Walter
　1940　*Spiritual Revolution in the East.* London: Lutterworth Press.

Fuller, Columbus C.
　1908　"The industrial missions." *Australasian Methodist Missionary Review.* August, pp. 3-4.

Fullerton, Leslie D.
　1969　"From Christendom to pluralism in the South Seas: church-state relations in the twentieth century." Ph.D. dissertation, Drew University, Madison, N.J.

Garrett, John
　1974　"The conflict between the London Missionary Society and the Wesleyan Methodists in 19th century Samoa." *Journal of Pacific History* 9:65-80.

Gilliland, Dean S.
　1973　"The indigenous concept in Africa." *Missiology* 1:343-356.

Gilson, Richard P.
　1970　*Samoa 1830 to 1900: The Politics of a Multi-Cultural Community.* Melbourne: Oxford University Press.

Gladwin, Thomas
　1970　*East Is a Big Bird: Navigation and Logic on Puluwat Atoll.* Cambridge, Mass.: Harvard University Press.

Goldie, John F.
　1914　"The Solomon Islands." In *A Century in the Pacific,* edited by J. Colwell. Sydney: Beale, Methodist Book Room.

Goodall, Norman
　1954　*History of the London Missionary Society.* London: Oxford University Press.

Government of Western Samoa
　1938-1967　Department of Justice. Land and Titles Court files, Mulinu'u, Western Samoa.
　1954　*Population Census 1951.* Wellington: Government Printer.
　1962　*Population Census 1961.* Census Commissioner's Office,

Prime Minister's Department. Apia, Western Samoa: Government Printer.

1968 *Population Census 1966.* Census Commissioner's Office, Prime Minister's Department. Apia, Western Samoa: Government Printer.

Goward, W.

1900-1902 "Report of work in the Tokelau, Ellice and Gilbert groups, London Missionary Society: September 1900 to September 1902."MSS. On file in the J. E. Newell Papers (Box 5), Council on World Mission (formerly London Missionary Society) Archives, London.

Goyau, Georges

1938 *Le Christ chez les Papous.* 3rd ed. Paris: Beauchesne et ses fils.

Grattan, Clinton H.

1963 *The Southwest Pacific Since 1900: A Modern History.* Ann Arbor: University of Michigan Press.

Grattan, F. J. H.

1948 *An Introduction to Samoan Custom.* Apia: Samoa Printing and Publishing Co.

Greenberg, Joseph

1946 *The Influence of Islam on a Sudanese Religion.* American Ethnological Society, Monograph 10. Seattle: University of Washington Press.

Gregory XVI

1836 "*Omnium Gentium.*" In *Origines Maristes (1786-1836),* edited by J. Coste and G. Lessard, vol. 1. Rome: Society of Mary.

Groenewegen, K.

1972 *Report on the Census of the Population, 1970.* Honiara, Guadalcanal, British Solomon Islands Protectorate: Western Pacific High Commission.

Groves, William C.

1940 "Report on a survey of education in the British Solomon Islands Protectorate." Tulagi: n.p.

Guiart, Jean

1962 "The millenarian aspect of conversion to Christianity in the South Pacific." In *Millenial Dreams in Action: Essays in Comparative Study,* edited by Sylvia L.

Thrupp. Comparative Studies in Society and History, Supplement 2. The Hague: Mouton.

Gulick, Luther and Orramel Hinckley
  1918 *Pilgrims of Hawaii.* New York: Revell.

Gunson, Niel
  1962 "An account of the Mamaia or visionary heresy of Tahiti, 1826-1841." *Journal of the Polynesian Society* 71:209-253.

Gunson, W. N.
  1964 "Missionary interest in British expansion in the South Pacific in the nineteenth century." *Journal of Religious History* 3:296-313.
  1969 "The theology of imperialism and the missionary history of the Pacific." *Journal of Religious History* 5:255-265.

Gutierrez, G.
  1972 *The Theology of Liberation.* Maryknoll, N.Y.: Orbis.

Haddon, A. C.
  1901 *Headhunters, Black, White and Brown.* London: Methuen.
  1908 *Sociology, Magic and Religion of the Eastern Islanders. Reports of the Cambridge Anthropological Expedition to Torres Strait,* vol. 6. Cambridge: Cambridge University Press.

Hagen, Everett
  1962 *On the Theory of Social Change.* Homewood, Ill.: Dorsey Press.

Hambruch, Paul
  1932 *Ponape.* 3 vols. *Ergebnisse der Südsee-Expedition 1908-1910* (II B7). Edited by G. Thilenius. Hamburg: Friedrichsen, De Gruyter & Co.

Hames, Inez
  1972 *I Remember... Personal Memories of a New Zealand Missionary in Fiji.* Wesley Historical Society (New Zealand) Proceedings, vol. 27, no. 5.

Hanson, F. Allan
  1973 "Political change in Tahiti and Samoa: an exercise in experimental anthropology." *Ethnology* 12:1-13.

Harwood, Frances
   1974 "The Christian Fellowship Church: a revitalization movement in the Solomon Islands." Ph.D. dissertation, University of Chicago.

Heine, C. R.
   1913 C. Heine to E. Bell. Letter in the collection of the American Board of Commissioners for Foreign Missions. On file in Harvard University Library, Boston. 20 February.

Hernandez, Faustino
   1955 "Missions in the Carolines and Marshall Islands." Mimeographed. Maldonado, Madrid. On file in the Jesuit Archives, Fordham University, New York.

Herskovits, Melville
   1948 *Man and His Works*. New York: Knopf.

Hilliard, David
   1966 "Protestant missions in the Solomon Islands, 1849-1942." Ph.D. dissertation, Australian National University.
   1969 "The South Sea Evangelical Mission in the Solomon Islands: the foundation years." *Journal of Pacific History* 4:41-64.
   1974 "Colonialism and Christianity: the Melanesian Mission in the Solomon Islands." *Journal of Pacific History* 9:93-116.

Hogbin, Herbert I.
   1939 *Experiments in Civilization: The Effects of European Culture on a Native Community of the Solomon Islands*. London: G. Routledge.
   1947 "Native Christianity in a New Guinea village." *Oceania* 18:1-35.
   1965 *A Guadalcanal Society*. New York: Holt.

Holden, Horace
   1836 *A Narrative of the Shipwreck, Captivity, and Sufferings of Horace Holden and Benjamin H. Nute . . .* Boston: Russel, Shattuck, and Co.

Holmes, Lowell
   1974 *Samoan Village*. New York: Holt.

Hopkins, Arthur I.
   n.d. "Autobiography." MS. On file in the Melanesian Mission

Archives, Auckland, New Zealand.

Horton, Dick
  1970 *Fire over the Islands.* Sydney: A. H. and A. W. Reed.

Hosie, J.
  1971 "The French mission: an Australian base for the Marists in the Pacific to 1874." Master's thesis, Macquarie University, Australia.

Hosie, S.
  1967 *Anonymous Apostle: The Life of Jean Claude Colin, Marist.* New York: Morrow.

Hurst, H. Leonard
  1937 *Report by Reverend H. Leonard Hurst after Secretarial Visit to Papua, September 1936-January 1937.* Sydney: Australia and New Zealand Committee of London Missionary Society.

Illich, Ivan
  1970 *The Church, Change and Development.* Chicago: Urban Training Center Press.

Ivens, Walter, G.
  1927 *Melanesians of the South-East Solomon Islands.* London: Kegan Paul, Trench, Trubner & Co.
  1930 *Island Builders of the Pacific.* London: Seeley, Service and Co.

Jacomb, E.
  1914 *France and England in the New Hebrides.* Melbourne and Sydney: George Robertson and Co.

Japan
  1925, 1933, 1937 *Annual Report to the League of Nations on the Administration of the South Sea Islands under Japanese Mandate.*

Jaspers, Reiner
  1972 *Die Missionarische Erschliessung Ozeaniens; ein Quellengeschichtlicher und missionsgeographischer Versuch zur Kirchlichen Gebiets Aufteilung in Ozeanien bis 1855.* Münster: Aschendorffsche Verlagsbuchhandlung.

Jayawardena, C.
  1968 "Ideology and conflict in lower class communities." *Comparative Studies in Society and History* 10:412-446.

Journal de la Société des Océanistes
   1969a Volume 25. December.
   1969b "Données statistiques concernant les missions du Pacifique Sud." 25:1-41.

Jupp, Kathleen M.
   1958 *Report on the Population Census 1956: Territory of Western Samoa.* Wellington: Government Printer.

Kahn, E. J.
   1965 *A Reporter in Micronesia.* New York: Norton.

Keesing, Felix M.
   1934 *Modern Samoa: Its Government and Changing Life.* London: G. Allen.
   1945 *The South Seas in the Modern World.* Rev. ed. New York: John Day.

Keesing, Roger M.
   1967 "Christians and pagans in Kwaio, Malaita." *Journal of the Polynesian Society* 76:82-100.
   1968 "Chiefs in a chiefless society: the ideology of modern Kwaio politics." *Oceania* 38:276-280.

Kent, Janet
   1973 *The Solomon Islands.* Harrisburg, Pa.: Stackpole Books.

Keys, L.
   1957 *The Life and Times of Bishop Pompallier.* Christchurch: Pegasus.

Keysser, Christian
   1921 *Was die Braunen dawider zu sagen wuszten.* Neuendettelsau: Verlag des Missionshauses.

Kingdom of Tonga
   1967- *Annual Reports of the Department of Education.*
   1969 Nuku'alofa: Government Printing Office.
   1970 *An Economic Survey of Tonga.* Nuku'alofa: Government Printing Office.

Krämer, Augustin
   1906 *Hawaii, Ostmikronesien und Samoa.* Stuttgart: Strecker and Schröder.

Lambert, Sylvester M.
   1941 *A Yankee Doctor in Paradise.* Boston: Little, Brown.

Lanternari, Vittorio
   1965 *The Religions of the Oppressed.* New York: Mentor

Books.

Laracy, Hugh M.
1968 "The archives of the Marist fathers: an untapped source of material on the history of the Pacific." *Journal of Pacific History* 3:165-171.
1969 "Catholic missions in the Solomon Islands, 1845-1966." Ph.D. dissertation, Australian National University.
1970 "Xavier Montrouzier: a missionary in Melanesia." In *Pacific Islands Portraits*, edited by J. W. Davidson and D. Scarr. Canberra: Australian National University Press.
1971 "Marching Rule and the missions." *Journal of Pacific History* 6:96-114.

Lātūkefu, Sione
1974 *Church and State in Tonga: The Wesleyan Methodist Missionaries and Political Development, 1822-1875.* Honolulu: The University Press of Hawaii; Canberra: Australian National University Press.

Laufer, Carl
1959 "Fehlbeurteilung der Eingeborenen-psyche in der Südseemission." *Neue Zeitschrift für Missionswissenschaft* 15:51-59.
1961 "Die Religionen Neubritanniens und ihre Auswertung durch die christliche Mission." *Priester und Mission*, pp. 323-337.

Laurent, Charles
1900 *Les Missionaires de la Nouvelle-Calédonie au sujet de l'enquête administrative de Wagap... Réponse et défense de la mission.* Paris: Firmin-Didot.

Lawrence, P. and M. J. Meggitt (eds.)
1965 *Gods, Ghosts, and Men in Melanesia: Some Religions of Australian New Guinea and the New Hebrides.* London: Oxford University Press.

Leach, Edmund
1966 "Ritualization in man in relation to conceptual and social development." *Philosophical Transactions of the Royal Society of London* 251:403-408.

Lebeau, Henri
1911 *Otaheiti, au Pays de l'Éternel été.* Paris: Librairie

Armand Colin.

Leenhardt, Maurice
- 1922 *La Grand Terre; Mission de Nouvelle-Calédonie.* Nouvelle edition. Paris: Société des Missions Évangéliques.

Lehner, Stephen
- 1922 "Anknüpfungen für die Predigt im papuanischen Heidentum." *Allgemeine Missions Zeitschrift* 49:363-375.

Lenwood, Frank
- 1925 *Modern Problems in the South Seas.* London: London Missionary Society.

Lessa, William A.
- 1966 *Ulithi: A Micronesian Design for Living.* New York: Holt.

Lévi-Strauss, Claude
- 1966 "Anthropology: its achievements and future." *Current Anthropology* 7(2):124-127.
- 1969 *The Raw and the Cooked: Introduction to a Science of Mythology.* Vol. 1. Translated by John Weightman and Doreen Weightman. New York: Harper & Row.

Lewis, David
- 1972 *We, the Navigators.* Honolulu: The University Press of Hawaii.

Lewis, F. G.
- 1935 "Methodist Overseas Mission, New Guinea District, the first sixty years." Mimeographed. Rabaul.

Logan, Mary
- 1884 "Letter of November 24." *ABCFM Papers*, vol. 7. On file at the Houghton Library, Harvard University, Cambridge, Mass.
- n.d. *Last Words and Work of Reverend Robert W. Logan.* n.p.

London Missionary Society (LMS)
- n.d. Reports, New Guinea Boxes. Microfilms located in the National Library, Canberra, Australia.
- n.d. Correspondence, New Guinea Boxes. Microfilms located in the National Library, Canberra, Australia.
- 1920 *A Day of Good Tidings. Being the Annual Report of the Gilbert Islands and Nauru Mission, South Seas, for the year 1920, the Jubilee of the L.M.S. Work in*

the *Southern Gilberts. From Darkness to Light, 1870-1920.* Roñoroño, Gilbert Islands: London Mission Press.

London Missionary Society, Islands Committee (LMS, IC)
   1943   "Minutes." 28 June. On file in the Council on World Mission (formerly London Missionary Society) Archives, London.

London Missionary Society, Samoan District Committee (LMS, SDC)
   1923   "Minutes." May. MSS. On file in the Congregational Christian Church of Samoa Archives, Apia, Western Samoa.

Loomis, Albertine
   1970   *To All People: A History of the Hawaii Conference of the United Church of Christ.* Kingsport, Tenn.: Kingsport Press.

Lovett, Richard
   1899   *The History of the London Missionary Society 1795-1895.* Vol. 1. London: Henry Frowde, Oxford University Press Warehouse.

Luxton, C. T. J.
   1955   *Isles of Solomon: A Tale of Missionary Adventure.* Auckland: Methodist Foreign Missionary Society of New Zealand.

Malinowski, Bronislaw
   1932   "Pigs, Papuans, and police court perspective." *Man* 22: 33-38 (art. 44).
   1967   *A Diary in the Strict Sense of the Term.* New York: Harcourt, Brace.

Marchant, William S.
   1940   H. Luke to W. Marchant. Marchant Papers, Miscellaneous No. 48. On file in the Alport Barker Library, Suva, Fiji Islands. 10 August.
   1941   H. Luke to C. Parkinson. Marchant Papers. 14 May.

Marcus, George E.
   1974   "A hidden dimension of family development in the modern Kingdom of Tonga." *Journal of Comparative Family Studies* 5:87-102.

Marshall, Mac and Leslie B. Marshall
   1976   "Holy and unholy spirits: the effects of missionization

on alcohol use in Eastern Micronesia." *Journal of Pacific History* 11(3 & 4):135-166.

McFarlane, Samuel
 1888 *Among the Cannibals of New Guinea.* London: London Missionary Society.

McHugh, Winifred
 1965 "Memoir of Reverend A. J. Small." Mimeographed. On file in the Methodist Church office, Suva, Fiji Islands.

Mead, Margaret
 1956 *New Lives for Old.* New York: Morrow.

Merton, Robert
 1957 *Social Theory and Social Structure.* Rev. ed. Glencoe, Ill.: Free Press.

Metcalfe, J. R.
 n.d. "Our time at Teop." MS in the possession of S. Lātūkefu.

Methodist Church Correspondence from the Solomon Islands District (MC, CSID). Files located in the Methodist Overseas Missions Archives (housed in the Mitchell Library), Sydney, Australia.
 1910 J. Goldie to B. Danks. 3 March.
 1913 M. Davey to B. Danks. n.d.

Methodist Church of Australasia, Board of Missions (MCA, BM). Papers on file in the Methodist Overseas Missions Archives (Mitchell Library), Sydney, Australia.
 1931 "Minutes." 11 September. MS.
 1932 "Fiji District Chairman's Report." MS.
 1933 "Commission to Papua," MS.

Methodist Church of Australasia, Fiji District Synod (MCA, FDS). Papers on file in the Methodist Overseas Missions Archives (Mitchell Library), Sydney, Australia.
 1930 "Minutes (European Session)." 29 October. MS.

Methodist Church of Australasia, Methodist Missionary Society of Australasia (MCA, MMSA)
 1923 *Commission re: Native Church: Information Collected for the Consideration of the Commission.* Melbourne: Spectator Publishing Co.

Methodist Church of New Zealand (MCNZ)
- 1920 *Report of Representatives to the Solomon Islands Mission District.* Christchurch: Lyttleton Times Co.

Methodist Mission, Fiji, District Chairman's Correspondence (MM, FDCC). Papers on file in the Methodist Archives (Western Pacific Archives), Suva, Fiji Islands.
- 1907 G. Brown to A. Small. 29 April.

Missionary Herald (MH)
- 1855 Vol. 2 (January). Boston: American Board of Commissioners for Foreign Missions.

Missionary Notices (MN)
- 1851-1871 *The Wesleyan Missionary Notices Relating to the Missions under the Direction of the Australasian Wesleyan Methodist Conference.* Sydney: Joseph Cook and Co. On file in the Mitchell Library, Sydney, Australia.

Missionary Reports (MR)
- 1860-1878 *Report of the Australasian Wesleyan Methodist Missionary Society with an Account of the Contributions.* Sydney: Reading and Wellbank. On file in the Mitchell Library, Sydney, Australia.

Missionary Review of the Methodist Church of Australasia (MRMCA)
- 1910 "A Susulu, or Cremation in the North of New Mecklenburg, Bismarck Archipel." 20(1):11-13.

Missiones Catholicae (MC)
- 1907 *Missiones Catholicae cura S. Congregationis de Propaganda Fide Descriptae Statistica.* Rome: Ex Topographia Polyglotta.
- 1927 *Missiones Catholicae cura S. Congregationis de Propaganda Fide Descriptae Statistica.* Rome: Typis Polyglottis Vaticanis.

Morrell, William P.
- 1960 *Britain in the Pacific Islands.* Oxford: Clarendon Press.

Moss, Frederick J.
- 1889 *Through Atolls and Islands in the Great South Sea.* London: Sampson Low, Marston, Searle, and Rivington.

Muller, Max
- 1875 "On missions." In *Chips from a Geman Workshop.* Vol. 4. London: Longmans, Green and Co.

Nason, James D.
- 1970 "Clan and copra: modernization on Etal Island, Eastern Caroline Islands." Ph.D. dissertation, University of Washington, Seattle.
- 1975 "The strength of the land: community perception of population on Etal Atoll." In *Pacific Atoll Populations*, edited by Vern Carroll. ASAO Monograph No. 3. Honolulu: The University Press of Hawaii.

National Opinion Research Center Study
- 1972 *The Catholic Priest in the United States: Sociological Investigations.* Washington: United States Catholic Conference.

New Zealand Methodist Foreign Mission Board (NZMFMB)
- 1958 "Minutes." 21 October. MS. On file in the Methodist Archives, Auckland, New Zealand.

New Zealand Missionary Conference (NZMC)
- 1926 *Report of the New Zealand Missionary Conference Held at Dunedin, 27-29 April 1926.* Dunedin: New Zealand Missionary Conference Committee.

Nicholson, R. C.
- 1925 *The Son of a Savage: The Story of Daniel Bula.* New York: Abingdon Press.

Nobili, de Roberto
- 1971 *Adaptation.* Edited by S. Rajamanickan. Palayamkottai, Madras: De Nobili Research Institute, Saint Xavier College.

Nottage, Basil R. C.
- 1940 *New Hebrides Calling.* Auckland: Presbyterian Church of New Zealand.

O'Brien, Ilma E.
- 1971 "Missionaries on Ponape: induced social and political change." *Australian National University Historical Journal* 8:53-64.

Oceania Province (Society of Mary)
- 1971 *Acts and Decrees of the Provincial Chapter.* Located in the archives of the Marist Fathers, Suva, Fiji.

Ogan, Eugene
- 1972 *Business and Cargo: Socio-Economic Change among the Nasioi of Bougainville.* New Guinea Research Bulletin no. 44. Canberra: Australian National University Press.

Oliver, Douglas
   1961   *The Pacific Islands.* Rev. ed. Garden City, N.Y.: Doubleday.

Oram, N. D.
   1971   "The London Missionary Society pastorate and the emergence of an educated elite in Papua." *Journal of Pacific History* 6:115-132.

O'Reilly, Patrick
   1963   "Chronologie de Wallis et Futuna." *Journal de la Société des Océanistes* 19:12-45.

Owens, J. M. R.
   1968   "Christianity and the Maoris to 1840." *New Zealand Journal of History* 2:18-40.

Pacific Islands Monthly
   1932   "Anglicans withdraw from trading." 3(August):14.

Parratt, J. K.
   1975   "Religion and the migrant to Port Moresby." *Missiology* 3:177-189.

Parsons, Talcott and E. Shils (eds.)
   1951   *Towards a General Theory of Action.* Cambridge, Mass.: Harvard University Press.

Paton, Frank H. L.
   1913   *The Kingdom in the Pacific.* London: London Missionary Society.

Philip, John
   1828   *Researches in South Africa.* 2 vols. London: J. Duncan.

Phillips, Clifton J.
   1969   *Protestant America and the Pagan World: The First Half Century of the American Board of Commissioners for Foreign Missions, 1810-1860.* Cambridge, Mass.: East Asian Research Center, Harvard University.

Pilhofer, Georg
   1963   *Die Geschichte der Neuendettelsauer Mission in Neuguinea.* 3 vols. Neuendettelsau: Freimund Verlag.

Pius XII
   1951   Encyclical letter *"Evangelii Praecones."* 2 June. In *Acta Apostolicae Sedis.* vol. 18.

Power, J.
   1971   *Mission Theology Today.* Maryknoll, N.Y.: Orbis.

Pratt, M. A. Rugby
 1922 "Kava ceremony in Tonga." *Journal of the Polynesian Society* 31:198-201.
Presbyterian Church of the New Hebrides, General Assembly (PCNH, GA)
 1958 *Minutes* (Minute 101). On file in the Presbyterian Mission Board Office, Sydney, Australia.
Presbyterian Mission Synod of the New Hebrides (PMSNH)
 1907 *Minutes.* 2 May. On file in the Presbyterian Mission Board Office, Sydney, Australia.
Pro Mundi Vita, International Research and Information Center (Brussels)
 1973a *Pluralism, Polarisation and Communication in the Church.* No. 45.
 1973b *Pluralism and Pluriformity in Religious Life: A Case Study.* No. 47.
Raucaz, L.
 1925 *Vingt-Cinq Annés d'Apostolat aux Iles Salomon Méridionales.* Lyons: Vitte.
 1928 *In the Savage Solomons: The Story of a Mission.* Lyons: Vitte.
Redfield, Robert
 1953 *The Primitive World and Its Transformations.* Ithaca, N.Y.: Cornell University Press.
Reed, Stephen W.
 1943 *The Making of Modern New Guinea; with Special Reference to Culture Contact in the Mandated Territory.* Philadelphia: American Philosophical Society.
Rivers, W. H. R., ed.
 1922 *Essays on Depopulation in Melanesia.* Cambridge: Cambridge University Press.
Roach, K.
 1963 "The Marists and Pompallier 1836-1848." D. Hist. Ecc. dissertation, Gregorian University, Rome.
Rogers, Garth
 1969 "Comments on the 'Report on the Results of the 1966 Census,' Kingdom of Tonga, 1968." *Journal of the Polynesian Society* 78:212-222.
Ross, Harold M.

Ross, Harold M.
- 1973 *Baegu: Social and Ecological Organization in Malaita, Solomon Islands.* Illinois Studies in Anthropology, no. 8. Urbana: University of Illinois Press.
- 1976 "Bush fallow farming, diet and nutrition: a Melanesian example of successful adaptation." In *Measures of Man*, edited by J. S. Friedlaender and E. Giles. Cambridge, Mass.: Peabody Museum Press.

Rowbotham, Arnold H.
- 1966 *Missionary and Mandarin: The Jesuits at the Court of China.* New York: Russell and Russell.

Rowley, Charles D.
- 1966 *The New Guinea Villager: Impact of Colonial Rule on Primitive Society and Economy.* New York: Praeger.

Rudge, P. F.
- 1968 *Ministry and Management: The Study of Ecclesiastical Administration.* London: Tavistock.
- 1974 "The sociology of conflict and ecclesiastical life." *Concilium* 1(10):100-108.

Rutherford, Noel
- 1971 *Shirley Baker and the King of Tonga.* Melbourne: Oxford University Press.

Sabatier, Ernest
- 1939 *Sous l'Équateur du Pacifique. Les Îles Gilbert et la Mission Catholique (1888-1938).* Paris: Editions Dillen.

Sandars, George E.
- n.d. MSS. in J. Boutilier's possession.

Scarr, Deryck
- 1967 *Fragments of Empire: A History of the Western Pacific High Commission 1877-1914.* Canberra: Australian National University Press.

Schiotz, F. A.
- 1950 "Dr. F. A. Schiotz's visit to New Guinea, February 1950. A summary of Dr. Schiotz's report to the Executive Committee of the Board of Foreign Missions." Mimeographed. On file in the American Lutheran Church Archives, Minneapolis.

Schloesing, E.
- 1952 *Rapport de M. E. Schloesing sur son Voyage en Océanie (Novembre 1951-Mars 1952).* Paris: Société des Missions

Évangéliques de Paris.
Sharp, Gerald
1917 *Diocese of New Guinea: Its Rules and Methods.* n.p.
Shorter, A.
1973 *African Culture and the Christian Church: An Introduction to Social and Pastoral Anthropology.* London: Geoffrey Chapman.
Smith, Michael G.
1974 *Corporations and Society: The Social Anthropology of Collective Action.* Chicago: Aldine.
Society of Mary
1971 *Declarations and Decisions of the General Chapter of 1969-1970.* Located in the archives of the General Administration, Marist Fathers, Rome.
Solomon Islands
1920 King's Regulation, no. 10.
1922 *British Solomon Islands Protectorate, Blue Book.* Colonial Office Series, no. 723, vol. 3.
1931 *British Solomon Islands Protectorate, Blue Book.* Colonial Office Series, no. 723, vol. 11.
1934 "Precis of Education." WPHC, IC 951/1934.
1939 *British Solomon Islands Protectorate, Blue Book.* Colonial Office Series, no. 723, vol. 19.
1965 "Educational Policy," White Paper. BSIP 3.
"Some Remarks about the Religious Views of Our Islanders"
1915 Anonymous manuscript by a missionary on Truk. On file at the Micronesian Seminar Library, Truk, Caroline Islands. Mimeographed.
Somerset Magistrates Book
1871- MSS. On file in the Oxley Memorial Library, Brisbane,
1877 Australia.
Sommers, T. V.
1966 *Religion in Australia.* Adelaide: Rigby.
South Pacific Missionary Conference (SPMC)
1948 23-28 February. "Reports of Commissions, I-X"; "Conference Resolutions"; and "Questionnaire on Commission Subjects and Replies to Same from Each Area." MSS. On file in the Australian Council of Churches Archives, Sydney, Australia.

Spindler, Marc
    1967   *La Mission, Combat pour le Salut du Monde.* Neuchatel, Switzerland: Delachaux et Niestlé.

Spiro, Melford E.
    1952   "Ghosts, Ifaluk, and teleological functionalism." *American Anthropologist* 54:497-503.

Stanner, W. E. H.
    1953   *The South Seas in Transition: A Study of Postwar Rehabilitation and Reconstruction in Three British Pacific Dependencies.* Sydney: Australasian Publishing Co.

Sterr, Joseph
    1950   *Zwischen Geisterhaus und Kathedrale; unter steinzeitmenschen der Südsee.* Edited by Joseph Sterr. Mödling bei Wien: St. Gabriel-Verlag.

Stevenson, Robert Louis
    1900   *In the South Seas.* London: Chatto and Windus.
    1973   *Travels in Hawaii.* Edited by A. Grove Day. Honolulu: The University Press of Hawaii.

Strong, William E.
    1910   *The Story of the American Board.* Boston: Pilgrim Press.

Sturges, Albert
    1854   A. Sturges to Anderson. Letter in the collection of the American Board of Commissioners for Foreign Missions, Boston. 3 April.
    1873   A. Sturges to Clark. Letter in the ABCFM collection, Boston. 30 September.
    1881   "Letters from Micronesia." *Missionary Herald* 77(1): 18-19; 77(4):143.
    1882   "Letters from Micronesia." *Missionary Herald* 78(11): 498.

Sydney Morning Herald
    1907   Article on Papua. 15 June.

Teilhard de Chardin
    1965   *The Divine Milieu.* New York: Harper & Row.

Threlfall, N.
    1975   *One Hundred Years in the Islands: The Methodist/United Church in the New Guinea Islands Region 1875-*

1975. Rabaul: Toksave Buk.

Tiffany, Sharon W.
- 1974 "The Land and Titles Court and the regulation of customary title successions and removals in Western Samoa." *Journal of the Polynesian Society* 83:35-57.
- 1975a "Giving and receiving: participation in chiefly redistribution activities in Samoa." *Ethnology* 14:267-286.
- 1975b "The cognatic descent groups of contemporary Samoa." *Man* 10:430-447.

Tinney, J.
- 1892-1902 "Diary." MSS. in the possession of S. Lātūkefu.

Tippett, Alan
- 1967 *Solomon Islands Christianity.* London: Lutterworth Press.

Tupouniua, Mahe 'Uli'uli
- 1958 *Report on the Results of the 1956 Census.* Nuku'alofa: Government Printing Office.

Turner, George
- 1861 *Nineteen Years in Polynesia: Missionary Life, Travels, and Researches in the Islands of the Pacific.* London: John Snow.

Tylor, E. B.
- 1958 *Primitive Culture.* Vol. 2. New York: Harper Torchbooks.

Valencia, Antonio
- n.d. "Memoria de Palaos." MSS. On file at the Micronesian Seminar, Truk, Caroline Islands.

Valentine, Charles A.
- 1958 "An introduction to the history of changing ways of life on the island of New Britain." Ph.D. dissertation, University of Pennsylvania, Philadelphia.

Vatican II Ecumenical Council
- 1966 *The Documents of Vatican II.* Translated and edited by W. Abbott. London: Geoffrey Chapman.
  "*Ad Gentes*" (Decree on Church's Missionary Activity).
  "*Apostolican Actuositatem*" (Decree on the Apostolate of the Laity).
  "*Christus Dominus*" (Decree on the Bishops' Pastoral

Office in the Church).
"Dignitatis Humanae" (Declaration on Religious Freedom).
"Lumen Gentium" (Dogmatic Constitution of the Church).
"Message to Humanity" (Issued at the beginning of the council by its fathers with the endorsement of John XXIII).
"Perfectae Caritatis" (Decree on the Appropriate Renewal of the Religious Life).
"Sacrosanctum Concilium" (Constitution on the Sacred Liturgy).

Verguet, C. M. L.
    1854 *Histoire de la Première Mission Catholique au Vicariate de Mélanèsie.* Carcassonne: Imprimerie de P. Labau.

Vernier, Charles
    1964 "Les structures agraires en Polynésie Francaise." *Journal de la Société des Océanistes* 20:1-3.

Vidich, Arthur J.
    1949 *Political Factionalism in Palau.* Coordinated Investigation of Micronesian Anthropology, no. 23. Washington: Pacific Science Board.

Viner, O. J., G. J. Williams, and Frank Lenwood
    1916 *Report of. . . Deputation to the South Seas and Papua (with a Chapter on the Organization in Australia), June 1915-June 1916.* London: London Missionary Society.

Vogt, Evon Z.
    1964 "Ancient Maya concepts in contemporary Zincantan religion." *VIe Congrès International des Sciences Anthropologiques et Ethnologiques* 2:497-502.

Wagner, J. F.
    1964 "The outgrowth and development of the cargo cult. A paper prepared by assignment of the Lutheran Mission, New Guinea, for the 18th field conference, 1964." Mimeographed. On file in the American Lutheran Church Archives, Minneapolis.

Wallace, Anthony F.
    1956 "Revitalization movements." *American Anthropologist* 58:264-281.

1970 *Culture and Personality.* 2nd ed. New York: Random House.

Walsh, A. C.
1969 "A Tongan urban peasantry—conjecture or reality?" In *Pacific Peasantry: Case Studies of Rural Societies,* edited by I. G. Bassett. Palmerston North, New Zealand, Manawatu Branch, New Zealand Geographical Society.

Watters, R. F.
1959 "The transition to Christianity in Samoa." *Historical Studies* 8:392-399.

Weber, Max
1930 *The Protestant Ethic and the Spirit of Capitalism.* Translated by Talcott Parsons. London: G. Allen.

Wench, Ida
1961 *Mission to Melanesia.* London: Elek Books.

Western Pacific High Commission, Inwards Correspondence (WPHC, IC). Files located in the Western Pacific Archives, Suva, Fiji Islands.
1898 C. Woodford to G. O'Brien. 28 December. WPHC, IC 49/1899.
1899a C. Woodford to G. O'Brien. 26 June. WPHC, IC 49/1899.
1899b WPHC minute on C. Woodford to G. O'Brien. 26 June. WPHC, IC 49/1899.
1907 E. Rason to E. im Thurn. 10 October. WPHC, IC 128/1907.
1913a C. Woodford to B. Sweet-Escott. 11 September. WPHC, WPHC, IC 200/1913.
1913b J. Goldie to C. Woodford. 5 November. WPHC, IC 223/1914.
1926 N. Kidson to E. Hutson. 26 April. WPHC, IC 1432/1926.
1930a F. Ashley, Recommendations. 25 June. WPHC, IC 2594/1931.
1930b F. Ashley to M. Fletcher. 29 October. WPHC, IC 3561/1930.
1931a F. Ashley to M. Fletcher. 5 October. WPHC, IC 2594/1931.
1931b F. Ashley to M. Fletcher. 9 October. WPHC, IC 2594/

1931.
1931c N. Deck to F. Ashley. 29 October. WPHC, IC 2594/1931.
1931d M. Fletcher to Ld. Passfield. 2 December. WPHC, IC 2594/1931.
1932a F. Ashley to M. Fletcher. 29 February. WPHC, IC 2594/1931.
1932b J. Barley to M. Fletcher. 11 November 1932. WPHC, IC 3905/1932.
1932c J. Barley to M. Fletcher. 9 December. WPHC, IC 2594/1931.
1933a J. Barley, "Memorandum on Missionary Influence in the British Solomon Islands Protectorate." 24 November. WPHC, IC 3808/1933.
1933b R. Garvey, note. 27 December. WPHC, IC 2877/1933.
1937a F. Ashley to A. Richards. 20 August. WPHC, IC 3052/1937.
1937b A. Richards to W. Ormsby-Gore. 30 October. WPHC, IC 3052/1937.
1938   W. Ormsby-Gore to A. Richards. 23 March. WPHC, IC 3052/1937.
1939a H. Vaskess to W. Groves. 13 February. WPHC, IC 3052/1937.
1939b Minute by H. Luke. 21 June. WPHC, IC 2463/1939.
1939c W. Groves, Interim Report, no. 4. 21 October. WPHC, IC 2736/1939.
1939d W. Groves, Interim Report, no. 6, 5 December. WPHC, IC 2736/1939.

Wetherell, David
- 1973 "Monument to a missionary: C. W. Abel and the Keveri of Papua." *Journal of Pacific History* 8:30-48.
- 1974 "Christian missions in eastern New Guinea: a study of European, South Sea Island and Papuan influences, 1877-1942." Ph.D. dissertation, Australian National University, Canberra.

Wetmore, Charles H.
- 1886 "Report of a visit to the mission of the Marshall and Caroline Islands." Pacific Collection, Gregg Sinclair Library, University of Hawaii, Honolulu.

Wheen, J. G.
- 1923 "A statement of missionary policy endorsed by the general conference." *Missionary Review of the Methodist Church of Australasia* 33(4):2-3.

White, Gilbert
- 1917 *Round about the Torres Straits.* London: Central Board of Missions.

Whitman, Samuel
- 1817 "Blessedness of those who shall ascend to the glory without dying." Sermon delivered before the Hampshire Missionary Society at their annual meeting in Northampton, 21 August 1817. On file at Houghton Library, Harvard University, Cambridge, Mass.

Williams, Francis E.
- 1935 *The Blending of Cultures: An Essay on the Aims of Native Education.* Anthropology Reports, no. 16. Port Moresby: Government Printer.
- 1944-1945 "Mission influence among the Keveri of southeast Papua." *Oceania* 15:89-141.

Williams, John
- 1838 *A Narrative of Missionary Enterprises in the South Sea Islands . . .* London: John Snow.

Wilson, Bryan R.
- 1967 "An analysis of sect development." In *Patterns of Sectarianism: Organisation and Ideology in Social and Religious Movements,* edited by Bryan R. Wilson. London: Heinemann.

Wilson, C.
- 1932 *The Wake of the Southern Cross.* London: John Murray.

Wilson, Ellen
- 1935 *Dr. Welchman of Bugotu.* London: Society for the Promotion of Christian Knowledge.

Wiltgen, R. M.
- 1968 "Catholic mission plantations in mainland New Guinea: their origin and purpose." In *The History of Melanesia,* papers delivered at the Second Waigani Seminar, Port Moresby. Canberra: Australian National University Press.
- 1971 "How the Marists were sent to western Oceania." In

Verbum S.V.D., 12(2):133-152.

Winthuis, J.
1929 *Zur Psychologie und Methode der Religiös-sittlichen Heidenunterwiesung auf Grund eigener Erfahrungen in der Südsee-Mission.* Feldkirch: L. Sausgruber.

World Almanac
1900 New York: World-Telegram.
1930 New York: World-Telegram.
1960 New York: World-Telegram.

World Christian Handbook
1962 London: Lutterworth Press.

Wylie, Mabel G.
1955 "A study of polygamous marriage with special reference to North Australia and Papua-New Guinea and the attitude thereto of administration and Christian missions." MSS in M. Wylie's possession, Sydney, Australia.

Young, Florence
n.d. *Pearls from the Pacific.* London: Marshall Brothers Ltd.

CONTRIBUTORS

GERALD A. ARBUCKLE is lecturer in social anthropology at Mount Saint Mary's Seminary, Taradale, New Zealand. He attended the University of Saint Thomas in Rome (Ph.D. 1960) and Christ College, Cambridge University (M.A. 1963). His field research includes a study of the socioeconomic effects of credit union development among Fijians and the effects of social change on residents of the Chatham Islands, New Zealand.

JEREMY BECKETT attended University College, University of London (B.A. Honors Anthropology 1954) and the Australian National University (M.A. 1958, Ph.D. 1964). He has taught anthropology at Auckland University, New Zealand, at Monash University in Australia, and at Queens College, City University of New York. Presently he teaches at the University of Sydney. In addition to his field research in the Torres Strait Islands, he has conducted research among part-aborigines in Australia, in the Cook Islands, and in the Muslim Philippines.

PETER W. BLACK attended the University of California at San Diego (M.A. 1971) and conducted doctoral research on the Tobian world view. He has taught anthropology at Pomona College, Claremont, California, and is currently assistant professor of anthropology at Wayne State College, Wayne, Nebraska.

CONTRIBUTORS

JAMES A. BOUTILIER is assistant professor of history at Royal Roads Military College, Victoria, British Columbia. He attended Birbeck College, University of London (Ph.D. 1969) and taught at the University of the South Pacific from 1969 to 1971. He conducted historical research in Fiji and the Solomon Islands in 1972, 1973, and 1975.

KENELM BURRIDGE is professor of anthropology at the University of British Columbia. He attended Oxford University (B.A. Jurisprudence 1948; Diploma in Social Anthropology 1949; B. Litt. 1951) and the Australian National University (Ph.D. 1953). He was a founding fellow of Saint Cross College, Oxford. He has conducted field research in New Guinea, Australia, and Malaya.

DOROTHY AYERS COUNTS is associate professor of anthropology at the University of Waterloo, Waterloo, Ontario. She attended Southern Illinois University (Ph.D. 1968). Field research took her to West New Britain, Papua New Guinea, in 1966-1967, 1971, and 1975-1976.

SHULAMIT R. DECKTOR KORN attended the University of Cape Town (B. Social Science 1962), the London School of Economics (M.A. 1965), and Washington University—Saint Louis (Ph.D. 1976). She has taught anthropology at Brooklyn College, City University of New York. In addition to field research in Tonga, she has conducted research among kibbutz adolescents in Israel and urban migrants in the United States.

CHARLES W. FORMAN is professor of missions at the Divinity School, Yale University. He attended the University of Wisconsin (Ph.D. 1941) and served as a missionary in India from 1945 to 1950.

FRANCES HARWOOD attended Newnham College, Cambridge University (Certificate in Social Anthropology 1964) and the University of Chicago (Ph.D. 1971). She was assistant professor of anthropology at Wesleyan University from 1969 to 1975 and visiting fellow in the anthropology department, Harvard University, in 1975-1976. She conducted field research in the Solomon Islands in 1966-1967.

CONTRIBUTORS

FRANCIS X. HEZEL attended Fordham University (M.A. 1963) and was ordained a Jesuit priest in 1969. He has been a member of the Micronesian Mission for ten years. He is director of Xavier High School, an experimental school sponsored by the Catholic mission, and director of the Micronesian Seminar, a pastoral-research institute in Truk, Caroline Islands.

DANIEL T. HUGHES is professor and chairman of the anthropology department at Ohio State University. He attended Catholic University (Ph.D. 1967) and has conducted field research in Ponape and in the town of Malolos in the Philippines. He is coeditor of *Political Development in Micronesia* (1974).

SIONE LĀTŪKEFU attended the University of Queensland (B.A. 1957, B.Ed. 1961) and the Australian National University (Ph.D. 1967). He is the author of *Church and State in Tonga* (1974) and *The Tongan Constitution: A Brief History for the Celebration of Its Centenary* (1975). He is associate professor of history at the University of Papua New Guinea. Field research has taken him to New Zealand, Fiji, Samoa, Tonga, Australia, Papua New Guinea, and the Solomon Islands.

JAMES D. NASON is associate professor of anthropology at the University of Washington and curator of ethnology and chairman of the anthropology division at the Thomas Burke Memorial Washington State Museum. He attended the University of California at Riverside (B.A. 1964) and the University of Washington (Ph.D. 1970). He conducted field research in the Caroline Islands in Truk District in 1968 and 1969.

GOTTFRIED OOSTERWAL studied anthropology and theology at Cambridge University and at the University of Utrecht (D. Litt. 1961). He worked in West Irian from 1956 to 1963 and in the Philippines from 1964 to 1968. He is professor of missiology at the Seventh-Day Adventist Theological Seminary and professor of anthropology at Andrews University, Berrien Springs, Michigan, where he is also director of the Seventh-Day Adventist Institute of World Mission.

HAROLD M. ROSS is associate professor of anthropology at the University of Illinois (Urbana-Champaign). He attended Harvard

University (Ph.D. 1970) and has taught at the Massachusetts Institute of Technology and the University of Hawaii (Manoa). His field research includes ethnographic work in Malaita, Solomon Islands, in 1966-1968, participation in the Harvard Peabody Museum Expedition physical anthropology project in Bougainville and Malaita in 1966 and 1968, and the conduct of a comparative survey of socio-economic development programs in Indonesian Irian Jaya, Papua New Guinea, and the Solomon Islands in 1972.

SHARON TIFFANY is assistant professor of anthropology at the University of Wisconsin at Whitewater. She attended the University of California at Los Angeles (Ph.D. 1972). Her field research includes twenty months in the Samoan Islands in 1969-1971 and 1973.

WITHDRAWN
from
Funderburg Library